Real, Honest Sailing

Great Lakes from space. *NASA photo*

It was Christmas, and I was going to go through the Straits of Mackinac. I called Sarnia traffic and said I was upbound and headed for Lansing Shoal and will be there at such-and-such a time. "What traffic are you going to have going through the straits?" I was thinking there might be ice breakers or there might be another vessel coming through so I could get information on ice. The dispatcher said, "As far as I know right now, I think you're the only vessel moving on the Great Lakes." What a lonely feeling.

– *Captain Gary Schmidt*

Real, Honest Sailing
With a Great Lakes Captain

Capt. Gary W Schmidt

By Captain Gary W. Schmidt
with Warren Gerds

Warren Gerds

Allouez, Wisconsin

ISBN: 978-1-4675-8114-1
Library of Congress control number: 2013944690
Warren Gerds: gerds.gerds@gmail.com

Cover and book layout/design by
    Loralee L. Olson-Arcand
    Word Services Unlimited
    N9034 Lanetta Drive
    Brillion, WI 54110
    920.540.4656
    WrdSvcsUnlmtd@new.rr.com
    www.wordservicesunlimited.com

Fourth Printing (December 2013) by
    Seaway Printing Company, Inc.
    1609 Western Avenue
    Green Bay, WI 54303
    920.468.1500

Printed in the United States.

Introduction

Some people build ships in a bottle. Captain Gary Schmidt and I built a ship in a book.

We know each other through family. The question his wife, Mary, hears often from family members is, "Where's Gary?" Mary will mention the name of a port on the Great Lakes, and eyes sometimes will glaze over because places like Ashtabula, Calcite, and Marblehead are off our mind's radar. We know Captain Gary is somewhere on the Great Lakes on a mystical, mysterious adventure (to us) that includes a lot of grunt work and importance in the shipping industry.

For many years a while back, Captain Schmidt was at the helm of the tug Triton and barge St. Marys Cement.

For many recent years, his name is attached to the larger tug Dorothy Ann and barge Pathfinder.

His tug is more than a tooty-toot-toot toy in a bathtub. His barge is more than a helpless hulk pushed and pulled from dock to dock. You will find out how they work, while reading colorful stories along the way.

The structure of this book has to do with the Pathfinder. The vessel provided the answer to a question: How do you organize interviews that run from Point A to X to M to B to Q to back to A to P, D, Q, and sometimes Y? You structure the book based on the five cargo holds of the Pathfinder. What typically are sections of a book are called Cargo Holds. In the book, they match the Pathfinder's cargo holds as IA, IB, II, III and IV. Each of the book's Cargo Holds has a theme – Basics, Necessities, Voyages, Operations, and Maneuvering. Instead of chapters, the book has Hatches. In other words, Hatch = Chapter. Why? It is a nautical book, and we wanted to keep a nautical flow. The book has more Hatches than the Pathfinder has hatches, and they are numbered differently in the book. It's called artistic license.

For the most part, I am a bystander in "Real, Honest Sailing." The book is dominated by the words of Captain Schmidt. Think of him speaking as you read text like this – My favorite thing is maneuvering. *My introductions and observations are in italics. There is an exception in a large section, but you'll figure it out when you meet the Flower Lady.*

From the start, the concept of the book lay in a simple statement: What it's like to be a captain on the Great Lakes today. It's like ... whew ... read on, and enjoy.

– Warren Gerds

About the authors

Gary Schmidt was born on Washington Island in Door County, Wisconsin. Sailing has been part of his life ever since he can remember. He grew up in Sturgeon Bay, Wisconsin, where ships large and small are built. Little did Gary suspect when he bought his first boat – a row boat – that he would sail all over the Great Lakes in a 711-foot vessel made in his home town. Gary has been sailing for more than 40 years and has been a captain for most of those years. Gary resides in Allouez, a village adjacent to Green Bay, Wisconsin, home of his beloved Green Bay Packers.

Warren Gerds is a native of West Allis, Wisconsin. He grew up in Milwaukee. He is critic at large for WFRV-TV in Green Bay. For 45 years prior to WFRV, Warren wrote and edited stories for the Green Bay Press-Gazette daily newspaper, 35 years as critic at large. He has three other books: "My Father Lives in the Drawer," "Tales of a Newspaperman: Ice Bowl and Lombardi Through Time," and "The Legend of Taylor Rapids." Warren's sailing consists of rowing a 10-foot plastic folding boat on a remote river in northern Wisconsin. He resides in Allouez.

Contents

Appendix

Dedication

This book is dedicated to my special people.

Thank you to my dear wife, Mary, who has shared so much through fair weather and foul. Mary always is in my heart and mind. All should know the dedication this captain's wife put to taking care of our family and oh so much else. Nothing can compare with a caring voice on the other end of the line for a guy far away from home. How rich my life has been because of the patience, understanding, and love of my Mary.

My children, Joe and Kate, bring joy. And pride. We may have missed many moments together with me being gone on boats so much, but Joe and Kate are in my thoughts always. I smile now thinking of them.

Here's to the crew of the Dorothy Ann. This book is about the Dorothy Ann and me, but I wouldn't be as good on the boat if it wasn't for them. What a really, really great bunch of people to work with – and so very, very good.

– Captain Gary W. Schmidt

Acknowledgments

Loralee Olson-Arcand
Kevin Bower
Rod Burdick
Robert Dorn
Irene Earl
Monica Gerds
Kathleen Gerds
Jennifer Holland
Amy Mazzariello
Jeremy Mock
Captain Brad Newland
Emily Rock
Kramer Rock
Christine Rohn-Tielke
Mary Schmidt
Carmen Tiffany
Mary Stroba
Tom Wynne

It only took one day to realize that this was a real boat. That you can work on the Dorothy Ann and let your effort speak for itself. No games, just real, honest sailing.

– Kevin J. Bower, Dorothy Ann crewman

The Great Lakes. *U.S. Army Corps of Engineers map*

Cargo Hold 1A – Basics

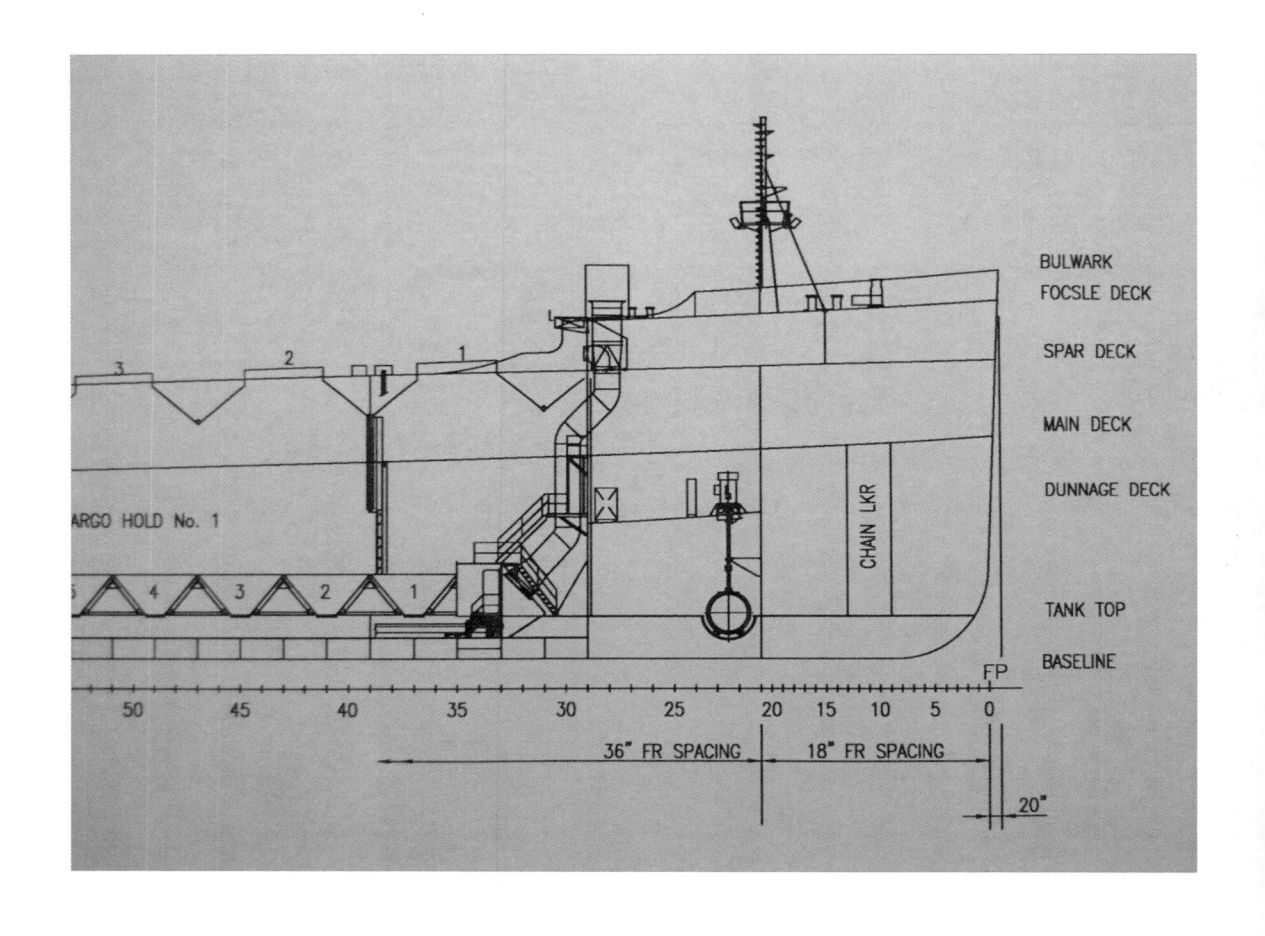

Hatch 1

"Cap"

Most of the people on the boat call me "Cap." That's just a title of respect. I'm a captain, I'm master of the vessel. Both. I don't have a preference. It depends on what I need to sign the title as. It doesn't really matter.

I've been the captain of the Dorothy Ann since March 2000.

My main cargo is stone – various sizes of stone, various types of stone. I also haul taconite, which is iron ore pellet. Haul coal. Those are my main three ones. But I do haul coke, slag, mill scale. Anything that can be run gravity fed we will run.

For loading and unloading, it's a 24-hour operation. It makes no difference if it's night or day, if it's raining or snowing or if it's sunshine or if it's a full moon. It doesn't matter.

The Dorothy Ann has two main engines for propulsion, and each one is independent of the other. Each engine is a 645 EMD, Electro-Motive Diesel. They're 20 cylinders. They were primarily made for railroad engines, but the company also has a marine division. We have a marine diesel. Each engine is 3,600 horsepower, and it has turbo blowers on it for extra power. The turbo blowers force air through, and that makes the engine burn the fuel more efficiently – gives a little bit more power. It's a total of 7,200 horsepower that's connected to a shaft that goes up to a compass drive.

A compass drive is a propulsion system that acts like the old outboard motors that can spin completely 360 degrees. There are no rudders. If you want to kick your stern over one way, it will push your bow the other way. How you steer is basically with the propulsion system, as in an outboard motor. But this outboard motor turns 360 degrees. You've got two of them. It's extremely maneuverable this way. I can spin the vessel within its own length. I can turn it right around 180 degrees within its own length within a very short period of time, less than a minute. I have done it. When you go to stop it, instead of reversing the engines you turn the pods the other way and just pull it backwards. It stops very fast. It stops within its own length in emergency shutdown.

The Dorothy Ann/Pathfinder unloads on the Cuyahoga River in Cleveland, Ohio.
Photo courtesy The Interlake Steamship Company

1

Some standard freighters would take miles to stop. If I turn the vessel, I can stop it within almost its own length. If I'm going full ahead and I decide to go 180 degrees to do an emergency turn, it'll turn within itself. I can stop it within 600-700 feet. And it will stop. I have done Coast Guard testing. We have gone from full ahead to a full stop – it's just by turning the engine – in 1,700 feet, which is just spectacular. If we were to take a steam vessel, to stop it would probably take a half a mile or more to do the same thing.

There are many tug and barge combinations on the Great Lakes. At more than 700 feet, the combination of the tug Dorothy Ann and barge Pathfinder is the largest vessel to go up and down the Cuyahoga River at Cleveland, Ohio. It's about 80 feet longer than the next vessel that goes up there. It means you get more cargo up there. It's more maneuverable than other vessels because of the compass drives, and it does it in the same amount of time. What it takes a shorter vessel to do, I can do in the same amount of time with this larger vessel.

Being a captain on a freighter has its attractions, but it's not for me. Not after being on this thing. This one's just too sweet. But what I enjoy other people don't enjoy. I enjoy handling. I like the close quarters and the challenge of doing a difficult river like the Cuyahoga. Other people would just as soon avoid the close-quarters handling and not have anything to do with it. And that's just a preference. A lot of them are very good boat handlers and could very well do the job, but a lot of them just don't like the constant pressure that you are under or the adrenaline rush that you get with it. And I do. You're making 90-degree turns and as much as 180-degree turns.

Dorothy Ann/Pathfinder at dock in Marquette, Michigan. *Rod Burdick photo*

The Cuyahoga is a very curvy river. The best speed you're going to do going up there is 2½ to three miles an hour on straight stretches. When you're going around some corners, you're down to less than a mile an hour and just doing a lot of maneuvering. You might have as little as 30 feet over your stern and 20 feet on your side and maybe 45 feet over your head. If you go into a curve too fast, you're going to hit something or come up against something, and you don't want to touch anything in the river. You just want to be able to maneuver. It's real tricky to maneuver in and out. It's really tricky to maneuver in and out. It's extremely difficult, and I like it a lot.

Way back when, I didn't give captain a thought at all. It just kind of happened. I aspired to be a sailor. I enlisted in the Navy in 1964 and was in for four years. A good part of that was overseas, which I enjoyed very much. When I got out of the Navy, I went to work in a factory in Sturgeon Bay, Wisconsin, for a short time. In the spring, a good friend who was in the Navy at the same time I was, said, "Hey, I'm working on a tugboat, you want a job?" I said, "Yeah." I thought about going sailing because that's what my dad also did. He worked on the ore carriers, and he spent 38 years doing it. So I was familiar with it. I knew what it was about. But I just went there to work.

As I got on a boat with Curly Selvick, I could see how he was handling the boat. It piqued my interest. I watched every move he made all the time. One day, after working as a deckhand and then becoming a mate and working my way up to first mate, he had hired somebody to do a job, and the guy couldn't do the job. Curly came back and said, "You're the captain." I had a lot of learning to do at that point, which I did. I've been running a tugboat or various other boats since 1973. Been a sailor since 1964.

I just like it. I like what I do. It's not a standard 8 to 5 job.

You're confined in a small space in a big area. There are magical things out there sometimes that you see. Just picture this: You're going up the lake, and you have clear skies. The stars are out. On the horizon, you can see the Aurora Borealis. Just the colors and the greatness of it. When you are in the northern part of the lakes, there are no lights around, you can see the Aurora Borealis really well. It's just majestic. You have that feeling of freedom and big, wide-open spaces.

Pilothouse of Dorothy Ann. *Gary Schmidt photo*

Hatch 2

Access limited

These days, the closest you're likely to get to a Great Lakes commercial vessel is from a railing when you get out of your car to watch a ship come through an open bridge. Don't expect to be able to get aboard a docked vessel. Access usually is denied. The ships are closed, secure entities.

To the general public, yes, nobody can come aboard. And we have to keep an eye out. We're supposed to be vigilant for anybody who tries to get close.

All this is because of 9/11, the attacks on America of September 11, 2001, and the resulting Homeland Security regulations. No more do Captain Schmidt and others aboard Great Lakes vessels get many chances to meet with the public on their journeys.

Not so much anymore. The public used to have the opportunity. We'd tie up at a dock, and people could come right down to the docks. And they'd always strike up a conversation with you and ask questions. Most of the time if you weren't busy, you didn't mind. I enjoy telling people about my craft and what I do. I didn't have a problem with any of that. Homeland Security put a clamp on that, so people just can't do it anymore.

Additionally, the public generally is not invited aboard.

That doesn't mean there isn't a way to get aboard the vessel. But the general public is not invited unless there's some kind of an open house or a christening or something on that order. With Homeland Security, it's really hard to get aboard vessels anymore. You have to get on a security list. You have to either have a TWIC *(Transportation Worker Identification Credential)* card or be escorted aboard by somebody who has a TWIC card. And it has to be agreeable with the facility that we're at. It's a combination of things. It's possible to do it. We don't do it, just for Homeland Security reasons because it is such a big hassle. But family gets to come down. We do allow family aboard.

For safety and security reasons, Great Lakes vessels are not certified to carry passengers for hire. It is impossible to buy a ticket.

My company sometimes invites business people for a cruise on one of their larger vessels. But basically not so much.

The only chance for the general public to take a cruise is through non-profit raffles donated to the various groups by the shipping companies.

Unless there are special circumstances, the general public just cannot walk aboard a vessel anymore. That's not going to ever happen.

Every port we go to now is fenced in. They used be open. People used to be able to go down to the docks and fish. You can't do that anymore. There are exceptions. Some of the docks you can get pretty close. Like the Shiras Dock in Marquette made an agreement when they built the dock that the public had access to fishing off of their dock. It went right into the laws there. They have a fence right around the dock in a certain area where we go to dock that nobody can get to. But the rest of the facility they can get to. So you can probably get within 20 feet of the ship down there.

Dry dock facilities may have restrictions.

You can still get in, but you have to be escorted by somebody who has a TWIC card. You have to be on a security list before you can get in there, which is given to the authority. It depends upon the facilities. Homeland Security – the Coast Guard – will not side with the vessels. They will side with the facility. If a facility says, "We don't allow anybody in or anybody out," you don't get on or you don't get off the ship. It's just plain and simple. If a facility is a little bit easier on stuff like that and wants to go through the rigmarole of signing people in, signing people out, escorting people to the vessel, and stuff like that – and a lot of them do – then yes, you can get aboard.

Hatch 3

Leaving

Beginning a season, I'm anxious to get back to work because I do like it and I've had an absence from it. I enjoy what I do. But it's also difficult to leave loved ones behind. It's very difficult for my wife, and it was hard on the children, too. But you've still got to bring home the bread. As much as I like my job, it also pays the bills. So it's hard to leave.

At the same time, you're anxious to get back to work. And it's the same way when I'm on the boat. You're comfortable on the boat, you're back into a routine, and now it's hard to leave the boat to come back to the family.

At the same time, you're anxious as hell to get home and see everybody that you miss and love. It's difficult both ways.

A rotation is about 60 days on and 30 days off. I might go to work for a month or maybe a month and a half and take a short vacation, a two to three-week vacation. Then I'll go back to work and work 60 days, and then I'll take a longer vacation of 40 or 45 days off. Sometimes I'll work 90 days to take the 45 off.

It's been a custom of mine to take off the last week in June, all of July, and, if possible, the first week of August. Other than that, the other vacation I take is my daughter's birthday in October. I try to work somewhere between 60 and 90 days, no more than 90 days and take off 30 to 45 days at a time.

Captains and Quarterbacks

Being a captain on the Great Lakes is like being a quarterback in the National Football League.

Both are given a game plan. A captain knows what he has to do at the helm of a ship. A quarterback knows what he has to do running a team.

Both deal with multiple moving parts.

Both deal with unknowns. What will an opposing team throw at the quarterback? What will the weather throw at the captain?

Both have to execute the game plan.

It takes years of training, knowhow, and specialized skills to be a quarterback or a captain.

A quarterback faces onrushing players and has to make snap decisions. A captain makes snap decisions in the face of high winds and rolling waters that would top a house.

Both are part of an established business. A goal for both is to make money, in the big picture for the business to survive and thrive and in the smaller picture for them to prosper from their can-do abilities. A quarterback answers to coaches and top brass. A captain answers to headquarters and top brass.

Both rely on instant communication. Both are responsible for others — their success and their safety.

A quarterback plays in large arenas — a league on a national scale, important to fans in a region, and in a stadium that holds tens of thousands of people. A Great Lakes captain operates in large arenas — five giant lakes that are crucial in the nation's economy, important to livelihoods across regions, and in a vessel that is much longer than a football field and, in one load, carries cargo that weighs more than three times that of all the people at a game at Lambeau Field in Green Bay, Wisconsin — home turf for our captain, Gary Schmidt.

Hatch 5

Captains

Our captains live everywhere. There's some from Florida, Michigan, Minnesota, the East Coast. Captains and engineers and deckhands and whoever on the vessel – there's no particular spot they're from.

Some are academy people. I think there are more mustangers than there are academy people. One of the captains was the first one who came out of the Great Lakes Maritime Academy at Traverse City is the captain on the Hon. James L. Overstar. A lot of the other captains worked their way up.

I see them once in a while, like in Marquette, Michigan. There might be two of our vessels in at one time, and we'll go from one vessel to the other and just shoot the bull for a while. Or on the dock, we'll talk to one another. Or we've already gone off the boat to get breakfast, just to get away from the boat. Just to talk, a friendly talk. Just to get away from the boat for a while.

I've had a few captains visit me in Green Bay when they knew I was off.

In passing, we always go out on the bridge and wave at one another. We usually give a captain's salute. And we talk. The captains talk. We talk on the radio or via telephone. We have conversations. "Go over to channel 8. Hey, what's the latest gossip? What's going on? How's the family? How's everything going?" Sometimes it's information we need. "What time are you going to be down at the Rouge?" "Are you going to be cleared by the time I get down there? Blah, blah. How much room is down there? Is there a lot of room for cargo?" Other than that, if something's happened, we like to hear details. "What's going on? What happened with this over here? And this and that. Oh, yeah, OK." Get the information.

No two captains are alike, and everybody runs his ship differently. And there's not a right way, and there's not a wrong way. Well, there are a lot of wrong ways, but there's a lot of right ways also.

Captains and Chiefs of Interlake Steamship Company pose at their annual meeting, which in March 2013 was part of the company's extensive 100th anniversary celebration on Marco Island, Florida. The sailing season just started, so not all of Interlake's Captains and Chiefs are in the photo. *Photo courtesy The Interlake Steamship Company*

There are some advantages to being a mustanger, there are some advantages to going through the academies. And who's better? It's personnel. It's how a person handles the job. It's just like the military. Whoever handles the action succeeds. That's what it is. Exactly.

Hatch 6

Credentials

United States Coast Guard
License
To U.S. Merchant Marine Officer
This is to certify that Gary Wayne Schmidt, having been duly examined and found competent by the undersigned, is licensed to serve as Master of steam or motor vessels of not more than 1,600 gross registered tons (domestic tonnage), 3,000 gross tons (ITC tonnage) upon near coastal waters; master of towing vessels upon Great Lakes and inland waters and western rivers; also; radar observer (unlimited).

Getting this license was a relief. "I did it. That's the end of a lot of studying."

I don't think I really did celebrate. I was just was happy to have it.

It's one of two absolutely necessary licenses to run the Dorothy Ann/Pathfinder.

They are that 1,600 ton license, masters — and you have to have a towing endorsement. You have to have a master of towing. Two things. But I have a lot more certificates and licenses.

Oh God, there's a lot involved. I have a Western Rivers License for uninspected towing vessels. I have an Inland License, 1,600 ton masters. I have a 1,600 ton masters Near Coastal License. And I have a Great Lakes Uninspected Towing Vessel License. An uninspected towing vessel is one that's usually less than 200 gross tons and is not inspected. I also have an Unlimited Radar Observer License.

I have a lot of certificates, like Bridge Resource Management that I've taken. ECPINS *(Electronic Chart Precise Integrated Navigation Systems)*, that I'm certified in ECPINS, that I have watch standers 95. I have a lot of certificates of classes that I've taken over the years. I have my radio telephone license; I have a Class 1 and Class 7. Class 7 is for GMDSS, which is Global Maritime Distress Safety System. I have an Able Bodied Seaman's certificate.

You have to take tests for all of this. I went to a couple of the small marine schools. Going to them helps you study for a test. I did my Great Lakes on my own, just studied on my own and passed that one. I went to sea school, called Master, Mates and Pilots School in Memphis for my Western Rivers License *(The River School, for Coast Guard license preparation)*. For my Near Coastal License, I went to Sea School in Daytona Beach, Florida.

For taking exams, you go to a Coast Guard regional exam center. There are many people taking exams. The closest regional exam center to my home in Green Bay is Toledo, Ohio.

You have to put in an application to the Coast Guard to take the exam. You have to pay for a background check and everything. You have to do certain things, a sign-off that they can look at your driving record and all that kind of stuff. And once all that has gone in there, they approve it, and they'll now say you're good for testing.

Then you make an appointment at the regional exam center to go and test for whatever you want to go for. If it's Unlimited, if it's a Pilotage, Engineer, Assistant Engineer, First, Second or Third Engineer, Chief Engineer, if it's 1,600 Ton or if it's Uninspected Towing Vessel – whatever you apply for, then you can go test for it. That goes for credentials, too. That goes for your upgrade to Able Bodied Seaman or Person in Charge Tankerman or Qualified Man in the Engine Department. All those ratings. They also have Water Tender. There's a lot of different smaller classifications on the license side. You still have to take a test for it all.

The licenses have to be renewed. Every five years, they're renewed, as long as you have been working and you are current on your license. That means that you've been working up so much time out of the year or whatever or so many years out of the last five years, that it's kind of a formality.

Yes, Interlake Steamship Company looked at my credentials before they hired me. They'll sometimes send you a rules of the road that you might have to look up and write down, just so that they know you looked through the rules of the road, but then they'll renew you. And, again, for a price. Nothing is free.

You have to show documentation before you walk on any vessel. And it has to be available to the Coast Guard at all times.

If you were to hire somebody as an electrician, you wouldn't hire anybody off the street. You'd have somebody who's a journeyman or at least has some kind of a license for it. I would think, anyway. That's like a bus company hiring somebody to be a bus driver. That's a special license also. I'm sure that they would check credentials.

Pursuing licenses is ongoing. This is a winter layover job that I have now, but other ones were time on/time off jobs where I worked year-around. I worked winter, summer, spring. A lot of my studying when I went for my first license was right on the vessel, and I went and took a test for it. It was OK.

Then my next one was that I wanted to be able to move up higher to operate larger tugs and larger vessels, so I went and did an upgrade. The one for Memphis was because I needed Western Rivers and I need a Western Rivers License to do the particular job I was after. So I had a Great Lakes and a Western Rivers License, and that gave me the opportunity to work the Chicago Sanitary and Ship Canal and all the western rivers. And I did work. I worked on the Upper Mississippi, all the way up to St. Louis, Minneapolis, St. Paul, all the way down to St. Louis, Cairo, Illinois. I've been up the Illinois River, right to the mouth of the Ohio. Up through the Illinois River up into Chicago and out onto the Great Lakes.

The experience was valuable. Working the Mississippi River teaches you a lot of close-quarter maneuvering because you know you're around vessels, you're maneuvering all the time, you're moving around other vessels, and you have to plan things. That gave me a lot of my close-quarter handling experience. It gave me a lot of handling experience, period, which helps out a lot.

When it came time to take exams, a lot of the stuff was experience. But at the same time there's a lot of stuff that you have to know that you very seldom use. And even though I have my Near Coastal License, I don't work the coastal, so I don't need to know tides and currents as much as some other person would. But you have to learn it. You have to know how figure it out. You have to know stability. You know some of it, but you still learn a lot more from the books. Rules of the road, general seamanship, a lot of that stuff, you know just from being on a boat.

Captain Schmidt wears this hard hat aboard ship when called for.
Warren Gerds photo

For my first license, I was working a tugboat for Selvick Marine Towing out of Sturgeon Bay, Wisconsin, and I got an Uninspected Towing Vessel License. Then my second license was the Western Rivers because I wanted to work for another company and needed the Western Rivers License for it. So I went to work on the Western Rivers to target the company I wanted to work for. That worked out, and I did get the job. Then while I was working for that company, I could see if I wanted to move up I'd need a larger license again. So I went and wrote the 1,000 Ton Master Freight and Towing License which was upgraded to a 1,600 Ton license later on by the Coast Guard. That's the next highest thing to having an unlimited license. An unlimited is what most of the Great Lakes sailors have.

We'll sidetrack here a little bit. The tonnage only counts for the tug. The barge counts for nothing. This is something that doesn't make sense to me with the Coast Guard – that you're moving two pieces of equipment, and they want to limit your tonnage. I'm moving a barge that is as large as any of the steam vessels out there, not the 1,000-footers, but it's a big, self-unloading vessel that I'm connected to solidly – and only the tug counts as tonnage, even though I'm moving 23,000 tons of cargo at a time, plus the weight of the steel and everything of the barge itself. It's a lot of weight.

Aside from the Dorothy Ann and Pathfinder, I could operate any tug on the Great Lakes, any vessel that's 1,600 tons or less. And I have the Master of Towing, which is pretty important nowadays, as someone who operates a 1,000-foot vessel, if he doesn't have the towing vessel endorsement, can't operate the Dorothy Ann. It used to be that they could do that. Now at least the Coast Guard recognizes that it's kind of a special thing, that operating a tug and a barge as two units is a little more difficult than operating one vessel.

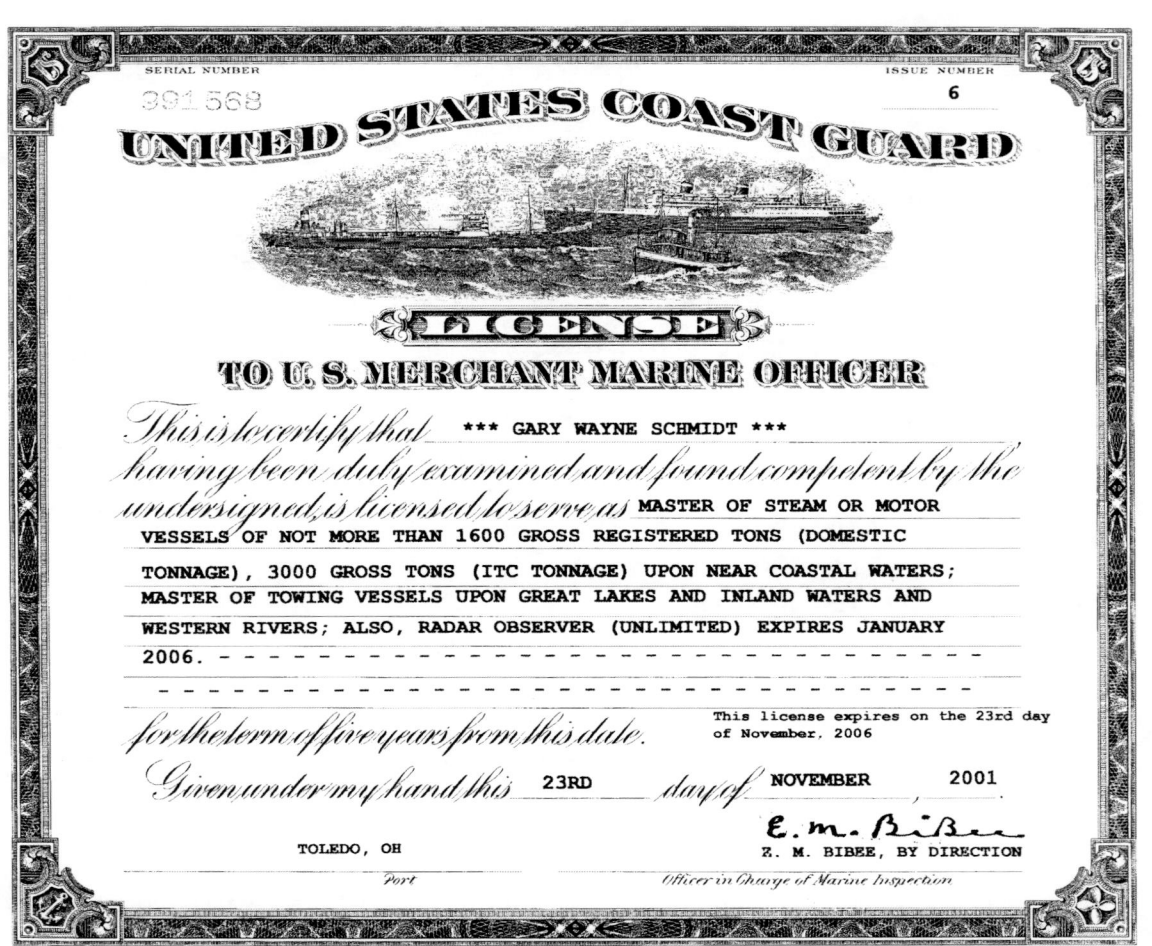

SERIAL NUMBER
391 568

ISSUE NUMBER
6

UNITED STATES COAST GUARD

LICENSE

TO U. S. MERCHANT MARINE OFFICER

This is to certify that *** GARY WAYNE SCHMIDT ***
having been duly examined and found competent by the
undersigned, is licensed to serve as MASTER OF STEAM OR MOTOR
VESSELS OF NOT MORE THAN 1600 GROSS REGISTERED TONS (DOMESTIC
TONNAGE), 3000 GROSS TONS (ITC TONNAGE) UPON NEAR COASTAL WATERS;
MASTER OF TOWING VESSELS UPON GREAT LAKES AND INLAND WATERS AND
WESTERN RIVERS; ALSO, RADAR OBSERVER (UNLIMITED) EXPIRES JANUARY
2006. -
- -

for the term of five years from this date.

This license expires on the 23rd day
of November, 2006

Given under my hand this 23RD day of NOVEMBER 2001

TOLEDO, OH
Port

E. M. Bibee
Z. M. BIBEE, BY DIRECTION
Officer in Charge of Marine Inspection

Among Captain Schmidt's many credentials is this prime license that he continues to renew.

Dorothy Ann/Pathfinder timeline

Then

⇨ **Original name of Pathfinder:** J.L. Mauthe

⇨ **Namesake:** J.L. "Pete" Mauthe (1890-1967). James Lester Mauthe was president of Youngstown Sheet and Tube Company, one of the largest manufacturers of steel in the world. He is namesake of the Mauthe Bridge in Poland (Ohio) Municipal Forest. The structure is a steel and wood suspension bridge over Yellow Creek. A captain of industry, Mauthe is namesake of other places, such as a park in Youngstown, and of at least one scholarship. Mauthe is a member of the National College Football Hall of Fame. Pete Mauthe played fullback for Penn State from 1909 to 1912 ('12 team captain), averaging seven yards a carry. He also was punter and place kicker, once kicking a 51-yard field goal, a rarity for the era. The undefeated 1912 team outscored opponents 285-6, with Mauthe scoring 119 of them. He graduated from college with a degree in metallurgy. In 1964, Mauthe received a Distinguished Alumnus Award from Penn State. He served on the board of trustees of Penn State and Youngstown State University and established a scholarship at Penn State for engineering students.

James Lester "Pete" Mauthe was a football hero at Penn State before becoming a captain of industry and having a Great Lakes freighter named for him. *Penn State Hero Decks playing card*

⇨ **Entered service:** April 2, 1953

⇨ **Memory:** Curt Balko, deckhand in first year of service: "It was a beautiful ship, everything was sparkling new, and it was a great privilege to serve her."

⇨ **Builder:** Great Lakes Engineering Works, River Rouge, Michigan

⇨ **Owner:** Interlake Steamship Company, Middleburg Heights, Ohio

⇨ **Type vessel:** AAA, a class designed for the Pittsburgh Steamship Company. The "AAA" designation was an internal U.S. Steel accounting code. Ships were differentiated by size as a way of setting pay scales. Officers aboard larger and more powerful vessels were generally paid more. The Arthur M. Anderson, Cason J. Callaway, Philip R. Clarke and John G. Munson fit similar criteria. Four other bulkers built in the early 1950s of the same design, size, and power were the Edward B. Green 2 (1952), J.L. Mauthe (1952), Reserve (1952), and the Armco (1953). The shipping industry generally classified the eight vessels as the "Pittsburgh class."

⇨ **Hull number:** 298

⇨ **Dimensions:** 647 feet in length, 70-foot beam, 36-foot depth

The J.L. Mauthe was different than other members of her class with a small after deckhouse and slightly different arrangement for the forward cabins.

⇨ **Visual characteristics:** Trim lines and distinctive profile for her class, a favorite among boat watchers in her later years.

⇨ **Power:** Steam turbine

⇨ **Cargo:** Taconite pellets (particularly early years) and grain. Interlake's iron ore routes ran between Duluth-Superior and lower lake ports.

⇨ **Historical notes:** By 1979, other members of the AAA class were lengthened by 120 feet, to 767 feet, and all but one (the William Clay Ford) was converted to a self-unloader. By the early 1980s, the Mauthe carried only occasional loads of iron ore and was used more for carrying grain. By the early 1990s, the Mauthe's use as a grain carrier fell off.

⇨ **Out of use:** On July 5, 1993, the J.L. Mauthe laid up for the final time at Fraser Shipyards in Superior, Wisconsin.

⇨ Inactive: The vessel did not sail while plans were made for her conversion in the wake of successful projects in the 1990s. Former straight-deck bulk carriers and other vessels were re-configured into barges, with powerful tugs fitted into a notch at the stern. During 1996, similar plans were completed for the Mauthe.

⇨ **One more destination:** On Dec. 31, 1996, the Mauthe left Duluth-Superior for Bay Shipbuilding Company in Sturgeon Bay, Wisconsin.

⇨ **Conversion:** Work was done during most of 1997. The vessel was made into a self-unloading barge.

⇨ **Completion:** March 1998

⇨ **Re-named:** Pathfinder, a name revived from Interlake's past.

Now
Barge

⇨ **Present name:** Pathfinder

⇨ **Official number:** 264738

⇨ **International Maritime Organization (IMO) number:** 5166768

⇨ **Namesakes:** Whaleboat steamer Pathfinder was active around the turn of the 20th century and into the 1930s. It carried 4,100 tons and towed the barge Sagamore. The Sagamore sunk in a collision in

In Captain Schmidt's home is the artist's rendition drawing for the construction of the Dorothy Ann/Pathfinder. *Warren Gerds photo of drawing by Paul C. LaMarre*

1927. Another Pathfinder was the freighter Samuel Mather, which was built in 1906. It was sold to Interlake in 1913 and renamed Pathfinder in 1925 and subsequently was known as Goderich.

⇨ **Owner:** Interlake Steamship Company, Middleburg Heights, Ohio

⇨ **Manager:** Interlake Steamship Company, Middleburg Heights, Ohio

⇨ **Dimensions:** 606 feet, two inches in length, 70-foot beam, 36-foot depth

⇨ **Capacity:** 26,700 gross tons

⇨ **Conversion design work:** Northeast Technical Services, Inc.

⇨ **Basic conversion:** Propulsion machinery removed. Forward cabins removed. Stern removed and replaced with a notch to accommodate the specially designed pushing tug. A 260-foot aft-mounted loading boom installed for the automated unloading system. Key is the Continental Conveyor & Equipment Company's HAC (high angle conveyor) sandwich loop belt system that allows a variety of material sizes (from dust to a foot thick) to pass through the system.

⇨ **Entered service:** March 21, 1998, with first cargo at Escanaba, Michigan.

⇨ **First season:** Delivered 112 cargoes totaling nearly two million tons.

⇨ **Cargo:** Stone, pumice, grain, coal, cement

⇨ **Memory:** "This is an impressive ship. My wife and I were cruising the Black River in Lorain, Ohio, (on July 3, 2011 and) passed within 50 feet." –Mike Weigand

⇨ **Historical notes:** Dorothy Ann/Pathfinder became the largest tug/barge combination to travel the navigable section of Cleveland's Cuyahoga River. She is the only commercial vessel that can back into the Rouge River without tug assistance. In the winter of 1998-1999, cargo slide slope plates were installed, allowing the vessel to carry cargoes in a wider range of sizes than other lakers. This reduced the amount of cargo the barge carries but speeds up unloading to 6,000 tons an hour with the all-gravity system.

Tug

⇨ **Name:** Dorothy Ann

⇨ **Official number:** 1081409

⇨ **International Maritime Organization (IMO) number:** 8955732

⇨ **Flag:** United States of America

⇨ **Namesake:** Dorothy Ann Tregurtha Croskey of Minneapolis, Minnesota. Nicknamed "Dory," she is the daughter of Paul R. Tregurtha and Lee A. Tregurtha. Paul R. Tregurtha is vice-chairman of the Interlake Steamship Company.

⇨ **Home port:** Cleveland, Ohio

The christening of the Dorothy Ann/Pathfinder took place June 28, 1999, in Cleveland, Ohio. Susan Tregurtha Marshall christened the Dorothy Ann by smashing a bottle of champagne on the tug's hull. April S. Barker then christened the Pathfinder.
Photo courtesy The Interlake Steamship Company

⇨ **Power:** 7,200-horsepower Z-drive. Two EMD (Electro-Motive Diesel) 20-cylinder 645 engines that turn out 3,600 horsepower each.

⇨ **Speeds:** Dorothy Ann can travel at 16 miles an hour, and Dorothy Ann/ Pathfinder can reach 11.5 miles an hour loaded on the open lake.

⇨ **Dimensions:** 124 feet in length, 44-foot beam, 24-foot depth.

⇨ **Range:** The Dorothy Ann/Pathfinder unit fits into locks of the St. Lawrence Seaway system. She operates all over the Great Lakes.

⇨ **Design:** Ocean Tug & Barge Engineering of Bellingham, Massachusetts.

⇨ **Construction:** Hull construction started January 1, 1998, at Bay Shipbuilding Company at Sturgeon Bay, Wisconsin. Hull, main engines and Z-drives were towed out of Bay Shipbuilding's dry docks and delivered to Escanaba, Michigan, on September 16, 1998. Outfitting was performed by Bark River Towing of Escanaba, Michigan; Weld All of Menominee, Michigan; and Marine Accommodations of Jacksonville, Florida.

⇨ **Vessel historical notes:** The Dorothy Ann is the largest Z-drive tug built to date in North America. Her twin Ulstein Z-drives enable her to turn completely within her length and move easily in any direction. The Dorothy Ann/Pathfinder unit can navigate tight turns and reach docks in tight quarters. The Dorothy Ann is fitted with a pin-type connection system for attaching the Pathfinder's notched stern. The AT/B tug-to-barge connection was manufactured by Hydraconn of Escanaba, Michigan. Two hydraulic rams project from the sides of the Dorothy Ann's bow and lock into receptacles in the Pathfinder's stern. This permits the Dorothy Ann to pitch freely within the notch in response to various sea conditions.

⇨ **Navigation and communication equipment:**

⇨ **Features:** Elevated pilot house has a height of eye of 70 feet. The Dorothy Ann has a large, spacious ship-like bridge with 360-degree visibility. The vented tower is designed to spoil trailing air drafts. Air conditioned private cabins with semi-private bathroom facilities for 14 crew members, a lounge and owner's stateroom. The Dorothy Ann includes a large galley and mess area and extensive heating, ventilating and air conditioning (HVAC) equipment. The air to her engine room passes through filter units on the 01 deck. Despite her height, the Dorothy Ann has a positive stability range of 85 degrees.

⇨ **Christenings:** June 28, 1999: The Dorothy Ann was christened by Susan Tregurtha Marshall, daughter of Paul R. Tregurtha. The Pathfinder was christened by April S. Barker.

⇨ **Entered service:** Late June 1999, carrying a load of taconite from Escanaba, Michigan, to Huron, Ohio.

⇨ **Concept historical notes:** The articulated tug/barge idea grew out of a demand for low cost, safe, reliable and more rapid marine transportation. The use of the conventional towed barges was weather dependent and not reliable in some weather conditions. Towed barges were slower than the ships they often replaced. With automated self-unloading equipment, economies were accomplished in crewing.

⇨ **Interlake background:** Fleet of nine self-unloading vessels. Interlake's Paul R. Tregurtha is the longest vessel on the Great Lakes at 1,013.5 feet (105 foot beam, 56-foot depth) and capacity of 68,000 gross tons. The Dorothy Ann/Pathfinder, at 730 feet (70-foot beam) has a capacity of 26,700 gross tons and "is small enough and maneuverable enough to fit in the tightest of spots," Interlake marketing says.

Proportions

- Length of Dorothy Ann/Pathfinder: 711 feet = more than length of two football fields.
- Dorothy Ann's capacity is 95,000 gallons of diesel fuel = more than 13 tanker trucks of fuel. One tanker truck can carry 7,000 gallons.
- If diesel costs $3.50 a gallon, the Dorothy Ann burns an average of $17,000 a day in fuel.
- Pathfinder holds a maximum of 23,800 tons of cargo. That's 47.6 million pounds. In car weight, that's equivalent to 8,000 Cadillac Escalades or 14,922 Toyota Camrys. In money, that's approximately 8.6 billion pennies. A railroad car carries from 61 to 63 tons of product, so it takes 378 to 390 railroad cars to load the Pathfinder.

Section 2

Cargo Hold 1B – Necessities

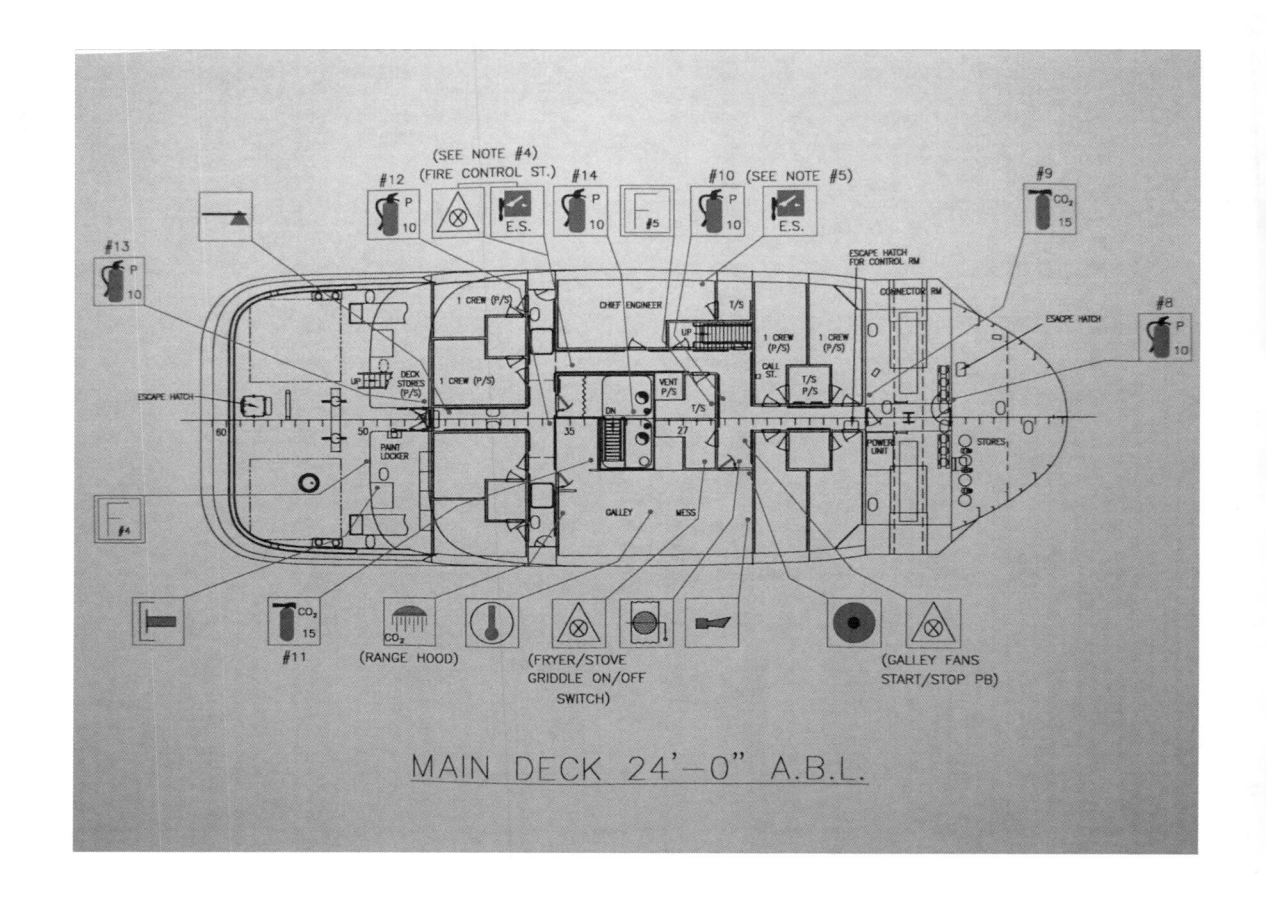

MAIN DECK 24'-0" A.B.L.

Hatch 7

Drinking water

We make our own water. We bring in lake water, and we have a reverse osmosis water system that's constantly making water.

We shower with lake water. The sanitary water is just brought in when we're on the lakes. It's filtered, and that goes right to the showers and also to the toilets.

We try not to take in water in industrial areas. I don't take in any water in rivers. I always take it out in the lake. When in the Cuyahoga River for extended periods, we take in water from the dock. There's a service with potable water.

Our reverse osmosis system makes water 24 hours a day. That fills our tanks up. That's what we normally do. The potable water goes to the sinks where you brush your teeth, and it's drinkable water. In the lake, we draw water into what we call our water maker. Once it fills up, our water maker tank overflows into the sanitary tank.

We probably use about 3,000 gallons a day. That's with the cooking, washing dishes, laundry, showers. It might not even be that much.

The water is stored on the Dorothy Ann. There is no potable or sanitary water on the Pathfinder.

The lake water is cleaner in some areas than other areas. But through that reverse osmosis process, it goes through a pre-filter, and then it goes through the osmosis system. It's very drinkable water.

Hatch 8

Garbage

We create plenty of garbage. Garbage is taken care of by compactor. The compactor is on the outside of the vessel on the stern.

Galley garbage is chewed up and run through our sanitary system, by which the bugs *(beneficial bacteria)* eat it up and it goes through a process. But packaging, cardboard, stuff like that we get rid of.

Bags of compacted garbage are kept near the compactor on the stern of the Dorothy Ann's stern. *Jeremy Mock photo*

All our garbage is compacted into great big compactor bags. It is sent to shore, where it is disposed of by the companies that we hire to do that. One of them is the mail boat, J.W. Westcott II. Whenever I pass under the Ambassador Bridge *(connecting Detroit, Michigan, to Windsor, Ontario)*, the mail boat will come out. I'll give it my mail. It will give me supplies and the mail for the Dorothy Ann, and then we'll drop off the garbage. The company gets the bill for that. The engineers take care of that paperwork. The mail boat takes care of some of our garbage when we're on the lower lakes.

***

SIDE TRIP: J.W. Westcott II is kind of an interesting thing, too. It has its own ZIP Code (48222, with mail addressed this way: *Vessel Name,* Marine Post Office, Detroit, Michigan, 48222). The J.W. Westcott II comes out and meets every vessel upbound and downbound and delivers mail and supplies. Interlake is contracted with it to also bring supplies out. It's not a Postal Service vessel. It's J.W. Westcott Company, who contracts with the U.S. Postal Service. But it is the mail boat. I think it's the only one anywhere, not just on the Great Lakes. It's unique.

***

When we go to the upper lakes, Soo Marine Supply takes our garbage and disposes of it. It takes our garbage when it brings stores to us.

I like to get rid of garbage every opportunity I have.

The bags are huge – three feet by three feet by three feet – full of pressure-compacted garbage. That's a lot of garbage. Normally, I have between two to four bags of garbage when I get rid of it.

Waste oil is taken off by truck or at some fuel docks. A few fuel docks take the waste oils and re-refine them. I'm sure that where we dispose of the waste oil it all gets re-refined. We either dispose of it into tank trucks when we are unloading or loading at a dock or at fuel docks where we take on fuel.

We throw nothing over the side. There is nothing discharged into the water whatsoever.

Hatch 9

Septic system

We have a sanitary system on the boat that returns the water to 99 percent pure, yet you often cannot release it into the water. It has some chlorine in it and stuff like that, but they say you can drink it. I'm not going to do it.

We have a bug-eating system. It's sort of like a municipal filtration plant. Treatment goes through two or three stages. The waste comes in, it breaks up the solids – the bugs eat the solids – it goes through an aeration process, it goes through a chlorine process, and we pump it from the tug to the barge. The barge has a filter system, and it does the same thing again. It's almost pure water when it goes back out. There are certain areas where we can discharge this into the water. In other places, we pump it into trucks.

We maintain the system. A sample is sent in and inspected. It's a process. When we get in there, we take a live sample and get to the inspecting place within four hours. We're all up to snuff on stuff like that.

Regulations about discharging that water are state by state. Some states allow it, some specifically don't – zero. There are places that you can – Canadian waters, Ohio waters. You cannot discharge anything in Michigan waters at all. Wisconsin is pretty strict. There are only a couple of places in Wisconsin waters where you might be able to. Illinois and Indiana – one you can, one you can't. That's the stuff that drives you nuts. It's not common sense.

***

SIDE TRIP: *State boundaries don't end at the shoreline.*

Boundaries extend out into the waters. Wisconsin-Michigan boundaries in Lake Michigan run pretty much down the center until you get up to Rock Island and Washington Island, where the boundary comes down between the two, then it goes down around, but not including, Chambers Island into Marinette-Menominee.

Then you've got the international boundary water between Canada and the United States.

***

To empty our septic system, a truck comes down to the dock and picks up that water. When we do the shuttles in Cleveland all winter long, we have a truck come every third or forth day and take a load away. What the truck takes away is water. It's 99 and something percent pure. The only bad thing that's in the water is chlorine. It's chlorinated.

Hatch 10

Food

Meal hours are standard. Breakfast is from 7 to 8 o'clock. Lunch is from 11:30 to 12:30. Dinner is from 5 to 6.

Now, we do work strange hours, and the cooks will accommodate and extend hours or feed early. And it's our job, if the men are out working through a load, we relieve the guys and get them in to get something to eat.

Our watches always change at noon. They change at 8 o'clock in the morning and at 4 o'clock in the afternoon. So guys who are on at 4 to 8 in the afternoon are the ones who need to take a break from their work job to go in and eat supper and then come back out to their work. But most of the time, you do it on your own time.

In the galley, we have a table that seats five people at a time. That's the mess area.

There's tons of food that's available 24/7. The stove and oven are in the back part of the galley. They're electric. In the forward part where we sit is a steam table where the food is set in. Next to it are a couple of coolers. The cooler above is where the desserts and salads are. It's a glass cooler that you can look into. The other one is the milk cooler, where milk, juices, and condiments are. On the other side is a table that has all the fresh fruits, which are usually in bowls. And there are snacks – potato chips and other things. A microwave oven is there. There's a coffee machine.

Also in the galley are a sink and dishwasher. There's a center prep area for the cook. And then he's got a counter on the other side and also a pantry. In the back, the cook has a stove, a grill, a deep fryer, and a big oven.

Dishes are made for a shared meal. There are two entrées plus several vegetables. If you don't like any of it, eat snacks or eat something else. There's cereal. There's everything else that you could want if you're not satisfied with what the cook has out at that time.

We often have certain meals on certain days. Usually, Saturday night is steak night. Sunday is turkey or chicken or ham. The cook usually has fish at every dinner meal and some other entrée and casseroles. There's a lot of food.

We get good food, good quality food, and it's up to the cooks to do a good job cooking it.

Dorothy Ann crewmen gather in the mess. *Gary Schmidt photo*

Cook Mangus Hines cleans up in the galley of the Dorothy Ann. *Gary Schmidt photo*

Certain ports have chandlers that supply vessels. There's not a lot of ship chandlers around the Great Lakes. There used to be a lot.

Allouez Marine Supply Company in Duluth *(Superior is the company address)* is a big supplier. There's Marine Market in Alpena. There's one in Chicago, Cleveland, the Soo Marine Supply, and Escanaba. The one that used to be in Toledo has been taken over by the one that's in Cleveland to supply the whole Lake Erie area. Detroit basically doesn't have one. There are some in the Canadian ports. If you're going through the Welland Canal, you can order a certain amount of stores. There are regulations on how much you buy in Canada, and there might be a tax on it.

Interlake pays for the food. I don't have to deal with that. The bill goes right to Interlake. On a computer, we have a list of just about every grocery item that you might need. If items are not on there, we still can order what we call a non-stock item. There's a separate way to order it.

The groceries are checked by the office. There are certain things Interlake won't buy. The company won't buy unlimited lobster tail or crab legs. You get that stuff at holidays. The company will buy that. It doesn't buy your soda.

If we know we're going to go up to Marquette and we're going to go through the Soo Locks, we'll put in our grocery order and say, "All right, deliver it from the Soo." We order three, four days in advance, so you've got to know what you're ordering.

Hatch 11

Supplies

Supplies such as engine parts are often ordered at the same time as groceries. But aboard the Dorothy Ann, a different take on picking up side items while shopping at a supermarket.

If you need light bulbs, if you need a bearing for the engine, or if you need cable – lines, heaving lines, whatever it is – you order from specific companies. They are sent to a place like the Soo Marine warehouse, and then that operation delivers the order to the boat. The place in Cleveland is called Beacon Hausheer *(Marine Co., which is historic).* We'll order marine supplies from Samsel Supply – for shackles or for ladders or whatever we need – and Samsel will deliver them to the Dorothy Ann or to Beacon Hausheer, and Beacon Hausheer will bring them down to the vessel.

Groceries and other supplies for the Dorothy Ann/Pathfinder are hoisted aboard from the supply boat Ojibway. *Jeremy Mock photo*

We take on supplies every three or four days – stores, galley supplies, and many, many boxes of groceries. These guys eat well. We have a hoist that will bring everything aboard, but then all of this is hand-carried into cargo spaces down below. There are dunnage hatches where you can get stuff down into storage spaces. Really heavy stuff like oil drums is lowered with a hoist, but your normal grocery boxes are all hand carried.

***

SIDE TRIP: There's petty cash on board in case you need to buy stuff in an emergency. There's draws. People want advance in pay. I have to write out checks for that. I keep track of petty cash, and that goes for buying stamps or, if we're in between chandlers, when the cook gets milk or something like that. If the engineers need something from a hardware store in an emergency-type situation, we go buy it. Or maybe office supplies. Anything we might need for the boat that we can get at a store. We try to order everything through the office, but at times when you need stuff now, you can just go buy it. But it's usually small stuff. Nothing major.

***

I need fuel and water and supplies to keep the vessel running, and the company supplies all of that stuff.

The company doesn't buy your personal hygiene items. The company will buy soap, but it doesn't buy your shampoo, it doesn't buy your toothpaste.

Hatch 12

Fuel

Many people fill up their vehicle at a corner gas station. Fueling the Dorothy Ann has whole other dimensions. For one thing, there's no filling station right around the corner.

We burn an average of 5,000 gallons of diesel fuel a day. That's considering running time and loading and unloading time. If we were to run 24 hours steady on an engine, we'll burn 7,000-plus gallons a day. That is equal to about one gallon per horsepower per hour per day.

We get our fuel at various places. We get some at the fuel docks in Canada. We get it at a fuel dock in Detroit. We have a barge that will come out and load us with fuel. Sometimes in certain areas when we cannot get a barge or we cannot get to a fueling facility, trucks will come down to the boat. A truck holds about 7,000 gallons. You need a lot of trucks. A lot of times, we'll just take enough fuel to get us through 'til we know we're going to get to another fueling facility.

When fueling, we do our own connecting. The fueling people have the hose that they either deploy with a boom or, if it's a truck, a heaving line is thrown across and we drag the hose. Any connections on the shore side are the shore side's responsibility. And you have to have what's called a Person in Charge. That requires a Tankerman's certificate. It's officially called a Person in Charge (PIC) of a Fuel Transfer. For engineers, it comes with their license.

Fueling stations are on either side of the stern of the Dorothy Ann. You can connect lube oil and fuel oil.

We have two methods for fueling. We have a system that automatically measures the tank. A device goes down into the tanks, and we have somebody watching that all the time. Plus you have somebody sounding the tank from above. If the oil gets within so many inches of the top, the fuel fillers stop pumping. They know exactly how much fuel is going in there. The facility shows you how much it is pumping to you at a time. There's a guy in the engine room who is watching the gauges down there that tell him how much he's got coming into the tank, and we've got one guy sounding. The chief engineer is in charge of the whole thing. The guys all have communication radios for this.

The Dorothy Ann takes on fuel on the Cuyahoga River with Cleveland Browns Stadium in the background. The vessel is secured to the dock by a line on an H bit at left. *Gary Schmidt photo*

Many times, we'll take on more than 50,000 gallons, and that will put us down another couple feet in the water. The tug will get lighter as the fuel burns.

There are a lot of variables in how often we fuel up. If we have a long run coming up, we want to make sure we're topped off so as not to run out – though you're never really going to run out because there are many ways of fueling.

If I'm on Lake Erie and doing seven or eight trips, I can run for more than a week. But if I make a run on Lake Erie and I unload at Marine City and I head up and maybe load at Stoneport or Drummond Island and go up to Marquette and unload, re-load and head back down, I will burn up on that particular trip somewhere between 30,000 to 40,000 gallons. That depends on delays if we are discharging and loading because the barge burns quite a bit of fuel when we're running the big generator on the barge for loading and unloading purposes. So if I do that kind of a trip, I'm using probably close to 40,000 gallons, and that'll be over a six or seven-day period. Capacity is more than 95,000 gallons. We usually run right around 91,000 gallons. If we get into a sea *(rough water)*, we don't want any spillage. Fuel oil will expand with heat and contract with cold. So it depends – summertime, wintertime – the amount of fuel that would probably take on. But what we try to do is, once we get back down to Severstal Steel, where we're going to unload, we'll have a fuel barge come up and bring fuel to us.

Fuel barge operators want us to take a minimum of 40,000 gallons. Out on the Detroit River, we can take smaller amounts. We go right up to the fuel dock. We can take 20,000 or 30,000 or 40,000 gallons. But most of the time when we go in there, we try to minimize our down time for fueling. So if we can take a fuel barge on and stay unloading all the time, we are saving ourselves two hours, which is a lot. They charge a little bit more by barge, but it's still more economical to do it that way.

We can take fuel on by truck, which we do when we're in Cleveland when we're on a shuttle run because we can't get to a fuel dock. You can fuel in a lot of places by truck. A lot of the docks allow it.

***

SIDE TRIP: A lot of the docks allow you to discharge the waste oil into trucks. Some don't. Some don't want the responsibility because you have to have a PIC, or Person in Charge, of pumping oil. It's a tanker with PIC, and that's an extra expense. Some docks don't want to deal with it.

***

The company has a person in charge of our fuel, Ed Priem. He runs out of our Duluth office. He sends out an Excel spreadsheet, tells us how much our average burn is, and what we have burned. We send in a fuel report every day. He coordinates with what our orders are at the time. Orders change a lot of times. He'll look at the different fuel docks and look at prices and try and coordinate us to take on fuel at a certain dock with a certain price. He negotiates the price before we go in.

It's still not a done deal whether the Dorothy Ann can fuel at the arranged place, if the load schedule has changed considerably.

Getting fuel factors into my time, my ETAs *(estimated time of arrival)*. It factors into a lot of different things. Down time or not down time. Sometimes where I get fuel is negotiable because the office does change orders. Sometimes when someplace is set up, it's a case of, "I can't do this. They've changed orders. I need fuel. I don't have enough. We're going to have to make a special stop or do something." And there's a lot of options.

Interlake gets the bill. There are some contracts where the fuel price is passed on to the customer because of the volatile market with the prices going up and down. There are some surcharges on some of that stuff, but that's out of my league. I don't know anything about that.

Fuel is a major expense. Labor used to be the most expensive thing on a vessel. It is now fuel.

The price shifts, like with gasoline for cars. It goes up and down a lot.

***

SIDE TRIP: We buy a lot of lubricants. We usually buy about 1,000 gallons of lube oil at a time. That goes into a big tank. The engines hold maybe 300 to 350 gallons of lube oil in their pan.

***

Here are fuel mileage exercises for math class — or not.

If we are running 24 hours straight, we burn 7,200 gallons. That's about one gallon per horsepower per day. If we travel 12 miles an hour – you can do the figuring from there – you burn so many gallons per hour. If you're loaded, you're going to make less mileage. You're going to do just a little under 11 miles per hour, depending on the size of the load you have. Then you can figure it out ton miles. We normally haul somewhere between 20,000 and 22,000 tons. If we're running at 22,000 tons, we'll do about 10.5 to 10.7 miles an hour.

The engines sound the same with a full load or with a light load, but there is what is called slippage. That's water that goes past the wheels as they're turning. They're turning the same, the racks are full on the engines, they're burning the same kind of fuel, but with the depth of the water you might have slippage, and you just get less miles. Depending upon the pitch and the size of the wheel, you can figure out how many feet you're supposed to travel per revolution. There's a formula for it. I don't know what it is right off hand. How many feet you travel per revolution is how it's logged on an ocean vessel. But we don't get into it that much.

Hatch 13

Habits

There's no drinking aboard the vessel whatsoever. Not on board. You can go out on the street and have a drink or two, but, according to Coast Guard regulations, you can't have a drink within four hours of your watch. Your blood alcohol has to be below .04 if you're on watch. It's just about zero tolerance. There's not much leeway. And it's not a bad thing, either.

You can smoke, but you can only smoke outside. You can't smoke inside. There are smokers, more smokers than I like. Some tried to quit. Some quit three, four times and are back to smoking. Some are not. It's a struggle. They all know they should quit. It's tough.

***

COMPLICATIONS: Crew members on the boat who have had a DUI *(driving under the influence conviction)* in the United States cannot go into a Canadian port. They are banned because it's a felony in Canada for a DUI. Canadians, on the other part, who are coming into the United States with a DUI have no problem. *Differing laws about pot use complicate matters in the two countries.* So between Customs and Immigration, it's a real pissing contest, and they are strict on these two rules.

Canada has our *(court system)* data base. So if you had a DUI, they can stop you at the border – even if you're driving – if they recognize your name in their data base.

If we have a crew member with a DUI and the company wants us to go into a Canadian fueling station, I either have to get that person off the boat and he meets me at the next port, or, if he's a necessary person who can't get off the boat, we can't take fuel on at a Canadian fueling station. We would have to go to a U.S. fueling station.

Hatch 14

Laundry

For our crew of 14, we have a couple of laundry facilities.

There are three washing machines and three dryers.

One laundry facility has a toilet, washer and dryer, and a deep sink. The other one has two washers and dryers, a deep sink, a folding table, and some cabinets.

Water is from our water maker tank.

With 14 people, you just take your turn. If it's busy, you wait 'til that person is done. You wait a half an hour, and it's your turn. It's not a big deal.

On certain days, you do certain things. Sunday is basically our main cleaning day. This is the day that we do a lot of sanitary work. We don't work the crew. We don't do any painting or hard work of any kind if we can avoid it on Sundays, other than loading and unloading, which has to be done. We try to give the guys a break on a Sunday. That gives them personal time to do their laundry and clean their rooms. We call it Sunday on the run if we can do it. Sometimes you don't get that Sunday on the run. A lot of times you have to work through that Sunday or a holiday.

Hatch 15

Sleep

There are times when the whole crew is up. We have drills when everybody is up and about and all hands are required. Most of the time, not everybody is up because of different work hours.

If you're a deckhand, sometimes you work six hours on, six hours off. You don't get eight hours of sleep in a row. But you can get eight hours of sleep – or you can get more than that. We're only working six and six when we're on Lake Erie when we have short runs that don't even take 12 hours one way. The deckhands usually get five hours of sleep on one watch, and they may get five hours on the next one. Some guys sleep that way. When I was working six and six – and I did it for 20 years – basically, I used to sleep five hours on one watch and two hours on the other watch. About all the sleep I ever needed was a little bit. And sometimes I didn't get that much.

Normally for the watchmen, it's four hours on and eight hours off. And the same with the mates.

The engineers are day workers. They work more than eight hours a day, and usually they average about 10 hours a day. They get a lot of straight-hour sleep. And they get a lot of interrupted sleep also. They're on call. They're day workers, but if something does go bad, then they have to get up and take care of it.

The deckhands are the guys who work six and six. Nobody else does. Usually we only have a maximum of five trips on Lake Erie in a row, which is about five days, maybe a week, of six and six. Then we'll do some long runs. And then the deckhands are called out. They'll be on eight hours in a 24-hour period. So they might get 10 or 12 hours of sleep in a row if they want. They'll get called out for unloading or if we're going to have a long lake run we'll not call them out depending on what time they've gone to

Loading the Pathfinder at night can mean odd sleeping schedules for crew aboard the Dorothy Ann. *Gary Schmidt photo*

bed. We'll let them get their eight hours sleep, and then we'll get them up and work them for eight hours. That'll be when we're cleaning tunnels. If the tunnel is clean, we'll do painting or other maintenance work that they can do during the daytime and then go back to bed and get their eight hours of sleep.

Just as astronauts do when they're in space, Captain Schmidt has trained himself to sleep when he must before a busy time coming up.

Pretty much. I can relax, and I can go to sleep when I need to do that.

There are times that you can't, of course. Everybody gets into a spot where you're kind of restless. But I pretty much sleep at will.

It used to be harder. But over the years, I've gotten to the point where I can. I darken my room. I don't have any light coming into my bedroom. I close the port lights. I make sure the curtains are closed, and it's totally black. I can trick myself into thinking it's nighttime any time.

The humming of the engines helps you sleep, or the generators running all the time. There's always noise on the vessel, and you get used to it. When that noise changes, that'll get my attention. I can tell a slight change in engine RPMs. I can tell when a generator's been switched. I can tell a lot of things by the sounds that are going on around me. You're aware of them.

I also have a ship's clock that rings every half hour. I don't have to get up and look at a clock. I can always tell what time it is by counting the rings. I hear them all the time, but I really don't pay attention to them all the time, just sometimes when I need to know what time it is I can kind of hone in on it.

I'm pretty much on my feet the minute that I'm called for a job. You have to be in emergency situations. You're always on the ready. I always seem to be able to be called, and I'll answer the phone within one ring and be alert to any questions or what's going on. It's pretty much been that way for a lot of years.

My room is on the 02 level. 01 level would be the main deck. There are 91 steps to the pilothouse from the main deck. It takes me less than a minute to get up there. No elevator. It's all walking, all running. You are out of breath by the time you get up there at a good pace. Even at a slow pace, a lot of people can't walk those steps very well.

Distractions abound aboard the vessel. Here are a few wakeup noises:

HORN: When I'm leaving a dock, I usually blow the loud whistle up forward on the bow of the Pathfinder. The horn on the tug can be heard so much on the tug that and it's much easier to use the one on the bow away from the sleeping quarters. It doesn't bother people as much.

ICE: There's very little sleeping for some of the crew members. It's real hard on them. Usually when we're going through the ice, I'm driving, so it doesn't really bother me as much. But when you're off watch and your relief guy is in the pilothouse going through ice, it is hard sleeping.

You don't hear the sound of the ice as much on the Dorothy Ann. The Dorothy Ann is in the notch all the time, and you're not breaking the ice with the tug. You're breaking the ice with the barge. You're pushing the ice ahead. There are some noises. Some pieces are pushed down by the barge and come up and hit the bottom of the tug and make noises. When a chunk of ice goes through the wheel *(propeller)*, then it does vibrate and it reverberates through the boat. Yeah, it makes a lot of noise.

Ice fields shift and crack as they contract and expand, making loud, rolling noises. You can hear the ice cracking if you have your window open. It's like thunder that moves. It occurred more when I was on a tug like the Donald C. Hannah because you are right there, just right there in the ice, breaking it. With the Dorothy Ann, I'm 600 feet from where the barge is breaking ice, so I don't hear it quite nearly as much.

BELL: The Dorothy Ann has a ship's bell. Some people walking by it and give it a good ring, and then the guys who are sleeping get real ticked off about it. So it doesn't get rung very much.

***

SIDE TRIP: *The crew is on water and in motion much the time.* I don't get seasick/motion sickness. The only time that I really came close to motion sickness was when I first quit smoking. For some reason, the first year after I quit smoking I'd get a little queasy once in a while, not really sick but queasy. But after that, I really don't get motion sickness. Some people do. Oh yeah, there are some people who are really sick.

I had one guy who – we'd leave the dock, and he could almost be flat out. I think it was just the thought process. But he'd get sick, and he was like this for like a year-and-a-half going on to two years until he finally was over the seasickness. When he got over the seasickness, he quit sailing.

I think you can adapt to it after a while. I don't know. I had an engineer who had the Dramamine patches he'd stick behind his ears. Four hours before we leave the dock, on goes the sticker.

Hatch 16

Communications

Great Lakes vessels boast up-to-date communications equipment and systems. And, at times, they still communicate in old-fashioned ways. Whatever gets the job done. Pilothouse roofs have telltale signs of communication needs, plus they have a whole lot more going on. Take the roof of the Dorothy Ann.

Up there are many antennas. There are three VHF radios. You have two antennas for radars. You have three antennas for GPS. I have three on one antenna for GPS gyro. I have a little antenna, a satellite antenna for Sirius Radio. I have one for my AIS, which is transponders so the Coast Guard and other vessels can keep track of us – vessel movements.

That's a lot to absorb, so let's take a systematic approach.

PERSONAL

TELEVISION: *One antenna is for satellite TV.* That goes to everybody's room, the lounge, the galley, and everywhere throughout the ship. We've had it ever since I've been on the Dorothy Ann.

We have DirecTV on the boat. We have the NFL package, so we get to watch a lot of games and shows. Sometimes we've gotten the hockey package, and we've gotten the baseball package a couple of times.

It used to be back in the day, if you had a TV set and you were close enough to shore and you had an antenna, you could watch TV. We had one in the galley. Or if you were lucky enough to be on a boat that had a lounge area, you had a TV set in a lounge area. I was never that lucky. So we had one in the galley.

As time went on, people bought their own TV sets to put in their rooms. Then you'd have to put up an antenna or connect with an antenna system. If you were lucky enough to be close enough to shore to get the old VHF/UHF channels, you could watch TV. At that time, you'd meet in the galley. People would be playing cards or sitting around watching TV. There was a lot of camaraderie throughout the crew.

A lot of times, you could go for a whole day without seeing TV at all. There was just no TV signal in the area. So you'd get together and play cards or checkers or backgammon or whatever.

Now, in this modern day and age, everybody has a computer, everybody has a TV in their own room, and it's hooked up to a satellite system, DirecTV, which you can get anywhere out on the Great Lakes. You always have great service. And you don't see as much of the people congregating in the galley or just getting together and talking and stuff like that. It's more of an individual thing now.

The roof of the Dorothy Ann supports many communication necessities. *BoatNerd.com photo*

Key:

1: GPS gyro/compass
2: Annometer
3: TV antenna
4: Radar
5: Antenna for satellite radio
6: Satellite antenna for telephone
7: VHF radio antennas
8: Horn
9: Loud hailer speaker

10: 2 Thermometers
11: Spotlight for dock workers
12: Forward search light
13: Stern search light
14: GPS
15: Radar
16: Starboard running light
17: Masthead lights

TELEPHONE: More people can communicate with their families versus years ago when there were no cell phones. Today, a crew member can speak with or send an email to family members from just about anywhere. There are certain cellular wastelands where you can't get out, but most places you can. Guys like to go up to the veranda on Dorothy Ann's tower because they get better reception on their cell phones. They like to go out there and have some privacy. They get up high enough where they get good service.

COMPUTER: *Games, movies, emails – you name it – crew members have choices.* A lot of the guys have Skype *(video phone)* on their computers. They can actually see when they're talking. It's quite amazing what you can do nowadays.

Separation from families is less harsh. It definitely helps, having communication. I can talk with Mary every couple of days when I'm away. She doesn't call me so much because she doesn't know if I'm awake or not awake and stuff like that. But I do call. Or she'll call me when something important comes up.

RADIO: I have an antenna for satellite radio, which we use in the pilothouse constantly. We listen to music. The crew likes to listen to various types of music and programs. We have Sirius Radio. The company doesn't pay for Sirius Radio. I pay for that myself. The reason I got that is so when I'm in the pilothouse I can listen to a Green Bay Packers game because it comes across on Sirius. I listen to the local feed. Sirius plays all the local feeds from all the NFL games, which is very nice. We get to listen to Larry McCarren and Wayne Larrivee.

ON BOARD

WALKIE-TALKIE, ETC.: We have a pretty good communication system. Everybody on the vessel has a walkie-talkie that they use at some time or another. We're in constant communication that way.

But the engineers sometimes in machinery space would not be able to hear the walkie-talkie, and would not carry it. Other times when you are way down in the bowels of the ship, down into the void spaces, you may not hear a walkie-talkie. At that point, we have sound-powered phones and a loud hailing system throughout the vessel, which you probably would hear and you can hear in the engine room even when we call for somebody. So if I call for an engineer and he's down in the engine room, he will be able to hear it. Also, with the engine room telephone, every time it rings, a light goes off, so that the engineers know they have a telephone call. The light corresponds with the ring.

Other than that, every mate, all the engineers, all the major rooms – the lounge, the galley, the engine room, pin room, Z-drive room, captain's room, all the mates – all have in-house telephone system.

We also, in case of emergency, have the general alarm, which rings throughout the vessel. At the same time you ring an alarm, you'll ring the ship's whistle, which also is the sound for emergencies.

If you just wanted to get somebody's attention on deck, a short blast of the whistle sometimes gets their attention, and they'll listen to their phone after that. There's a lot of ways to communicate on the vessel.

Walkie-talkies are used in many ways, such as when fueling, maneuvering through tight quarters, docking, and loading and unloading.

COMPUTER: We have computers in the first mate's, chief's, and captain's room, pilothouse, and engine room, and we can email one another. If I know that I can't get a hold of one of them, if he's down in the engine room or out on the barge doing some work where I can't get a hold of him and it's not important enough to really track him down, I'll send him an email with whatever the message is or whatever came in, and so when he gets it he'll read it. Unimportant messages.

TELEGRAPH: We have a telegraph system in case communications go out or steering goes out and the engineers have to steer from the engine room. I have a half ahead, full ahead, quarter ahead, half astern, full astern, quarter astern, and stop telegraph for which I just hit a button. An engineer has to answer in response in the engine room.

WIND GAUGE: The anemometer has heaters on the spikes so ice melts off. I have had to go up there. If the heater has not been on or the breaker on it goes and it gets a freezing rain on it, you can't go up there and tap it because they are hard antennas and they'll break off. You have to go up there with a little torch, and you have to be careful to melt it off properly. We have a 10-foot step ladder.

Communication with the engine room at times is through this telegraph system.
Gary Schmidt photo

LOUDSPEAKER: We call it a loud hailer. It's a speaker. It's so I can talk to crew members outside.

AFAR

COMPUTER, ETC.: Computers used to be just on board. They didn't communicate with the office. But now they communicate over Verizon wireless, and you can communicate with the office every day over computers. The company used to do it through a satellite system. It's gotten cheaper and much easier to do it with Verizon wireless or Sprint or whoever. We happen to use Verizon.

Captain Schmidt is in contact with the office every day. Directly or indirectly. A lot of times, if I've been up all night maneuvering in the river or sleeping, the mates will take the message, and write it down. When I get up, I'll read all the messages from the company. It communicates to me personally via emails to my computer. And if the office needs to get a hold of me, the mates will wake me up. That's not a problem. I will communicate with the office at any time. Basically, in one form or another, we communicate every day. Several times a day usually.

I'm immediately answerable to everybody in that office. Essentially, that's the way I feel about it. I answer to any and all. But I communicate mostly with somebody in marketing or dispatching. They tell us where to go and what to do. They are not my boss, but I work closely with them and I respond to them.

The company system is in-house, so to speak. Ours is unique to us. It's our system.

TELEPHONE: A smaller antenna is for telephone. I have satellite telephone communications anywhere on the lakes.

With the office, if it's an immediate need, we use wireless telephone, Verizon, for instance. If it is out in cellular wasteland where there is no Verizon, we have satellite telephone, and we can always get through. If it's not urgent, it goes through our email system, which is wireless Verizon again.

POSTAL SERVICE: There is ship's mail that I send out at the mail boat, the J.W. Westcott II. For instance, I send a hard copy of payroll to the office via ship's mail or just send it off at some port that I'm at. I might go to the post office and send it off, and it's usually express mail or priority mail in a hard envelop, flat rate. I also send the same payroll off via our email system. I make a copy of it and send it off so the office has an early copy of it so it can get some of the work done. But not all the ship's mail goes through emails. A lot of it has to go by snail mail.

RADIO: We have at least three VHF radio antennas. *These are used for communicating with other vessels, bridge tenders, traffic systems, docks and more.*

NAVIGATING

RADAR, ETC: Our radars used to be just a radar – you looked and you saw stuff out there. Now with the new technologies, they have ARPA, which is an automatic system that finds a target, tracks a target, marks a target, and tells you which are the most dangerous ones that you'll be coming into contact with.

Our radar masts are redundant. They are both Furuno Radars. One is a little smaller than the other one. They do the same thing. They do ARPA (*Automatic Radar Plotting Aids*), which is automatic plotting. They are both full range – more than 100-mile range, down to about a quarter-mile range. I have both on.

We usually have one set on close range when we're under way and one on further range. You might have it fine tuned when you're in closer so you pick up smaller boats. The longer range is for seeing larger ships as they're coming down the lake toward you. If it's a 1,000-footer, the distance it comes in depends on atmospheric conditions. But if you have a clear day, you can pick somebody up 100 miles away and even farther than that. If the conditions are real bad, you usually pick them up at between 24 to 48 miles easily.

I'll know who it is. I'll have it on my ECPINS (*electronic charts*), and that tells me the name of vessel and gives me its course. I can put the plot on him, and that will give me my closest point. When I get close to him, I know that he's going to be a mile off on my port side or he's going to be a mile off on my starboard side or he can be a mile off as we're heading on. We have time to make a decision and call him up and say, "Hey, what side would you prefer?" or "Where are you headed?" I give him one whistle or two whistles. One whistle means I'm going to direct my course to my starboard. Two means I'm going to direct my course to the port.

Unless it's in a confined area, like at one of the shoals, I usually direct that we're going to be a mile off. Sometimes it's a little bit closer or farther away, depending on where you are going. But you make arrangements, and you both alter course just a little bit and you pass.

If you're driving in a river, sometimes you're only 200 feet away. So I'm comfortable with a mile. But out in the open water you have more room to play, so you just make the room. In case something happens. In a confined area, you don't have much choice. Sometimes you might slow down. Somebody might slow down for you if you are passing them. You make arrangements to do something. But you're close. Sometimes you're a boat width apart of somebody as you're coming around a bend.

Sighting of pleasure craft depends upon the sea state. If there's sea *(rough water)* out there, you get some kind of a sea return on the radars. There's an adjustment on the radar set, and you adjust the picture to some degree. But when you do that, it takes out the small boats, too. That's why I keep one radar on a close range, and I'll fine tune that one and it will pick the a small craft up fairly decent, maybe three or four miles in kind of bad conditions. Sometimes you can't pick them up at all. I try to adjust the radar so I can pick up buoys. If you pick up a buoy, most of the time you can pick up a small craft. The small craft can help themselves just by putting some kind of piece of metal somewhere, and I mean something that will reflect, on a pole. Radar will reflect really well off a piece of metal. It could be tin, but it will reflect the radar transmission really well. I wish more boaters had it or had it built in to their boats. For the closer range radar, I usually set it at six miles. The long range I normally carry it on 24 miles. With the short range, on the radar screen, I can pick up images just about to the boat. It's just a matter of 100 feet.

CAMERAS: I have a wireless camera system with pictures transmitted from the bow to the stern. The cameras are adjustable. They rotate either way 180 degrees. I can't keep winding a camera. It has stops on it. I use it a lot. With the cameras on the bow, I have monitors in the forward pilothouse and in the after pilothouse. So if I'm backing up, I'll turn the camera around so it's facing back and I can see how my stern is approaching a bridge and stuff like that. It's a very, very handy piece of equipment. My camera is very good at night. It does not have the infra-red light, but it does have lunar vision.

Also, off each side of Dorothy Ann's stack is a remote camera so the guys in the engine room can see what's going on. It goes

Camera monitors (top center) communicate distances to the captain at his command position. *Gary Schmidt photo*

right down to the engine room. They can see where we're at, how we're docking, or how we're leaving. They're not totally blind.

I have an ECPIN – the electronic charting – that the engineers can see on their computer down there. They can see where we are and, if we're in a river, how we're maneuvering.

They have cameras by each engine and by the generators so they can tell in the control room if anything looks wrong – if they see smoke. These are stationary.

GPS (Global Positioning System) GYRO/COMPASS ANTENNA: That has three separate antennas on the one antenna and triangulates off the satellites. It's very, very accurate. It's better than my regular gyro that is a gyro compass. You don't lose the signal in rain and snow. It's very good.

It seems to be more accurate until you get into rivers when you get underneath a bridge and you lose the signal. It'll carry you for a little while. You'll get a warning that it's aborting. I'm not really using the gyro in the river at all. I'm doing everything visually.... You don't lose the signal in rain and snow. It's very good.

HORN: I use it mainly as a danger signal. I also blow when I have small or large craft that I meet in the river. The rules state that I can either give a whistle signal or I can talk to them on a VHF radio, which is also considered a signal. With the larger boats, we usually make an agreement over the radio. With the small boats, because most of them don't have the radios or you don't know if they have a radio or you don't know who they are to be calling them, I just give a whistle signal. That happens quite often. Either one or two whistles.

Also, when I blow that whistle, there's a little light that goes on. An amber light goes on. That's for nighttime, so it's visual as much as it is sound.

DEPTH MONITORS: I have a depth sounder on the tug, and I have a depth sounder on the barge. It all comes to the pilothouse through a wireless system now that I don't have to plug in because the plug-in types would corrode. It's kind of nice. I use that all the time.

RADIO: To communicate as we're coming into a port, we give security calls on Channel 16 VHF, our radio, to let other vessels know that we're coming in. When we are talking to the facilities, our company has already told them that we are coming in, then I give them a final, sometimes 12-hour ETA.

SEEING AND BEING SEEN: The vessel has searchlights forward and astern and running lights on both sides.

Uniform

Almost all the time, I wear khaki pants and a nice shirt that has the Interlake logo on it. So do all the mates. Some deckhands wear coveralls that say Interlake. Some wear them, and some don't.

I also have a dress uniform. It's been a tradition at Interlake. If you look at early Interlake photos, uniforms were worn just about all the time in the early days. The company was more strict with uniforms. It was a tradition. Not so much anymore. It's more relaxed now. Normally, I wear my dress uniform once during the course of a year. It's for a function for the company.

Captain Gary's dress uniform has four stripes on the sleeves.

The stripes indicate rank. The rank is captain, four stripes. If you are a first mate, that's three bars. Second mate would be would be two. And third mate would be one. The anchor on the sleeve represents deck department.

On the front of the dress cap is a medallion with a bald eagle standing on a U.S. shield with a rope and anchor superimposed. The anchor and shield are enclosed in a wreath.

Side buttons on the cap band are of an anchor and two stars and anchor rope. The brim is patent leather.

It hasn't happened to me, but if you're the first vessel through the Soo Locks for the season, the vessel is given the top hat award. Usually, the captain will put on his uniform and go out and have photographs taken.

If you're invited to a christening of a ship, you would wear your dress uniform.

At the company meetings, we have a formal dinner. We all dress up for that. Our masters and chiefs wear our uniforms. The executives wear suits.

I have a story. I recently had my dress uniform altered. We went to the Men's Wearhouse to have it done. When they went to charge me, they told me that uniforms are a reduced rate. When I paid for everything, I got $35 off the uniform alteration, and they also told me I was doing a great job overseas. I haven't been overseas since 1968, when I was in the Navy.

I've worn the dress uniform when I've gone to court for the company.

Here's another uniform story. A few years ago, I am going to court for Interlake on a lawsuit. This is in Detroit.

Captain Gary W. Schmidt in his dress uniform. *Turba-Schroeder Photography*

I'm sitting out in the hallway waiting my turn, as a witness for the company, and one of the federal judges comes out and addresses me and tells me what a fine job we're doing over in Afghanistan and Iraq. And he keeps on telling me what a great job we're all doing and stuff like that. Instead of explaining to him that I'm a merchant marine and embarrassing him, I just go ahead and say, "Thank you, sir."

When I came back from Vietnam, the public reception wasn't especially nice. But I came back early enough before the real bad protests took place. And I could understand both sides of the protesting. I could understand the patriotism of the servicemen. It was a real hard time back in the early '70s. But I was out of the service before the really bad stuff started happening with the protests.

Today, people respond to the uniform. It is nice recognition. The uniform I wear is not distinctive except for the anchor on the sleeve and the four captain's stripes. But I don't have any medals or anything like that on my chest. Even at that, it still looks like a Navy uniform pretty much.

Hatch 18

Flags

I usually go through about two American flags a season, maybe three.

They're changed because they get wear and tear. They're up all the time. From the stacks, they get some carbon in them, and they don't look bright enough. The wind flapping on them all the time shreds the ends.

We'll do things to keep the flags from wearing too fast. Where seams are sewn on the end, I've taken a thin layer of silicon and gone over them, and that prolongs the flag a little bit before it starts to tear.

Our flag is flying on the stern of the tug.

The company flag is flown forward on the barge. I fly the company flag on one side. When we go into Canadian waters, we're flying the Canadian flag on the side that Canada is on, usually. And the company flag on the other side.

We fly the Canadian flag out of courtesy. Just like any vessel that comes to the United States will be flying an American flag. If you go into somebody else's waters, you usually fly their flag.

Any of the numerous flags we have we can fly underneath the flags on the bow of the barge – except the Don't Tread on Me *(a spiraling snake)* which is a U.S. flag. It gets flown higher than the company flag or any other flags.

My relief mate likes that Don't Tread on Me flag. It's not my thing.

The Dorothy Ann/Pathfinder approaches the Mackinac Bridge in northern Michigan. *Gary Schmidt photo*

It's fall as the Dorothy Ann/Pathfinder is served in the MacArthur Lock downbound at the Soo Locks at Sault Ste. Marie, Michigan. *Gary Schmidt photo*

Westbound in the Straits of Mackinac, the Dorothy Ann/Pathfinder follows in the track of a thousand-foot vessel ahead as it is passed on the right by the freighter Philip R. Clarke, which is having its way cleared by an approaching U.S. Coast Guard icebreaker *Gary Schmidt photo*

On Lake Erie, big waves crest over the Pathfinder's deck line, which is about 15 feet above the water in calm conditions. *Gary Schmidt photo*

The boom is raised on the Pathfinder to ease loading of iron ore at Marquette, Michigan.
Photo courtesy The Interlake Steamship Company

Iron ore pours from the Pathfinder's boom at Severstal North America on the Rouge River in Dearborn, Michigan.
Gary Schmidt photo

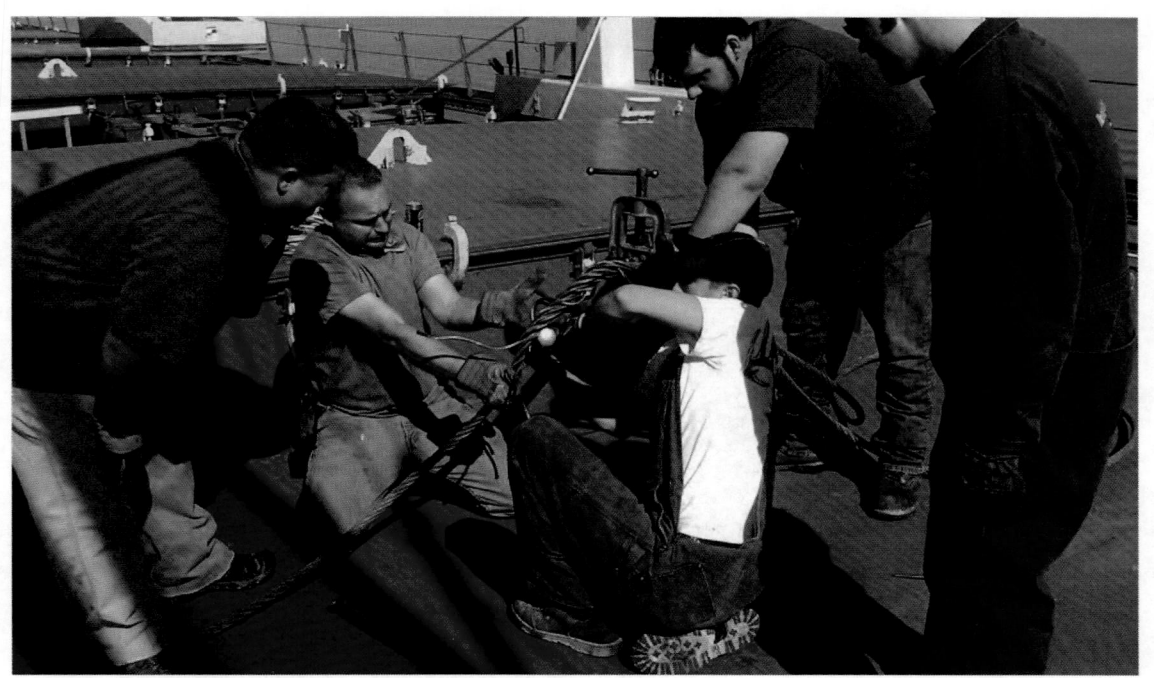

Crewmen team to splice a cable that has become worn. *Gary Schmidt photo*

As part of fire safety training, crewmen spray one another with hoses to demonstrate how waterproof their gear is. *Gary Schmidt photo*

The sun sets with the Dorothy Ann/Pathfinder docked at the Lake Superior and Ishpeming Railroad South Dock at Marquette, Michigan. *Rod Burdick photo*

Snow has fallen as the Dorothy Ann/Pathfinder docks at the Lake Superior and Ishpeming Railroad North Dock at Marquette, Michigan. *Photo courtesy The Interlake Steamship Company*

Captain Schmidt works in his office in his quarters aboard the Dorothy Ann. *Gary Schmidt photo*

Captain Schmidt poses in his work hard hat.
Warren Gerds photo

Captain Schmidt poses in a discarded fireman's hat that he rebuilt into a hat to wear to Green Bay Packers games at Lambeau Field in Green Bay, Wisconsin. *Warren Gerds photo*

It's a rainy day, and the river current is fast as the Dorothy Ann/Pathfinder is docked, hatches open, at the West Third Street Osborne Dock on the Cuyahoga River in Cleveland, Ohio. *Jeremy Mock photo*

Snow has fallen since the photo at the top of the page, and the Dorothy Ann/Pathfinder, hatches closed, is still at the same dock. *Jeremy Mock photo*

Sturgeon Bay, Wisconsin, is dressed in autumn colors in this photograph taken through a periscope that's among the attractions in Door County Maritime Museum. "The water tower is my neighborhood," says Captain Schmidt. "That's where I used to live." The Dorothy Ann was constructed at Sturgeon Bay, and the Pathfinder was converted to a barge there. The bridge in the left foreground is on the National Register of Historic Places. The rescue of the Michigan Street Bridge from demolition is the inspiration for the annual Steel Bridge Songfest, which features an eclectic array of musicians from around the world. The building with the red roof in the right foreground is the Holiday Music Motel, owned and operated by singer-songwriters melaniejane and Pat mAcdonald. As part of the duo Timbuk 3, mAcdonald created the 1986 hit song, "The Future's So Bright (I Gotta Wear Shades)." "At the base of the bridge, when I was a kid, was a bait stand," Captain Schmidt says. "That's where I used to work. During the summer, I would pick nightcrawlers, and I would go out and trap minnows in the rivers. That's how I got my first boat. I picked nightcrawlers the whole summer and bought a rowboat." *Monica L. Gerds photo*

Cargo Hold 2 – Voyages

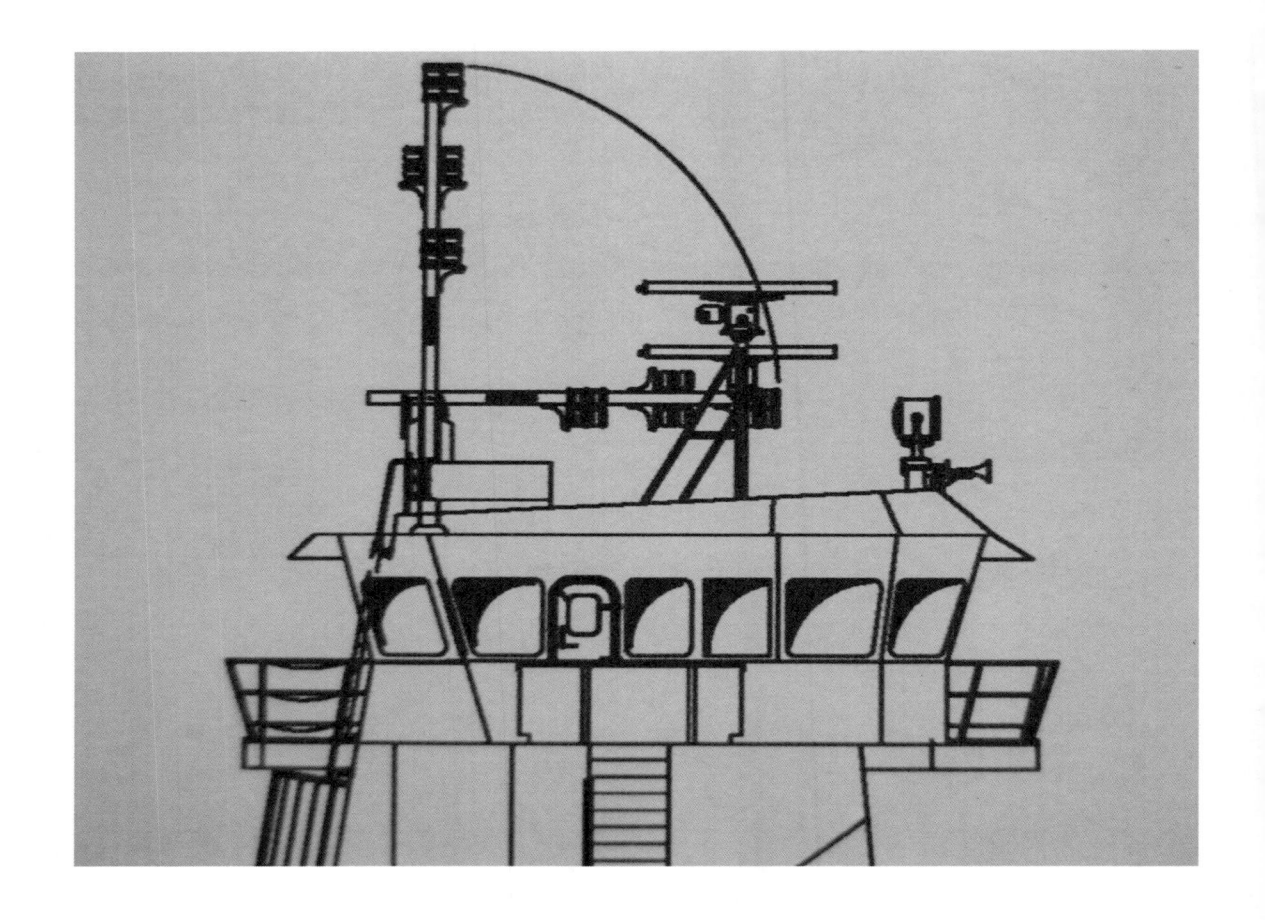

Hatch 19

Plotting

In this chapter, we learn that Captain Schmidt has developed a sophisticated system for charting courses using prime technology.

We also learn that Captain Schmidt is like Starship Enterprise captains, boldly going where few vessels the size of the Dorothy Ann can go.

Hang on.

ECPINS came into my life the minute that I walked on the Dorothy Ann. I had never worked with it before.

ECPINS stands for Electronic Chart Precise Integrated Navigation System. It's electronic charting.

Another thing I like is AIS, which is short for Automatic Identification System. This system gives you an idea of where all the boats are. You can go by the name of the vessel, and the system will show you where is and its direction and speed. You can switch from satellite view to a chart. The system shows you all the Great Lakes, and you can see where all the boats are. I use these tools all the time. These are on web sites. Anybody with a computer can get on them.

We do have software, though, and other tools that are hooked into our radars. They automatically plot other vessels. This system tells you when you're going to be in a collision situation or close-quarter situation, and it gives you an idea when your closest point of approach is and how far off you're going to be and more. And you can plot what to do to avoid a situation, and it's all automatic. That's software.

We also have the electronic charting, ECPINS. That software pretty much shows you what's on AIS – gives you a chart and it shows your position as you're moving along exactly where it's at. It also shows all the other boats like on AIS. You can also click on the vessel, and the system gives you plotting information.

Interlake sent me to a school on a one-day ECPINS course to learn as much as I could, and I fell in love with it. It's a very, very useful tool. It's one of the best navigation tools there is around right now.

I have three GPSs on the vessel, other than the GPS gyro.

That stands for Global Positioning System, and it's a satellite navigation system

The captain has an ECPINS monitor in his room.
Gary Schmidt photo

that's non-magnetic and is used to automatically find geographical direction using satellite triangulation.

GPSs are nice. They're very accurate. And just recently, ECPINS computers and software have been upgraded to hold all of the charts. It used to be there wasn't enough memory, and you would be cramped for how many charts you can put in at one time. The programs have caught on to the size of the computers. Programs have advanced. ECPINS is a very handy system. You can go to any route you want. Cleveland to Marblehead, Cleveland to Toledo, Cleveland to Lorain, Cleveland to Fairport.

Over time, Captain Schmidt has put together routes throughout the Great Lakes that include approximately 300 waypoints, which are GPS and/or visual points of reference. The routes and waypoints are compiled electronically and in print – and indexed so he can more simply chart courses.

The zero range is for Lake Huron. I have 34 waypoints on Lake Huron. The 100 range is Lake Michigan, with at least 98 waypoints. Lake Erie has more than 50 waypoints. Lake Superior has about 40 waypoints. I don't go to Lake Ontario often, so I bring that waypoint index out only when needed.

This is what the ECPINS electronic chart looks like when the Dorothy Ann/Pathfinder is docked at the Shiras Generating Plant at Marquette, Michigan. *Gary Schmidt photo*

On a chart, you just put a point right where you want to be. That would be a waypoint. That waypoint might correspond with a lighthouse, it might correspond with a buoy, it might be off an island, or it might correspond with two miles off a certain point where you want to make a haul. It's any Lat. and Long. that you want it to be. When you put it down, you name it as waypoint number one or waypoint 365. It doesn't matter. It's just numbered. A waypoint could be where I will make a steering change. Or I have some marked where I have to do something like call in Sarnia traffic. That waypoint matches up with the Salt Dock Light in the St. Clair River. And it's not that I have to make a course change there, because I don't have to, it's just a reminder that this is a point where I have to call in.

So waypoints can be used for many things, not just hauling points but can be used for references for other things. A waypoint could be just a starting point. Coming out of Cleveland, a starting point would be at the break wall. My next waypoint might be a mile off. I always put a mile-off reference because I use that as a checkpoint as I'm coming back in. It lines you up with the break wall or, with the system that I have, as a lineup point to come through a break wall. Those last two waypoints usually direct me straight in. But they're still generic.

If I'm going to Marblehead, I'll have a waypoint off of Vermilion Point of five miles. That keeps me clear of all obstructions. It keeps me clear of all the sailing vessels that like to have races. I stay outside of their race zones, and I try to miss most of the traffic of that kind. And that waypoint keeps me away from all shoals. Then from there, I can set a course for Lorain, I can set a course for Sandusky, or I can set a course for Marblehead.

The waypoints are set up for upbound traffic and downbound traffic. Depending on which way you're going, you make adjustments off waypoints as to how you want to meet traffic.

The Lake Superior routes will run to the St. Marys River. The St. Marys River is a route by itself. Once I get down to the bottom of the St. Marys River, I'll have a route from De Tour to wherever I'm going. De Tour can go down Lake Michigan, it can go down Lake Huron. But if it goes down Lake Michigan, it'll go from De Tour to any port on Lake Michigan.

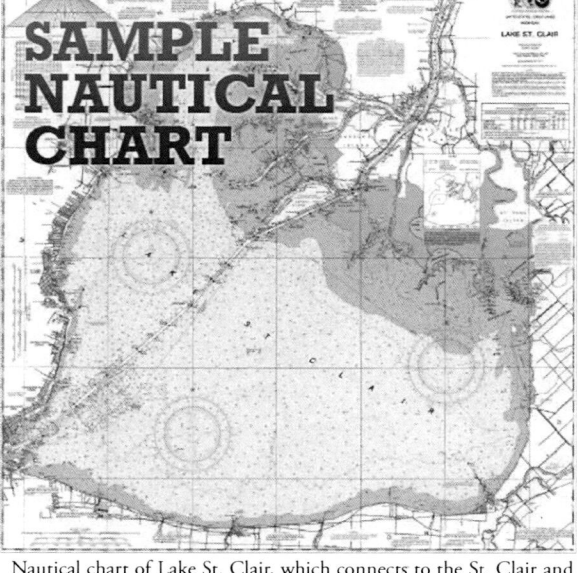

Nautical chart of Lake St. Clair, which connects to the St. Clair and Detroit River. The area is familiar to Captain Schmidt.

My routes will go from De Tour to Huron Cut Buoys 11 and 12. That is the start of the St. Clair and Detroit River. I will run a route for the St. Clair and Detroit River. It has 80-some waypoints in it just by itself. When I get to the bottom of the Detroit River, which is at Detroit River Light, then I make waypoints from Detroit River Light anywhere on Lake Erie all the way over to the Welland Canal. At the Welland Canal, that's another route. I don't have a route for the Welland Canal because the canal is really narrow and movement is from lock to lock to lock. You're not really using a GPS.

Once you get in at Port Colborne *(Lock 8)* and travel out at St. Catherines *(Lock 1)*, then I have routes for Lake Ontario all the way up to Cape Vincent at the start of the St. Lawrence River. I don't have any St. Lawrence River waypoints because we always take a pilot. A pilot has his own set.

***

SIDE TRIP: You need pilots when you go into a foreign country.

For example, I was in Canadian waters off of Lake Ontario going up the St. Lawrence Seaway. Because I'm not familiar with that area, I took on pilots from the pilots association.

We started our voyage from a dock in Ohio. We signed out. We had to get Customs clearance to go into Canada. I took the vessel east on Lake Erie and went through the Welland Canal and across Lake Ontario. Once we got to Cape Vincent, New York, which is at the source of the St. Lawrence River, we picked up pilots. The pilots can be Canadian, or they can be U.S. It doesn't matter. A pilot is a pilot. We're crossing borders along the way. We're in Canadian waters on one side and American waters on the other side going up almost all the way up to Montreal. Once you get to Montreal, it's all Canadian waters going the rest of the way up.

So we picked up U.S. pilots at Cape Vincent. Because I am two vessels – I am a tug and a barge and I have two IMO numbers – two pilots are assigned, one for each IMO number, which is really ridiculous. We went all the way to Montreal with those two pilots. In Montreal, I picked up two totally Canadian pilots. We went to Trois Riviers and changed pilots. The next pilots took us all the way to Quebec City. Once we loaded our cargo at Quebec, we notified the pilots association, and we had pilots going back out. Again, they changed at Trois Riviers and again at Montreal. And we dropped the pilots off at Cape Vincent on the way back.

All the while, I'm responsible for the vessel, but the pilots give sailing directions to whoever is steering the vessel. Pilots know the river better and have better local knowledge than I could ever read up on or get. I rely on that person for direction. But if I see something wrong, I'm responsible for taking over. It does feel odd, and you're up for a long period of time.

***

Let's take a route. Let's say I'm in Milwaukee, and I want to go over to Stoneport. I'm empty because it's not a loading port. I'm going to Stoneport to load. The weather is going to be out of the west, but it's not going to be strong. I have options. When I come out of Milwaukee, I can go up to Lansing Shoal, go across, under the Mackinac Bridge, down the South Channel, around Presque Isle Light, and right to Stoneport to load. If the wind is strong out of the east, I would shoot across for Little Sable Point, ride the east shore of Lake Michigan up to Manitou Passage at Sleeping Bear Buoy, go through Grays Reef Passage, to White Shoal, over to Mackinac Bridge, down the South Channel, and to Stoneport. That involves dead reckoning.

You would plot everything out before you left. You would make a route. I write down waypoints. Waypoints are in Lat. and Long. *(Latitude and Longitude)*. Waypoint 1 would be Milwaukee break wall. Waypoint 2 would be three miles off Milwaukee. Waypoint 3 would be Little Sable Point. The next waypoint would be Big Sable Point. The next waypoint would be Point Betsy. If I'm far enough off, I could go right to Sleeping Bear Buoy, which will take me through the Manitou Islands up to North Manitou Light. At North Manitou Light, I would change course and have a straight shot for Grays Reef Passage/Grays Reef Light. That would take me up to White Shoal Light, the next waypoint. From there to the Mackinac Bridge would be a waypoint. I would be coming down through the South Channel. There's a straight shot all the way down to Cheboygan Traffic Buoy. At that point, you make a haul for Poe Reef Light. When you come out of Poe Reef, you pass Cordwood Point, the next waypoint. From Cordwood Point you would take a shot all the way down to Presque Isle Light. Then I would just shoot right down for Stoneport.

Those waypoints are on my GPS. Also, on my ECPINS, I have the same ones, which shows me the charts, shows me where the waypoints are. As we are going along, the monitor shows me a picture of my waypoints, of my routes, in big red lines. It's a light red line until I get on it. When I'm on that line, it turns a dark red so you know that you are on that waypoint line. It gives me a warning. It tells me before I get to the waypoint that it's time to change to the next waypoint. I can set that warning up to wherever I want it. I can set that up for two-tenths of a mile, three-tenths of a mile, four-tenths of a mile.

And then I have my book, and I have my routes numbered. As you look up the route that you want, that number, you go to the route, once you get to that route, it gives you all the waypoints on it, all the names of the waypoints, the distance to the waypoints, and the degrees that you have to steer for waypoints. That's in a book, so you can have that in front of you at all times. But it's also in both of the machines. It's like a three-way backup system. It's something I built.

Off of those routes, I can make variations or changes. They are all put into a route system in a GPS. So all I have to do is pull up Route number 006, for instance – from Huron Cut buoys to Calumet Harbor in south Chicago. It will give me all the waypoints that I have figured out. I have generic waypoints for Presque Isle, two miles off; for Middle Island; for Harbor Beach. For whatever point there is, I'll give it a number. And then I assign those numbers into the route itself, the waypoints. That will be a waypoint number, and those waypoint numbers go into a route, which I have named. Huron Cut Buoys 11 and 12 to Calumet Harbor and it will be Route 006.

I have a book, so anytime that I need to go from any point – Marquette to Detroit – I just look up what route that is. The routes are broken up where rivers are. I have a route for the river, but there's too many waypoints in a river to make a complete route.

***

SIDE TRIP: *Captain Schmidt has a Route 66, but his Route 66 is quite different than the famous highway from Chicago to Los Angeles.*

It's Port Inland, Michigan, to Marinette, Wisconsin – or the other way around *(and it's on page 10 of Captain Schmidt's book)*. Going upbound to Marinette, waypoints are the Port Inland break wall. This is a tough port. You get to one mile out to where the buoy is, go to Seul Chioix Point, which is 2.8 miles. You head down to Rock Island Pass for 51.1 miles. You get over to the top of Washington Island, which is Boyers Bluff, and you make a haul. You go down to Chambers Island, which is 28 miles. You're going to be 2½ miles west. You shoot from there to Marinette, one mile off, and then you start in the channel to Marinette break wall.

***

There are three monitors for the ECPINS. Two are in the pilothouse. There's one in the front window and one in the back window. There's one in my room. From those, I can change a route. There is another part that goes to the server, and other people on board can see ECPINs but not get into the system. There's one in the chief engineer's room, one in the engine room, and one in the cook's room. That's part of their computer system. On the monitor, they can see where we're at in live time.

Mariners of old would be dazzled by such a system.

Back in the '70s on the small tugs that I was on, we had a gyro. Some of the boats had radio detection finders, and most of the major break walls on Lake Michigan had a distinctive radio call – dot dash, dot dash – different for different places. You would hone in on them. You would do your plotting with pencil on paper, adjusting for wind-blown routes. Every two hours, you would plot your course on the lake so you would know where you're at. ECPINS has made it so much easier – real, live time you know where you're at exactly all the time. Back then, when you did the plotting, you looked at your radars, which weren't too good. If the weather was good, the radars were good. If the weather was bad, the radars were bad. They weren't so good. If you had an electrical storm or snow, you were just screwed.

***

SIDE TRIP: I'm not a tech person by any means. I have no idea about a lot of computer stuff. But I learned to use the computer to my advantage. I made it my business to know a little bit about computers.

Years ago, a relative gave me an Apple 2 when she got a new computer, and I took the Apple 2 aboard the Triton with me to play with and to learn something about computers. I figured out some of the programs and some of the things I could do. I started to fill out forms with computer, like all our payroll forms. That made the job easier. The more time you can commit to things other than paperwork, the more you can get done.

***

When I started on the Dorothy Ann, this capability was there, but I did not have all of this. ECPINS existed and the vessel had some routes in the system that some of the mates made up. From Marblehead to Cleveland, there might have been five different routes. I wiped them all out.

I started from scratch and built this system.

I put down my waypoints. I started out with the ones that I knew we were going to use right away and built a base of waypoints and built the base of everyday routes. As we expanded to more ports, I would build more routes and I put them in the system.

At first, I was putting the routes in alphabetical order. But then as I was building so many routes, the alphabetical order was too hard to change everything around in the system, so I numbered each one. As I added on, I could number a route and put it on a page and put a page number to it. It made the system easier to add on routes, and now I'm to well over 200 routes.

Plotting is much simpler. I have a big base of waypoints. And I have not added very many more waypoints. So if we do change to a different port or from one port that I've been to before but going to one that I've not been to from the previous port, I can make a new route using all the waypoints I have. It's very simple. I can build a route in a matter of minutes. It takes no time, and not a lot of effort.

Then I just enter the information into the ECPINS and enter it into my GPS, and it's there permanently. Then I come back and I add it on to my list in the computer. Then all I have to do in my book is replace the page that I had to change or add on to or add another page.

So I have it several different ways. I have it by routes and what page they're on. In the beginning of my book, I have an alphabetical listing. If I want to go from Alabaster to Port Huron, it's alphabetical but the route might have a different number reference to it. It's alphabetical so you can find a route faster in the index. I have maybe 300 waypoints total, and off of those base waypoints, I can make as many routes as I want. I just number them differently. If you wanted to print out the computer version, you could have it in front of you as you're going down a lake. You know what your next waypoint, your next route is.

This is a system that I kind of built for myself. It's one that they use on the Dorothy Ann. My relief captain knows and loves the system. The mates know and love the system. Other people have used it and take it to other boats and put it on their personal computer like I have. I bet 100 people have one, but this is my original one. It's not unique. Other captains might have a similar system. I don't know. This is what I came up with.

Some vessels have little use for such an elaborate system. For instance, the 1,000-footers go to fewer ports.

They don't need many routes.

Captain Schmidt is given pause by the next consideration: By comparison with the Dorothy Ann…

I don't know if I have the most routes of the Interlake fleet. I may have the most. But I may not. I have a lot because of the maneuverability of the vessel.

While the system that Captain Schmidt came up with is customized for him and his relief mates, he doesn't view it as exclusive.

It's not necessarily specifically for the Dorothy Ann/Pathfinder.

Other captains have borrowed my book. Other captains have their own system, their own books, and their waypoints may not be the same as my waypoints. These are waypoints I am comfortable with, that I have researched, that I have put up in the system, that I am safe and feel safe with anybody running them. They could be for a thousand-footer. They're kind of generic.

If you are going through Southeast Shoal, there are buoys, there are many courses that run to Southeast Shoal from different angles. I put a generic in my system *(Captain Schmidt tosses off technical details).* Other captains asked for my information, and I gave it to them.

The screen shows information available by way of ECPINS electronic charting. Note the wind speed of 62 miles an hour. *Gary Schmidt photo*

I do not have a copyright on it, but I thought about publishing it at one time. And I also at one time thought about publishing a waypoint and route book for small craft – how to avoid large vessels and stay off the main courses – but I never did get to it. It was a thought and I started to work on it, but it was too massive to undertake. I give the information to anybody who wants it. I don't have a problem with it. I know of at least three people who have the system. Do they use it? I don't know that they use it. They have it, but I don't know if they use it. And maybe more have it. A lot of captains share information. They share their points of where they make turns in rivers and stuff like that, and it's passed around. That's a good thing. The more information you have, the better you can do your job.

While Captain Schmidt may chart course for a trip beforehand for him and his relief to follow, the route is not chiseled in stone. Storms can factor in, especially if a turn is required in open water to reach a necessary point.

If a wind is off the stern, or you're head on into it, you're riding pretty good. And I mean riding. You might have some action with the stern of the tug going down a little bit. The bow of the barge might move a little bit up and down but not too bad. You can head into 12 to 14-foot seas and not be too bad off. And the same with the stern wind.

You can ride a stern wind. It can push you along, and you won't feel the wave action so much until you have to make that turn. It's different once you take the wind on the beam, once you take one of those 20-foot seas on the beam. For instance if you're coming from Marquette and we're eastbound on Lake Superior and you've got a west wind, you'll ride real nice until you have to make the turn to go onto Whitefish Bay. Now, I've had 20-foot seas on my stern, riding good, and then at some point in time you can be one to two miles off of Whitefish Point and you've got to make that turn and you're going to be in the beam for approximately two miles or three miles until you get out of that beam sea. It can be pretty tense at that time. Then you're looking at water, maybe blue water shipping right over the deck of the barge. And you just hang on. That's what you do.

There's no stopping and waiting until this blows over.

You can't stop. Once you're going, there's no stopping. If you run out of water *(that's deep enough)*, you're going to hit the shore, so you have to make the turn. You get to a point and you either have to turn into the bay or you have to go straight and ride it, and then pretty soon you run out of water. You have to make that turn.

When the going gets rough, the captain is at the helm.

I go up to the pilothouse. Any turns into a beam sea, I'm going to be up there. I'm going to do that.

It's never my watch, so to speak I'm up there anytime. The mate would still be up there. I would go up there and supervise the move. I would tell him that, "Wow, we can't take this big of a beam sea. Maybe we'll have to cut it back and run a little bit further on kind of an angle. We'll take it the best we can until we can get around the corner and get into shelter." That's what I go up there for.

You can't just turn 90 degrees and go right into a beam sea. If you're coming into a point, let's say, and you know you have to go down to another point no matter what, you might start just easing the angle over a little at a time so you don't roll too much until you can get past that point and you lose some of the angle. It may be a longer ride, more than if I turn at a sharper angle and have only a mile or so to go. If I angle it less, it might affect me for several miles, but it'll be a better ride and you wouldn't roll the ship.

Some vessels have little use for such an elaborate system. For instance, the thousand footers go to fewer ports.

When you're plotting a course over open water, you use dead reckoning. Places like the Cuyahoga River are line of sight. Things change – water level, current.

We'll get into the Cuyahoga in greater depth later. For now, ECPINS will lead us to a new topic.

Computers are a curse and a blessing. They make your job so much easier *(as with ECPINS)*, but because it's easier, more stuff can be piled on you. There's a lot of it. The paperwork has piled on and that has to do with everybody being more aware of their surroundings.

***

EPILOGUE: Lighthouses play a role today to a little bit of a degree. We have to know that they're there, and you have to know their characteristics. It's all part of piloting, to know the different lighthouses and where they're at. But with the electronic charting, and with GPS and pre-determined routes, you don't pay as much attention to them except maybe the ones on the end of the break wall as a visual guide as you're coming in. But for the most part, something like Lansing Shoal Lighthouse, you know it's there, but if it's foggy, you don't even see it. They served their purpose. And they still serve their purpose. But with the new electronics, I don't think they're quite as important as they were.

Hatch 20

The pie story

We were coming with the Triton and St. Marys Cement *(barge)* from Bowmanville, Ontario, with a load of cement. It was 1992 or 1993. We were headed for Milwaukee. The weather was getting bad. I could have run some more down the east shore, but I couldn't tow the barge into Milwaukee Harbor because the seas were too large. It would have been too dangerous to take the vessel across Lake Michigan. So we pulled into Ludington, Michigan, for safe harbor and to tie up for the night. It just happened to be Thanksgiving. We didn't have a cook on the boat. Dave Fitzpatrick, my second mate, and I did most of the cooking. Between the two of us, we always cooked for the holidays. We would put out a big meal. We would put out the turkey with all the dressings, lobster tail or crab legs, shrimp. We made hors d'oeuvres. We worked hard at a dual job. We had to run the boat and be the cook and try to put out a meal.

The meal wasn't such a big meal because there were only six of us on board. There were three mates, two engineers, and a deckhand. So we got into Ludington, and we didn't have pie or pie material.

There were always curiosity seekers who came down to the dock. There were always boat nerds, and we had some that day. They wanted to know about the boat. So we went out and talked to them. "Yeah, this is a cement boat, this is what it looks like." People are interested in the tug. They're interested in diesels, big motors, big engines. Most people are the most interested in those. We took these people aboard and showed them the engine rooms. They said, "Wow, those are big."

Eventually, I asked, "Is there a bakery open where we could go and get some pumpkin pie? We need some pie for our Thanksgiving Day meal." A guy said, "There's a bakery up there that might be open." So the guy drove me up to a bakery, and we went in. "Oh no, all pies are spoken for, we have not a pie left." We went to another place, and it was closed. Nobody had pies. There was not a pie to be had in Ludington. So we went back to the boat, and I said, "That's fine, we can have our big meal without pie."

A little while later, somebody came down to the dock. I was sitting in the galley, and I could hear, "Hey! Hey!" Well, there's the guy who took me up around all over town. He came back with two homemade pies. All we had to do was bake them. They were apple and, I think, pecan. They weren't pumpkin. But it was pie. So there we were with pies to eat for Thanksgiving.

His wife made them up, and he brought them back down. I have no idea who he is to this day. I don't remember his name. He was just somebody who came down and said, "Yeah, I'll give you a ride up. Let's go look and see if we can find you a pie." He drove me around. I said, "Can I give you any money for the ride?" "No, no, no, that's all fine and dandy." "Well, the next time I see you around here I'll take you out and buy you a beer or something." I went back aboard the boat and gave it no more thought until he came back yelling, "Hey! Hey!"

Hatch 21

Soo passage

The Great Lakes have major obstructions to navigation. One is a height problem between Lake Superior and Lake Huron, which are joined at Sault Ste. Marie, Michigan, USA/Sault Ste. Marie, Ontario, Canada.

There's typically 16 feet between the two water levels. But it could run 19 feet, and it could run less. I probably do about 20 trips a year to Marquette, Michigan, so that means that I go through the locks about 40 times a year.

***

SNAPSHOT: Each year, more than 4,500 vessels maneuver through the Soo Locks, according to the U.S. Army Corps of Engineers. There are two locks for commercial vessels. Built in 1968, the Poe is 1,200 feet long. Built in 1943, the MacArthur is 800 feet long. During the 2013 winter shutdown, crews repaired watertight doors and miter gates, upgraded concrete, and installed gate fenders and an air bubbler suppression system for the MacArthur Lock. The Poe Lock got a new hydraulic system to operate the gates, booms, and valves.

***

Come on along as Captain Schmidt walks us through the process of sailing to, into, and out of the locks.

Going upbound through the locks system, you come in at De Tour, Michigan. One hour before you get to De Tour, you have to call the traffic system in the St. Marys River. It's called Soo Traffic. You report your vessel name, your cargo, destination, and your draft. At that point, you are monitored as you go through the system. At certain points in the system, you have to call in and report that you're at that point. The call-in points upbound – or westbound when we're going through Lake Superior – start at De Tour Reef Light. After the initial one-hour pre-call to De Tour Reef Light and then a call in at De Tour Reef Light, there's Munuscong Lake Junction Buoy – we call it Mud Lake. At Nine Mile Point, which is nine miles from the locks, we also call the lockmaster and give him our destination, cargo and draft. There are two separate entities. This one is for the Soo Locks. You also have to let them know if there are any security issues, like if you have any crew members coming aboard or getting off. Or if there's anything else that they need to know about, you report it at that point. Then you call in at Mission Point, which is just below Sault Ste. Marie Harbor, or just below the locks. At that point, you also call the Coast Guard and the locks. There are more call-in points if you don't have AIS for your vessel to be tracked.

The lockmaster will tell you what lock you're going to get – the MacArthur Lock or the Poe Lock – and if there's any traffic, or if you're going to have to tie up and wait or if you have a clear lock and you can go on up through. All that information is passed. Let's say that I'm going up on ballast *(with no cargo load)*. I'm usually going up on ballast, but a lot of times I'll take a stone load up to Marquette. My vessel is the size that will fit the MacArthur Lock. Most of the time, they give me the MacArthur Lock. The Poe Lock is a much larger lock that accommodates the big vessels, the thousand footers. Any vessel longer than 730 feet and anything 75 feet or wider, they're Poe Lock-size. Anything under the 730 by 75 is a MacArthur Lock size. But if you have several boats going through the MacArthur Lock and one's in ahead of you, the lockmaster may give you the Poe Lock even though you're a smaller size vessel. And it's first-come, first-served on your boat size to the lock. So if you've got somebody who's called in above the locks coming down and has called in at his points and he's going to be there before you, he has the right of way before you get your upbound slot.

So at that point, let's just say he says you've got a clear lock and it's the Mac, I come up into the lock area maneuvering. I'll put my bow on the approach wall to the lock, and I will put men off board and put them on the dock. They're line handlers. They help the lockmen handle the lines as we're going into the locks. We swing our guys off. We have a swing with a chair on it. With a pulley system, we swing the chair out over the edge of the dock area and drop them down slowly to a standing position on the dock. The vessel's moving, but

very slowly. They get back on board when the boat rises and reaches the right level in the lock. They just step over onto the vessel.

There are two or three lock personnel at each lock, and my two crewmen. So there are four or five people involved. And there's a lockmaster up in the tower, where the traffic in and out is controlled, who watches the operation.

I don't know who opens the gates, or where they open them from.

In a view from the Dorothy Ann, the Pathfinder makes another trip through the Soo Locks at Sault Ste. Marie, Michigan. The vessel is in the MacArthur Lock. *Gary Schmidt photo*

Gates let the water in or let the water out for different levels. There's somebody behind the scenes doing that. They've got to make sure that the gates close properly and are sealed before they do any water operation. They either let the water in from Lake Superior or they let the water out of the lock – if they're dropping the water level down into the lower pool, the water comes out. It's a matter of opening which gates and closing which water gates.

When I'm in the lock, the engines are running but I'm not engaged. I'm watching the mooring lines. You can surge in the locks, depending on how the gates are opened. A vessel going into the other lock can affect the way the water is going into the gate that you're going in because it's pushing water forward sometimes, or vessels are pulling water away from you as they're leaving. And it does affect you a little bit. So you kind of keep an eye on the lines. If you start moving and the winches aren't holding the cable properly, you might have to give it a little propulsion to stop that action, or give it a kick ahead, or something. Even though the vessel is at a dead stop, I'm on duty. I'm in the pilothouse watching everything. From the time that you're tied up in the locks until you're departing the locks is only about 20 minutes, or a half an hour at the very most if you have little delays. It doesn't take long to raise or lower the vessel.

The locks operate 24/7. They operate, I believe, from 00:01 in the morning on March 25 through January 15. I've never heard of the locks closing early, but I've heard of them extending.

With the lockmasters, it's pretty much all business. Every once in a while, there's somebody on another vessel who knows a lockmaster. I don't know the lockmasters well enough to converse with them. My visits are pretty much business. But I do hear others who do know the lockmasters, and they talk and call one another by name.

When the lock is filled, the gates on the upper end will open. Once I get the light there – a white light goes on when the arrester boom is all the way open – I give the whistle a toot, which means throw the lines off, and the lock personnel come out to turn the lines loose. My crew is already aboard. Once they're done, I start pushing out.

Once I get above the locks, there's a call-in point for the Coast Guard which means I've cleared the locks upbound, and then I call the Soo Traffic and say, "All right, I'm clear of the locks." My next call will be at Gros Cap, which is a light that's in Whitefish Bay. It's out of the river, and it's the beginning of Whitefish Bay on Lake Superior.

There's a speed limit throughout the system. You cannot go drag racing. The speed limit from the time you get in at De Tour is 14 miles an hour until you get to Everens Point. It's nine miles an hour when you're going around Johnston Point up to Reed Point. Then it's 10 miles an hour up through the Stribling Dike area until you get to Light 62. Then it's 12 miles an hour to Light 80, which is Nine Mile Point. At that point, the speed limit drops down to 10 miles an hour until you get to Six Mile Point, where it drops down to eight miles an hour until you get to the lower reaches of the St. Marys Canal, which is part of the power plant system, the hydro plant, where it drops to six miles per hour until you get to the locks. You cannot enter the locks at more than 2½ miles an hour.

When you're leaving the locks, you can drive up to six miles an hour until you're clear of the locks. After that, it's 14 miles an hour out the rest of the way until you're clear at Gros Cap, and then it's unlimited speed.

From there, there are recommended courses, on the Great Lakes. But the courses are just what they say – recommended courses. You can deviate from that. There are upbound courses and downbound courses, and you try to stick to them because that avoids collisions. But weather dictates a lot, and you can deviate from a course anytime.

There can be a lot of traffic at the Soo Locks. There have been waits of two to three hours. There are waits in the St. Marys River. They'll close the river for fog or visibility. If you have a blinding snowstorm, they'll close the river because they don't want somebody going aground and blocking up the whole system. That is one of the traffic schemes that does shut down. Now, when we go down the St. Clair and Detroit rivers, that's also a traffic scheme, and that's run by the Canadian Coast Guard Sarnia Traffic. But I've never been down through there where they closed that system for weather. They close the system for events, like when they have the Freedom Festival at Detroit and Windsor *(Windsor-Detroit International Freedom Festival)* and put a line across the river and have a tug of war. It will be closed from 12 to 2 or 12 to 4 or something like that.

Now, come on along as Captain Schmidt takes us east from Lake Superior, or downbound, through the Soo Locks.

You call in at Whitefish Point downbound. You call the traffic system and give them a pre-call. An hour after that, you're going to be abreast of Ile Parisienne, and that's when you call the lockmaster. The next call for the Coast Guard is at Gros Cap. The next call for the lockmaster is at Big Point, which is just above the locks. The lockmaster will tell you which lock you'll enter and if you've got to wait, slow down, tie up on the wall and wait for traffic, or do whatever you've got to do. Usually, you're in a loaded position. Coming off of Lake Superior, I've never been in a ballast situation *(carrying no cargo)*. Lake Superior usually means I've gone to a loading port and am coming downbound loaded.

Once I get through the locks, I have to call the Coast Guard again when I've cleared the locks downbound. The speed limits are in effect after that.

Going downbound with a load is different than coming up upbound. You have a traffic separation. The Middle Neebish Channel is one way upbound, and the West Neebish Channel downbound is one way, and they meet at the Mud Lake junction point. They separate or come together again at Nine Mile Point.

Downbound leaving the locks, the speed limit is six miles an hour. Once you get to the lower reaches of the St. Marys Canal and the power plant, the speed limit is 10 miles an hour on the way down to Winter Point, which is just above Mud Lake junction buoy. After that, it's 14 miles an hour. I can't make 14 miles an hour, so it's full speed ahead.

There are no fees for any vessels going through the Soo Locks. There are tolls at the Welland Canal and for vessels using the locks of the St. Lawrence Seaway.

I have been on land at the Soo Locks, but I've never gotten off a vessel or gotten on a vessel there. I like that area. I've gone up there for a vacation.

***

SIDE TRIP ONE: During a short vacation in 2012 to the Soo, Mary and I went into the Alberta House, a place where artists hang out and sell their wares. We were flipping through pictures and looking at books and all the stuff the store has. We were looking through prints, and Mary said, "Here's one of the Dorothy Ann." I said, "I've never seen this one before." It's a snowy picture. It's a fall picture. We are coming down from the locks in the Soo. We're headed downbound, coming up on Mission Point. The painter had made a print, and it was signed number two of 100. I bought it. I was thinking, "Wow, it would be nice to give one to my relief captain. He would like one."

The painting is by Mary Stroba, who lives in Sault Ste. Marie, Michigan. Back home, Captain Schmidt's Mary contacted the artist and inquired about print number one.

Artist Mary Stroba's painting of Dorothy Ann/Pathfinder near the Soo Locks found its way to the home of Captain Gary and Mary Schmidt. *Warren Gerds photo*

She said, "Print number one is gone, but I have the original painting. How would you like the original painting?" So Mary gave her the history that I'm the captain on the boat, and she was very interested. We went ahead and bought the painting, which we had framed. I gave the print to my relief captain. He was very interested in it.

In a note, Mary Stroba wrote that the painting of the Dorothy Ann "is where it belongs."

In the painting, the vessel is at a distance, and no name is visible on the bow.

I could tell right away it was the Dorothy Ann by the general shape of it because there's no other vessel that looks exactly like that

***

SIDE TRIP TWO: *Mary says when she and Captain Schmidt stay overnight at lodgings near the locks, Captain Schmidt, without seeing them, can recognize ships by the sound of their engines as they pass.*

Some of the vessels have a deep-throated diesel sound. If it's a steam engine, it has a different sound. If it's a variable-pitched vessel, you can tell by whether it's loaded or empty just by the way the prop rolls around. Those are sounds that I've noticed over the years. You might be at a dock and you're lying in bed and you hear a vessel going by. Now, just by listening to it, I can tell if it's a Canadian vessel because they're the ones mostly with the variable-pitch system. And then you know which vessels possibly would run this route. By sound and knowledge of which vessels are running which route, you can make an educated guess. I've told my wife, "Listen, that vessel is Such and Such coming through right now," and sure enough, pretty soon you can see the name of it.

And I can tell vessels from far off by silhouette. Or I can tell what class of vessel they are. With thousand footers, there's a Bay Class thousand footer versus a Lorain thousand footer class. They are built differently in profile. There are only so many Lorain vessels that are built, and you can take an educated guess because of what route they're running and where you are.

I can pick out the sound of the Dorothy Ann. Certain diesels make certain sounds. With EMDs *(Electro Motive Diesels)*, when you rev them up and go with them, it's like hearing a train. Ever hear a train engine, how it powers up when it's leaving? It goes bubb, bubb, bubb, bubb, bubb, bubb, bubb. You can tell by the sound it's some kind of a

20-cylinder EMD diesel. Which I am. They sound different than a Pielstick or another one that's like a six-cylinder diesel – great big cylinders.

When I was on the John M. Selvick, we had what we called "Thumper." It had a distinct sound that no other tug had. It had a 1928 Fairbanks Morse engine, and it had what's called a scavenger pump that picks up air and feeds it more into the engine to burn the fuel a little bit better. It would go, "thump, wheeeeeze, thump wheeeeeze," so we called it "Thumper."

***

Going through the Soo Locks is different in winter than in summer.

It's the ice. You'll be told to do a winter landing. That means that they want you to stay kind of in the middle and, right at the last minute, stick your bow into the dock at a soft angle and then ride it in so you don't have much ice between you and the lock wall. When you get in there, one side will have ice on it, and the other side will be up fairly tight. They don't want a lot of ice between you and the wall. It's more difficult to open the gates. You also don't want a lot of ice between you and the wall when getting your lines out. If we can stay up as close as we can to the lock wall, we can get our guys off for tying up the vessel. And we've got to get them back aboard when we want to leave. If the vessel is far away from the lock wall because of ice, we can reach with ladders or gangways, but it's more difficult. Thick ice makes it more difficult to push in. It's more difficult for the lock people to open the gates. A gate has to open so it's flush against the wall. Ice can build up and get in the way. They can open valves at the bottom and flush things out, but sometimes the shot of water doesn't flush ice away. They'll get pike poles out and have to move the ice chunks out from between the pocket and the gate.

Ice builds up more above the locks. It's hard to get into the channel that leads to the lock. It can be very tight sometimes, and you have to push very hard to get into the lock. That's just one difficult part of making a winter landing.

Going through the Soo Locks in winter provides extra challenges. *Gary Schmidt photo*

Hatch 22

Welland Canal

Captain Schmidt has said of the Welland Canal, "It's our legacy."
A tremendous number of vessels go through there.

In recent seasons, we've seldom gone through the Welland Canal. I did when I was with St. Marys Cement. I made between 25 and 30 trips a year through the Welland Canal.

That's a different experience because, rather than going up or down once, there are more stages. There are eight locks. The first one is not much at all, around two to three feet. Sometimes they don't even tie your vessel up in the lock. You just go in there, the boat slowly lowers, they open the gates, and away you go. You don't even put lines out. When you go down to Lock Seven, now you've got a drop of about 50 feet. The whole stage between Lake Erie and Lake Ontario is more than 320 feet. That's quite a drop.

***

SNAPSHOT: *The Welland Canal was built for ships to get around Niagara Falls. The canal is in Canada. It is 27 miles long and runs between Port Colborne, Ontario, and St. Catherines, Ontario. Ships ascend and descend the Niagara Escarpment in stages. Seven of the eight stages are between 43 and 49 feet – equivalent to a four-story building. The current canal system was completed in 1932. In places, road traffic travels under the canal in tunnels.*

***

I liked going through the Welland Canal with the *(tug)* Triton and the *(barge)* St. Marys Cement. My vessel wasn't fast, but it was quick. I could maneuver very well, and I could go up and down at a fairly decent pace if I didn't have other vessels in the way. But there are a lot of vessels that transit that area, and that's what really slows you down. It's more traffic than anything else.

But going into a lock and coming out of a lock used to be fun for me. That's the kind of stuff I like to do – handling, maneuvering.

There are lockmen at each lock. They take care

At Welland Canals Centre Lock 3, visitors can see a model of the area that includes a freighter entering the lock. *Warren Gerds photo* of everything. You don't put any personnel on the dock. The only time you put somebody on the dock is if you have to tie yourself up to wait. But going through the locks doesn't require anybody aboard in the lock to help the lock personnel with lines.

Once you get into the Welland Canal, there's channel 21 Canadian alpha for communication going one way, and they use another channel going the other way. It's one up and one down, and you're always talking to the lockmasters as you go through. They'll tell you to tie up at the upper locks or wait for somebody to come up before you proceed down.

It is an amazing system. The first one was built back in the 1800s, and the equipment and how the canal had to be dug had to be labor-intensive work.

You should see the Welland Canal. It's very interesting.

Hatch 23

Typical day

There is no typical day.

I'm a fairly early riser. If it's a non-work day for me – which means not having to be in the pilothouse or maneuver or a close-quarter situation – I usually get up between 6 and 7 o'clock in the morning. I will start my day by catching up on some of my paperwork and getting ready to talk with the mate about the loads that we have coming up.

The first mate is on watch on the eight to 12 watch on the Dorothy Ann. *(The standard watch format is 8-12, third mate; 12-4, second mate; and 4-8, first mate, Captain Schmidt says.)*

The first mate is the one who tells the crews what he wants done for the day or positions the guys to do their work. Let's say we've left the loading dock and we cleaned up and we're on a longer run, he'll assign – "OK, today we're going to paint the dunnage room, or we're going to paint this, or we're going to clean this. We'll do sanitary work from the top to the bottom. Or let's clean the pipe room up and get it squared away. Rewind the winches, make sure all the wraps are equal and straight on the winches." We are our janitor service. That's the kind of work stuff that he assigns to the crew on the day that you're going out on long runs.

You try to work the crew during the daylight hours versus the nighttime. The only time we do nighttime work is if we're loading, unloading, when we are leaving the loading dock and we have to clean the tunnel before we get to the next port. If it's a certain time and we've got enough time to do it before we get to the next port, we'll wait until the next morning and then call the guys back out and do daytime work.

But there's so much maintenance that has to be done other than just getting the vessel prepared to load and unload. All the deck equipment has to be greased every so often. With the unloading system, rollers might have to be replaced or repaired. That takes people to pull the rollers out and put new rollers in. There's constant maintenance going on, and that's what the personnel are for.

Besides loading and unloading – which is the most important part of the vessel – you still have to maintain it so everything works throughout. Everybody has to have knowledge of the equipment. The conveyorman is in charge, but he'll say, "Hey, I need a couple of deckhands, we've got to change out so many rollers." And then the oil has to be changed in the gears. There's just a lot of work that's constantly going on and on and on.

Through the Interlake office, Captain Schmidt has some idea of how a week may run.

The dispatcher sends out a daily position report on where the vessels are and what their next two or three loads are with an estimated time – if everything goes on schedule. Things very rarely run exactly on schedule.

There may be a breakdown in the loading situation, or it might take a little longer because of the type of material loading. Many times, a plan runs on schedule, and you can almost predict a week in advance where you're going to be. But then again, if there's a conflict – like if there's two vessels going to the same loading port, and you have to wait for one to finish loading before you can go in to load – that might set you back. If it's going to be a race where you both get there at the same time, the first one will go in, and usually the second one will be deployed to a different loading dock – and then that shoots your whole schedule for the week. Then everything changes. So nothing's written for sure.

The vessel is usually busy except when the economy is bad, if it's laid up, or if it's wintertime when navigation shuts down. But the object is to keeping that vessel moving at all times.

There are times when weather interrupts us, and we have to go to anchor. We can't maneuver, we can't load, we can't do anything. That's an idle time. When we have idle times or down times like that, then there's time for maintenance and doing a lot of other things.

The people aren't idle, the boat is once in a while.

When we are under way on a long run and the decks have been cleaned and the sanitary work is done, we knock the people off. They only work eight hours a day, and they'll have 16 hours off. That happens. That doesn't happen that often with this vessel.

This vessel is a short-run vessel, so it's always on the move. Some of the other vessels in our fleet, Stewart J. Cort, for example, loads up in Duluth, runs down Lake Superior through the St. Marys River, down Lake Michigan, to Burns Harbor, Indiana. It

Captain Gary peels an orange during "a typical day" in the pilothouse. *Jeremy Mock photo*

unloads. It takes 16 to 18 hours to unload. It turns around and goes back all the way up Lake Michigan, all the way up the St. Marys River, all the way over to Duluth, and reloads. That's its only run. That's all it does. It can stay on top of its work because it has enough people on board to keep it well maintained and well painted.

The Stewart J. Cort does maybe 30 to 40 trips a year. The vessel I'm on, we may do 100 more than that. It's constantly busy. We put as much cargo across our belts as those big vessels do. We just do it in short bursts. We did 2.8 million short tons of cargo in 2012.

Loading and unloading takes place at any time day or night – or day of the week.

You work holidays. Every day. It's 24/7. I take that back. One dock did shut down for a holiday. We didn't shut down. The office sent us to another port that wasn't shut down for a holiday. But that was years ago. I can't remember ever shutting down for holidays. I know some facilities might. And some do. But as far as ships coming in, I think most of the docks aren't going to say, "You can't unload here on a holiday." Because you can't. They will. Somebody will.

Potentially, Captain Schmidt could work all the time because he's virtually always aboard the vessel. So he consciously plans to shut down.

I pretty much know where we're going and what we're doing. When I do, I plan my day accordingly. Let's say I know that we're going to be downbound from Marquette, and we're going to be getting into the St. Clair/Detroit River area at 1:30 in the morning. I will shut down at 1830 at night after dinner and take a nap and shut down and get my rest because I know I'm going to be up for the next nine or 10 hours after we get there.

Those kind of "up" days sometimes string together.

It's pretty often. It is quite difficult. When you get a lot of them in a row, it's quite hard. I don't mind it. I kind of like it. I like being busy. I don't like the long runs where I'm trying to invent stuff to do that I don't need to do.

■ **Hatch 24**

Season

The season for the Dorothy Ann/Pathfinder is from sometime in March to usually mid-January. It depends.

For a season, the ice never shuts you down. The closing of the Soo Locks for maintenance is the main thing.

The seasons have gotten longer over the years. When my dad sailed when I was a kid, he was usually home by Christmas or at least somewhere between Christmas and New Year's. Now, the normal is a layup around after the locks close on January 15, and I've seen some vessels run a lot longer than that. Some vessels on the Canadian side run salt. They don't have to go through the locks, and they're running just about all winter long.

Seasons vary for Interlake vessels. Dorothy Ann/Pathfinder has sometimes been the first one to lay up, and it's also been the last one to lay up. And the same with all the other vessels. It depends upon how many cargoes we have, and if we have satisfied our customers, or if the weather is so bad that we can't run or the ice is too thick to continue. Then they're done for the year. It depends on where what ship is at what time. They might be in position to make the last trip of the year and be the last one in. That's happened to me. I was supposed to be the first one in, and I was the last one in.

Interlake would like us to run most of the season right up until the locks close for Lake Superior, and the locks have stayed open as many as 10 days past January 15. Usually, the season for the locks is only extended three, four, or five days.

My shortest trips in the 2012 season were about four hours. They were from Marblehead to Lorain. The longest one this year was Marquette-Rouge-Stoneport-Milwaukee-Calcite-Conneaut. Once I made a six-day round trip from Ohio to Quebec City and back.

Once aboard, Captain Schmidt is on board the vessel 99 percent of the time. I'm on call at all times. Even if I'm off the vessel, anyone usually can get hold of me by cell phone if there are any questions to be answered. I very seldom get off the boat because I just don't like getting off in these way-off ports. I get off in Marquette, Milwaukee, and Cleveland once in a while. But other than that, when I get on the vessel, I'm usually there for the whole period.

Crew

You are a man of grace and polish
Who never spoke above a hush
All at once you're using language
That would make a sailor blush

That's the rap that sailors get in the song "I'm an Ordinary Man" in the classic musical "My Fair Lady." Is it a fair rap?

I have a mix of family guys and single guys, and I think we older guys are probably the saltier ones. There are some of the younger guys who cuss up a storm, but most of the guys don't cuss too much anymore. The language used to be pretty salty, but I think it's settle down a lot. I think with women sailing – I've had as many as three women crew members at one time, and a lot of time I've had a female cook also – and that seems to tame the guys down. They don't use the salty language as much.

Imagine living with everybody you work with every day all day, all week, for weeks on end. Talk about close proximity.

Sometimes you want your privacy, so you go back to your room or you find your solitude somewhere. Sometimes guys will be just hanging out in the galley just talking and just having a good time. When that's done, it's time to take a nap or get ready for your next watch or just have some solitude time.

Dorothy Ann/Pathfinder has a 14-man crew. They are the captain, or master; three mates – first, second, and third; two engineers, chief and assistant; conveyorman; six deck hands; and cook.

We have replacements for when people go on vacation. Hiring is done by Interlake through the union. If the union can't supply people, then hiring of new people usually comes from a resume that's been sent in to the office.

Crewmen gather for a safety meeting in the crew's lounge aboard the Dorothy Ann. *Gary Schmidt photo*

With reliefs, we probably have as many as 25 people in a season. That can vary. So it's 14 plus maybe 11 people.

Where crew members live is all over the map. Of my most recent crew, several were from Michigan – Rogers City, Alpena, Middleton, Traverse City, Cedar River and Escanaba. They also came from

Sandusky and Cleveland, Ohio; Green Bay and Madison, Wisconsin; Portland, Maine; Terra Haute, Indiana; and near Bradenton, Florida.

Crewmen don't punch a clock – there is no clock to punch – but you have to be on time. If you fall back asleep and show up late for a watch, the guy you're relieving is going to let you know that you owe him time. It's up to an individual to keep track of his hours and have them approved. The first mate assigns work, and he keeps track of work. You write up your time. I have the guys come up to the pilothouse and fill out their timesheets. Once the timesheets are approved by the mate, they're sent on to me, and I just look through them for a final go-over. Each department sends its timesheets to me. The first mate sends the deck's side of it, the chief sends me the engineer side of it, and the cook has his own. They all send it to me, and then I approve it all. It's bookkeeping. There's a lot of bookkeeping, actually.

We get paid every two weeks. Everybody is away from home, so that's a factor. There's direct deposit for some people. Some people like their checks sent to the boat. Checks are usually issued on a Wednesday. They usually reach the boat within a week of whenever they're issued. Sometimes if we're in the Cleveland area, somebody from the office will come down to the boat with the check, and it's right there. It's there the same day. But you just don't know where you're going to be, and the office has to find out where to send the check. The check is usually overnighted wherever they send it. It's usually pretty quick. But sometimes it gets sent to the wrong place or your orders are changed. You were going here, now you're going over here, and now you have to wait for the mail to catch up to you. That happens.

During free time, some guys like to go for walks, get off the boat and go up the street. Maybe have a drink or two, but they can't drink a lot because you just can't do that anymore. It's my job if I let somebody on the boat who's drunk. It could be my job, not just theirs. If we're under way and the guys have time, most of them on their time off will play euchre up in the crew's lounge. Or they might play video games. I like to plays cards when I'm invited, but not video games. Guys play mostly for the heck of it, no big stakes.

Other than that, leisure time is relaxing in your room watching TV or even playing video games.

There's a site on their computers that they go to, BoatNerd, if you want boat news. It has a news channel so you get what's going on around the lakes. For instance, right now it says, "Great Lakes coal trade down 3.5 percent in November." It tells where the ships are. "Corn state strong as demands drop. Futures look stable."

The guys are political as anybody else. Some are die-hard Republicans, and some are die-hard Democrats, and some don't care one way or the other. But most of them have an opinion.

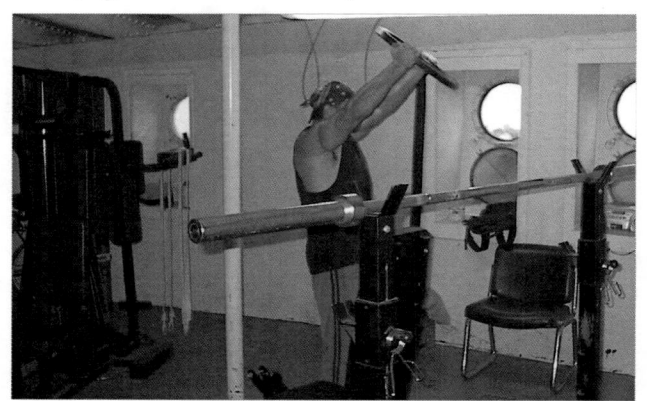

A crewman lifts weights in the exercise room of the Pathfinder.
Gary Schmidt photo

Sometimes guys will work out in the weight room on the barge.

A lot of them are calling home or on their computers. They use Skype. Sometimes the Internet service we have gets little overloaded, gets pretty slow. That's usually on long voyages and along a shoreline and we can get Internet.

We have sports packages on satellite TV. That's part of our safety incentives from the company. If you go a whole year without an accident on the boat, the company pays for one sports package. If you go two years, you get two sports packages. Three years, you get three sports packages. I get to select. The only one I select is the NFL Network package. But if there are several, I'll let somebody else pick.

With Sunday often being the day for time off, the guys watch NFL games. They're interested. Saturday also. There are a lot of people who are interested in college football. Those two days, if they can, the guys like to watch games. If they can't, well, they can't. But they're always interested in sports.

***

SIDE TRIP: Over the years, we've had storytellers aboard. There were some good ones. They'd start a story, "This one guy, something happened with him, but he's dead now," or, "He blew himself up." They'd always give you a hook right off the bat and get you interested in the story.

Dave Fitzpatrick was with me for a long time, on the Triton and the Dorothy Ann. He is a storyteller. The things that happen to him are just totally unbelievable, like how he blew himself up one time. He was working for a company and got gasoline on his clothes. He put the clothes in the wash machine and washed them. He went to open the door, the whole thing blew up because the gasoline went to the top and was ignited by a little micro switch that shuts off the machine. He wasn't wearing clothes on the upper part of his body, so when it blew him – almost through a wall – he had burns, but he wasn't burned really bad because he didn't have clothes on to catch on fire. It burned the hair off his body. And he drove himself to the hospital in that condition. He didn't call 911. And his wife worked in the hospital. "You know your husband's here, don't you?" "Oh yeah, he's coming to pick me up." "No, you know he's here as a patient, don't you?"

He had what we called Dave-isms. Like with a deckhand, who said, "You know, Dave, I was thinking..." "Hey, listen here, I'm the one who gets paid to think. You just get back out there and start shoveling." When he got kind of tired, his short-term memory would start to lose a little bit. He'd say, "Tell Thing to go do this." He couldn't remember the guy's first name right off the bat. We named a tool after him, The Thing. When we're loading, sometimes dirt gets into one of our specialized chocks and it can't be turned. We had a tool – just a bar with two prongs sticking out – that you'd put on the chock and give it a wrench, loosen it up, get the dirt worked out, and give it some squirts of grease to get it working again. Dave would say, "Go get The Thing so we can loosen up this chock." So somebody took a welding rod and welded "The Thing" on the bar.

***

You're allotted so many vacations a year, and the company picks up the travel expense per the contract. In the officers' contract, it's all picked up. In the deck department, I think the company picks up up to $300 round trip, which covers some of the crew's expenses. That means they probably drive more than they fly. That more than picks up for a rental car, but it doesn't pay a full fare flying price. And a lot of the guys get off close to home to try to keep travel expenses down. Let's say we're going to Stoneport near a guy's home. He will try to get off there because he only lives within a 30-mile radius of that dock. But there are no guarantees. Sometimes guys will get off in Ohio and have to drive up to northern Michigan. But they try to figure what works best for them. Like, "All right, I'm taking vacation on our next voyage up to Marquette. I'll get off at the Soo." And the next guy who's coming on is usually from that area also. Deckhands are pretty much congregated in northern Michigan. Sometimes the men will work it out among themselves. Guys talk and say, "OK, we're going to be up there on a trip in about a week. How does that sound for you coming back and relieving me?" They work it out, and they work it out with us. We try to do the best we can to accommodate and keep the expenses down.

We try to accommodate as best we can to get certain guys off so when we do hit port they can go up and get their personal items. They may need toothpaste or a haircut. You try to accommodate them at the next port. You have somebody else fill in that spot, and you work him a different hour so you might be able to let him go.

Also, when we know that we're going to a port where there's family, they

Being a Great Lakes sailor often means spending such holidays as Thanksgiving aboard a vessel. (The turkey was neutered for the sake of the photo.) *Gary Schmidt photo*

have to be put on a security/crew list because of Homeland Security to get on the vessel. We do allow family to come down to the boat and visit. We try to work it out.

I basically have the same crew for a season, from sometime in March to usually mid-January, dependent upon how the economy and everything's going.

At the company masters meeting in early March, the personnel department says, "Here's the starting crew. This guy is going to be starting a vacation cycle." When I go back to work, I get a rotation going. We get a basic vacation schedule. It doesn't mean it's in stone, but basically when you want off for vacation for the season. We do that for the engineers, for the captains and for the unlicensed people. We have a basic fill-in plan, so we have a flow so I don't have too many of the permanent people off at the same time. I can let as many as three of the six deckhands off at one time, but I want three experienced guys on the boat. So we try to make a rotation, and we try to make a flow. "This guy's getting off this slot in the calendar. If you want to start a vacation and you need to be off for this date, well you have to work it in to take this slot of time off." And the next guy will take that kind of slot off. And then we have our relief people – and relief people are the ones who can get bumped. If all the regulars are back, relief people are, just what they are, relief people. Although the relief people work just as much. We do work it out so everybody has time off, everybody has at least three vacations a year if they want it.

You're starting out a season with a basic crew that's been there already. It's not like you're starting over again. It's not like you're replacing a lot of people.

First of all, personnel at the office gives me a little bit of a rundown on the relief person getting on board. Personnel tells me if a guy's coming out of one of the academies, if he's a walk-on the first time on a boat, or, if he's come from another vessel, what kind of experience he's had. So I have a little bit of an idea. Then I sit down and talk to him to some degree and find out what his last job was and why he left it or out of curiosity what his history is on some stuff. We have an orientation day. The first mate or the second mate will take this guy around to the whole boat. He goes through everything, including the fire stations, the station billet, what he has to do in case of emergency. And that's the first day he walks on the boat. From there, he's given a hard hat and told where the first mate is and go see him for his work details. And that's how they start out. And then from observing and how he does, he has 90 days to make it to a permanent roster spot or for me to decide whether I want to keep him or not keep him.

I do have influence on who can stay and who won't stay. I don't mess with the engine room. I let the chief engineer do his thing.

Over the years, the crew has gotten very good at teamwork. There are times when somebody is not having a good day, and I've got to tell them, "You're not giving me good distances. I need better distances. Refocus," or something like that. But it's teamwork. We're working with a tremendous amount of weight. There are trust factors on both sides. The crew trusts me to get them home safely, port to port, without injury. And I trust them to help me maneuver, to make sure they do their jobs. You're not constantly checking them out, but if there are miscues, yeah, then you would check things out. But there are trust factors both ways, and it works back and forth.

From season to season, some people will quit or move on or transfer to a different position. The people who were in the relief deckhand position will move into the deckhand position. Or a mate will move to another vessel, and another mate will come on. You determine, as the new person comes on, who is fit to stay and who is not fit to stay. It's a decision. Most of the time, you're pretty good at picking them out. Every once in a while, you get one that you let stay too long, maybe, that doesn't fit in with the crew. But eventually you weed them out. If you don't like somebody, either he will conform a little bit, or he'll fit in somehow, or he'll leave.

The crew can transfer to any vessel within the fleet. They can also change positions from deck to engineer or even over to cook, which is the third department on board. And some do. I've had a deckhand who went over to the cooking side. He went to school and came back and is our cook now. You can move around. There's a lot of opportunity to move up. If you start as a deckhand, your next step up is to become an able bodied seaman in the deck department. From that, you have to work for so long before you become a mate. And then you work so long at mate and work your way up through the ranks to finally become a captain or a master.

Hatch 26

Packers

Captain Schmidt is to Great Lakes sailing as Green Bay is to the Green Bay Packers football team. Sometimes the two ways of life converge and become visible in the form of an oversized blow-up balloon Packers player who wears number 00.

When at home during the Packers season, Captain Schmidt has put what he calls his great Packers player up in his front yard. The sight is not that unusual in Green Bay. There, Captain Schmidt is just another Packers fan. The town lives and breathes its team – and well knows its unique place as the only community-owned major franchise anyplace.

That great Packers player also goes places. Captain Schmidt packs it up and blows it up for display as he sails Dorothy Ann/Pathfinder into places where he knows he will get a rise out of folks in one way or another.

With "the great Packers player" proudly displayed, the Dorothy Ann/Pathfinder makes its way up the Cuyahoga River past Cleveland Browns Stadium. *Jeremy Mock photo*

Captain Schmidt poses with his precious rummage sale purchase, "the great Packers player," that has traveled the Great Lakes with him. *Jeremy Mock photo*

I bought the great Packers player at a rummage sale. I've had it out on deck. I've had it on the veranda under the pilothouse.

I've displayed it going through the Soo Locks. People will respond to it. I get thumbs up. A lot of people like it. I get a mixed reaction. But there's always something out there.

I've displayed it going up and down the Detroit River, especially in front of Detroit.

On the Cuyahoga River in Cleveland, we go through The Flats area where there are taverns – Shooters and places like that. I get a lot of reaction. Cleveland Browns Stadium is near. I have a little sign, "Go, Pack, Go," just to get the reaction rolling. I like to give it to them, too, with the ship's whistle. I get boos every time I go through there. "BOOOOO!"

Once I put it up in my room. I left my door open, and the guy who has the room right across from me said it scared the hell out of him.

I've always been a Packers fan. I went to my first Packers game in 1963 for my 17th birthday. It was a Vikings game.

If the Packers are playing when Captain Schmidt is sailing and in the pilothouse, he'll tune in the game on satellite radio to listen to the local feed with announcers Larry McCarren and Wayne Larrivee. Back home...

I have my own Green Bay Packers helmet. I made it from a fireman's helmet. One of the firemen's hats on the boat got damaged, and I tried to order inner parts for it but couldn't get the parts. So I just kind of kept the outer shell. I had it for four years as a broken helmet. So I had an idea. It's a nice Packers yellow, so I brought it home and decided I'd make a Packers helmet out of it. I got some green and white tape to make the stripes on it and some decals for the side of it. I had another helmet that I put on the inside of it so it would sit on your head properly. I put that helmet in with rivets. It seems to work pretty nice. My brother Dale wore it to a Packers game at Lambeau Field and got a lot of compliments on it.

Captain Schmidt's head gear when he is on the boat is a white hard hat that includes a tip of the hat to another Wisconsin favorite.

My captain's hat that I've had for years and years and years has a couple of Badgers stickers on it.

A good part of the Dorothy Ann's crew is Cleveland fans, a good part of the crew is Detroit fans. And sure, there are little rivalries there, little kidding. And there are a lot of Packer fans, Colts fans, New England fans – because everybody's from everywhere. They all have favorites.

You can be serious so long, but you've got to have a little lighter side to things. It's a job, but the guys are people you are friendly with. You're not just a boss all the time. You communicate with these people, sit down and have lunch with them, sit down to dinner with them, and you talk about various things. We talk a lot of football. We have a football pool. We get the jabs in. We get to kid around. If it was a 24/7 job where you were just serious all the time, I don't think anybody could take that.

In the off season, Captain Schmidt likes to get into poker and cribbage tournaments. He has gone to Reno, Nevada, to play and meet folks from all over the country. They talk.

I show them pictures of the big Packers player on the ship going into Cleveland Harbor, which is just great. They love that piece. They like the Packers or they hate the Packers.

Hatch 27

Time off

Captain Schmidt heartily agrees with old line, "All work and no play makes Jack a dull boy."
When I'm home on vacation or winter breaks, I love to go to cribbage tournaments. I play a lot of cribbage. And I play a lot of cribbage on the boat. There are a couple of guys I play with a lot. And every once in a while, you'll have a poker game on the boat. It's not very often anymore, but once in a while. Some of the guys get together who like to play euchre. We've got some northern Michigan boys who like to play euchre, and I'll play with them once in a while. I like playing cards a lot. Also, I like backgammon a lot, too. And poker. I like to go to small tournaments that we have in Green Bay on Monday nights. On the boat, for recreation, after supper sometimes I'll play with the conveyorman. We've been playing cribbage for many years, 10 years. And it comes out pretty even. We play for a buck a game, just to keep track, that's all. Nothing exotic. No big stakes.

A few years ago, Captain Erik Sawyer came to work at Interlake. He was a captain with another company, and he decided he wanted to switch over. He's a relief captain, and he was working on my vessel as a third mate. Captain Sawyer was on for 30 days, and we played 250 games in the time he was there, and we were separated by 11 games at the end. Of course, I was victorious. That's all that really mattered. I didn't matter if it was one game. I had bragging rights.

***

SIDE TRIP: Once there was a really good cribbage player. I just walked on a boat. He asked, "Do you play cribbage?" "Oh yeah, I sure do." "You wanna play?" "Yeah." "Five dollars a game?" "Not a problem." So we played five games, and I beat him five straight games. He says, "Well, let's play for double or nothing." "Okay." I beat him again, so now he owes me $50. He says, "I'll play you double or nothing one more time." "Okay." I skunked him. That means he has to pay me doubles. Now he owes me $150. But I told him before we started that game, "This will be the last time we're playing double or nothing. Eventually I'll probably lose to you. You'll get good hands, and I'm going to lose. This is the last double or nothing." So when I skunked him, his face almost went white. I said, "Here's what I'm going to do. I want to say I'm going to forget about double or nothing and the skunk. It's going to be eight games that you owe me – $40. You pay me $40, and we'll forget the $150 altogether. And from now on we'll not play for more than $2 a game, but I like to play cribbage." We ended up playing for $1 a game, to keep score. Nobody gets hurt, and it's a fun game."

***

For other entertainment for myself, I like sports, and I watch a lot of sports. We have DirecTV on the boat. We have the NFL package, so we get to watch a lot of that. I'm a football fan. I like professional football and college football and basketball (*and for a time was a season ticket holder for University of Wisconsin-Green Bay men's basketball games*).

When I get a chance, I read. The spy novels and the mysteries are my favorites. There's plenty of dry reading that I have to do all the time, which is Coast Guard information and local notices to mariners. There's plenty of stuff from the office coming through. For entertainment, my favorite author for a long time was Robert Ludlum. After that, I like James Patterson and I really like the ABC books (*"alphabet murders"*) of Sue Grafton. I like most of the newer mysteries.

Captain Gary's Tom and Jerry recipe

For those seasons when Captain Gary is home for the Christmas-New Year holidays, he whips up a batch of Tom & Jerrys for guests. He combines what he likes best from two Tom and Jerry recipes that have been passed down through his family.

His version of the hot drink features rum, brandy, and spices in a party-size batch. Ta-da:

Captain Gary's Tom and Jerrys
1 dozen eggs (separated)
2 pounds powdered sugar
Cinnamon
All spice
Ginger
Cream of tartar
Nutmeg
Rum
Brandy

White part: Beat egg whites, adding 1½ pounds powdered sugar and ¼ teaspoon cream of tartar. Beat until very stiff.

Yellow part: Beat egg yokes until lemon color: Add ½ pounds powdered sugar, 1 teaspoon cinnamon, ¼ teaspoon all spice, and ¼ teaspoon ginger. Beat until very stiff. Fold yellow mixture into white. Put 2 tablespoons of mix into a hot mug. Add 1 shot rum, 1 shot brandy. Fill mug with hot water. Sprinkle with nutmeg.

Hatch 28

Forces of nature

You get a feeling for weather. You kind of know when storms are coming, and with the modern-day technology, you can really tell.

In days gone before, you got a weather report every six hours. It may or may not be very accurate. I'm talking back in the '70s and the '80s. They weren't exactly the best forecasters back then. You took a lot of chances. You'd try to hit the directions (*of "smoothest" passage*), you'd try to hit the weather just right. But nowadays, I can advance the weather (*by computer model*), I can take a look to see what's coming ahead – and it's fairly accurate. You can tell pretty much what the weather is going to do. You can plan your route accordingly to avoid the harshest weather.

You're always going to get some weather. Sometimes you've got to go in weather that's uncomfortable but not extreme. There's a lot of uncomfortable weather out there. It happens a lot.

I'm not even talking about temperature. I'm talking about wave heights. Atmospheric conditions – I never really pay too much attention to that. I don't care if it's raining, I don't care if it's snowing. I don't like fog, but I don't really care if it's foggy out there. I can maneuver through it, and I can get around fog. I can go through fog. I can go through snow and rain and sleet and all this other stuff. But not when you're talking about waves getting to 18 to 20 feet or when (*the 2012 storm*) Sandy was around and they were talking about waves of 28 and 30 feet on Lake Superior. When you're talking about big seas and strong winds, those are the ones that you're watching out for.

I got stuck in Marquette, Michigan, because Sandy reached all the way there. As Sandy hit the East Coast, I made it to Marquette, but I couldn't get out of Marquette to get to the north shore to get away from Sandy. It was pretty rough in Marquette. We were snapping wires and breaking lines. These are nylon lines that are 2½ inches in diameter and 1-inch cables. It's all-steel cable with wound wire – 19 or 25 wires to a cable. They're heavy wires. They weigh a lot. They're mooring wires. We were breaking them. Another boat there, the Buffalo, was breaking more wires than I was. He was on the north side. There was surging in the harbor. To alleviate violent boat action from the surging, we put all the nylon lines one way and put the wires the other way. The nylons have give. You would pull against the nylons and keep things as tight as you could so the boat wouldn't surge. As long as the boat doesn't move, you're not going to break wires. But you have any run (*looseness*) on it, that's when you walk through (*systematically snap*) wires and lines. We tied nylons one way, put wires the other way, and pulled against the nylons and kept things as tight as we could.

The sound of a line breaking is like a shotgun going off. It's loud. The cables don't make much noise. Nylons stretch, and, when they break they sound like a shot. And if they hit somebody, they'll probably kill 'em.

***

SIDE TRIP: Sailing's a risk in the things you go through and you put yourself through. Going out there into storms and into big waves, things can happen. Because you have a boat that's not stable that you're walking on all the time – you're rockin' and rollin' – and things could just happen. Things move. You try to secure everything, but there are always risks of doing anything on any kind of an unstable platform. But our safety meetings help. You try to do things as safely as possible.

***

We've seen hurricanes that have come up from the Gulf of Mexico. Once they hit the warm water of the Great Lakes, they intensify. A low pressure might combine with another low pressure coming in from Canada, and that's what makes a great storm on the Great Lakes. As a hurricane that has lessened to a tropical storm moves up into the Lakes and combines with a Canadian low, it can hit the warmer waters of the Great Lakes, which aren't really warm, but they're warmer than the land mass. That big body of water can intensify those storms, and they can blow quite hard again. I can remember several storms where that was the case. Sandy was a real special case the way it came in. It came in and came right over the Great Lakes. According to BoatNerd, the vessels in the Great Lakes fleets during that storm lost a total of 2,000 sailing hours.

Wind can be a major headache. You're dealing with it all the time. It's something that's just part of sailing.

I know that I can operate most of the time in a wind that's a Force 4 (*28 to 33 knots*) or Force 5 (*34 to 40 knots*). Anything over that, then you really start to pay attention to which direction and where it's coming from and where you are going – if you can get any kind of a lee (*downwind, or a somewhat protected angle*). If you can't, then you kind of settle down and wait for the storm to ease.

***

SIDE TRIP: Another weather tool is the MAFOR Code. (*It stands for MArine FORecast*). It gives you five numbers in a row in a code. By sequence, the first number is for Great Lakes, the second for the time period, the third is wind direction, the fourth is for wind speed, and the fifth is for atmospheric condition. (*See page 317 in Appendix.*)

***

If you're at an open dock, sometimes a Force 2 wind (*17 to 21 knots*) or Force 3 wind (*22 to 27 knots*) can blow you off the dock, and you can't stay there to load. The wind is just hard enough that it's a nuisance enough that you can't stay steady. If you're making (*coming into*) a dock and the wind's on the beam (*at 90 degrees or a high angle*), a nuisance wind would be close to 30 miles an hour. After that, the vessel is kind of hard to operate. Up to that speed, I can hold the vessel into the wind to make a dock where I'm not going to do damage.

All the lakes have their own challenges. They're different in different ways.

When you get a big sea (*large waves*) on Lake Erie, the sea beats you to death because the wave periods are close together. You get one wave after another wave after another wave hitting you.

On Lake Superior, as the waves get larger, the wave period extends a little bit. You get a longer wave action, so the waves get much bigger, and you get a lot more blue water, or bigger volume, hitting you at one time. It's a larger lake, and, with the way it's configured, it's got a big reputation as being harder in weather.

I pay attention to forecasts. I look at the lows as they're combining and how close the isobars are together. The closer they are, the stronger the storm, the tighter the isobars wind up. I try to figure out where the low is. Then you can figure out which direction the wind is going to come from and if that storm is going to be a problem. On Lake Huron, for instance, it could be a real mixed bag. But if the storm is off to one side or the other, you can predict which direction the wind is going to go, and you can make a choice of which side of the lake you want to run to be in the lee of the shore and get a better ride out of it. You pay attention to all that.

If you have an east or west wind on Lake Michigan, you could take either shoreline. You can just follow a shoreline and probably have a good ride up and down. If the wind is north and south – if you're on the wrong end of a north wind or on the wrong end of a south wind – it can be quite challenging. A north wind is more challenging. Usually a north wind is not a summer wind. A summer wind is a south wind, and it doesn't seem to be quite as hard. But a north wind is colder, with a colder wave that seems to pack a stronger punch. Cold water seems to pack a harder punch than warmer waters. So usually if it's a south wind, it's a summer wind or fall wind or spring wind. It's not a winter. You very seldom get the south winds in the wintertime.

***

SNAPSHOT: *The density of water changes with temperature and pressure.*

There's a difference between 70-degree water and 32 or 40-degree water. The water condenses with colder temperatures and becomes heavier, and you get a heavier hit with a wave. In the summertime, you might have the same size wave, and it doesn't seem to affect you nearly as much. You can feel the battering effect of a colder wave more than you can a warmer wave.

***

The National Weather Service provides wind advisories for small craft. Winds of 25 to 38 miles an hour trigger an advisory.

The alert may not necessarily take small boats off the water. If the wind is blowing off the shoreline, the boats will be out there anyway. The risk depends on the direction of the wind and sea size, sea state.

In certain cases, folks in small craft and pleasure craft would be off the water if they had any sense, but Captain Schmidt still would be out sailing.

Oh, I'd still be out there, absolutely. Small craft warnings wouldn't really affect me too much as far as wind. We'll go into winds up to 50 miles an hour, and heading into them, if it's not too long of a way to go. But if the winds are head on for 200 or 300 miles, then you might not go in that situation. But if it's 50 miles an hour and it's off the shoreline, the waves are only going to get up to five or six feet, and you're going to be two to four miles off the shoreline, so that's not going to affect you much at all.

On trips with rough wind and seas, a dock looks really nice.

Oh, yeah. You get in, and you know that you've got seven or eight hours to unload or load, and that's just fine. It's real nice before you have to go back out into a sea again. Rough weather can last. Sometimes it's 12 hours. Sometimes it's 12 to 36 hours. I've anchored for three or four days and not moved. I've gone into Marquette, and sometimes it's not so much the force of the wind, it's the direction, and it kind of locks you in there. Sometimes you just can't head into a 16-foot sea. Sometimes it's just the wrong angle to take on or the destination in those seas is too far away. You've just got to wait for the weather to subside a little bit before you head out into it.

I give Interlake updates every day, and I tell them what my forecast is – what I think is going to happen. Most of the time, my forecast is the way it does happen, but sometimes the weather just doesn't cooperate with me.

The Interlake office realizes that, too. It's the company's business, so Interlake relies on its captains and knows that it's the captain's call "out there."

Interlake has been in business for 100 years, and it has heard reports of bad weather from ships for 100 years. It knows. It doesn't like it anymore than I like it. The thing I hate worst is laying for weather. It's just not a productive thing, and it drives me nuts. I like to be on the move.

To high wind and rough water add ice. Seasons start with icy conditions that last for months. Seasons end with icy conditions that last for months.

There are all kinds of different kinds of ice. In the open water, a lake freezes over. Let's take Lake Erie, for example. There are some dangers in Lake Erie. You come out of the Detroit River, and now you're in kind of a shallow western basin. It freezes up quite fast. If the wind isn't too strong, you can break through the ice, and you can maintain some kind of a track. As one vessel goes through, the next vessel will follow your track, and everybody follows that track. Once the wind starts blowing, it'll move that ice. A lot of times, ice will cover buoys. The ice will go over the top of buoys. It'll cover the old track, so you're breaking a new track all the time.

Sometimes if you get stuck in the ice, you'll move right with the ice. The ice will take you. So you've got to be aware of all that. As the ice stops moving somewhere, and the ice behind it wants to keep moving, it piles up and makes what we call windrows. As the ice is building up, it'll build a windrow. You'll see windrows building one, two, three, or four feet above the water. Well, there's two times that amount of ice underneath the water. So, when you hit one of those windrows, it will slow you right down. It will stop you a lot of times. You might have to back up and crash through the pileup a couple of times to get through. And, again, wind just makes everything worse with ice. The wind keeps things moving. At nighttime, it's hard to follow tracks. You're kind of guessing. You want to take the softest ice as you can, and a lot of times you can read the ice. You can see where it might be a little softer. Sometimes it'll be white. White might indicate soft. Clear or black will indicate very hard ice. That depends on the time of year. But you try for the softer ice or stuff that's been broken. Once the ice is broken, sometimes you'll find leads. As you go into a lead where the ice might open up just a little bit of clear water in between the cracks, as you hit the ice, it keeps opening up in front of you, and you can keep going pretty well. Once that wind comes, all bets are off. You just don't know what's going to happen.

Saga of freezing horns

In the wintertime, the horns freeze up. In some cases, your whistles don't blow. A horn will be frozen, and it won't open at all. In some cases, your horns freeze open.

You have to have communication with other vessels, tell them, "Hey, I'm trying to blow you one whistle," or something like that, "but my horns are all frozen up." And it takes time to thaw everything out.

They're air horns. What happens is compressors make moisture. They send a little bit of moisture into the air horns. The minute that you open a solenoid to let the air go through, that air might freeze that solenoid open, and your horn will just continually blow. The horn that's on the barge is a big, self-contained Kalhenberg, which has its own compressor that's all in one unit. (*Kalhenberg is a commercial brand of air and electric horns built for military and heavy-duty commercial use.*) That horn usually doesn't freeze up if I can cover the front with some kind of a cloth so the water doesn't get inside of it.

The horn on the Dorothy Ann is on the top of the pilothouse (*at a height of about 80 feet*). It's outside, at the top, in the open. It's up there a ways, and it's hard to get at and take care of. There are ladders that lead to it, but you still have to climb and get up there. The ladder is icy. The tug's roof is icy. And the horn is blaring away.

The horn on the barge is on the forward mast. That one's not so hard to get to in general. It's got steel ladders going to it. But when it's all icy and slippery, that makes the climb harder. You have a better shot at stopping that horn than the horn on the tug. If it gets stuck open, you can and turn off its compressor and the horn will stop blowing because it's a self-contained unit.

But the one on the tug is different. You can't stop the horn once it starts blowing. It's kind of a mechanical device that's open, and the air that flows to it is the air that services all the tug. It doesn't have its own compressor, so you're not going to run out of air. The horn will keep blowing until you get that solenoid cleared. Or there's a valve that we can shut off the air going up to it. But you want the horns functional. They have to be thawed out. That's your danger whistle. You use that also for your general alarm. That's your abandon ship whistle. You use it for a lot of things. To thaw out the horn on the tug, you usually take a little, hand-held propane torch to the roof of the pilothouse. You're up there in the wind and snow. You're out in the elements. You're cold. There's no wind protection whatsoever.

The horn could freeze up again. To try to take care of that, we have an air drier. What happens when the horn freezes is the pellets in the air drier get saturated. Part of the process is to change the pellets in the air drier. That will solve some of the problem for quite a while.

But it seems to happen every winter a couple of times that a horn will freeze open. When it happens, I call the engineer.

It's not so much the thickness of the ice, but the wind and pressure on it. If there's pressure on the ice, it doesn't take much to slow you right down to nothing. On a nice day when there's no wind, you can break through a fair amount of ice with no problem, maybe up to a foot. Sometimes it's a lot more difficult. When the wind is blowing, it creates those windrows.

Or when the ice is shifting and moving, then it's more difficult. For a season, the ice never shuts me down. The main thing is usually the Soo Locks closing. Some of it is because the weather has turned really bad, and it just doesn't pay to lay that much and then try again to get through heavy ice.

The Coast Guard helps out with icebreaking, but it only does that during daylight hours. It will not operate at night. You have to kind of work to the Coast Guard schedule. Those guys will get up and say, "OK, we're going to start work at 8 o'clock in the morning, but first we have to take on fuel and take on supplies, and then maybe we'll be down to your position in four hours." Well, you don't want to wait for that.

A lot of times, you just try to back up and keep on ramming, keep on going through the heavy ice. It takes a while, but usually you break yourself out of it. Sometimes you can't. Sometimes you do need the icebreaker.

Being able to deal with ice makes a difference if you're carrying a load of cargo or not carrying a load. It's the weight. If you get the weight moving, the momentum can take you through a lot of ice. The weight and momentum will help out going through the ice. But once you stop, then it's hard to get that momentum up again. You have to back up quite a way and hope that the water stays open in front of you as you take another run at the ice and see if you can keep going. Usually if you get through the tough spot, then you'll find some softer ice and go for quite a while and hit another tougher spot. You've just got to work through it. It's a lot of time in the pilothouse, and you're usually up a lot of hours when you're in the ice.

The winters of '78 and '79

I don't know what was with those seasons. They were really cold and long. I was working for Hannah Marine. We were moving tank barges – usually fuel oil, gasoline, fertilizer, stuff like that.

I remember going into Escanaba, Michigan. There was about five inches of ice on the bay, and I was pushing through it OK. John Selvick was coming out with another vessel that he was assisting. Selvick Marine Towing had an ice-breaking tug up there breaking ice. He said, "How about if I make a couple of circles around you, and then you can follow my path going back?" I said, "OK," and he made a circle around me. And then all the ice started moving. The ice shoved up against me so hard that you could hear the ribs on the barge bending. You could hear the "RRRRRR," creaking noise. The ice started piling up on my side. It broke my facing wire, which I was pushing with. The wind was blowing about 40 miles an hour. It was below zero. The wind chill had to be around minus 40. Really, really cold. It was just raw. The guys had to get the cable out of the water because it had broken, and they had to get it out of the water before I could break away and use my wheels (*propellers*) to get away from the barge.

They could only work a short time. The guys would get out there, and they'd work for a little bit, and then they had to get out of the wind for a while. Then they got the other wire off, and we got the wires changed out. I finally broke loose out of a big windrow and got in front of the barge and put it on a short tow line and started pulling the barge. I was OK. I headed right into the wind until I got the vessel up close to the shoreline. I was coming through Rock Island Passage, and Selvick got stuck. He said, "Come over and help me get unstuck." I said, "God, I can't right now." The ice was piling up and almost picking his tug up out of the water. That was a real bad year. It was below zero a lot that year. And then with the wind, the wind chills were really really bad.

Ice builds up on the vessels. You have to watch for freezing spray, which is very dangerous. It can put you on a list. It has sunk boats. I remember one time when I was on the tug Donald C. Hannah, the sea was just big enough to be trouble. It was very cold out. This was back in a pretty bad year – '78 or '79 – and I was going from Chicago to Ludington. I was out in the open water. I had gone straight across Lake Michigan, and just a little bit of a wind came up. It was just enough wind that every time I hit one of those little waves – two to three feet – water was spraying up. I kept on building ice up. I built so much ice up on the decks that when we got into the port, we had to steam the ice off with the dock's steam-making equipment. It took us a whole day to just clean the ice off. We were pretty heavy with it. There was so much ice built up you could hardly walk between the gunnel and the house.

The ice doesn't really affect handling. It's just extra weight. What it does cause is extra work.

When ice builds up on the deck of the Dorothy Ann/Pathfinder, it builds up on all the hatches. All the hatches have clamps. All of this has to be broken loose with sledgehammers or picks. You have to chop it. We have what's called a donkey boiler. It's a boiler that heats water. We take hot water, and we go out there and spray off the majority of ice. That's how we get rid of snow, too – just wash it off with hot water. But that takes a lot of extra time. That's time that you're not loading or unloading or moving product.

Slinging a sledgehammer takes a lot out of the guys, too. If it's really windy and blowing hard, you have to give the guys enough breaks so they don't freeze their hands or toes or get wind burned so bad that it's just as bad as sunburn. And they have to do their normal job on top of it. There's a lot of work. Day or night.

In the wintertime, there are some operations that the Coast Guard names that are near the Straits of Mackinac. Once the ice forms, it has Operation Oil Can, which is for tankers or tank barges that go through straits. It has Operation Coal Shovel. That's for coal boats. And then it has Operation Taconite. We have to report in to the Coast Guard at pre-arrival to ice areas. For instance, if we were going up through the Straits of Mackinac, coming up Lake Michigan, you would report in at Rawley Point. If you are upbound on Lake Huron, you would report in at Thunder Bay. If you're downbound on Lake Superior, they already know that because there's the traffic system in there. They want to know when you're going to arrive at a certain point, or about. Then if you get stuck in the ice, you report to them on how you're doing. Then you report back in before you get to Round Island, before you get to that area before you get to the Mackinac Bridge.

Usually you have pretty much open water up until you get to Boblo Island, or what is called Bois Blanc, up in the straits. The south channel is closed because of icing. You have to go upbound on the north side of the Bois Blanc Island because of closures. They close Grays Reef. They close the south channel in the Straits of Mackinac, so you have to go up through Round Island Passage. You usually don't encounter too much ice until you get to Round Island Passage. Then from Round Island to Mackinac Bridge – it's only a matter of three or four miles – it's pretty heavy ice, and it can be jammed because of currents. Then, when you get through the bridge, it's pretty much iced up until you get to Lansing Shoal. In some of the harder winters, it would be frozen all the way down along the shoreline.

Normally, you have pretty clear sailing up to Lansing Shoal. Then you have Lansing Shoal to the Mackinac Bridge, which is about 40 miles, and that's all ice covered. And then five miles through. And if you have ice on the other side of Round Island, it's usually not too heavy. But between Mackinac Bridge and Lansing Shoal, it is really affected by the wind. If you have a lot of wind making windrows, that makes it harder to navigate. That's when most of 'em get in trouble.

An ice lift

One year when I worked for Hannah Marine, I had to come up to northwestern Michigan to help one of our tugs out. Coast Guard boats were in because jet fuel was needed for Traverse City air station for the Coast Guard. We brought a load in there by barge. The going was pretty good headed in, but when the tug and barge were coming out, the captain wanted me to wait at a point for his vessel to come out and start breaking ice in the lake so we could get into open water.

It was quite an operation. We had a helicopter up there, two 140-foot ice breakers, and myself. Every time our tug and barge would get stuck, I would break up the windrows so they could push through. The helicopter crew was able to read the ice and was reporting to us where the light ice was.

Well, we sat there at night and just sat in the ice waiting on it. I was off duty and in bed when the wind picked up. I could feel us moving. I could feel that the ice was pushing in on us, and it was lifting us. I went up to the pilothouse and said, "Let's start these engines up." Because if the ice gets down around the rudder, if it starts pushing, it'll bend your rudders, it'll do a lot of damage. It could bend your wheels. It can put you in a bad situation. What you do is head into the wind. Instead of the ice pushing sideways on you, you're headed into the wind, and you just run your wheel. You're not going anywhere. The ice may be pushing you backwards a little bit, but you're not in any real danger, and the wheel wash keeps the ice away from the rudders. That's a precaution.

It was the Donald C. Hannah. I was the captain on that for 10 years. It was very exciting. I enjoyed it. And I loved ice breaking. To me, ice breaking was one of my favorite things to do. I was very good at it, for one thing. And I could maneuver well in ice. Some people weren't so good at it because you have to do anticipating. You have to anticipate when you're going to break through a windrow so you don't put your bow into the barge.

All of the machinery is affected if it's not warmed up to some degree with oil. The oil lubricates everything. Most of our machinery has heaters for wintertime. For instance, the unloading generator on the barge – if we're not using it, we put heaters on it to keep the oils warm and keep the water circulating. We keep the generator warm all the time so that when the deckhands start it up, we can use it right away.

It's the same with all the gears and everything on the unloading system. All of them have either oil heaters or some kind of heating system.

That's the same with our hydraulic winches. They have heaters.

Heater systems are built right into the machines. You can turn the heaters on or turn them off with a switch. It's not like you have to have a separate heater. Ship operators have learned from past experiences how gears are slow and it's hard on the gears if their oil is not warm. Because of the scale of the heating system on the vessel, I think the oil we use is pretty much the same. We don't change it by seasons. In a car, you go from, in the winter, a 10W 30 to 5W 30 oil or 10-40 to 5-30. But ours are pretty consistent. They don't change much at all.

The Hon. James L. Oberstar makes its way through ice and snow. *Gary Schmidt photo*

Wind whips the waves on Lake Erie near Fairport Harbor, Ohio. *Gary Schmidt photo*

Mother Nature puts on another spectacular display. *Gary Schmidt photo*

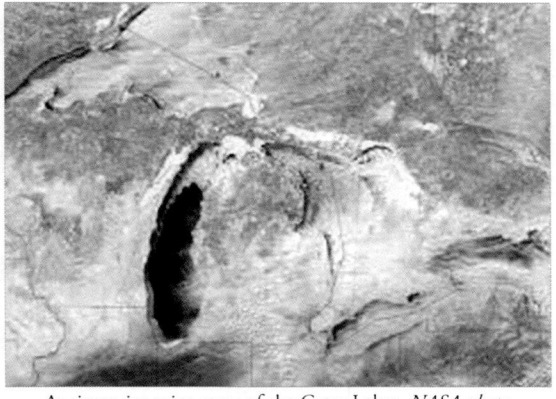

At times, ice grips most of the Great Lakes. *NASA photo*

Hatch 29

Navy

I enlisted in the Navy in 1964 and went to boot camp in San Diego. I wasn't thinking about the war too much when I enlisted. Vietnam wasn't really heating up too much yet. It was really in the early stages, and the American role was more as advisors than anything. I wasn't really aware of Vietnam, but I know I didn't want to be in the Army. The Navy was the way to go for me.

I went from boot camp to a base in Stockton, California, and was waiting for a chance to go to school in Treasure Island, San Francisco. I was there six or seven months. I went to school for electronics – radar and radiomen – but that wasn't my calling. I didn't care for it. I was sent to the Philippine Islands, and I was just a Seaman there. They sent me to a Navy magazine, which is an ammunition place. The magazine grew while I was there. It was early Vietnam times, and we were stockpiling ammunition. We would supply Navy ships with ordinance. They went right to Vietnam.

After the Philippine Islands, I went on board the USS Chicago, a guided-missile cruiser. I was pretty much just a Seaman on it and went mess cooking and discovered I liked the galley part of it. I stayed there and became a commissary man. The recipes were for 100 people at a time. It wasn't any gourmet cooking. It was your meat and potatoes and vegetables.

The Chicago had 1,200 men aboard. It was a pretty large ship. She was nearly 700 feet long. It was like a little city. I became a baker. I would bake about 300 loaves of bread a night. I'd do the morning pastries. I forget how many dozens of donuts or sweet rolls we used to make. We made a lot. That was my night job. I did cooking in the galley. I especially enjoyed the breakfast part. I'd have a grill about the size of this table *(four by six feet)*, and I'd just whip out dozens of eggs at a time. And I enjoyed it. I really liked cooking. I did that until I got out in 1968.

The Chicago went to a lot of ports, but most of our time was spent in Vietnam. I got on board in San Diego, California. We made a cruise to Seattle, Washington, for a sea fair there in 1967. On our way to Vietnam, we stopped in Hawaii and then Midway Island and then went on to Vietnam.

We were right on the DMZ line *(demilitarized zone)*, and we were to fire at any MIGs *(North Vietnamese jet fighters)* that would cross over to the south from the north. We stayed 12 or 13 miles off the coast, and we just patrolled up and down. It seemed like the only time we could be involved in action was when we were fueling, and we'd have to break off. They seemed to know – and I don't know this for a fact – but my theory was always that years later we found out about the Walker spy family and the stuff that was fed, we were wondering if some of that went over to the wrong people. I don't know if the Chinese got a hold of that or North Vietnam, but information was fed to the Soviet Union. And who knows who the Soviet Union was feeding information to. I always thought that it was just odd that the minute that we would hook up to take on fuel or to take on supplies, that's the exact time that the MIGs would fly, and we'd have to break off. Of course, by the time you break off and get ready to fire, they were gone. But they seemed to be aware of it.

You'd put 45 days on the line, and then you'd get some to R&R *(rest and recreation)*. On our R&R, we went to Hong Kong a couple of times, went to Singapore, and back to the Philippine Islands. We were supposed to go to Australia, but as we were nearing the end of our time in Vietnam, our 45 days on the line, the Pueblo was seized in Korea, so we sailed to Korea. We went from 95-degree weather in Vietnam to 20 below zero on the north side of Korea, and it was pretty bad.

***

SNAPSHOT: *The seizure of the spy ship USS Pueblo and its crew created international turmoil. The 82-man crew eventually was released, but the vessel still is held by North Korea. The Pueblo was built at Kewaunee, Wisconsin, and launched there in 1944.*

***

It was pretty tense off Korea. I think it was more tense than what it was for us in Vietnam. I think things were really ready to explode up that way. We were on duty stations, more aware of what was going on than even in Vietnam. It was a whole different tension up there. It was February 1968. We were part of the task force.

Going into the Navy was eye opening. I was from a little town, Sturgeon Bay, Wisconsin, and just going to boot camp in San Diego was an eye opener. San Francisco was a real eye opener. There's a whole lot more to the world than little Sturgeon Bay, and I was pretty naïve, I guess, when I went in.

The Philippines was kind of neat. You talk about a small world. When I was stationed in the Philippines, a ship came in, and another guy from Sturgeon Bay was aboard. He was running the river boats in Vietnam, and he was in for R&R. And another guy I knew was in Subic Bay. So two guys I went to high school with ended up meeting me in Olongapo Bay, Philippine Islands, which is Subic Bay basically. And two more guys from Jacksonport in Door County were there, too. There was a picture in the Door County Advocate *(newspaper)* of the five of us meeting up in Subic Bay. It was pretty amazing that we could all meet up one night in the Philippine Islands. And it was a fun night, too, what I remember of it.

But being a cook in the Navy or driving a truck and a forklift at an ammunition dump really didn't have too much to do with what I do now.

Hatch 30

Lassoin' a deer

I was working for Hannah Marine on the tug Donald C. Hannah. It was February, and it was cold. Steam was coming up off the water. It was hard to see. With my tug, I was going from one barge to another in the Chicago Sanitary Canal. I was headed upstream to pick up another barge miles away. The Donald Hannah threw a big wake, somewhere between six and eight feet when I was in the canal. The Chicago Sanitary Canal is only about 160 feet wide. I was barreling up the river. It was 10 o'clock at night. There was no other traffic around, and I was moving right along, somewhere around 14 or 15 miles an hour. I was throwing this big wake, and it was almost going to the top of the walls. The tug's water line was about 10 feet from the top of the walls. One of my mates was up in the pilothouse talking with me as we headed upstream. He was looking out the window, I was looking straight ahead, and he said, "Wow, we just passed a deer in the river." I said, "No, no way. You're crazy." He said, "No, no, it was a deer. I'm positive." I continued on a way, and he said, "We ought to check on it." I said, "All right, we've got time." So we turned back. At the same time, we were thinking the section of the sanitary canal we were in was at least four miles long with high walls. If it was a deer, we were concerned about how it was going to get out and how it was going to survive. I didn't think one would. There was no way for a deer to get out except in a couple of areas. And we didn't know how bad off it was. As we got to it, my mate said, "Yeah, that's a deer." And I said, "Oh, yeah, that's a deer." There it was, paddling down the Chicago Sanitary Canal. So we ordered the crew on deck. We were deciding what to do. The deer would have had to swim three to four miles to get out. The mate said, "Let's kind of herd it over to the side and see if we can lasso it." So I brought the tug in and squeezed the deer toward the wall as it was swimming along. Guys threw a rope, one of our heaving lines, over its neck. They pulled it up out of the water, and as they did that, they tied the legs so they wouldn't get kicked with the hoofs. They got the deer aboard and secure. It was a doe, maybe 105 pounds, not real big. It was exhausted. We took it down river about two miles. There was a break in the wall where the walls fell in. The Donald Hannah had a flat stern, so I backed the tug into the wall. We untied the deer. Everybody was standing on the sides and herding it off. The deer got off the stern of the tug. It was not very steady. When we first untied it, the deer was not sure what it wanted to do. Then it got onto ground and started go up the hill, it couldn't make it at first. Then it did a little trot and up and away it went. It took off. So that's my lassoin' a deer story.

Hatch 31

First tugs

I started out on a single-screw (*propeller*) boat with a rudder. I worked a twin-screw boat with rudders. I've operated a single-screw boat that had a right-turning wheel (*propeller that spins clockwise*) and one that had a left-turning wheel (*propeller that spins counterclockwise*) – and it makes a difference.

Left: What happens when you come into a dock to your port side, when you back with a left-turning wheel, the force of the propeller wash will pull your bow away from the dock as you back up. The bow will start to swing out because, the way the pitch is on the propeller, the wash will pull you that way. So that's how you learn how to use it. You come in to the dock at a certain speed. As you're getting close, you give it a little backup, let 'er run again, give 'er a little backup, and that pulls your stern over, and your bow will kind fall up against (*the dock*). You get a line out (*to the dock*), and you can work your way in.

Right: With a right-hand turning wheel, it's just the opposite. When you maneuver into a dock on the port side, if you back on it, the propeller wash is going to throw your bow into the dock, so you have to maneuver in a little bit flatter and then back up and let that bow fall over and back up again, and get it stopped until you get a line out, and then you can work ahead on it.

Now, I worked on the tugboat John Purves, which had twin screws and an extended rudder. And that was not the way to go. It's a narrow boat, and it didn't have a lot of room on the stern. So the designers put the rudder so there would be wash from screws, which they thought would help, but it really didn't do a very good job because there wasn't enough wheel wash on the rudder. You couldn't maneuver the vessel.

***

SNAPSHOT: *Today, the John Purves is an attraction at Door County Maritime Museum in Sturgeon Bay, Wisconsin. Guided tours take visitors from stern to bow, engine room to pilothouse.*

***

The Donald C. Hannah was a twin screw with flanking rudders. Flanking rudders are rudders that are forward of the prop (*propeller*). When you backed up, you could maneuver it a little bit because you could throw wash one way or another. But it became problematic when you were out in the open water because if you didn't have the rudders exactly straight in front of you – they're off a little bit – it slowed you way down, and there was a lot of turbulence. So eventually the flanking rudders were taken off, and it was just a plain old twin screw.

I also picked up a boat for Hannah. It was called the City of Toledo. It was an excursion boat. It was a big aluminum crew boat, and it had triple screw twin rudders. You had a rudder on the outside of both of the outside screw and the middle screw was for maneuvering. You could get into position. And then you could come ahead or go astern a little bit to make a dock, which was kind of nice.

Captain Schmidt's tug and barge timeline
(On Great Lakes unless otherwise noted)

⇨ *1969: Tug: Lauren Castle (1,200 horsepower). Barge: Sea Castle. Deckhand for Penn-Dixie Cement.*

⇨ *1971-1974: Tugs: Lauren Castle (1,200 horsepower), John M. Selvick (1,500 horsepower), Telson Queen (450 horsepower). Barges: Sea Castle, Mel William Selvick (sometimes both barges at once). Mate and captain for Selvick Marine Towing.*

NOTE: *The 2012 TV series "Great Lake Warriors" on the History channel spotlighted Captain John Selvick aboard the tug John M. Selvick.*

⇨ *1975-1976: Various tugs (1,200 to 3,600 horsepower). Multiple barges (sometimes 15 at once), either pushing or towing on the Western Rivers (upper Mississippi River and Illinois River). Captain and mate for Mississippi Valley Line and Twin City Barge.*

⇨ *1977-1986: Tugs: Donald C. Hannah (2,400 horsepower), Mary E. Hannah (3,600 horsepower), James A. Hannah (4,000 horsepower), Margaret M (1,800 horsepower), Tugboat Hannah (1,200 horsepower), Daryl C. Hannah (2,000 horsepower), Mary Page Hannah (2,000 horsepower). Multiple Hannah tank barges (sometimes two at a time) of 2,000 to 6,300 barrel capacity, either pushing or towing on the Great Lakes and Western Rivers. Captain and mate/Hannah Inland Waterways/Hannah Marine/Tampa Towing.*

⇨ *1987-1999: Tug: Triton (4,000 horsepower). Barge: St. Marys Cement. Captain for Merce Transportation.*

⇨ *2000-2013: Tug: Dorothy Ann (7,200 horsepower). Barge: Pathfinder. Captain for Interlake Steamship Company.*

The Mary Page Hannah, one of the tugs Captain Schmidt worked on in the 1970s and 1980s, still is in service. Here, it is docked adjacent to the Door County Maritime Museum in Sturgeon Bay, Wisconsin. *Monica L. Gerds photo*

Inside an engine

When I went aboard the Donald C. Hannah, it had just come out. The engine was pretty good. On an EMD (*Electro Motive Diesel*), you usually run somewhere between 30,000 and 35,000 hours before you do a major overhaul. And it was time for a major overhaul on the engine, so Hannah Marine hired a company that does that.

That company came with a crew of seven people, three people working on each engine and a supervisor watching the whole thing. They tear down the engines completely. They tear out all the power packs; take out what we call jewelry on the top, all the lifters; the cam shafts; rocker arms, all the stuff that's vital to the intake and outtake of the gases in the cylinders; head cocks. They go underneath the engine itself and disconnect the rod arms off the main crank shaft that move the pistons up and down and are attached to a flywheel. They take the flywheel off. They take the clutch assembly off. All you have left is the bare block. They clean out the sumps, in bottom, in oil pans that hold 250 to 300 gallons of oil. The engine parts are cleaned up, gaskets are scraped, everything is cleaned. Then they come in with fresh power packs – fresh bearings, new jewelry for the top lifters, cam shafts, water pumps, oil pumps, starters. All that is put in new. They're just like complete brand new engines when they're done.

The gears on the front end have overspeed trips. That means that if the engine starts to run away from you, it shuts itself down. The engine has fuel pumps and injectors. It's really involved. I wanted to be on one of these overhauls just to see what went in and what went out and to have a little bit of a knowledge of the engines.

The engines were warranted for six months on workmanship.

An engineer makes an adjustment on one of the Dorothy Ann's two 3,600-horsepower engines. *Gary Schmidt photo*

We ran for a while after the overhaul. We went through sea trials and broke things in properly. We did all the maintenance that had to be done. After so many hours, we had to re-tighten bolts to specs, to a certain tightness. There is a wrench that tells you how many pounds you're putting on a bolt so you don't over-tighten it. We did all of this stuff, and it was logged.

After five months, we were headed up Lake Michigan, and all of a sudden you could hear a noise in the engine. That means something was going bad.

The engineer caught it right away. He was in the process of shutting down the engine. There's a lever that, if you push down hard enough, will stop the engine. All of a sudden, a rod came through the side of the engine. He got a hold of us and said, "Hey, we've got to turn this thing around. We've got a major engine problem."

And we were lucky. Usually when you open up that hot oil to the atmosphere, it causes a crank case explosion, and you get a fireball that comes out. We didn't get that crank case explosion because we'd just been getting under way, and I don't think the engine was really hot hot. Otherwise, we would have had an engine fire on top of it. That could be a real disaster. Hopefully, you've trained your crew well enough to fight fires. But engine room fires are more difficult. If you have any oil in the bilges – underneath gratings or underneath plates where you're walking – and you get a fire under there and it spreads around, it's really hard to get it out. You have to use what we call Purple K *(dry chemical fire extinguisher)*, which retards the fire from flashing back. It puts a coating on everything.

We called the overhaul company. The engine was, indeed, under warranty. The company figured out one of the bolts on one of the bearing baskets was the wrong size and let go. That's when the rod separated from the crank shaft and was thrown outside of the engine,

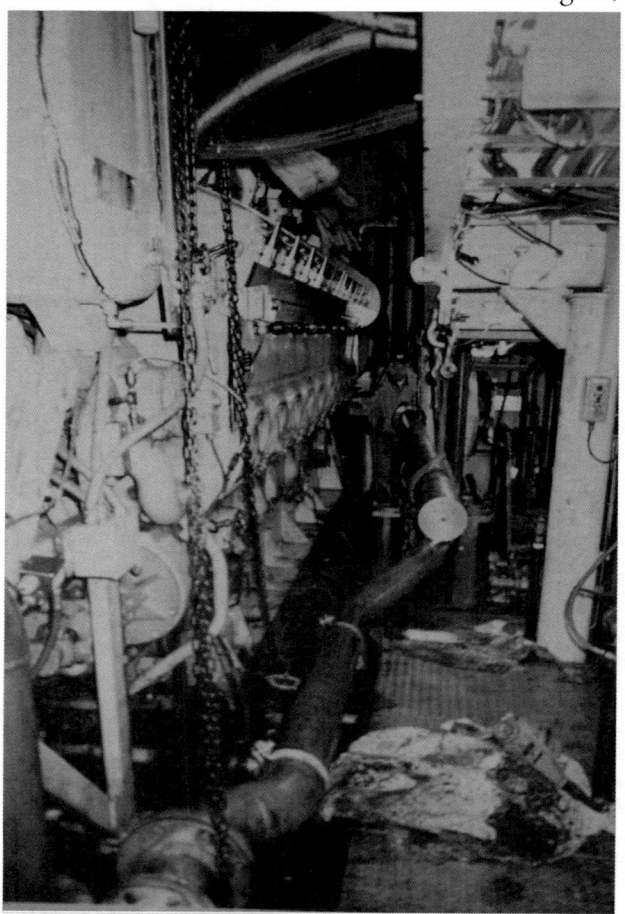

right through the block. The piston had come down and come back up before the engineer could shut the engine down, and it egg-shaped the liner seat. It also burred up the crank shaft. Once a crank shaft's burred up, that can't be fixed. That's a throwaway.

The company came in with another crank shaft and made sure all the specs were good. The guys on the repair crew split the engine in half. They separated it from the oil pan. They cut holes in the deck. They had cranes with spreader bars down there. Once they unbolted the engine and parts, they lifted up the half with chains. They put in legs between the two sections so you could get inside. The crank shaft is as long as the engine is from one end to the other, for all the pistons. The guys kind of walked the crank shaft out with chain falls and took it out through a hole in the roof.

All the power packs had to come out. Part of the engine had to come off, and other parts had to be pulled up.

Captain Schmidt examines a shaft that's been removed during a dry dock of the Dorothy Ann in February 2002 at Sturgeon Bay, Wisconsin..
Warren Gerds photo

Everything had to be disconnected from the shaft. Then they cleaned out sump really good. They cut out in the block where rod came through the side, and they welded in a whole new piece, and it looked like new.

They got inside the engine to work on the liner with the egg-shaped seat. A welder added steel to the seat. He welded it with many passes. The area can't be overheated. The guys came in with a machine that looks exactly like a liner that sets down inside and re-grinds the seat. It's a specialized machine just for doing that. This is all close quarters.

I got inside engine. I could see what the inside of an engine looks like and how the liner seat was oval shaped from the piston hitting it. I was curious. I wanted to see. I wanted to know. I just went in to look at what the inside of an engine looks like. I could have taken a layoff, but I came to clean parts and to see the ins and outs of an engine. I wanted to see how it was done.

It's very interesting to sit inside of a main engine. You crawl in. You put your feet down and sit on one of the pedestals and look up underneath. I was seated, but the guy doing the welding was not. He was on his hands and knees and working hard.

The repair took a week. It took three days to take the engine apart. They worked around the clock on the repair.

On the overhauls, I learned a lot about engines. When an engineer would come up and tell me what a problem was, I understood what the problem was, and that was great. It made better communication between me and an engineer.

Hatch 33

Fire

One of my last years with Merce Transportation in the late '90s was rather trying. It was a long year, and I was physically and mentally exhausted. I don't remember if it was from the heavy ice or what, but I just remember I was tired out. Curly Selvick gave me a call and said, "Do me a favor. Can you run up to Escanaba and break ice and help assist some ships in?" I said, "I'm physically and mentally beat. I can't do that for you, Curly." He said, "I'm running thin on people. How about just running a tug from Sturgeon Bay to Green Bay? We have to break some ice and assist some other boats in later on, and I just want to get the tug in position." I said, "All right, I'll do that for you." Just running a light tug – no barge – from Sturgeon Bay to Green Bay and tie it up I thought should be five or six hours at the most.

Well, I get up to Sturgeon Bay early in the morning, and we jump on the tug, and we start breaking. There was a lot of ice out there, with plenty of ice in the southern end of Green Bay. We were breaking our way into Green Bay and just about to Green Bay Harbor Entrance Light (*about 10 miles from the mouth of the Fox River in the city of Green Bay*). At that point, a fuel line busted in the engine room, and it squirted fuel oil right onto the exhaust manifold and caught afire. The fuel line was steel. Through vibration, the metal can weaken. This was not a break but a spraying leak. If it was a complete break, the fuel might not have caught on fire.

So now we have three guys on the boat – an engineer, a deckhand, and myself – and we weren't anticipating any big problems. The manifold is up kind of high where the fuel is squirting. In the upper part of the engine room, which we call fiddley, we had some towing lines laid down to thaw them out and let them get dry. Well, these nylons caught on fire, so now we've got a real toxic smoke. There's a doorway from the engine room that goes right up the stairway to the pilothouse. The smoke was like a chimney effect. If I opened up the door, it brought everything right up through the pilothouse, and I wouldn't be able to stay in the pilothouse because of the smoke.

The engineer was afraid that the boat was going to blow, and I told him it wouldn't. But he was going to jump off the boat and walk on the ice over to Green Bay Harbor Entrance Light. I told him, "No, you can't do that." I didn't fear that we were going to burn up in the fire. We were probably within a quarter mile of Green Bay Harbor Entrance Light, and it was all ice. There was a chance that we would have jumped off and taken a ladder with us and walked it across there so that, if you do go down, you have something to hang onto to get up. That was a plan that we had established. But I told the engineer, "You're not jumping off of this boat. You're not leaving because if you do go through the ice, there's no way that we're going get you back."

I got a message out to the company and the Coast Guard's Mobile Bay, which was in the area breaking ice and working the buoys. She came out to give us assistance.

We shut all the ventilation to the engine room, but we didn't have a remote shutoff for the engines. This was an older tug. So we just shut everything up so it didn't get any more air for fire.

The Coast Guard boat came up alongside and gave us a Purple K unit. Purple K is a fire retardant that will keep the fire from flashing back. It's great, especially with a bilge fire. Our fire never got to the bilges. It never got down that low. It was always a high fire. It burned up the electrical wiring that went into the steering system, so we didn't have any steering. We had generators, and everything else was working fine. But all the wiring was burned up going to the steering systems, going to whatever else we needed for navigation. We couldn't do anything.

At one point, the Coast Guard wanted to fill up the smoke stack with water to shut down the engine, and I said, no, that would just ruin the engine. We opened up the engine room and sprayed Purple K in there. The fire was out, we let the smoke run out, and then I went down there and turned the engine off.

At that point, the Coast Guard gave us a tow to Sturgeon Bay, and Selvick came out with the rest of his tugs, which were headed for Sturgeon Bay. Once we got to Sherwood Point, he came out with another tug and towed us back to the dock and tied up.

So what I thought was going to be a five or six-hour job turned into 20 hours later.

For a totally exhausted person that I was, I was really exhausted. I was already tired before I took the job. But that's what you do when you do favors.

Selvick still needed to get a tug to Green Bay. But not me. That was it for me. And he offered: "Hey, I'll give you a free trip down to Florida for a vacation." I said, "Curly, if I could do it, I'd do it, but I'm really tired." And there wasn't anything I wouldn't do for that man because I really liked Curly Selvick a lot. He gave me a start. (*See "Best teacher," page 301*.) When he asked for a favor, I normally would do it, but that year I was just exhausted.

Hatch 34

Star tug

Once upon a time, there was a Hollywood movie star with a tugboat that carried her name – Daryl C. Hannah. The tug was named by her father, Donald Hanna. Daryl was a child at the time. Captain Schmidt worked for Hannah Marine from 1977 to 1986.

We were aware that there was an actress daughter in the family. Absolutely. We had her first movie on the boats, and everybody knew who Daryl was, especially after "Splash." I ran the Daryl C. Hannah a few times. She was already a star.

During the time Captain Schmidt was with Hannah Marine, Daryl starred in such movies as "Splash," "The Pope of Greenwich Village," Roxanne," "The Clan of the Cave Bear," and "Steel Magnolias."

The name kind of attracted people to the tug. Sure it did – "Oh, Daryl Hannah!" Absolutely. You bet. It made a difference. It was a conversation piece – "Oh, that Daryl Hannah."

Hannah Marine was out of Lemont, Illinois, and that's right where the Chicago Sanitary Canal connects with the Calumet-Sag Canal. The company owned a triangle plot of land where it had a shipyard. It had quite a fleet at one time, a lot of tank barges. We moved oil, we moved any liquid products – liquid fertilizer; chemicals; heavy oils; crude oil; crude oil with gas in it; calcium chloride, a byproduct of making fire brick, a salt product used in thousands of things, for dust control, salt for roads, and ballast for tractor tires. And I moved a lot of that stuff. Donald C. was the father. Daryl was from Donald's first wife. The tug was named when she was a child, and that was before I worked for Hannah Marine.

James A. Hannah was the founder of the company. He was a trucker. He was loading trucks, and he was loading them into barges and saw the potential of how many trucks it took to load up a barge and how economical it would be to… so he bought a tug and a couple of barges and started moving stuff that way and developed Hannah Marine. Eventually, Donald C. became the president of Hannah Marine. All of the tugs are named after family members.

With the Daryl C. Hannah, we moved oil barges. We went all over the place. On the Daryl C. Hannah, I was moving oil barges between Chicago and Indiana Harbor to Escanaba, Ludington, and Cheboyan.

I took the Daryl C. Hannah on a trip a long time ago before the steel mills shut down in Lackawana, New York. I took heavy oil to Lackawana. I'd run Lake Erie with it. I've been into Toledo with it. Been all over, actually.

EPILOGUE: *Daryl Hannah today is an environmental activist.*

Hatch 35

Talkin' tugs

Tugs just happened to be available at the time that I got out of the Navy. I was thinking about sailing. My dad worked on the bulk carrier Richard J. Reiss. There was an opening on it, and I could have gone to work with him. At the same time, a job came up on a tugboat. I was thinking of going where my dad was, and I was thinking we'd be better friends if I didn't. So I took the tug job. Once I got into the tugs, well, that's just the direction I went. I could have gone either way.

Say "tugboat" to most people, and an image may pop to mind of a harbor with a small, rugged boat pushing a large ship toward a dock with not much speed but a whole lot of effort. That stand-alone tug differs from the vessels in Captain Schmidt's career.

Those tugs are for assisting vessels in and out of ports. But my tug is matched with a barge and is part of the ship.

A stand-alone tug in Green Bay for ship assistance would have two to three people on it. With me, with the self-unloader and product, I have 14 people, sometimes 15, riding the boat.

The crew of the stand-alone tug wouldn't live on it. The tug just goes to the dock when the job is done. The crew will fire the tug up a couple of hours before a ship is coming in. The ship's company will call a tug office – whatever towing company – and say, "Hey, we've got ship coming in there tomorrow. We're going to need tug assistance. We're going into the Reiss Coal Dock." And the tug office will say, "OK, we'll have a tug ready for you. Where do you want us to meet, at the entrance to the river or when you get up to Such-and-Such Bridge?" And that's where the tug will meet the ship. Sometimes the tug crew will put a line on the ship. Sometimes the tug will just maneuver the ship to the dock.

The Dorothy Ann is called a tug because it can tow. We can tow our barge, the Pathfinder. It's considered towing whether pushing ahead or towing astern. Or alongside. That's still considered towing.

The Dorothy Ann is a different tug in that the crew lives on it. The Dorothy Ann is a mobile home.

Yeah. So was the Triton. That one I towed with most of the time, but I pushed sometimes. Took it on the side sometimes. On the Triton, I had a crew of six.

∗∗∗

SNAPSHOT: *There are distinctions between large-operation tugs. The 1,000 foot Presque Isle is an integrated tug and barge (ITB) because, for all practical purposes, it's a single unit. The Dorothy Ann/Pathfinder is an articulated tug and barge (ATB) because they are separate units.*

∗∗∗

The Triton was a World War II Army tug. The barge the St. Marys Cement that I pushed around was built in 1986. It was 360 feet. With the tug and a notch, we were 400 feet overall. I was captain for 14 years. They are still around and strictly Canadian. The Triton comes to Green Bay. It doesn't come all the way up the Fox River. It just comes in the mouth where St. Marys is, just below the first railroad bridge, just through Tower Drive and before you get to the first railroad bridge, just below the limestone dock.

For 14 years, Captain Schmidt sailed the Great Lakes at the helm of the tug Triton.
Gary Schmidt photo

The Triton and St. Marys Cement was a push-pull kind of barge where the tug was just connected by wires to the barge when I pushed it. In fact, in any seas over five feet or six feet, I would have to pull the barge. I would put it on a tow line behind me and run it probably 1,200 to 1,400 feet behind us in rough weather.

On the Triton, we eventually replaced most cables with Kevlar lines, which are stronger than steel cables and lighter. The 1½-inch cable that we were using was so heavy that it was hard for the small crew that I had to pull those lines. With the Kevlar lines, one guy could lift it off. It's that light. It would take two to three guys to lift off the other cable.

On the Dorothy Ann/Pathfinder, we are mechanically connected with hydraulics, and I never have to pull the barge. I can pull the Pathfinder. I have the capability of pulling it in case something fails, but it would have to be catastrophic to have to do that. We can push it in all weathers with waves of up to 20 to 25 feet.

With St. Marys Cement, you just control with the wire that's behind you. We had a cable – 2 or 2 1/8-inch diameter steel cable – that was 2,000 feet long that we could tow with – two fifths of a mile. You don't really have a real good control until you shorten the tow line. At 1,200 feet, the barge will follow a path. It might move around a little bit. The weather might affect it. That depends on which side the weather is coming from. It might blow the barge down a little bit or pick it up a little bit depending on whether the barge was loaded or empty and what direction the wind is coming from. As you shorten up the tow line, as you're coming through a break wall and you have to tow the barge through a break wall, you shorten it up to maybe 100 feet behind you or less, maybe 60 or 70 feet. Then you have a lot more control. You can just give it a little pull to the north or pull to the south, and that'll affect how that barge comes in through a break wall. You have a lot more control then. Once you get in through a break wall, you take the barge off the tow line, you get the tug back into the notch, and put facing wires on that are connected between a tug and a barge when you are in a notch and pushing it. You have great control over it then. The barge had a bow thruster on it, so once I was in the notch, I could control the barge pretty well. Once we got into the notch, we made electrical connections to the barge to control its bow thruster right from the pilothouse. The tug

Because of space at the Bay Aggregate Dock at Bay City, Michigan, the Dorothy Ann is docked next to the Pathfinder during unloading. *Gary Schmidt photo*

was twin screwed, which gives you more maneuverability.

The Triton was about 4,000 horsepower. It had pretty much the same kind of engines that the Dorothy Ann has, except they were 16 cylinders instead of 20 cylinders for the Dorothy Ann.

The Triton had straight drive shafts with rudders behind. The Dorothy Ann has shafts in a configuration that looks like a Z.

There is much better control with the Dorothy Ann. With the Z-drive versus twin screw with rudders, the Dorothy Ann can outmaneuver the Triton, even though the Triton was smaller. The Triton could do a lot. It was very maneuverable, but the Dorothy Ann is still more maneuverable.

Overall, the Triton and St. Marys Cement were a little over 400 feet, and Dorothy Ann in the notch of the Pathfinder is a little over 700 feet. So it's a 300-foot difference.

The Triton's pilothouse eye level was about 27 feet. The Dorothy Ann eye level is about 70 feet. From the water line to the top of the mast is 95 feet.

The speed on the Triton was around 9 miles an hour loaded and around 11 miles an hour in a light condition. The Triton wasn't fast, but it was quick, and I could maneuver very well. I would slow down if towing with it. If pushing, the Triton was a little bit more efficient – about 15 percent as far as fuel consumption and speed. If you're towing, that includes a tow line dragging in the water that slows everything down a little bit.

On the Dorothy Ann, I travel approximately 12 miles an hour in a ballast situation (*no cargo*) and, when loaded and depending on what cargo I have and how deep I am, around 10½ or 11 miles an hour.

The Triton didn't have a pin system, no connection. The connection with the Triton was by wires and cables. The Triton went into a notch. We had bumpers on the side. We had room to move. So we wouldn't break wires, we had rollers on the stern of the tug that guided the cables that connected to the barge.

When I stepped on Dorothy Ann, it was like, "I'm learning all over again. This is something new." Not only is it a pin system, but it has the Z drives. I like the pin system because you're just solid, and it's easy to get used to. It's nicer than being on a cable-and-tug barge. It's a lot easier to control your vessel. I had no experience with the Z drives with no rudders. When I walked on the Dorothy Ann, I thought I was doing all right with a tug and barge with an overall length of a little over 400 feet, and now I'm on a tug and barge with an overall length of more than 700 feet. My eyes went from wide to saucers. "Whoa, did I bite off more than I could chew?" And, as it turned out, I did not. It was pretty interesting. Being about to handle a boat that size with that kind of quickness and that kind of maneuverability was just totally awesome.

Hatch 36

Trip up the Fox

The thing about being a Great Lakes captain is he's going someplace. He's moving. He's going places most people don't see because the places are off shore. He lives in his office, but he's going someplace in his office and seeing places with exotic names. Not only is he going someplace, it's his job to go someplace. It's an everyday thing for him. He likes going places and seeing mansions on the shore, mansions in the sky, and all things vigorous that make sailing sailing. And there are memorable trips, favorites.

A trip that I took that I thought was really fantastic I did for Selvick Marine Towing. I took a tug and a barge from Sturgeon Bay all the way down to Neenah on the Fox River. What was interesting about this trip was that we took a Yankee Dryer, which is a big dryer for the paper mills that's polished stainless steel that came from France.

When you go up the Fox River, you have 17 locks you have to go through. You had to double-lock every one of them. And not only that, but we had to open our own locks. We had to send a crew from lock to lock. And they were old, turnstile locks, so once you got in there, you dealt with hand-operated locks. It was very interesting.

Normally, I'd be sitting in the pilothouse, from which you couldn't see much of anything. But we had an upper pilothouse, where you could sit outside in the open. There were controls up there. So I sat out, and we're going, and I could see around a little bit.

I have a chart, and I see where the buoys are, and I stay within the buoy system. But it's a six-foot controlled depth, and our draft was right at six feet. We had to put chain on the tug to tip it (*with the heavy weight*) so the stern was less than six feet and the bow was less than six feet. We had to tip the tug because the tug draft was about seven feet on the stern and about four or five feet on the bow. We tipped the bow down and then made up (*fastened*) to the barge.

As we went along, around Wrightstown there were cows in the water grazing. So here you're

A Yankee Dryer arrives aboard a barge in Green Bay, Wisconsin. This is the dryer that Captain Schmidt delivered to a paper mill up the Fox River. *Gary Schmidt photo*

going up this place with a tug and a barge, and you look over here, and here are a couple of cows in the water. And it was fun.

It took the whole day to get up there. We started in the early morning at daylight, and we got there, and we were all settled in and had the Yankee Dryer up to the landing spot and it was nighttime. Then we just left everything sit. We tied up everything.

It took four or five days to get the Yankee Dryer off of the barge. It was lifted onto the barge real easily at Bay Shipbuilding. The ship that came in with the Yankee Dryer took it right into the big engraving dock, a big dry dock there, and used the overhead crane to pull the Yankee Dryer out and move it back. And then the ship went out, and we brought the barge in and loaded it onto the barge. But at the paper mill, a crew had to use some kind of a mover to come and get onto the barge, pick the Yankee Dryer up, and roll it real slowly up into the mill, where they put it to use.

It was one of my most interesting trips. I really enjoyed it a lot. And to prepare for that trip, I took my own boat through all the locks past Appleton. There were five step locks.

Hatch 37

Kate's birthday

One year, I told Kate that I'd be home for her birthday. And we're coming from Bowmanville, which is on Lake Ontario (*and about 50 miles east of Toronto*).

We were on the Triton, with the barge St. Marys Cement. It was kind of rough on Lake Erie, but I knew it was going to be really rough on Lake Huron and Lake Michigan. It was blowing pretty hard. It was full gale winds.

Once I got up to the Straits of Mackinac, the wind was against me, and I had about a 60-mile run to go through this weather that had waves of 15, 16, 17 feet in that area that I had to tow across and take the vessel into Rock Island Passage into the Bay of Green Bay. Once I got in there, I was all right, but from Lansing Shoal to Rock Island Passage was a very rough trip. Normally, it takes me about six hours. I took me about 12 hours to get that far. And we got into Green Bay before Kate's birthday on the 22nd of October.

The crew did remember it. They didn't like it too much.

Dave Fitzpatrick, one of the crew members who had moved over to the Dorothy Ann before I went to the Dorothy Ann, had told the company the story. So they already knew about it before I got over to the Dorothy Ann.

Hatch 38

Kids on board

My kids both have taken rides, and Mary has taken a short ride on vessels.

Joe was the first one to ride with me. I was on the Triton. The first time, he was pretty young yet, about seven. He got aboard the boat in Green Bay, and he rode it with me to Milwaukee.

Mary was very, very, "Oh, should I do this or let him go or let him not?" I said, "Well, he'll be fine." Of course, any time that he went out on deck, he had to wear a work vest, a life preserver. He wore a hard hat. But he really didn't want to go outside too much. He was just happy to be in Dad's room and watch TV. But he got to go out on the barge.

There were a lot of restrictions on him because of his age and how small he was at the time. But he enjoyed it very much.

We went through the Sturgeon Bay Ship Canal and straight on down to Milwaukee. That was about an 18-hour ride. Mary came down and met us in Milwaukee to pick him up.

I don't remember whose idea it was, but he wanted to be with Dad. So, yeah, we took him for a ride.

He took another ride on a similar route. This time, he was much older, 16. He got a lot longer ride. He was out on deck a lot. He interacted with the crew a lot, and they all remembered him from the time before when he rode when he was a little guy.

I was on the 6 to 12 watch so I couldn't do much, but one of the mates, Joe Tully, took him to Summerfest (*massive popular music festival in Milwaukee*). That was his first exposure to Summerfest, which he loved. Joe enjoyed that ride a whole lot more. It was memorable.

Kate rode on the Dorothy Ann with me. She got on in Holland, Michigan, where she and Mary were visiting an aunt of Mary's. Kate rode with me for six days. We went up to Port Inland and then to Bay City and then back to Stoneport, and then she got off at Alpena. Mary, her sister, Louise, and mother, Agnes, drove around (*Lake Michigan*) to pick her up.

While Kate was on the boat, she had a great time. She interacted with the crew. She ate everywhere. She was at the age, 10, when it was still okay to be with Dad. We thought about her riding one more time, when she was turning 11, and then Dad was a thing of the past. In the photograph of her aboard Pathfinder (*on page 152*), it's a foggy day. We just loaded at Stoneport. Kate's wearing my coveralls, tied off. She had to have my radio on. She's wearing my work gloves and a hard hat and is walking the rail for the hatch crane. That's the crane that takes the hatches off. So she's walking the hatch crane track, balancing, and just doing kid stuff.

She had a great time on the boat. She loved every minute of it. She had a nice, long trip. She enjoyed going down to the galley because it's sort of an open mess down there, and she could get something to eat anytime she wanted. She was up and down. The crew all looked after her. I had a female mate on the boat at that time, and they got along really well.

On other vessels, a lot of captains and mates bring their children. Some bring them on for a long time. It's not unheard of back in the day that they would bring them on for a summer or a month at a time.

Logs

Overall, this job has gone from just driving a boat and enjoying what you're doing and keeping a pilothouse log and engine room log to much, much more. So much more. The paperwork has just kept growing. You would think it would stop at some point, like when the government had the Paperwork Reduction Act, but that hasn't stopped it at all. It's increased since then.

First of all, we have our ship's log to fill out. That's a daily thing.

On a blank log book, which has headings, I draw my vessel's name on it, Dorothy Ann. We don't usually run out of pages before the season ends. I think I started a second book one year.

I start the log out on each trip. But then when mates are in the pilothouse, the mates maintain the log.

When a person gets on watch, comes off watch, he has to sign the book. In the book, you have every course change. That's a logging point. Arrivals and departures all go in the log. There are lots of course changes, positions. At the very top, across the top, I put in three different ports – your loading port, your discharge port, and your new loading port.

***

SIDE NOTE: Departure time is when we throw the last wire off and our crewman on the dock is aboard. When is my arrival time? When all the lines are secured. When I was in the Navy, arrival time was when the first line went out. But I have alongside time. That means I come up alongside the dock, and we're getting ready to secure our lines. At some docks, it takes about half an hour to tie up. So I log "alongside" and then "arrival."

***

The log book is handwritten. It's spiral bound, and it's a real big book. Each page when you open it up is one log day. If you can't fit it all in on that one day, then you continue on the next page.

This is written in ink. I write in the dates. I write in our departure time. I put in our course and heading, our wind speed and direction, atmospheric conditions, wave heights, wave

When visitors from Interlake Steamship Company headquarters climb aboard the Dorothy Ann, their presence is duly noted in the ship's log.
Gary Schmidt photo

direction, barometer reading, and any remarks I want to make. If there is an event – not necessarily catastrophic but really meaningful – you put it in there. I log our drills, meetings. We also log in the pilothouse log the fuel at the beginning of the day each day and the amount of cargo that we load. This is just the pilothouse log. We log the weather, any personnel getting on or off. Anybody from the dock or port who may get on is kept in a different log. There are different logs.

We also log in the pilothouse log the testing of equipment before you leave the dock – that the steering is working, that your running lights are functioning, that your whistle works, that your propulsion is working. It's all checked. I'm usually in the pilothouse. I turn on the radar and make sure the radars are working. The navigation equipment is usually always on, like the GPS and the gyro. But you look at it. You make sure that it's functioning. You do a test call on the radio, and you sound the whistle – whistle, horn, same thing, a very loud sound. But there is a whistle. It's called a Modoc Whistle, which is a high, screeching whistle that used to be used on tugs and other vessels for certain things. It isn't in use anymore. I don't have a Modoc Whistle on the vessel I'm on now, but I did on other vessels. The engine room has a log. The engineer logs different things. I really don't know what he all logs, but it's stuff like fuel, taking on water, and anything to do with engine temperatures.

When the log book is finished, it stays on the boat. I have logs that go back to '99. I always keep the last three years of the log in the pilothouse because you might want to look at a previous trip and maybe what depth you went into a dock at and see if there are changes here and there, or how long it took you. There are reasons to go back, and I do go back.

Then we have our EPA *(Environmental Protection Agency)* log. We inspect our water purifiers. Anything that gets shipped over the side has to go through a purifier and have less than so many parts per million residue. We even have to log rain runoff. We have to log any residue that's been washed off or cleaned, any spillage that bounces off the belts that we put on the belt. There are certain areas where you can discharge spillage into the water if it's clean limestone. That all has to be logged. We have ballast reports that have to be logged for the EPA. We have a cargo residue log so we can estimate how much that was on the deck that was swept up or not swept up and was washed over – so many pounds. How much spillage went off, so many pounds. Then there's a cargo residue log. Then there's our ballast report. Ballast report – the temperature where we picked up the ballast, the temperature of the ballast, and where it's going to be discharged in the next port. That's every trip that has to be done.

We have Homeland Security drills that have to be done monthly, quarterly, and yearly.

We have a safety meeting, and that's a special report by itself.

Lake levels change, but that's a separate log again.

There's a separate log book for loading. Crewmen write in there how much cargo went into each cargo hold and what type of material. For that, you check the water gauge when you started loading, and you check the water gauge when you're done loading, and then you write in what you loaded to, draft wise. And that's the load book. Now, when you go to the unload book, you log when you started up and when you stopped and for any shutdowns, and what the shutdown reasons were. Again, what the water gauge read when you got there, how much water you actually had, stuff like that. That's a separate log book again.

We also have a radio log book. You need to make a test call every day for your equipment. Any logs for Pathfinder would be for its functions, such as loading and unloading. It has start time and finish time – start loading, finish loading.

We also have a master's log that we fill out for the office, which is each trip. It tells everything – our arrival, our start time for loading, our stop time for loading, our loss time – if there's any down time is all logged as lost – our run time to the next port, fuel consumed, start time for unloading, finish time for unloading, rate of unloading. There's quite a few items. That's handwritten as well.

We send electronic reports in to Interlake – arrival report, departure report, position report. That's typed into the computer and sent into the office every morning.

With master's log, the first mate makes it out, and I just make sure that it's all done correctly and send that in.

In addition, we have a trip report, which is for the petty cash, fuel, start of the trip, finish of the trip. I get petty cash by writing a check for it. Somebody has to go to the bank. Either somebody I know cashes the check, or somebody on the boat will go to their bank, or I go to a bank. Somebody will cash it. Usually, I have the people who deliver the groceries cash the check. I'll tell the grocery man, "Bring me $500, I've got a check for you," and he does.

Birds and bugs

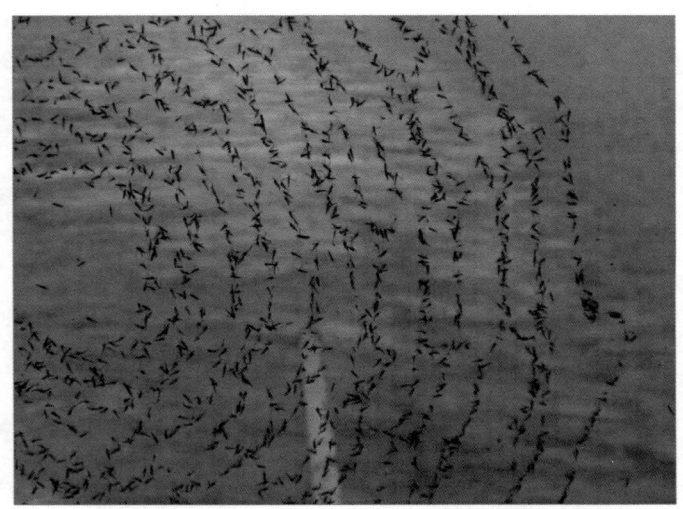

Lake flies caught in a spider web make a pattern in a window of the Dorothy Ann. *Gary Schmidt photo*

You get bugs, sometimes a lot of bugs. That's a main problem.

Especially in the springtime, you have all kinds of bug hatches. We're cleaning air filters about once a week. You can pull the filters out and hose them off, and you'd be just amazed at the amount of bugs that get washed out of these things.

We're on water, and that's the breeding area for bugs.

The white tower of the Dorothy Ann gets covered with bugs. You get the little black flies. I'm not talking about the house flies, the ones that bite. I mean the little black flies that look like mosquitoes. They just cover the whole A frame that's white. Sometimes the A frame will be totally black, just totally black.

It's like that at certain places at certain times of the year.

It's really neat when that does happen and we're coming down the St. Clair River because, as soon as we get near Port Huron, we pick up all of these swallows. And they are just an aerial attack on all these flies.

The swallows ride with us about 30 miles down river.

These birds can fly fast, and they're aerial acrobats. Some of the birds are martins.

***

SIDE TRIP: Many seagulls like us when we're in the Cuyahoga River at Cleveland. They fly near my bow thruster because I kick up little fish. Or they fly around my stern, where I kick up fish and whatnot. They have a place to eat.

***

It's neat to watch the birds in action on the St. Clair River. They'll go up alongside the tower and flutter and knock the bugs so that the bugs will start flying again, and the birds devour them.

The birds will land on the cable rails on the barge, and in certain spots you can see where they deposit a lot of what they've eaten. And it's pretty neat.

They'll land on the rails on the tug, too.

There are hundreds of birds. They'll ride for about 30 miles, and all of a sudden you don't see them anymore. We'll lose them all before we get onto Lake St. Clair. And they do this to a lot of ships. They might catch the next ship going upbound. I don't know where they go to, but all of a sudden they're gone from my vessel.

We're in the middle of the river, with 600 to 1,000 feet on each side of us. They've been doing this for as many years as I can remember, so it's ingrained in them somehow that this is a meal.

Seagulls by the hundreds follow in the wake of the Dorothy Ann in hopes a wintertime meal is churned up. *Gary Schmidt photo*

Hatch 41

Border crossing

We cross over Canadian and U.S. boundaries all the time in rivers and on the Great Lakes, and there's nothing there that we have to worry about. It's part of an international agreement.

Canadian vessels come over on our side, and American vessels go over on their side with no problems.

If you land on the Canadian side, then you have to file a Customs report. But if you don't do any landing – if you're just mixing the waters – there's nothing.

I have a passport. It's mandatory that everybody has to have a passport going into a Canadian port. It didn't used to be that way. Just your Seaman's card was good enough. But things have changed due to Homeland Security.

I have both a passport and an easy-access card. I never had to show either one yet. The border people never asked for either one.

I used my passport when Mary and I went across on a trip to Canada when I wasn't on a boat. But as far as being on a boat, the border people pretty much look at just your credentials. I do have to show credentials, to Canadians and U.S. both. They usually come down to the boat in a vehicle when we dock.

When we are ballasted *(carrying no cargo)* and we are going to go into a Canadian port for a load, I have to clear out in the U.S. There's what you call clearance. I have to tell Customs I'm leaving the country, and I'm going into a Canadian port. That does not require Customs to come down to the boat. We sometimes have to go to the port office and just submit the papers and bring those back. Immigration is not involved at that time. Customs just gives me clearance to go out of the country.

When I get into Canada, I have to file papers saying I'm coming into Canada to load. And then, once I'm loaded, I have to send papers saying I'm loaded and going into a U.S. port. When that happens, I also have to send notice to the U.S. port that I am coming back in with a load of Canadian goods. Canadians do most of their paper work with a fax machine and very seldom come down to the boat. Every once in a while, they come down as a surprise inspection. And they will go through the whole boat and inspect. That's happened to me a couple of times. They're looking for contraband. They are looking for pornography. You can't take pornography into Canada. It's against the law. If you bought anything in Canada, they want taxes. You can't bring more than 200 cigarettes into Canada, or so much tobacco. There are all kinds of regulations, little regulations. They go into each person's cabin and look through his personal stuff. They're afraid you'll bring in a laptop and sell it to somebody or bring in some electronics.

When you come back into the U.S., Customs always comes down to the boat and checks everybody who Immigration has not been checked or had his card inspected by

Immigration and Customs. That happens just about every trip down. Sometimes, American authorities go through the vessel in a similar manner to the Canadians. The searches are random.

Now, as far as what I look at it – and this is just strictly me, it's not the company, it's not anybody else – my observation is that you are the terrorist until proven innocent. And I really detest that. We came from a Canadian port one time into Chicago, and they boarded us. They had two boats. They had cars that came down. They boarded the vessel with 10 to 12 personnel. Carrying M16s. Herded everybody into the galley area and searched the vessel. It was under the guise of Homeland Security. I am a United States citizen, and I am not a terrorist. I don't understand it. Did they think we were going to smuggle people across or smuggle arms across? That's not going to happen.

Hatch 42

Traffic systems

If you drive from one state to another, some traffic laws change. If you sail from one area to another on the Great Lakes, some traffic laws change. The rules are for high-risk areas in which ships must take care. Radio is essential.

There are a lot of traffic schemes.

Vessels sail across state boundaries – which extend into the lakes – and they sail across boundaries between the United States and Canada. International agreements come into play. Various sectors are the responsibility of one or the other country.

On the U.S. side, there are rules written in the Great Lakes "Pilot" (*"United States Coast Pilot 6"*). You get a rundown of what a captain needs to know. It also gives you specific rules for things that you can do, like going through the Sturgeon Bay Ship Canal in Wisconsin. You can only tow at a certain distance behind you if you are towing.

The Coast Guard knows exactly where you're at all times. In the rivers, the Coast Guard monitors your speed, and it lets you know what traffic is coming your way. It is a safety system, and it works well in most cases.

If you're going from one traffic zone to another, the rules can change. The "Pilot" gives you the speed limits, like for the St. Marys River or the Detroit/St. Clair River. Those are two different things. You have a maximum speed in the Sarnia Traffic Zone, the Detroit/St. Clair River, where it's 12 miles an hour. There are a couple of places where the minimums come in for slow-moving tugs and barges where it might apply to the Dorothy Ann.

And then there are no-passing zones – no passing, no overtaking, or no meeting. There are some places where it's one-way traffic where you can't meet another vessel. You've got to wait your turn. And then there are rules on who has first at the no-meeting zones.

There are a lot of differences between the zones and what radio channels you're calling in on.

Separate radio frequencies cover such areas as of the Soo Locks, Sarnia, Soo Traffic, St. Lawrence Seaway, Welland Canal, Detroit and St. Clair River – sometimes with more than one frequency.

For example, going downbound from the Soo Locks: Once you've cleared the Soo area (*U.S. control*) and you're getting into the Sarnia traffic (*Canadian control*), you get down to Harbor Beach, and you give Sarnia a call and check into the system, giving Sarnia your ETA's for Huron Cut Buoys 11 and 12. Then you have to give Sarnia another call 30 minutes above 11 or 12. There are certain call-in points throughout the system. You're on channel 11. Soo traffic is on channel 12. Sarnia is on channel 11 until you get to St. Clair Lake Crib Light, where it switches over to channel 12…

At Southeast Shoal, you're still in the Sarnia system. You give an ETA for Long Point and for the Welland Canal, if you're going that way. If you're not going into the Canadian ports, then you're dismissed at Southeast Shoal, and you just go about your business, and you're not under any traffic scheme then. But if you're going through the Welland Canal, you are with Sarnia until you get to Long Point. At that point, you're in Seaway Welland, and you go through the Welland traffic system until you clear out at St. Catharines or maybe New Castle or Midlake, and then you come into a different traffic scheme, a Seaway system. And they have different ones of that, with different names.

In the Welland Canal, you use one Canadian channel going one way, and another Canadian channel going the other way for the locks. It's one up and one down, and you're always talking to the lockmasters as you go through. They'll tell you to tie up at the upper locks or wait for somebody to come up before you proceed down.

***

EPILOGUE: I was on the Donald C. Hannah, and it was a slow year, 1980 or 1981. It was Christmas, and I was going to go through the Straits of Mackinac. I called Sarnia traffic and said I was upbound and headed for Lansing Shoal and will be there at such-and-such a time. "What traffic are you going to have going through the straits?" I was thinking there might be ice breakers or there might be another vessel coming through so I could get information on ice. The dispatcher said, "As far as I know right now, I think you're the only vessel moving on the Great Lakes." What a lonely feeling.

Hatch 43

9/11 impact

Where were you September 11, 2001? As so many other Americans, Captain Schmidt remembers well.

I just left the port of Port Inland with a load of stone headed for Bay City. I was watching on TV. I watched the second plane live as it crashed into the tower. By the time I got to the Mackinac Bridge, a Coast Guard boat escorted and kind of watched us go under the bridge. Nobody said anything or did anything at that time. We went on and unloaded. Every time we came back up, we had a Coast Guard escort going underneath the bridge to make sure that we weren't going to blow up the bridge.

The next year after 9/11, the Department of Homeland Security came in. After that, there was a big buildup.

We had to have a security plan that was written up. Every company had to have one. So the Lake Carriers' Association wrote up a security plan and included all the companies in the association. The members approved the plan. Once that happened, we had to go through a Homeland Security class to learn about all the processes we had to go through and all the steps. And the plan built up. Every year, there has been a little bit more added to it. And things have changed over the years. It's added up to a lot of extra work through Homeland Security.

The Coast Guard is now under the Department of Homeland Security. Under the heading of Homeland Security, we have a Coast Guard inspection at the beginning of every year. The Coast Guard will go through the vessels and discuss whether they're within code. If not, you get a certain amount time to correct them. When corrections are done, we have to notify the Coast Guard.

The only other contacts with the Coast Guard would be if we have some kind of a mishap, whether it is with personnel or the vessel or an oil spill. The Coast Guard very seldom comes down to inspect, but they do once in a while.

Another part that's under the Department of Homeland Security is U.S. Customs and Border Protection, which comes down and inspects the crews.

Other than that, if something happens to the vessel – just say that internally a crack develops – you have to call the Coast Guard down along with ABS *(American Bureau of Shipping)* and have them inspect it. We repair it. We let them know. We're up front about it. We want to make sure that the corrections are done properly, for our safety as well as the vessel. It's just good practice to have them involved.

The Coast Guard provides some icebreaking maintenance. We see a little bit more of them in winter.

But they're on patrol out there. They're always watching little boats. They're always watching the borders or watching everything, especially on Lake Erie, where you have an international boundary, or in the Detroit and St. Clair River. You don't see Coast Guard vessels out in the middle of Lake Huron where the international boundary is but closer to shore where small boats can run back and forth. They're more of a presence there.

There are 43 Coast Guard stations all over the Great Lakes.

Hatch 44

Boat nerds

For thousands of reasons, people have a fascination with the big Great Lakes vessels. They take a lot of photos of the ships, and then they show off the photos. You can find hundreds of pictures of Dorothy Ann/Pathfinder at many ports it sails to where there are more people enamored of the sailing way of life.

I think it's a lot like the train nerds. The BoatNerd website has a discussion page. There are facts, figures, vessel passages. People can find out where all the ships are moving to. It's pretty interesting.

I had a deckhand who came on the boat, and he was a boat nerd from just a little kid. He made his mother take him down to the different docks and see boats. Eventually, he worked his way up. He's an Able Bodied Seaman now, but he's still a boat nerd. He knows facts and figures about every boat and ship, has pictures from everywhere. It's quite interesting. It's kind of neat. That's where I get my boat nerd information from – from him.

***

SNAPSHOT: *These are .com or .net websites where you can find photos of Dorothy Ann/ Pathfinder at work: boatnerd, eireshipnews, duluthshippingnews, shipspotting, flickr, saginawriverimages, flickriver, gallery.pasty, michiganexposures.blogspot, lakeshippics.blotspot, atdetroit, tugboathunter.wordpress, tugster.wordpress, maritime-executive, workboat, greatlakesdigitalimaging, flickrhivemind, youtube, wellandcanal.ca, marinelink, miningjournal, worldisround.*

***

There are a lot of photos of the vessel. A lot of people post them on BoatNerd, and they post them other places, and the company has a lot of photos.

It does hold fascination for a lot of people, and there are a lot of people who come down to the rivers just to watch the boats.

BoatNerd headquarters is in Port Huron. It's right at Vantage Point. It's right at the mouth of the Black River across from Sarnia Bay, and all the boats that come off of Lake Huron or go back up on to Lake Huron or go to the upper lakes pass that point. That's where many, many, many of the photographs are taken.

Hatch 45

A boat lover

Rod Burdick of Negaunee, Michigan, is absorbed by photographing Great Lakes vessels.

It's capturing the Great Lakes shipping industry, the changes, the history. I definitely try to capture the last remaining steamboats that are in operation. That's probably my main motivation, just trying to capture history for future generations.

Searching the Internet for a catchy image of the Dorothy Ann/Pathfinder for this book, I came across a photo by Burdick on BoatNerd.com. You can see the photo on page 2. In time, Burdick and I spoke by telephone, and what you are reading is excerpted from the interview. A starting point was a discussion of the image that appears in this chapter.

That photo was taken in the fall of 2009 at the lower harbor Shiras Dock in Marquette. That was a fairly slow year for shipping. It was probably just one of the opportunities to take some photographs in a pretty slow season.

That picture was taken at about 70 millimeters (lens size). There are fences around the Shiras area, so you usually have to shoot between the fences. You can't get too close anymore. The vessel was unloading limestone, which is transported to the Empire and Tilden mines on the Marquette Range. The stone is blended with the iron ore to create what's called a flex pellet.

Burdick photographs vessels a couple of times a week during the shipping season.

I live just eight miles from Marquette, so it's easy access.

As does Captain Schmidt, Burdick has an attraction to a unique configuration.

The Marquette Upper Harbor Ore Dock is a chute-type dock. It was constructed in 1912. It just celebrated its 100th year of service. It's almost original in terms of its design. There have been some updates to the loading chutes. Other than that, it's loading ore the way it was 100 years ago.

Unloading and loading offer sights and sounds.

Especially in Marquette, the most common sound is the crashing sound of the ore coming down the chutes. You can hear conversations between the mates and the ore dock workers. You can hear them shouting to each other. You can hear the sounds of the generators running the conveyor. In other ports, you can hear the belts of the self unloaders running.

Burdick also photographs at Escanaba, Gladstone, Munising, and Duluth-Superior.

Especially in Marquette, I like to capture the ore coming down the chutes and going into the hatches. At other places, I like to concentrate on whatever the action is in terms of the unloading or loading, some type of perspective of the port itself.

The number of photos I take each time depends on the boat and the situation. It could be as few as five up to maybe 30. If it is one of the older classic steam-powered vessels, there would definitely be more.

Burdick's connection to the Dorothy Ann/Pathfinder goes way back.

The *Pathfinder* is always, in mind, the *J.L. Mauthe*, which was always a favorite boat of mine. It was the only triple A (AAA class) that wasn't lengthened. She was pretty much in her original build when she was converted to a barge – obviously not the greatest aesthetics anymore in terms of looks, but still she does carry some history as the first tug/barge in the Interlake fleet.

And I was also involved during a photo shoot during her construction in Escanaba and Sturgeon Bay. I was on board her during her construction. And I was on board during her fit out as well. I was contacted through a maritime magazine to freelance photographs for the magazine.

Burdick's grandfather gave him a camera when he was in high school in the early 1980s. Today, Burdick maintains two websites, plus a Facebook site. He's had maritime photos published in magazines and books.

Since the early '80s, I probably have more than 10,000 images in my collection.

Through Facebook and BoatNerd, it's fairly easy now to make connections with other boat lovers. That's made it easier recently. In the past, if you ran into somebody taking pictures, you'd strike up a conversation and find a common interest.

Our local paper, the *Mining Journal*, has a daily vessel report in the paper. And also, with the start of the required AIS navigational systems on the freighters, most of the AIS signals will list destinations, which is helpful. Depending on weather and work, I'll go shoot.

I captured one of the *Kaye Barker* with a double rainbow. That's definitely one I'm very proud of. I also have a sunrise image from Duluth taken during my honeymoon, which is very special.

A goal is to compile a book.

My theme would be something about shipping in Upper Michigan, focusing on Great Lakes shipping and how it drives the economy here.

As a youth, Burdick had a yen to sail. That was short lived.

When I was in high school, the recession basically took its effect on the industry. Those dreams of sailing were pretty much put to rest when the Lakes fleet began to diminish, and the job opportunities were pretty slim.

He did sail once, and it was an invigorating experience.

I had a trip on the *St. Marys Challenger* in the summer of 2005. I won an online raffle. Given the *St. Marys Challenger* is the oldest steam-powered vessel operating on the Great Lakes, it was like walking back in time. She has an old Skinner Uniflow engine. It was just amazing to see the old gauges and gears and the machinery in the engine room and how it worked.

The trip as a passenger was wonderful, but in terms of being a worker on the boat, I would say no (to the life style).

I definitely have a respect and an admiration for sailors because I know it's a very difficult job, and it's an important job, obviously, for the Midwest.

Veteran Great Lakes photographer Rod Burdick captures the Dorothy Ann/Pathfinder unloading stone at the Shiras Generating Plant at Marquette, Michigan.

Snow has fallen as the Dorothy Ann/Pathfinder arrives at the ore dock at Marquette, Michigan. *Rod Burdick photo*

The Dorothy Ann/Pathfinder leaves Marquette, Michigan. *Rod Burdick photo*

Hatch 46

Rest in peace

Early in my career, I was a deckhand for Selvick. It was 1971. We were towing the barge Sea Castle with the tug Lauren Castle. We were headed to Petosky to get a load of cement. As we approached, we pulled in the barge with a capstan. We might have had nine people on the tug. It was very physical, manual to bring the barge on the capstan. Neil Claflin said he had heartburn. We went out on the stern and started pulling the cable, and Neil collapsed. He was down on his knees. We didn't know what happened to him, but we got him up and got him into a bed. We gave him CPR for a long time. We tried to get a hold of the Coast Guard on the radio. Nobody would respond to the calls that we had a problem. We couldn't raise anybody. Those were the days when the Coast Guard in a small station may not have had anybody listening to the radio at night. Our radios didn't carry as far. So nobody responded to us, so we had to disconnect from the barge – taking all this time – and run to the dock. Once we got to the dock, we had to go to a pay phone. We had to call the operator because there was no 911 back then. Once we got to the dock, it took a good 45 minutes for the emergency squad to get to the dock. We did CPR on Neil for more than an hour and a half. Once the ambulance crew got there, he was declared dead. It was really quite a shock for us all. And at the same time, even though you have a tragedy, the work load still has to go on. You still have to deal with it. You have to continue on. You have to load. You have to deliver things. It's not like you can just shut down an operation because this is something that involves other people and other companies, the need for the product. You do mourn it, you just don't have time to deal with it the way you should, it doesn't seem like. I know that once we got this load delivered, we all got off for the funeral, but it was that and right back to work again. Neil was 39 years old, wife Penny, and two young children. One of the guys who performed the CPR, Chris Larson, never sailed again after that. That was it for him. He was going to school. It was a summer job for him. But at this point, summer wasn't over. But he was done with it.

+++

There was an accident when I was working on the John M. Selvick. We're up in the Straits of Mackinac in the spring of 1974. The S.T. Crapo got stuck in the ice in the straits, and as the ice was moving, its rudder was bent and was inoperable. She was loaded with cement. We went up to pick her up and take her to Bay Shipbuilding. We were towing it in the ice, and we weren't making very good speed. The captain on the S.T. Crapo made a suggestion to the stern tug *(Lauren Castle)*. I was on the forward lead tug towing the S.T. Crapo, and there was an after tug with a bow line on it that was trying to keep the S.T. Crapo straight from wandering. The rudder was bent off to one side, and the S.T. Crapo took off to one direction, and towing was hard. The S.T. Crapo would slow us down to almost a stop, and then we'd start going again. The captain was trying to use his engines to help us out a little bit by pulling ahead through the ice so we could make a little bit better time. Finally, we broke out of the ice, but then the S.T. Crapo would sheer off one way or the other all the time. While I was lying down and somebody else was at the wheel, the captain on the stern tug and the captain on the S.T. Crapo got together and decided that they might do better if they went stern to stern so when the tug pulled it could pull with a little more power. But you don't ever do that because it's too easy to trip a boat. Once you start pulling it backwards, the tug has no way to steer itself, and all of a sudden you just pull it over. And that's what happened. Two guys on the stern, Mel Selvick and Ronald Smith, went into the water and were lost.

EPILOGUE: *The Lauren Castle sank Nov. 5, 1980, with the loss of engineer Bill Stephan. The Lauren Castle collided with the disabled oil tanker Amoco Wisconsin in Grand Traverse Bay. Resting upright in 390 feet of water, the wreck was pinpointed 30 years after the accident.*

+++

A third tragedy was when I was on the Triton and the St. Marys Cement. This was 1990. We were pushing down Lake Michigan. It was moderately rough. It wasn't real rough, but it was what I had pushed in many times. We were headed down the lake, and it was a nice ride. I was in the push mode instead of the towing mode. I got down past Rawley Point *(near Point Beach State Forest)* by Kewaunee. The way Rawley Point comes out in the lake, as the waves are coming down from the north, they roll down the shoreline and, as they come out off of Rawley Point, they kind of mix with what's already coming straight down the lake. They create a bigger wave, or they create mixed wave action. Once I got there, one of my cables broke on the push mode. I turned the tug around and headed into the sea, and we were getting the deckhands out on deck to release the other cable and get it back aboard so we could get the barge in a towing mode, get on the tow line. One of those people was my brother, Keith. The other one was Terry Jesse. They were the two deckhands. It was an emergency. We have life jackets and life preservers and work vests, but because they jumped into action so quickly when the cable broke, neither one of them put on a work vest. Everything was going good, we were getting everything set up, when one of those rogue waves came down the side of the vessel. I got the tug turned maybe a little bit too much and was not protecting them because of the sloppiness in there and I was in the notch and I was bouncing around pretty good at that point. And the wave came down and washed both of them into the water. The other guys who were aboard starting pulling the cables up. Terry Jesse was hanging on to the cable with both hands. We got him aboard. As I drifted off, I aimed a light down. I saw my brother, but he was already under the water. And once we got up close to him, I couldn't shine the spotlight down close to him to see where he was at, and we never did see him again. He was drowned. A year later, some fishermen were trawling off Rawley Point. They happened to pick up my brother in the net and got him aboard. So he had a proper burial a year later. He was single. He did have a daughter, but he was not married. Again, you don't have time to deal with the tragedies that you want to at the time. I mean, I was really broken up and I was bawling my eyes out. The hardest thing

I had to do was call my mother and tell her we lost Keith. That was very, very difficult. The Coast Guard came out with a rescue boat and went into a search pattern, and I went into a search pattern. They knew that they were not going to recover anybody at that point. I stayed in the area and did the same thing, looking, until they released me and told me to take the barge and head to Milwaukee and unload it. Then there's the paperwork that has to be filled out, the 2692. This is the time when you don't really want to fill out forms. This is the time when it's really hard to fill out forms. A loss of life is always difficult. When it was a family member, it was really, really difficult. And you've still got to remember to do all the stuff that you have to. You have to take a weather observation. You have to know your course and speed. You have to know night or day, weather conditions, how hard it was blowing, the sea condition. All this kind of stuff has to be recorded and put on a 2692. You have to do a pee test to make sure alcohol or drugs weren't involved. All this stuff you have to do at the same time you're trying to mourn. That's very difficult. Then I still had to get the boat and the barge into the dock and get it unloaded and then make arrangements to get off for a funeral. We had a memorial service for Keith because we really couldn't have a funeral. Companies showed up for the memorial service. I was surprised at the amount of people who came out for this. Other marine companies. Vendors. Other people who were involved in the marine industry. After that, getting back to work, I'm going along pushing and towing when I had to tow. I'm on the St. Clair River, going out into Lake Huron, and here's it's on the rough side again. I really got dry mouthed and wide eyed. I thought, "Wow, I've got to do this again. I hope nobody gets hurt." But you just have to do it. It's like once you get knocked off a horse, they say you have to get back on it again. That's what I had to do. I just had to put it on a tow line and hope for everything good and great, and it turned out fine. I wasn't so scared after that. I just kept doing it again. I didn't retire from it. It's something that… it's what I do. It was difficult. It was very difficult, the '90s. I thought the '90s were going to be the gay '90s, and it was anything but the gay '90s.

Hatch 47

Edmund Fitzgerald

A bridge is up in downtown Green Bay in November. A vessel glides slowly up the Fox River and nears the bridge. On the bow is its name, Arthur M. Anderson. It's a large vessel, a veteran vessel. Slowly, it passes through the open bridge. An image moves through the grates on the lifted bridge deck. Waiting in a vehicle on a bridge gives one time to pause and think. The bow reaches the other side. The name is visible again. Arthur M. Anderson. I know that name. Why do I know that name? I sift for a bit. And sift. Sometimes you don't know what history is when you are looking at it. Then it comes. The Edmund Fitzgerald. The Arthur M. Anderson trailed the Edmund Fitzgerald on Nov. 10, 1975, in a storm on Lake Superior. The last contact of the Edmund Fitzgerald was with the Arthur M. Anderson. To this day at memorial ceremonies, a bell is rung 29 times for the 29 souls who went down on the Edmund Fitzgerald.

I'd say the captain on the Anderson and one of the Ford boats that the Coast Guard asked to go back out into that storm after he had just plowed his way through it and then to go back out and look for survivors had to be one of the hardest things and the bravest things that that man ever did as far as I'm concerned. You're lucky to survive some of those storms and you say, "I hope I can get out of this," and then the Coast Guard asks you to go back out into it. And he turned around and went back out into it looking for survivors. In the teeth of a storm like that, that had to be just as hard as hell to do.
And the Anderson is still sailing.

***

SNAPSHOT: *Also responding with the Arthur M. Anderson were the U.S. vessels William Clay Ford, Armco, Roger Blough, Reserve, Wilfred Sykes and William R. Roesch. Canadian vessels responding were the Hilda Marjanne, Frontenac, John O. McKeller, Murray Bay and fishing tug James D.*

***

The anniversary of the Edmund Fitzgerald on Nov. 10 is always on everybody's mind to some degree, and especially when you hear the Gordon Lightfoot song.

***

SIDE TRIP: *I interviewed folksinger Gordon Lightfoot a number of times. He wrote and recorded a bunch of hits and is a member of the Canadian Songwriters Hall of Fame. In many people's heart around the Great Lakes, there is only one No. 1 Gordon Lightfoot song, "The Wreck of the Edmund Fitzgerald."*

Prior to an engagement at Green Bay's premier venue, the Weidner Center for the Performing Arts, he said, "I'll be thinking of the fact that the Edmund Fitzgerald was launched in Milwaukee in 1958. I love going around the Great Lakes area. That's where we feel at home with the song.

"The song never fails to get a huge response, and it's that way all over the States and here in Canada – and all over the planet for that matter," he said. "It came from an article I read in Newsweek magazine. That got me interested in the idea, and I went back and researched newspapers for whatever I could find so it would be in chronological order."

The song was tucked into the album "Summertime Dream."

"What happened happened spontaneously," Lightfoot said. "The responsibility that went with it has been interesting, too. I've met a lot of people, and I had to be attentive and pay attention and get involved, which I have done."

***

It's very eerie. But, at the same time, you don't pay a lot of heed to it. I mean, that was special circumstances and an extremely dangerous storm. There are only a few of those. And today's communications and weather predicting are much better than they were back in 1975, when the Fitzgerald went down.

At that time, those were fairly new boats – 20 or 25 years old – and they thought they were really well constructed and could take just about anything, which isn't always the case. Some of those captains really pushed the envelope a lot. Although I take calculated risks, I'm not going to go into a Force 8 storm, which the Edmund Fitzgerald did. And heavy weather was predicted – and they knew – but it was a little heavier than what even was predicted.

A damaged lifeboat from the Edmund Fitzgerald is on display at the Great Lakes Shipwreck Museum near Paradise, Michigan. *Warren Gerds phoot*

The Flower Lady

Some routes are very scenic. Even in open water, you can have very scenic days. You can have cloud banks or fog banks on one side and crystal clear on the other side. You see stuff that's pretty spectacular.

On shorelines, there are some very spectacular homes. And there are some unspectacular homes, too.

Along the Detroit River, boy, there are some mansions. Huge homes. Immense.

There's stars' homes along the river. We know where Bob Seeger's house is on the river. We know where a couple of hockey players from the Detroit Red Wings have their big houses on the river.

And there are other houses that are just big and beautiful houses that you see along the way. And then there's some really nice, old, beautiful houses. Some are like a starter castle. They have huge, huge trees for entrance ways. Very nice. If people are outside, they wave. We see a lot of people out there.

And then there's The Flower Lady in Detroit....

She has a flower business, and on all holidays, she sends every boat that goes by a bouquet of flowers. She lives on the St. Clair River, and we always give her a salute when we go by. Most of the time, she comes out and waves if she's home. They're very friendly. I don't know why they started doing this, but they started doing it years ago. And it's nice. For Father's Day, we get a big bouquet of flowers. On Mother's Day. On Thanksgiving. On holidays, there's always flowers there.

Arlene Earl is The Flower Lady. She lives on Harsens Island, Michigan. She was contacted by telephone for this book. This is Arlene:

Sometimes in two weeks time, I get 30 to 40 ships saluting.

This started many years ago. My husband, Richard Earl, used to sail the Great Lakes. He started with his uncle. At that time, the uncle, Norman Le Croix, was a

A greeting card sums up the story of The Flower Lady. *Image courtesy Arlene Earl*

Arlene Earl prepares bouquets for vessels that pass her home on Harsens Island, Michigan. *Photo courtesy Arlene Earl*

chief engineer aboard a ship. My husband started sailing just summer months when he was 15 to 17. After that, he went for a first mate license.

Richard was born and raised in the Harsens Island area. I've been a Harsens Island summer person my whole life. We're strictly what we call Islanders on that beautiful St. Clair River. We built a home there 37 years ago.

The uncle also was born and raised on Harsens Island. He maintained the license as chief engineer. He retired years ago and came to Florida. His health declined and had Alzheimer's Disease.

Families have to take care of each other, there's no doubt about it. His wife had passed, he had no children but three nephews, with my husband as one of them. We brought him back.

The name of my property is Sail By World because every ship around the world goes right past my house. Of course, Uncle Norman is a happy camper. He's on the St. Clair River, and the ships are going by. He stood out there for hours waiting for his ship. Well, there was no such thing as his because they were all his because of this terrible disease.

He'd come to the kitchen where I'd be making dinner, and he'd just be teary-eyed. He said, "They don't remember me." I said, "Well, what were you doing?" "I was waving the sailor's salute and stood there." It was very upsetting to him. It would be. Well, I said, "We'll take care of that."

So after a few times with the tears and all the disappointments for Uncle Norman Le Croix, I decided I would write some letters. This was well before faxes and computers and whatever is out there now that they use – myself, I hate computers. So I wrote handwritten letters to every ship and just said, "Now, we're on the St. Clair River between the markers of 11 and 13, and if you see a gentleman out there waving or a crazy blonde jumping up and down with him, please give him a salute."

Well, it worked. Now we have a ship that's going to salute, and, being that I own a flower shop, I decide to reciprocate a kindness – from the heart – from the flower shop.

First, I called the J.W. Westcott II, which is our mail boat in Detroit. I said, "I have this idea. I'd like to send flowers aboard as a thank you, blah, blah, blah." "Well, we have to charge you," because basically it's a postal service and has its own ZIP code. The Westcott said, "Well, we're going to have to charge you a fee because it will be posted." I said, "I didn't ask you that. I said will you do it?" "Absolutely!" I can't remember what I sent that particular day, maybe a pretty blooming plant from the greenhouse or a centerpiece. I wrote, "To the captain and crew of the... say it was the Middletown..."

Nowadays the mail doesn't like flowers. Well, I beg to differ with you – being in the business for about 57 years, born and raised, and our flower shop this year will be 130 years old and surviving.

Now, the ships do their turnaround. They deliver their cargo maybe to Detroit, Cleveland, who knows. On the return trip, it was daylight, of course, I'm out there waiting for a ship to come by. Now we get a salute – "Well done."

That's the good news. Then somebody else blows, so forth and so on. And the word got out – "All you gotta do is give that blue house a salute with a gentleman and the lady, if she's there, and they'll send you some flowers." Well, it boomeranged. It was a token of love, and it boomeranged.

I'm going back almost 35 years. Uncle Norman, of course, has gone on to heaven, but I still do this in his memory and honor. A great man. You know, some things in life – you can't dollar-tag everything. People say to me, "Oh, what an expense." Isn't everything?

Basically, what I do now is the ships get flowers three times a year or four. One is Easter, depending on when that falls. As soon as I know the ships are running and J.W. Westcott goes in the water, then we start. We'll give something suitable. I always send a balloon on that particular arrangement – "Welcome Back, We Miss You" – to every tug and barge and, for the thousand-footers, I try two gifts because of the two galleys, dining rooms. After that, it goes into Father's Day, and that's just a big day. They love that, and I address that card, "To all the dads aboard." Thanksgiving and Christmas I do together.

Not only have the flowers brought joy to the men out at sea, as they say, they miss their family. They do a special service for this country.

In fact, Uncle Norman Le Croix would have been very, very good friends with more than half of the crew of the Edmund Fitzgerald. Captain McSorley was one of his best friends. Here in Detroit, the Mariners' Church of Detroit puts on a remembrance service year around Nov. 10, and, of course, I'm part of it.

Arlene Earl rides aboard the J.W. Westcott II as the mail boat nears the passing Algosar near Detroit, Michigan. *Photo courtesy Arlene Earl*

Another delivery of flowers to a passing vessel complete, Arlene Earl steps off the J.W. Westcott II. *Photo courtesy Arlene Earl*

Years ago at the Mariners' Church of Detroit, the bishop was the one who brought in Gordon Lightfoot and got that bond going. Twenty-nine bell ringers are appointed, and during the service everybody would line up and we would ring the bell once when the bishop would mention that crewman's name. Now it's not called the service of the Edmund Fitzgerald as much as a pause of remembrance, and basically it's of all the shipmates who have gone down. It's just wonderful.

Of course, The Flower Lady – somebody out there nicknamed me that. I still go to downtown Detroit and work at the greenhouse.

Never thought she'd be invited aboard a Great Lakes freighter trip. You're talking one gal who's had 13 in the last 50 years, and I tell you what, no words ...

I have a monitor, Sarnia Traffic Marine Radio, at home and in my flower shop that's going 24/7. I hear the ships coming three hours before, and I've actually canceled appointments, "Oh, I've got a ship coming. I've got to get out there and wave." It's a very, very, very important part of my life. Somebody asked, "Well, how long are you going to keep doing this?" I said, "'Til the day I die." That's how that's going to be.

It comes from my heart, and I want to do it.

Fog shrouds the way as the Dorothy Ann/Pathfinder comes off of Lake Erie and, with the permission of Sarnia Traffic because there is no other traffic, heads upbound into the one-way downbound Livingstone Channel of the Detroit River. *Gary Schmidt photo*

The Dorothy Ann/Pathfinder heads toward another beautiful vista provided by the sun and clouds. *Jeremy Mock photo*

Quarters are close in the Rouge River near a Conrail bridge in Dearborn, Michigan, as the Dorothy Ann/Pathfinder is passed by the Charles M. Beeghly, which has since been renovated and renamed the Hon. James L. Oberstar. *Gary Schmidt photo*

The Pathfinder is being loaded with taconite at a dock on Whiskey Island in the Cleveland Harbor for shipment to the ArcelorMittal Cleveland plant up the Cuyahoga River. *Gary Schmidt photo*

Sunlight reveals the wear and tear of docking on the port side of the Dorothy Ann/Pathfinder. *Rod Burdick photo*

Supplies are lifted from the Ojibway ("The grub boat," Captain Schmidt calls it) to the stern of the Dorothy Ann.
Gary Schmidt photo

A storm with a descending funnel cloud brews on Lake Huron. "I've been in the middle of five, six, or seven water spouts at one time," Captain Schmidt says. "They don't have as much energy because they pick up too much water. I've never been hit by one." *Gary Schmidt photo*

Ice is thick as the Dorothy Ann/Pathfinder and U.S. Coast Guard icebreaker Bristol Bay pass one another on the St. Clair River. *Gary Schmidt photo*

It's another tight corner for Captain Schmidt in the Cuyahoga River at Cleveland, Ohio. *Gary Schmidt photo*

Cargo (stone or coal) is unloaded from the Pathfinder at the power plant at Marquette, Michigan. *Gary Schmidt photo*

Captain Schmidt stands in the compass drive pod of the Dorothy Ann during dry docking in February 2002 at Bay Shipbuilding in Sturgeon Bay, Wisconsin. *Warren Gerds photo*

Coal is unloaded from the Pathfinder at Manitowoc, Wisconsin. *Gary Schmidt photo*

With a storm in the air, the Dorothy Ann/Pathfinder is tied up and waiting for the weather to clear at the historic iron ore chutes at Marquette, Michigan. *Gary Schmidt photo*

The Dorothy Ann/Pathfinder is on another journey. *Photo courtesy The Interlake Steamship Company*

Captain Schmidt's blow-up Green Bay Packers player is set up aboard the Pathfinder as his vessel heads into Cleveland, Ohio.
Jeremyt Mock photo

Katherine Schmidt balances as she walks along a hatch crane track aboard the Pathfinder during a trip with her father.
Gary Schmidt photo

Section 4

Cargo Hold 3 – Operations

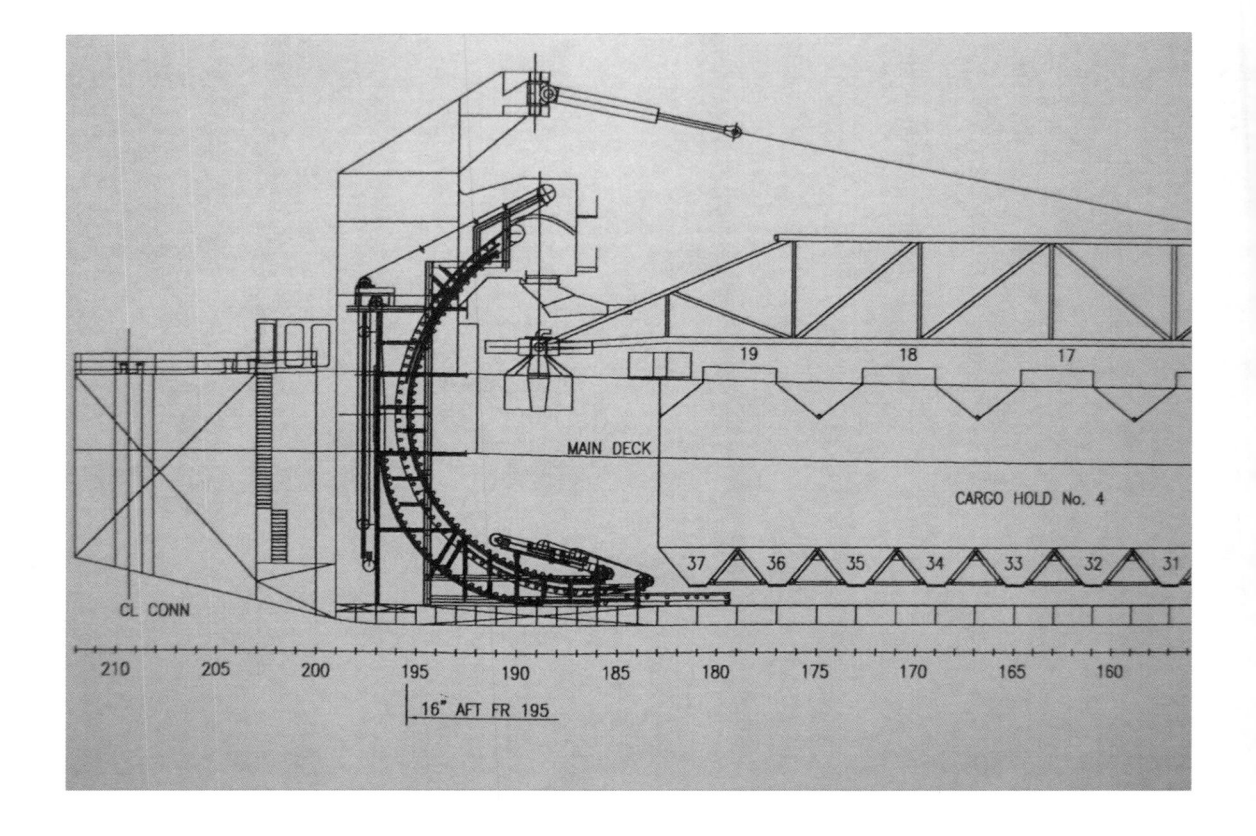

Hatch 49

Inside the Dorothy Ann

The tug Dorothy Ann is 124 feet from bow to stern. The width is 44 feet at its widest point.

Starting at the stern, on the deck in the back, we have towing bits to be able, in an emergency, to tow the barge. There's a hatch that goes down into the Z-drive room in an emergency. It's an escape hatch/entrance hatch. Also on the stern is a fire station for fighting fires. It has a hose that you pull out. That fire station also is for when you are at a dock when a fire department comes and wants to hook up to our fire system. There is a flange there and a pipe that the fire department can hook its system into our system. Also on the stern is a fueling station on each side where you can connect for taking on lube oil and fuel oil.

As you're going into the tug from the stern, on either side are storage rooms. One is our safety locker. That holds our turnout gear for fire and other safety gear. Included are extraction winches for somebody who might be hurt, a litter basket for an injured person, and flat boards for strapping an injured person and being able to extract him from a cargo hold or machinery space below via winch.

The other storage room on the other side is our emergency spill locker. In that oil response locker, we have oil booms that we place around the vessel in case we have an oil spill. We have soak pads. We have shovels. We have what we call kitty litter to sop up oil. There's a lot of other stuff in there for oil spill response.

Going up to the 01 Level on the stern, we have our compactor for all of our garbage. We throw nothing over the side. Everything is compacted into big compactor bags.

Up there also we have several drums of oil that we keep as supply. That's heavy gear, specialty oils that we don't have storage for down below. The drums are chained down and secured. We have two to four barrels there at any time.

On the port side are dunnage hatches where we can drop supplies in. We have two stiff-leg chain hoists or booms that go over the top of the holes, and we can drop supplies down.

MAIN ENGINE ROOM FLAT

The Dorothy Ann's engine room level is an important hub. *Warren Gerds photo*

Underneath that are two more hatches inside that go all the way right into the engine room. We can drop stuff all the way to the engine room from the 01 Level.

Also on the port side is the emergency generator room. It's just one generator. This is the third generator in our system. If two other generators fail, this one is for emergency steering and navigation only. It won't light up the rest of the boat. It won't give you TV, it won't give you anything else. It just strictly for steering and stuff that we have to have.

Going up the port side a little bit farther is another hatch that takes you inside the vessel, which will take you into the hallway to the officers' sleeping areas.

Beyond that, you come to the first pin, the port side connection pin station. You can push a button and extend the pins or retract the pins.

Forward, going around the bow, there's a winch on each side. They are called jockey winches. They help hold us into the notch when we're not connected by the pins. Just if we're loading or unloading, we want to stay there. It's not there to help you maneuver or anything else. It's just to hold you in place.

Going along the starboard side, from the bow going back, is the other pin station and another hatch going into the hallway that goes to the officers' sleeping quarters – captain, first mate, second mate.

On the opposite side from the emergency generator room is our CO_2 room that is our automatic fire extinguisher system for the engine room. If you had a fire in the engine room that was out of control and everybody was out, there's a remote way to close ventilation. You just open up the CO_2 room and it spills in CO_2 to put out the fire.

As you go into the back hatch on the main deck, you enter a hallway and you come to a T. Both ways from that T are crew's quarters and also another hallway to the port. On the starboard side if you go forward you run into the galley area. On the port side is a hallway that will take you past the chief's room. There's also a fire station on the starboard side right outside the chief's room where you have remote fuel shutdown for the engine room. You have remote fire pump startup. That's in case you can't get into the engine room. There's a door to the engine room also as you're coming in. If you go straight ahead, you'll go straight into the engine room down below.

So let's go down to the engine room. You go down two flights of steps, and you'll be to the upper part of the engine room. You'll see the top of both main engines, you'll see the turbos for both engines. There's part one of our two-part sanitary treatment system. Also in the forward part of the engine room are compressors. In the overhead are I-beams with rollers on them with chain hoists attached to them for pulling parts off the engine. For instance, say if you need to pull a power pack, which consists of a liner, a piston, a rod, and a head – a complete assembly pack for one of the 20 cylinders – it takes a couple of hours to pull one out. But the guys have to do it. Every once in a while, you'll might drop a valve inside of a head, and it will screw up the piston. You'll hear it knocking. Instead of changing out the head, they just usually pull out the whole thing. It's easier to pull out a pack that's all set up to pull out. You just disconnect the rod basket and the bearings and pull that off. There are what they call crab bolts that are holding the heads down, and you pull off all four of those, and then you pull out the ejector that ejects fuel. In the top of the piston, there's a little screw head, and you can take a rod down and screw it into the top of the piston. Once the rod is disconnected, you can pull the piston up, and you secure it in place so that the rods don't hit the crank shaft and score the crank shaft or do any damage to that. Once that's done, you can pull the whole power pack out. There's

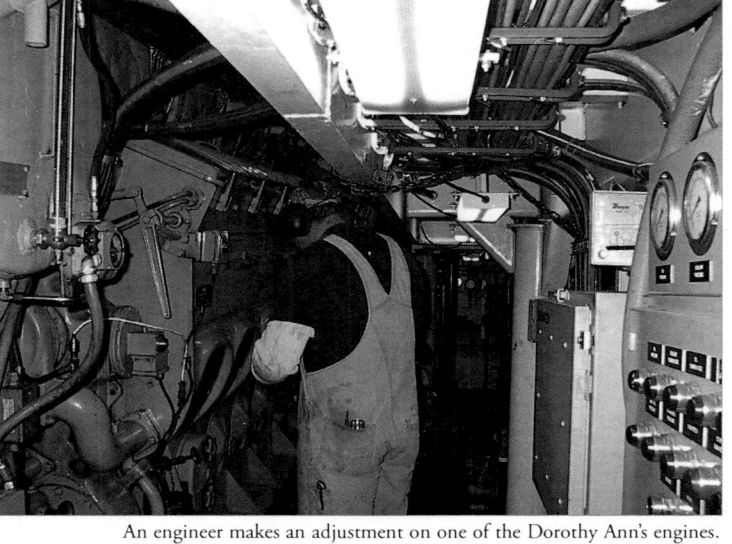

An engineer makes an adjustment on one of the Dorothy Ann's engines.
Gary Schmidt photo

a test cock that also has to come out. The test cock screws through the line into the piston chamber so you can get a reading off of it. It tells you how much pressure you have. It's also how you blow an engine down. You open it up, and, before you start an engine, you turn it over to make sure that no water has leaked into it so you don't blow a head or something on that order. So you pull it out, and you get a new one, and you drop 'er back in and assemble it back together. Usually the whole process for this, if everything goes well, can be done in two to four hours. I've seen it done in two hours, and I've see it done in a lot more than that when things don't go right.

Also in the engine room is the control room. It's the part where all the gauges are. It's also where all the electrical panels are. It's air conditioned. It's where the engineers sit. They can see what's going on. There's a company computer in there. There also are monitors that tell you exactly what everything is doing on the engines. You can see what the piston temperatures are, you can tell what the fuel pressures are. It gives you all kinds of information. I don't look at it all that often to tell you all that's down there, but it's a lot. And it means a lot to an engineer. You can keep on top of stuff like that. You can get the stack temperature. You can tell if fuel is being fed properly by the pyrometer readings on the stack. If it's reading low, it's not burning fuel correctly, it's not getting hot. If it's reading too hot, there's also a problem. There's something wrong if the engine is overheating. It's not getting enough oil or something. It always tells you something.

That's where they start the engine from – push the buttons to get 'er going. When we're in a port at a dock, we completely shut down the engines. To even idle those, it burns a lot of fuel. Every hour on that engine is wear. You usually get approximately 30,000 hours out of an engine before it needs an overhaul. And 30,000 hours can add up fast. I'm going to guess from three to five years. It depends upon you're runs, long runs. How heavy the loads are doesn't really affect it too much. You might burn a little bit more fuel than other times, but an engine hour is an engine hour.

The instruments in the control room also tell you about the temperatures on the shaft bearings. The instruments have a lot to do with Z drive monitoring, the gears and whatnot as the propulsion goes around. All your fuel information is down there. And all that information that's in the engine room is available to the chief in his room. He has the monitors and everything up there, so he's on 24/7 like me in a way, and he can see what's going on at all times.

Now we'll go back up to the galley level or the crew's level. Once you go past the chief engineer's room on the right side, there's a head and a laundry facility – with a toilet, washer and dryer, and a deep sink – on the right side before you come to a corner and go down another hallway. That hallway, if you go straight ahead, will take you into the galley. If you take a left, it will take you up forward to the pin room. Also up there are crew's quarters on both sides – the cook and the assistant engineer and the conveyormen.

As you leave the galley and go forward to the crew's rooms, you come into the pin room. A pin that we connect with is a massive piece of steel that's connected to a big hydraulic cylinder. Each pin weighs about 14 tons.

After the pin room, you go into the forward peak area. That is a storage room. That's where the cook keeps supplies – groceries. There are a couple of refrigerators and a freezer up there. And there are other supplies. That's where the hot water heaters are.

Underneath that forward room are where the fresh water tanks are, and the sanitary water tank. So there are tanks underneath that deck. We make our own water. We bring in lake water, and we have a reverse osmosis water system that's constantly making water. There's also an escape hatch from that room so you can get up and go outside.

Now we go back to the hallway right to where the bathroom and the laundry room are, across from that is a door and then ladder leading up. There's a hallway at the first landing, and that's where the other laundry room is. That one has two washers and dryers, a deep sink, and a folding table and some cabinets. In there, we also keep our cleaning supplies. In that hallway is an electrical panel. Those are breakers for the lighting systems on that level and the next level up. Also, there's a door that goes back through into the hallway for the officers' hallway and the two outside exits.

Going up from that landing are other stairs – if you don't go through into the officers' hall – and at the top are three rooms. One is an owner's or guest room, one is an officers room, and one is a non-officers, and then there is a lounge in there. There is an area where there are a couple of couches, a table with chairs where people can play cards, and a big flat-screen TV. That's where the guys have their Xboxes and other games and compete with one another. That's where we have our safety and security meetings. When the company comes aboard for our officers meetings, the meetings are held in that room. Sometimes the guest room is used by contractors who are doing work on the boat. Sometimes we'll have a cadet. We'll have somebody extra who rides the boat. We might be breaking somebody in in a new position, who's riding the boat, just learning. Sometimes somebody aboard will have a guest, and the guest can stay there.

On the next level up, we have two rooms. One is the HVAC *(heating, ventilating and air conditioning)* room. The other room is what we call our electronics room. It has computers for the steering system. It also has our gyrocompass in it. It had more. It used to have our company computer system, but things changed around a little bit. The main servers for our computers now are in the pilothouse. It used to be the main servers were in the electronics room. We also have storage in there.

Going up from that level, at the top of the next level is a door that takes you out into an area that's like a veranda or porch. There's one porch on top of the other, so you can go up, and there are two areas where you can kind of lounge around. Guys like to go up there because they get better reception on their cell phones. They like to go out there and have some privacy. They get up high enough where they get good service on their cell phones and talk up there. One guy used to hang a hammock up there and lie up there and read his books. Up there is where I put my big Packers player. Also at level is a kind of tower where the steps go around and keep going up. On the back side is a storage area for the crew's luggage containers. When the guys come aboard, they want to put their suitcases away. Or they'll use it when they leave the boat for vacation and don't want to take everything home with them and they have to clean out their room for the next person who's coming on board. They'll take their boat clothes and stuff like that and store them in there.

Now you're going to go up several flights, and they're just going around – one, two, three, four more flights – and you come to a landing. There's a bathroom there. That's the bathroom for the pilothouse. If you take a right, you go through a fireproof door. You go up one more flight of steps, and you're finally to the pilothouse. That's eight sets of steps. Some of them aren't real long. Some are going up part way, kind of like half a flight. But it's still 91 steps whatever way you want to look at it.

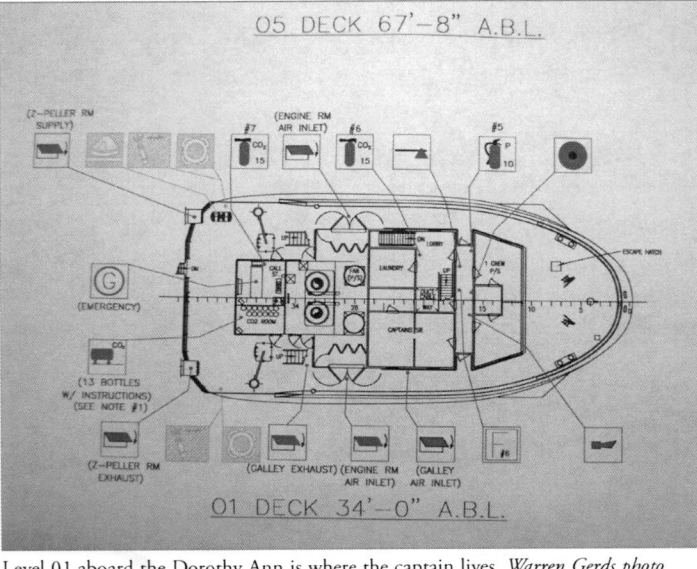
Level 01 aboard the Dorothy Ann is where the captain lives. *Warren Gerds photo*

Hatch 50

Captain's room

The captain's room is on the 01 level one deck above the main deck. There are 91 steps from the main deck to the pilothouse and 76 steps from my level to the pilothouse.

It's not actually my room, mine to own. It's the captain's room, for the captain on duty.

My space consists of a bathroom, a bedroom, and an office. The office is separated by a doorway to the bedroom. And then from the bedroom into the bathroom is another separate door.

My office includes a desk. On my desk are a computer, a printer, and a lot of switches so I can switch from my computer server to the computer for the ECPINS. They're on the same monitor.

***

SIDE TRIP: *The ringtone on Captain Schmidt's personal cell phone is "I'm Your Captain," a 1970 Grand Funk Railroad song written and sung by Mark Farner. People around Captain Schmidt often hear a high voice singing, "I'm you captain, I'm your captain."*

When I got my phone, I was thinking of an up theme, and I always liked the song, "I'm Your Captain." It was more of a joke at first when I put it on the phone – so I'd get the reaction of the people around me. It stuck. It was kind of fun after that.

***

Most of the time, any private discussions take place in my office. If a guy approaches me when we're out on deck, then we'll just go off to the side somewhere where we can talk. But most of the time, if I have to reprimand somebody or if I want a discussion with somebody in private, it's in my office. In my office, I take care of everybody who comes aboard. I check their credentials. I make copies of their credentials so I know that if they were to lose their credentials that I at least would have proof that I signed them aboard and have the credentials. If he's licensed personnel, I see his license. Everybody has to have a TWIC card when they come aboard. If they have a passport, I'll make a copy of it. And it's all there if the guys want a copy of it, too. It's easy enough just to print them out.

A safe is built into the desk so you don't see it. You don't even know it's there. It's where I keep real important stuff, like my big Homeland Security manual, and some petty cash. We don't carry a lot of petty cash on the boat because we can get it whenever we need it. I usually don't carry more than $500 at a time.

There's a settee for people to sit on. Under the settee are supplies. I keep extra radios, equipment that I might need here and there, office supplies, and other supplies you don't want all the time. Some are things that you hand out only when they're needed, For instance, for when it's really cold, we have what are called trackers *(cleats)* that you put on your shoes when it's really icy. People like to keep stuff like that, and they're kind of expensive, but not that expensive – except if you handed them out every time it froze out there. As people want the trackers, you supply them. You make them sign for them, and then they turn them back in.

During a tour of his vessel in February 2002, Captain Schmidt explains his survival suit that's laid out on the bed in his room.
Warren Gerds photo

Alongside the settee is a side table. On top of that, I have a small refrigerator for my personal use.

Above my desk are manuals. I have manuals just about for everything. One is the "Pilot," which covers the Great Lakes. I refer to if I go to any new port that I haven't been into for a while. It has a general description of the harbor, the length of the dock, who owns the dock, some phone numbers, the capacity of the dock, rules and regulations for specific waters, traffic schemes, and bridge hours. That's U.S. There is a Canadian manual. I have Canadian manuals for when I go through Canadian waters. There's also a Seaway handbook. I also have manual for the "Light List." It gives a description for every buoy and every light on the Great Lakes, when they're deployed, when they're decommissioned for the wintertime. In a loose leaf notebook is the "Notice to Mariners," which comes via the Internet, plus it is sent weekly through the office and sent with the ship's mail. There are manuals on fueling procedures. One is my ISO/International Safety Organization manual. I have first aid books. We get first aid CPR every year. You do the practice once a year. To get a refresher every year is very helpful.

I have a TV in my office. There's a TV in my bedroom. Sometimes when I'm sitting in the office, I just like to watch TV for a while. I don't want to go to the lounge to watch. If I'm waiting on going to a dock, I might have a couple of hours to go. I'm just up and about, watching TV there. You don't want to be lying down.

My bedroom is kind of small. It's has a double bed, but it's still tight quarters. There's not a real chair in there to lounge in and watch TV. If you want to watch in the bedroom, you pretty much are sitting up against pillows or lying down watching it.

***

SIDE TRIP: I've got lots of songs on my computer. Every CD I ever bought I put in a file so I have them on my computer and on the boat. On the boat, I have a decent set of computer speakers with a sub woofer for better sound than just coming off of the computer. I listen to music a lot. When I'm in the pilothouse, I bought Sirius Radio, so we have non-stop music all the time. I normally listen to classic rock.

***

In the bedroom, I have a table on both sides with a lamp on both sides. And I have everything secure so it can't tip over. Everything is Velcroed down.

Under my bed are compartments. One is for a survival suit. If we were ever to sink, you can put on the survival suit. It will keep you warm to a degree. It's a floatation device also. You can go into the frigid water, and it gives you at least a chance to survive in frigid water in the wintertime. Also, there is a life jacket under my bed. In another drawer is where I keep personal reading books.

In the room is a dresser with all my work clothes. I keep a set of clothes on the boat, and I keep a set of clothes at home so when I travel I don't have to bring clothes back and forth.

There's a closet for hanging clothes.

There are few supplies here and there. Sometimes when somebody gets off the boat who had a clothing allowance, like for coveralls, I keep a couple pair. If somebody new coming aboard doesn't have the proper clothes, I'll hand them out a pair of coveralls.

The bathroom consists of a shower, a sink, and a stool, and that's pretty much it. Nothing fancy. There is a medicine cabinet. Under the sink are places for cleaning supplies and toiletries.

The captain's room is different than other rooms because of the office, pretty much. And mine is a double bed. Most of the other beds are singles except for the chief engineer and the cook.

Everybody is responsible for the upkeep of their room. I change my sheets, I wash my clothes, I do it all.

I have my personal computer that I bring on the tug. It's a laptop. The company owns the computer on my desk. The relief captain has absolute use of everything in that room when I'm gone. It's his room. He's the captain, and he's in there.

For when I am off, I have big Tupperware boxes that I put my clothes in and stow them on the boat.

The room is beige. All the rooms are the same color.

I put up family photos on the wall. I have pictures of my wife, my son, and my daughter. Because the walls are metal, I buy a package of magnets with sticky backs. I put a little strip on the back of the pictures and then put them right on the wall. That's kind of nice.

Captain Schmidt once stuffed his oversize balloon version of a Green Bay Packers player into his room, left the door open, and scared the dickens out of a passerby. *Gary Schmidt photo*

I also have a couple of bulletin boards on the wall. I keep track of the personnel coming on and off. You put up all the information in case of emergency. Included are national response things, testing procedures for alcohol in case you have an accident – Canadian national response numbers in case you're in Canadian waters – and various U.S. Coast Guard information. Also hanging on the wall is a kit for any time that we are participating in a random drug program. I've been tested as close as two months apart and as far apart as three years. So the random is really random.

We have an in-house phone service. Everybody has a phone in his room except for the deckhands – chief, assistant chief, the conveyor men. My number is 107, and it gets called quite often.

That's one way of communicating with me. When I know I'm getting close to a port and we're going to be making a dock, a lot of times I turn on the walkie-talkie to see what's going on out there. A lot of times, somebody will get on and say, "Are you on the radio, Cap?"

When we're getting close to a dock, the crew knows where to find me, in one of three places. If I'm going out on deck or on the barge, I'll let them know I'm going out there in advance. Otherwise, I'll be in the galley eating, or I'll be in my quarters. I go to the barge just to take a walk around and just look at things, just to check. I do that quite a bit. I just take a walk around, to visually look at things and see that everything looks right to me. Or, if something needs my attention or needs the crew's attention, I'll let them know.

Hatch 51

In the pilothouse

Going to the pilothouse, 91 steps later, out of breath...

Walking in, it's not "task" that I'm thinking of. When it gets to the maneuvering part, that's the part I really enjoy most of all of my job. Now, if you're talking about filling out Customs forms, that's dreadful. That's hard for me. But to go up to the pilothouse and to do the maneuvering or make a dock, it's like, "Oh, no chore at all." That's like, "Yeah, this is what I want to do." When I'm zoned in, I'm making a dock, and the tougher the dock, the more zoned in I get on it, the more that I'm concentrated on it.

For maneuvering, I have a main control station and a stern station, for backing up. Everything nautical is duplicated at the stations. I have both of my throttles for steering at the stern station, for both engines or pitch control. I have a control station for the bow thruster. I can turn both the searchlights from back there, one on the barge and one on the tug. I have the same indicators as I'm backing up as going forward. There's a station for the tug. I have the same indicators as I'm backing up as going forward. There's a station for the camera back there. We can run the camera that's up forward. We can turn it around. You can watch yourself as you're backing up. You can watch how you are coming through bridges. That's real handy. Also, a stationary ship's radio is back there. I don't have radar at the stern station. Also what you don't have back there is the telegraph that goes to the engine room. If you're to lose your steering, you can tell the engineers what to do with the throttles. The telegraph is up in the front window. A lot of the indicators of what is going wrong — engine indicators — I don't have that monitor in the back window. I don't have the capability to re-start the engines from the back window, which I can do from the forward station. Or switch generators or start a fire pump. That's all forward. The stern station is mainly for backing up and making a dock. Out in an open lake, you wouldn't be maneuvering from back there. This is strictly a backing up maneuvering situation. You could switch to using the stern station in an emergency. You could activate many things from back. That would be a temporary station. You just have a button to activate the after station and one to activate the forward station. When one is on, the other is off.

Under way, 24 hours a day, there is at least one person in the pilothouse all the time. At a loading dock, the mate will be out loading, and I will leave the pilothouse and go down

The hard-working part of Cleveland, Ohio, along the Cuyahoga River provides a panorama from the Dorothy Ann pilothouse.
Jeremy Mock photo

and rest. Everything is shut down. It's the same with an unloading dock. When we go to an unloading dock, I only have four hours *(off duty)*. I've already been in the river for eight to 10 hours. I go down and take a nap. After the unloading, I'll go back up and do another eight or 10-hour stretch.

When I'm doing maneuvering, I have a second person in the pilothouse. It will be myself and a mate. Or sometimes I'll even have an extra deckhand up there. Also, when we're out in foggy weather, if we're out in the open lake, instead of me being up there all the time, we'll call the AB up there. In a fog situation, we have two people in the pilothouse and myself on call so if anything comes up I'm readily available.

Normally, there aren't many people in the pilothouse, but sometimes you could have four or five people in the pilothouse. A lot of times while you're under way, you'll have two guys come up there and start cleaning. You might have an engineer coming up there looking at something. Normally, you wouldn't.

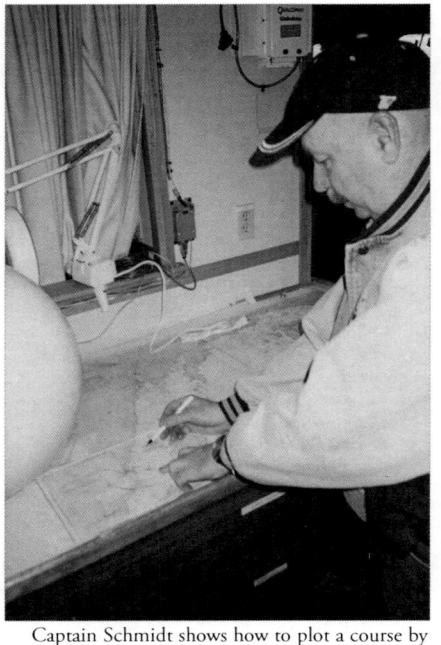

Captain Schmidt shows how to plot a course by pencil on a chart in the Dorothy Ann pilothouse. *Warren Gerds photo*

Sometimes, people watch Captain Schmidt at the controls.

I've trained a lot of people. I teach people how to handle, maneuver a vessel around. I think it's important that people get a chance to see handling and ask to do it. People have asked, "Can I do this?" I say, "Sure, I'll let you. I'll give you a shot." I give them simple tasks to start with. If they've got their license and I know that they're moving up into a position, then I'll give them harder and harder tasks to take care of. It's really hard to teach somebody because there's always a chance that they can do some damage maneuvering. You know exactly what you would do, and sometimes it's kind of hard to explain to somebody exactly how to make that maneuver. I can do it, but it takes patience and time. Sometimes you just have to bite your tongue and let them kind of make a little bit of a mistake – not enough to get them into trouble but enough to know that, "Oh, this isn't right, and I've got to do something else." That helps them out also.

In the pilothouse, we have printed charts and electronic charts. You have a chart in front of you on a screen, but you really get into information on a printed chart. Say, to pick a spot to go to anchor, I'll look at the depth. I'll see if it's a rocky bottom, I'll see if it's a muddy bottom, and you pick a spot where you might want to anchor and then you put a mark on it. I go over to the printed chart, and I get a fix on it. I fix what the lat and long *(latitude and longitude)* of that mark is, and I can enter that into the GPS. Once I enter that into the GPS, it takes me right to where I want to anchor. So I use paper charts all the time. I think they're going to be a thing of the past eventually. The chance of losing all your electronics at one time is kind of odd, but it could happen. You have redundancies. You have backup systems. You have backup electrical systems. So if you do lose your electrical

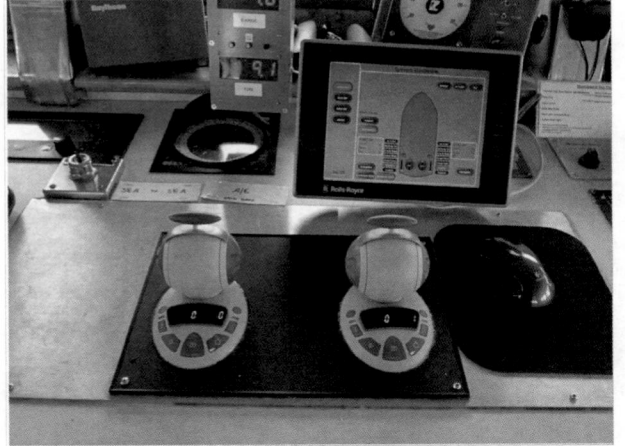

These controls are the center of action in the Dorothy Ann pilothouse. *Jeremy Mock photo*

system, usually there's a battery backup to everything.

When I have a new guy who comes on board who doesn't know the lakes as well as he should know the lakes, who doesn't know the places, I still make him plot on a printed chart where he's at every two hours. I say, "You're right here. Make a plot. I want to see it on paper. Put it in pencil." I want to see where he's at. Even though I can see it on the electronic chart, I want him to actually do it. This way he's looking at the chart. He gets to see that this point that he's off where he's making the X's – Sturgeon Point or 40-Mile Point or Nordmeer Wreck – a position. When you're looking at a chart like that, you pick up certain things just looking at it.

The charts are from the National Oceanic and Atmospheric Administration *(NOAA)*. The Interlake office has a deal with the J.W. Westcott Company, the mail boat, so every time that an updated chart comes out, it is put aboard the vessel automatically. If I wear out a chart or a chart gets damaged, then I can order a chart anytime through the Westcott Company. Also, we have a company that gives us updates for the paper charts and the electronic charts. Let's say the Coast Guard has decided to de-commission a buoy permanently and it's no longer going to be in existence, or it has changed the position of a buoy, or something has been dumped on the bottom and the Coast Guard knows the object is going to be there permanently. There's a change in the charts, and the company prints out the change in the charts on a stickyback. We can paste the change over the exact spot where it's got to be on the paper chart. We also have a book, and we make the corrections in the books as we go along so everything is corrected. All the charts are up to date, and I mean up to date. Every month, we have a new correction that comes up for every chart that we have.

A new day dawns in the pilothouse as the Dorothy Ann/Pathfinder approaches Cleveland. *Garch Schmidt photo*

Dredging information is different. That comes out on "Local Notices to Mariners" and also is on the U.S. Army Corps of Engineers website. The "Local Notices to Mariners" is published weekly, and you can go on line and get that and get the latest updates. We're aware of all the dredging. That's a different form. That wouldn't be shown on the charts, not necessarily. Channels are supposed to be dredged to a certain controlled depth chart datum, so, as the water levels go up and down, you're working off of chart datum.

Speaking of water and wet...

I thought about spilling coffee. When new controls were put in the pilothouse, I siliconed everything around the edges so coffee couldn't run down into the electronics. Water or spillages are bad for electronics.

There are only two windows that open in the pilothouse. They're on both sides. It would have to be a driving rain for water to reach the controls. But people have opened

The Dorothy Ann pilothouse provides a vantage point 70 feet above the water. *Gary Schmidt photo*

the windows at a dock and forgotten about them as we are loading or unloading. I am among the people who have left the windows open and left the lights on. With the bug hatches, the pilothouse has filled with bugs.

Hatch 52

Outside the Dorothy Ann

The top of the pilothouse is about 93 feet from the bottom of the Dorothy Ann.

Up there is the mast for all the lighting. I have to have a lot of lights up there. You have your fueling lights, not-under-command lights, towing lights, masthead lights, running lights on either side. And then you have vents. Everything is vented. Your water system venting, everything, comes up to the top of the pilothouse and is vented up there.

Also on the top are multiple antennas – including two for radars, three for radio telephones, one for satellite television, one for satellite telephone. Then there are whistle signal lights, anemometer, four GPS antennas, and more.

For the pilothouse, there's a walkaround catwalk that you walk around outside of the pilothouse. On the back of the pilothouse is a ladder. One way, you get to the roof of the pilothouse. The other way, you can use it for an escape route and get all the way down to the 02 deck, which can get you down to the lower deck.

Just below the pilothouse, there's a veranda or observation deck. There are two levels of the veranda. There's a hatch way that goes into the tower. The veranda is used by some guys just to sit and relax and look at things when we're under way. It's pretty noisy when we're unloading because the generators are running and all the equipment is going. But guys also use it for their cell phones because of the higher vantage point. I see a lot of guys go up there to talk in kind of privacy when we're under way. Of course, I put my big Packers player up there. That's where I tie him up when we go through the Soo Locks. Sometimes I put him on deck but not very often.

The Dorothy Ann is a home away from home for a crew of 14 for weeks at a time. *Gary Schmidt photo*

Inside the tower, we have the HVAC room, a storage area, an electronics room, lounge, two crewmembers' cabins and the owner's stateroom or visitor's room. Below that, we're getting down to the captain's and mate's area and then a laundry room and a stairwell going down to the main deck, the 01 level.

On the outside of the captain's room on the bow is the ladder that runs between the tug and the barge. You have a winch on the deck for a jockey line besides the one on the outside of the barge. You have a jockey line on both sides with a winch so you can maneuver the tug around a little bit if you want to pin the tug in sometimes. That's what this one does, too, besides holding us in place. We call it jockeying, so you can jockey it around so we can move the boat so the pins line up better to pin the tug into the barge. Also up here are our water stations for when we take on water. The manifold for taking on water is up here. Also on the port side of

The only way to get from the Dorothy Ann to the Pathfinder is this metal walkway. *Gary Schmidt photo*

the bow is a hatch that takes you down into the storeroom so you can put supplies down there. There's also a hookup for when we process our sanitary on the Dorothy Ann that we pump over to the barge, which has a second sanitary cleaning station for the water. There are a couple of vents up here so if our water maker makes too much water, it'll come out on the deck, just plain, clean water. But it's vented. There also are fuel vents for the tanks with a catch basin as big as a dining room table to catch any fuel that might slop out – one on each side.

Around the back side on the starboard side going astern, there's a hatchway that takes you into the crew's hallway where the captain and first and second mate are. Going further back, the first hatch leads to a vent room. The hatch going in is on the back side of it, and it has great big filters. Any air that goes to the engines is filtered before it goes into the engines. Along with dirt, we get a lot of bugs in those filters.

There's a hatch on each side that goes forward into that vent room. Behind that is another hatch that opens into what we call our automatic fire system for the engine room. It's all the chemicals for putting out a bilge fire. You can do it remotely so you can evacuate the engine room. That's on the starboard side. Right outside of that is a stiff-arm hoist. We have one on each side, exactly the same on either side. The hoists swing out over the side. This one we use for discharging our garbage over to the mail boat and other boats that take our garbage. It doesn't quite reach the dock if we're in the notch. If we swing our stern over to the dock, then this will reach the dock. The same with the other side.

Behind are what look like little stacks. They're air vents that go down into the Z drive room. They're made to look like little stacks to keep a theme going. They're decorative, but they have a function.

Also on the deck is a hatch opening so we can drop down supplies or anything that we need. There's one on each side. The one on the port side is larger for taking out larger items. On the other side as we're going around the stern of the stack is a trash compactor for bagging all our big bags of garbage.

Coming up from the stern on the port side on the other side of the stack is the emergency generator. It's a small generator. It just operates all the emergency things that we need. We can have steering, hydraulics for the steering, one of the compressors, all the emergency color lights. In the pilothouse, it operates one radar, one radio telephone, the gyro and GPS. Also, the emergency general alarm, all horn functions, and all navigation lights.

Going forward from that is the other door to come into the filter room.

Forward of that on the port side is the other door hatch going into the crew's quarters. And a hallway.

Then there's a door from the crew's quarters that goes down below to the 01 deck. Further on the outside on each side on the bow is where the pins extend into the barge. We do extend the pins manually by pushing a button. We'll watch the pins so that they're in the correct alignment.

Also on the bow is the company's logo, which is the Great Lakes. Underneath it is the ship's bell for ringing. You're supposed to ring it when you're towing in a snowstorm or poor visibility. It's not rung much. It's functional by law, but in the pilothouse I have a simulated bell system that will work just the same, and it's away from the crew's quarters. It's on a loud hailer. It rings out like a regular bell, and it sounds like a regular bell. So there's not really a need for the ship's bell, but all ships seem to have one. It's a thing of the past.

Also on the stern of the tug are floodlights. I have floodlights to light up my stern for backing up or for taking on supplies or when you need the lights back there for working purposes. There's a floodlight on the top of each of the stacks. I have a floodlight on the port side that you can swing so you can light up different things. We normally use it to light up the draft marks that are on the stern of the barge so we can see our depth at night.

On the 02 level, there's a hatchway that goes into the lounge, which is on the port side of a ladder. Through the lounge, you can go in and you'll see the third mate's, the deckhands', and the owner's stateroom or guest room.

From there you can go down the ladder again to the 01 level, which is the captain's level, and then from there you can get down to the main deck also. There's a ladder behind the stack that takes you down to the main deck. As you're coming down, there are the fueling stations between the stack and the ladder. Also, there's a fire station, above the fueling station.

There's a hatchway that takes you into the inside of the 01, the main level. On each side are hatches. On one side, outside of the main cabin, is storage for the turnout gear for our firefighting. On the other side is our emergency oil spill response locker.

Also back there on the stern are our H bits. We use these to tie off the stern of the tug. We also use the H bits if we would ever have to tow that barge. Coming down the port side on the barge is the emergency tow line that runs the full length of the boat. It comes around the notch over to the other side. There's a ball with a long line attached to it. If we had to tow the barge, we'd take this long tow line, run it down the outside, bring it around the stern, and hook it into the H bit. Now we would pop the pins, pull out, take off around the side of the barge – this is all just tied on with light string and would pull right out – and that's how you would attach to an emergency tow line. God help us if we ever had to do that. It would be a dire straits type thing. I wouldn't really want to do it.

Off the side of it is the capstan so we can retrieve our lines. This capstan also works for the anchor on the stern. This anchor is clipped in place. It has a drum underneath that's attached to a Kemlar line. It's a synthetic line. Very strong. Stronger than steel. When we drop the stern anchor, we would use the capstan to retrieve the anchor.

Over on the side is a hatch that takes you down into the Z drive room where the Z drives are.

Also along the back is where we store our ladder that we hang over the side. We have a gizmo that we put on a rail, and then the ladder hooks into it and it drops down. When we bring our work boat alongside, we're able to get people right up to this hatch area. We drop the work boat down from the higher area on the barge, too. But it works better off the stern of the tug. It's a little safer.

Also on the stern, there's a hatch on either side for getting people aboard or getting off or for a gangway when we lay up. We'll lay up against a dock, and we'll just run the gangway across it.

Inside the stack, there is a way to go all the way up to the top.

On each side of the stack is a remote camera so the guys in the engine room can see what's going on outside.

There's another fire station outside the 02 level. And there's a fire station on the forward end of the tug and one on the aft.

Hatch 53

In & about the Pathfinder

When docked, the Dorothy Ann and Pathfinder are held in place by what are called jockey lines. *Gary Schmidt photo*

On the bow of the Pathfinder is a capstan to tighten lines. There is the mast. On the mast are lights and the ship's whistle, the Kalhenberg. I use the whistle on the bow of the barge most of the time. It's a deeper-voice whistle. It's louder than the one on the Dorothy Ann. But, if I'm backing up, it's hard to hear that whistle up forward. If I'm going through a bridge, I'll use the ship's whistle on the tug. Otherwise, the tug can be detached from the barge, and, if I'm running with the tug, I need a whistle on the tug. I use the whistles simultaneously when we have the general alarm going off. I blow them for at least 10 seconds when we have a general alarm or when we have a boat drill and a fire drill. *(A boat drill and a fire drill are two separate drills that take place during the same drill session. The fire drill is first, and the boat drill comes second. It is an abandon boat drill.)*

When I'm leaving a dock, I usually blow the loud one up forward on the barge. Not only that, the one on top of the pilothouse is extremely loud in the pilothouse. So I don't use it as much, but I do use it.

Also up on the bow is a little house just for the bow thruster unit. It houses the bow thruster controls.

***

SIDE TRIP: If the tug is detached from the barge, which we used to do when we went to Charlevoix, the barge used to have to be maneuvered back into a slip by itself and go all the way up against the end of the slip because the dock crew wanted the boom back as far as they could get it for the cargo that we were unloading. I used to back all the way into the slip and just put out one cable and then take the tug out farther because we were in a channel and there wasn't enough room for me to be alongside the barge. There's a couple of sunken ships used for a break wall. We used to tie up alongside the two ships, and there was enough room for me to go alongside of them. The crew would pull the barge back in with the cable, and they'd have to shift cables as they went but we could control the barge's bow with the bow thruster. One guy would handle the bow thruster and move it around and keep the stern coming back in and the bow from sliding into the sides. And that worked out really well. It saved a lot of time. When I first went there, the crew used to just tie it off on the outside. The guys pulled the barge back with cables, and it took a whole crew to do this. I said, "There's got to be a better way to do it." And there was.

***

Behind the bow thruster house is a vent house where the big super fans are that pull air through the tunnels and discharge it outside. There's a filtering system in there. That's on the upper deck.

As you come down a ladder, there's the two landing booms for people going ashore. Also on the starboard side there's a chain hoist with a hatch underneath it that drops all the way down to the void space in the tunnel down below where we store rollers and supplies for the unloading system.

Then you can go inside the lower house. The anchor windlass is up forward in a room. There's a winch up there, the bow winch with a capstan on the side or what they call a gypsy-head winch. On the side of that there's the anchor windlass itself that handles the two anchors.

Outside of that room coming back on the port side, there's a workout room, a weight room. We have all our workout equipment. We have an elliptical, a treadmill, several weight systems. It's heated.

On the other side is the pipe room for a supply of steel pipe. We can cut it there, and we have a threader. We have other things. We cut and thread pipe when we have to replace something. We have pipes that run the length of the vessel on both sides for hosing out the cargo holds, and we use pipes for firefighting also. It's not what it's made for, but we could fight fires with it. It's metal pipe. One runs on the outside of the deck on the starboard side right up on top along the gunnel *(top edge of the side)*. The other one is underneath the deck. It runs the port side in the walk tunnel. They're two-inch pipes. We have two pretty big water pumps that supply water to them. That gives it a really good stream, very strong.

Also in the pipe room is extra metal that we might need for repairs. That would be flat bar, angle irons, sheets of plate steel that can be cut to whatever you want. You would use that if you have a crack in a bulkhead from being out in the sea *(heavy waves)*. You might crop the cracked area out and put in a new piece of steel. We have the steel on board. We have a repair person come in. ABS comes in, we report it, and they'll say, "OK crop this out and replace it." The Coast Guard comes down and inspects it after it's done.

Also in that room is a crew's lounge for the deckhands to take a break every once in a while.

Also up in that forward part is a bank of batteries for backup lighting.

Powerful winches aboard the Pathfinder serve many important purposes.
Gary Schmidt photo

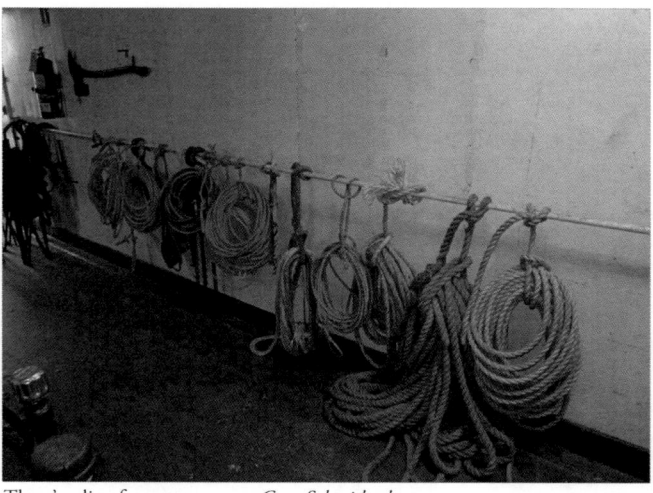

There's a line for any purpose. *Gary Schmidt photo*

When a generator goes out, the bank of batteries takes over, and the lights stay on.

Coming back, you see the hatches, 1 through 19. The hatches are 12 feet wide by 50 feet across. We have a hatch crane that can lift those hatches – put 'em on and take 'em off. It takes not even a minute to move the hatch covers. This is a hydraulic system with its own diesel engine on it. It rolls up the deck. You drop the hydraulics down, and it has two hooks that are matched up with the hooks on the cover. You drive the system forward, the hooks are there, you pick the cover up, bring it back to a space between the two hatches, and drop the cover. And then you go up and get the next one. Same thing. Sometimes you stack the covers on top of one another because some of the areas that hatches would go are smaller hatches that let you get down into the cargo hold with ladders underneath them that you can go down into the cargo hold. There's one on each side for each cargo hold. There will be one for Cargo hold 1A and 1B – 1A and 1B will be on port and starboard side. And you go back between 2 and 1, there will be one for 1 and one for 2. At each bulkhead there's one on each side that separates the cargoes.

On the decks, there are vents, what we call goose necks, in a half pipe that comes around, and they have flappers on the bottom. The pipes go right to the ballast tank and let the air escape when you transfer ballast in and out of each tank. Also, there are mushroom heads along the decks that open up. They just spin open or close. They supply straight ventilation to the walk tunnels that are just below the cargo decks on either side.

Going back to the stern, you have the unloading boom that sits down the middle of the deck. It's 260 feet long, from the base from which it spins. So it extends quite a way out over the docks.

The HAC – the High-Angle Conveyor – involves the A-frame. The HAC brings the belt up from below and drops material down into a hopper, which drops it down onto the boom belt.

On either side there's a boarding ladder.

The boom shack goes all the way from one side to the other of the barge, and you can walk around it. On the outside of that shack are the controls, a little box with which you can swing the boom and raise it and lower it.

As you come back a little bit farther on the barge, there are houses and what we call our stiff-legs hoist. We have a chain hoist on the end of these that can go over the side, drop things down or pick them up and then bring them over.

There's a hatch where we can drop stuff right down into the engine room on either side of the barge.

Coming back a little bit farther, there's the fan house and a stairwell on the inside that goes down into the engine room. Both sides are the same.

When the Pathfinder was converted, the back was squared off and sponsons, or wings, were put on both sides for greater stability. So a little bit of it was cut off, and a little bit of it was extended. The area where the engine was is still the engine room. It is where the generator room is now. It's also the pump room where the big ballast pumps are. There are two generators, electrical panels. It's pretty much still an engine room, with a pump room down below it. Part of it is used for the unloading system, the HAC. Part of it is hollowed out, and the high-angle conveyor goes through it from the tunnel. The conveyor is propelled with electric motors and big gears. It is powered by generator power.

In a view toward the bow, the Pathfinder is loading. *Gary Schmidt photo*

In a view toward the stern and the Dorothy Ann, a crewman washes out a cargo hold. *Gary Schmidt photo*

Coming around to the stern of the barge, there is a winch that controls a jockey line that, when we disconnect from the barge, holds us into the notch. That's a nylon line.

Also along the sides there are chocks and timber-heads at various places, I think five on each side.

Forward are the forward winches. There's a port and starboard, or two can go off the port side or off the starboard side.

Back aft are two more winches.

Also in the back is an entrance going down to the HAC, and there's a hatch on each side that takes you down to through the HAC into the tunnel or up through the HAC all the way up to the hopper, and outside there's a catwalk that goes around and takes you to where you can service the motors that run the belts.

Aft on the starboard side is where we store the work boat.

Holds, hatches, gates

The Pathfinder has five cargo holds. You have a very small 1A and part of the number 1 cargo hold and 1B. 1A will hold 700 to 1,000 tons, depending on the weight of the product. 1B will hold about 2,500 tons.

Cargo holds numbers 2 and 3 will hold more than 5,000 tons. Cargo hold 4 is just a little bit larger than the rest of them. It can hold up to almost 6,000 tons. Full capacity can run over those amounts.

For the five holds, there are 19 hatches *(on top)* and 37 gates *(below)*.

The cargo is gravity fed onto a belt, and that belt runs the whole length of the vessel.

We'll start with cargo hold 1 and 1-A/1-B. 1-A is just gate number 1, hatch number 1. 1-B is 2, 3, and 4 hatches, and then there is a separation bulkhead. These are gates 2, 3, 4, 5, 6, and 7.

Cargo hold 2 is hatches 5, 6, 7, 8 and 9 and gates 8 through 17.

Cargo hold 3 is hatches 10, 11, 12, 13, and 14, and it gates go from 18 to 27, underneath, on the belt.

Cargo hold number 4 has hatches 15, 16, 17, 18, and 19, and the gates are 28 through 37.

The gates are controlled hydraulically. Each gate has a hydraulic ram on it that pulls the gate back that lets the cargo release by gravity onto the belt, and it's closed with a valve. The guy just pushes the valve, and it will either open or close. We have a gateman down there.

Once the belt starts, it's running at a consistent speed. We open a gate, and we have a series of lights in the tunnel. There are four lights – blue, yellow, green, and red. Blue is just running, that it's in operation. Yellow means that you're low on cargo. Green is where you want to be. Red means you're overloaded and need to back it off. You try to maintain green,

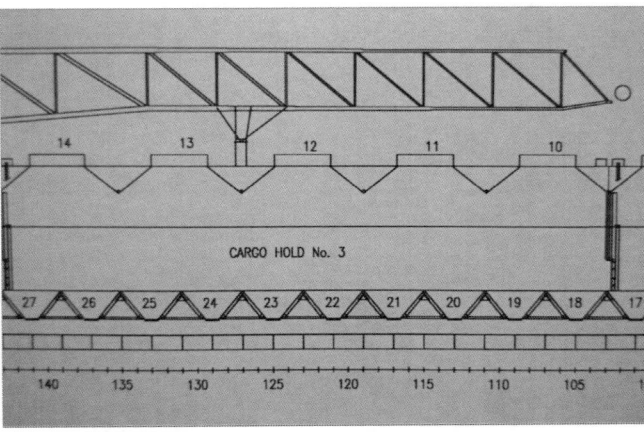

The interior of the Pathfinder is systematically numbered.
Warren Gerds photo

with the material four or five inches from the top of the belt, which is shaped like a "V." That depth will keep a steady light. You usually open three gates in a row. One's just barely cracked, one might be half open, and the third one might just be barely cracked to maintain an even flow. The guys up on top are washing stone down into the gate, and that drops onto the belt. As a gate finishes up, you open the gate all the way up and they clean it out.

Certain cargoes flow better than other cargoes.

Sometimes it's a little dusty, but you have circulation air blowing down there all the time. You have big fans and suctions.

The gateman is a crewman. He doesn't have to be Able Bodied. He can be just a regular seaman. But we break in just about everybody to be a gateman because you never know who's off or who's doing what. You need an abundance. You need a lot of people who can do that particular job. He has a walkie-talkie. He has a headphone set so the noise doesn't interfere with him. We communicate with him, saying, "OK, slow down the gates," or "Shut your gates," "Go into cargo hold so-and-so and start unloading that one."

You have to unload the boat in a sequence. Because we're multi-cargoed, we don't want to pull up too much cargo out of one area and put a stress on the vessel. As you're pulling out cargo, you're putting water into the ballast tanks for balance, and you might only take out half of one cargo hold and then go to another one

A crewman washes the deck near an open hatch. *Gary Schmidt photo*

In a tunnel of the Pathfinder, crewmen shovel fallen product back onto the cargo belt. *Gary Schmidt photo*

and take out half of it or maybe all of it and then go back to the other one and take out the rest of it. So if you have a split half-and-half, you'll have cargo in holds 2 and 4, and your sequence will be half of 2, all of 4, the rest of 2. And then when we're done with those products, we'll shift up the dock to another pile and unload holds 1 and 3. And you'll do the same thing again. You'll do half of 3, all of 1, the rest of 3 until you're done on that order so you don't put undue stress into the vessel.

For a multi-cargoed load, if you loaded one product in both cargo holds in the middle, you would probably break the ship in half. Or if you put the product on the ends, you'd break it in half. And that has happened to other ships.

Let's say we had four different cargoes. I would unload all of 3 first. Number 3 brings the vessel up bodily without tipping it too much. That means you have stern room. Then you go up and unload 1A and 1B. At the same time, we're replacing more than half the weight with water, so you're not putting undue stress on the vessel. Now I go back and unload 4. That will bring my stern up. Number 2 is a body hatch, and we'll go up there and unload number 2 last. I can do just the opposite. I can unload 2 and 4 and then do 1 and 3. Those are the sequences we unload.

Hatch 55

Bodies

I was on the Mississippi River. This was years ago, and we were pushing barges. On the Mississippi, you push multiple barges. They form what are called duck ponds. Barges have a rake on one end so they go through the water a little bit easier. On the back, they're usually flat, straight up and down. River barge guys put a barge with a rake on it in the forward position, with the stern facing aft, and then they'll take another barge and turn it around and put those barges stern to stern. Next is a bow, and the setup is bow to bow. So it's stern to stern, bow to bow, stern to stern – for 15 barges. When the barges are side by side, with the rakes facing each other, you get what they call a duck pond. The corners are rounded, and there's a space. You can see into the void area of the duck pond.

As you move along the river, you get turbulence. You pick stuff up off the bottom, and you get a lot of turbulence in that duck pond.

One of the guys happened to see something down there that was really white. Nobody knew if it was an animal or person at first, but he reported it. I wasn't on duty at the time. But the crew stopped and figured out that they'd have to call authorities. It was a white female corpse that was floating in the duck pond.

Another time, I was on the Donald C. Hannah going down the Chicago Sanitary Canal, and I was close to the city. It was at Ashland Avenue, so I wasn't in Western Rivers section anymore but in the Great Lakes basin of the Chicago River, south branch of the Chicago River.

It rained quite heavily a couple of days before, and there was a lot of flotsam in the water – branches. I was headed in to wait for one of our other boats to bring a barge in to me. It was going to be three or four hours for that tug to get in with the barge. So I was just light boating it *(traveling with the tug alone, not towing or pushing a barge)*, just goofing around.

I wasn't at full speed, just idling up the river. I saw branches floating in the river. There was a big, heavy duty fender on the front of the tug for pushing barges, and I was just steering and bumping those pieces of wood and branches in the river. I was steering on something, and some people on the bank got my attention, saying, "There's a body in the water." At the last minute, I avoided it. I went past, stopped, and called the Coast Guard.

The body was of a black male. He hadn't been in the water long because he wasn't bloated. His head was still small, but his body was getting bigger.

The Coast Guard said, "Put a line around him." I said, "No, I'll stand by, but I'm not putting a line on him. I'll stand by until you get here." I wasn't going to put a line on him. I would have had to fill out too many reports for the Coast Guard. And I was not equipped to handle it. If it's a body that's been in the water for a while, you don't want to be pulling it apart. I have no desire to handle something like that. I'll stand by.

Hatch 56

Lake levels

A big factor in loading in many seasons is lake levels – low levels. We lose approximately 100 tons of cargo space per inch of lake level lost.

You record the water gauge level when you start loading, and you record it when you're done loading. In the load book, you write in what you loaded to, draft wise.

Our deepest draft that we can load the Pathfinder to is 26 feet 2¾ inches. That's what my load line says, what my Plimsoll Marks tell me that I can load to at mid-summer. Now, if the water level is down, we may load to 25 feet. That means we're losing 14 inches of water. That means we're losing 1,400 tons of cargo, which is substantial. When your talking moving by ton miles or whatever, that's substantial. And that's everybody. It's not just our fleet. Every fleet feels this.

***

SNAPSHOT: *Lake levels are monitored continually. While levels fluctuate from year to year, the general trend is down, as seen at the U.S. Army Corps of Engineers website, www.lre.usace. army.mil. Among other numbers, the Great Lakes account for 4,530 miles of coastline, 95 percent of United States' fresh surface water supplying 40 million people with drinking water, 6 quadrillion gallons of fresh water, and 250 species of fish. Sources: U.S. Army Corps of Engineers, Great Lakes Environmental Research Laboratory, Great Lakes Information Network, International Upper Great Lakes Study, Department of Transportation Ports Economic Impact Report*

***

The water level is set by a low water datum or what is called chart datum. Lake levels rise up or go down against that chart datum. There's a station on the computer that I go to that gives me the water levels that I need to know for most of the ports. On those water levels, we have established to what depth we can load the Pathfinder in this port at a certain water level. According to that information, that's what we have to base our draft off of.

***

SIDE TRIP: *At this point, Captain Schmidt scans his computer for sample ports and finds the observed height of the water on a specific time and date.*

(On this day), when we load at Marblehead, we can load to 22 feet at a plus-20 inches. Now the water's down to 13.3 inches. I'm going to have to subtract seven inches from my cargo, and I'll lose 700 tons of cargo.

I can go into Harbor Beach at 19 feet 6 inches at zero. So I'm losing 17 inches. I can't even get in there. I would not be able to get in there. I just couldn't do it.

That's why you have to plan ahead and try to work that out.

***

The water gauge tells me the depth of the water at the dock.

The depth fluctuates on Lake Erie dependent upon weather. If the wind is blowing out of the west, it blows the water out of the western basin, and I've seen the water drop as much as five feet in Toledo, maybe two to three feet in Marblehead. Usually in mid-lake it might not affect it as much. It might drop a little bit if the wind is out of the south on the Lake Erie ports.

Cleveland, Fairport, and Ashtabula are not affected as much by the winds shifting. Buffalo may rise in water depth with a west wind by three or four feet.

If you have an east wind, it's going to have the opposite effect. It's going to build water up in the western basin, and we can load a lot more at Marblehead. But it's hard to load at the dock when the wind is out of the east because we tie up on the west side of the dock and the wind blows the vessel away from the dock.

We watch the water gauge closely, especially on Lake Erie.

Hatch 57

Loading

Our loading and unloading are not done the old-fashioned way. Everything is done by self-unloaders now.

We run a 24-hour operation. It makes no difference if it's night or day, if it's raining or snowing, if it's sunshine, or if it's just a full moon. It doesn't matter.

Depending on the dock and what product we're loading, the process usually takes four people – three deckhands and a mate out on the Pathfinder.

The cargo is loaded over the top. Most of the loading is by conveyor that dumps product right into a cargo hold and fills up.

Whether loading or unloading, the balance – or what we call trim – is a constant battle. You don't want to tip your vessel side to side too much. You might get two feet difference sometimes, and that's a lot. You don't want to go two feet. You have no center bulkhead as you're loading a hold, so you want to keep your load as level and balanced as you can going across.

You start loading in the middle of a hatch. As you load up the middle, you've got to start loading the outsides. You don't want a list.

The loader is a dock person. He's watching a series of trim lights. We've got them on both ends of the boat. White light means you're trim. The port side is a red light. Starboard is green. If you go to two green that might tell you that you've got a six-inch list. You switch your loading to the other side until you have a white light.

You have to keep a trim fore and aft also. You don't want to put undo amount of stress on the vessel. You load everything in a sequence. One way is to start with cargo hold three, then go to one, then load half of four, then all of two, and then fill four. We fill certain hatches as we finish loading. Our trim hatches are seven forward and 14 or 15 aft, depending upon what we are trying to finish up with.

We know exactly how many tons per inch we're loading. We have a trim gauge, and it tells you that you have so many tons per inch and how that's going to affect your bow and how much it's going to lift your stern up. So there's a balance there. That is how you trim a vessel up to your depth. That measurement

The Pathfinder takes on stone – and a lot of wind-blown dust and dirt that has to be shoveled up.
Gary Schmidt photo

For perspective, Captain Schmidt's hard hat is placed next to a rock that couldn't fit through a gate during loading. *Gary Schmidt photo*

does not depend on what the cubic weight of a cargo is. Our heaviest product is probably the steel product. The iron ore pellets are heavy. Slag is very heavy. Sand is heavy. But those are in cubic measurement – that's inside. Your trim on the outside is the total tons per inch for the cargo in the whole vessel but not for a specific hatch. This is a movement of the vessel. It's a little bit different.

The deckhands have to shift wires to be able to move the boat up and down the dock as we're loading cargoes, as the cargoes are shifted into different cargo holds. Two deckhands are on the dock. The mate, who's in charge of the loading process while we're out there, handles one of the winches. One of the ABs (*Able Bodied Seaman*) handles the other winch and helps move the vessel back and forth.

I'm just there for support. If they need me for anything, I'm there to do it. One thing is to check on the weather, to make sure that because of weather we're not going to be overloading the vessel or not going to load it to the bottom *(of draft)*.

The first mate makes up the loading plan, and he gives it to me for approval. From that, we make a contingency plan – if the water drops below a certain level, then we'll stop loading at a certain point. Or if the barge is dropping more rapidly than we thought it might, he'll give me a heads up and give me a call. If it looks like there's going to be maybe more water *(draft)* than we thought, we might take on a few more extra tons. We adjust to what the conditions are at that time.

***

SIDE TRIP: A ton is not universal. A ton, when you're talking about a short ton, is 2,000 pounds, or what we call a net ton. That is used by most facilities. A long ton, which is 2,240 pounds, is used by most of the steel companies. One of the stone docks used to use long tons, and it may still. Then the Canadians use metric tons, which is another ton. A metric ton is 2,204.6 pounds.

***

The barge is loaded by both weight and volume.

Sometimes we can't what we call cube out. That means we can't fill up the barge, so we have to fill to a certain draft. If you have something like coke, which is very light – it doesn't even weigh as much as the water we take on in ballast – we're lighter than we are in ballasted conditions. We'll cube out the boat – it will be completely filled with cargo right up to the top. Coal is like that also. But with stone, we can get close to filling up the vessel but not quite. With iron ore, we don't even come close.

Once we've loaded the vessel and we're headed for a loading port, it's just a matter of going in there, depending on how many products we have loaded. We can load more than one product at a time. We can load up to five different products in one load. It will be all stone – stone or sand or something related but not exactly the same stuff. We can go to more than one loading port with what we have loaded. There are a couple of places where we always take a split load. One of them is Marine City. There's a dock there that takes stone, and there's one up in Port Huron, which is actually Marysville, where we take stone. We usually take half a load to each place because the docks don't have the space to take full loads of certain products. Also, instead of going into Detroit to the Levy Dock, we go into two different docks there. We usually take a split load. Sometimes we'll take three cargo holds to one dock and one cargo hold to another. Or we'll take two and two. I have five cargo holds. They're all separated. I can separate but not contaminate all these products. We have hauled five cargoes at one time, and we have gone to three different docks with five cargoes.

The Dorothy Ann is disengaged from the Pathfinder every single time that we load. Every single time that we load, we have to take the pins out that connect the tug and barge. That's because, with the cargo going in, the barge settles in the water but the tug stays at the same level.

***

SNAPSHOT: The Dorothy Ann drafts run between 18 feet 3 inches and 20 feet 3 inches, depending on the amount of fuel that we have on or if we're de-ballasting or not de-ballasting. That depends upon circumstances, like levels in certain ports. But mostly the difference in draft is the amount of fuel that we burn.

***

When the barge is loaded, we re-pin the vessels, and we take off. When we get to the unloading port, we have to disengage the tug and barge because now the barge is going to rise in the water as it unloads and you re-pin it in at a different setting.

There are times that we physically get out of the notch because of where the dock boss wants cargo. If I get out of the notch, I can move the barge back an extra 100 feet by moving the tug out of the way to be able to unload the cargo.

Every dock we go to needs a security plan. That means that you have to have a list of the crew and of anybody who may be visiting the vessel or getting on or off the vessel. This is part of Homeland Security measures. We send a fax to the loading dock or the ore unloading dock.

Another communication is we have to send the dock boss a load plan – how we plan to load the vessel, so he has an idea how we're going to shift along the dock and what cargoes are going to go in which hold and in what amounts. That is also faxed.

At the same time, the loading docks have what they call a pocket list. For instance, if we go to Marquette, we're told how much product is in each pocket – each chute, or silo – that's there. Now you can plan your load, where you have to shift up and down the dock to get product. Sometimes a chute is broken down and out of use, and you have to work around that. You want to try to get so many tons in each hatch as you're moving along the dock. Most of what they call pockets, or the silos, that the ore is dumped into usually hold anywhere from two to 3½ railroad carloads per pocket. Each railroad car holds somewhere between 61 to 63 tons of product. So you count the number of carloads that go into each pocket, and that gives you an idea how much cargo you need to put forward or back or where it has to be in the vessel. And this way, you can plan your loading to start out at a certain area, and you progress to fill from all of its 19 pockets. You'll shift the barge back 12 feet, and you'll take the next 19. Then maybe you'll skip some pockets, and you'll go back and you'll take four in a row from one area or four in a row in another certain area. You'll load the barge up as you're going back. And then you might shift all the way back to get the end pockets, move up 12 feet and get all those pockets. Then you'll see how much cargo you have in the holds and which chutes are left and which ones you have to pick up and where you want to pick them up, how much you have to shift just to pick them up and get the cargo in the right area. You can't leave anything in a dock when you leave. The dock wants it all out, so when the next cargo comes in, the next boat comes in, it may change cargoes. There are two different types of ores from two mines that the dock can put in the chutes. So the dock wants the product all cleaned out. Just like when you're emptying out a ship, you want to clean it all out. That's the reason for faxing back and forth.

You also talk to the docks to give them a notice of your estimated time of arrival. At that time, they'll want to know what product you're starting with, just to have a little heads up in advance. Or they'll let you know, if there is no one at the dock at the time, how much delay there will be. And that's via telephone. Some docks have email access. Not too many. We may go to more than one dock, more than one port, on a trip. While we're on a time schedule, there may be delays. We give the docks an estimated time of arrival. If we're going to two docks, I give both a call and say, "Okay, we'll be at the first dock at such-and-such a time. We'll be there about 2½ hours, and then it takes us another hour-and-a-half to get up to your dock from there." It gives that dock boss a time schedule so he can call on his people. He'll usually say, "Okay, give us an hour call before you get to the dock also." That way he can have somebody there upon arrival.

Products

I'm mainly a stone boat. My cargoes are stone, various sizes and various types of stone. I also haul taconite, which is iron ore pellet, and I haul coal. Those are my main three ones. But I do haul coke, slag, mill scale – anything that can be gravity fed.

The stone is used for many, many products. Some of it is for roadbed, some for cement, some for decoration. Some of it is specialized stones for bridges and for crete span *(precast concrete)* for bridges. Some of it is cinder block. The stone is used in many, many products. And in large amounts. I would say most of it is used for road construction.

The washed stone which we move plenty of is for cement. What we call dirt stone – dirt with stone in it that was quarry-washed and is what's left over after stone is ground and made small – is used for driveways and road construction. Some of it is used for drain. Some of the stone we haul is used for making lime cement. Some of it is used for making lime, period. There's quite a variety.

The hardest stuff to unload is coal. It's very sticky. It doesn't want to flow very well. Another sticky cargo is gypsum, which is a very soft stone. It's used in making plaster board or drywall.

Sometimes the mill scale and certain sands are kind of hard to unload, but most of it flows pretty well.

The iron ore is made in Ishpeming, Michigan. It's made from a low-grade iron ore and put into a furnace and made into taconite, which is a higher-grade ore that can be put right into the furnaces. That taconite is shipped by railroad car to Marquette, and some of it goes to Escanaba. The railroad cars are run onto a great big loading dock, and the taconite is dropped from them into sort of a silo that's above the ground. Everything is loaded from the top down, gravity fed. The taconite dumps out of the train right into hoppers, for lack of a better word. From there, there's a chute that swings down onto the ship, and the guys there open up a gate, and the taconite all just runs into the ship.

Now, stone is brought from a quarry, and the big stones are brought to crushers and the big stone is dumped into the crushers and made into smaller

The Pathfinder takes on a load of taconite at the historic Lake Superior and Ishpeming Railroad dock at Marquette, Michigan.
Gary Schmidt photo

The Pathfinder is filled with coal for a short trip with its hatches open.
Gary Schmidt photo

stone. As the stone is filed through different screenings for different size stones, it falls on conveyor belts into different piles. From those piles there are tunnels underneath the ground where gates are opened up, and the stone falls onto belts that carry the stone off to the loaders at the ship's side. At most places, the quarry is fairly close, within a mile of the dock. Big trucks haul the stone to the crushers. At Port Inland, the quarry is a little more than three miles away, and the stone is brought by train to the crushers.

Grain comes to silos in ports via trucks mostly from farms. Grain is loaded overhead from the silos, and chutes distribute the grain inside the ship.

Coal comes from as far away as Montana, Wyoming, or wherever they mine coal. That's brought in by unit trains, and it's brought to facilities like Duluth or Chicago for the western coal. The eastern coal usually comes into Conneaut, Ashtabula, Sandusky, and Toledo. There, again, the coal is loaded into silos. Some of the facilties have what they call a reclaimer. With that, once the coal is dumped into a pile, a mechanism picks up the coal and dumps it onto a belt and then the belt ferries the coal sometimes to a silo or right straight onto a conveyor belt that goes into the ship. Now, at some facilities the train cars are brought right up into a dumper. Two railroad cars will be run into the dumper, which will turn the railroad cars upside down and dump the coal onto a belt, which carries the coal over to the shipside facility. It's really fun to watch as these big railroad cars, come in, are picked up, and turned over.

Other products are hauled. I don't haul them, but there are byproducts of the steel mills, like the slag. That's what's left over after steel is poured from the big kettles that have been lined with a kind of sand. The slag is brought by dump truck to a facility. The slag is put on front loaders, and there are little conveyors for loading into a ship.

***

SIDE TRIP: Coming into the vessel, the product is weighed by an electronic scale, and it's fairly accurate. As the product is coming across, it's measured by how much average that the bulk uses, and it's fairly accurate. It's within plus or minus two percent. But you also measure product by dead weight. You know the weight of your vessel. We have what they call a strapping table. It tells you that you are putting in this much of displacement, and that's going to equal that many tons. There's a way to figure that out from displacement.

We check the tonnages against what the scales say. Sometimes the scales are off. Some companies also have surveyors come down. They are people who take draft readings. They figure out how much water was left in after you de-ballasted the vessel. They figure out how much fuel weight you had, how much water weight, how much lube oil, how much storage weight and more. And they can figure very, very, very close to the tonnage of product. We can do the same thing with our books.

The surveyors are their own company. They're independent. The customer, or even our company, will hire a surveyor to come down and survey the vessel. How often depends upon the company. For instance, when we were hauling coal out of Chicago for DTE *(DTE Coal Services)*, a surveyor was always sent down. Before we'd start loading, the survey crew would take readings of draft marks, the ballasted position, and our water soundings. When we were done de-ballasting and the boat was loaded with cargo, they'd come back before we'd leave and take soundings again and try to figure out the fuel consumption. Basically, you might burn 1,000 or 1,500 gallons of fuel at a dock, which is going to be a ton. But the water sounding is the main thing. They know exactly what the boat weighs light. They have the strappings. But what the vessel weights light, what the vessel weighs loaded, it should say exactly how much cargo there is. It'll tell you how much cargo per inch. It'll tell you, if you have cargo that's on a slope, it's not going to be the same as you're first loading in as it is at the top. You're cargo-per-inch is going to be a lot less when you're starting out loading than it is when you finish. The surveyors call us before they come. Or the company will let us know, "You've got a surveyor coming." They can come on board. They come down and look at the vessel as you're making the dock. They'll grab the draft marks. And then we call them an hour or two before we're done, and they'll come down. Before you can sail, they'll take all the measurements again.

***

Which vessel in the fleet goes where is determined by Interlake. A lot of it has to do with the amount of cargo that a vessel can haul and the size of the vessel – if it can get into a facility. There might be a contract stipulating something, that this vessel will do. It's a combination of a bunch of things. Sometimes it's just who's available at the time.

You can say, "Hey, I want to do that," but that doesn't fly. I might say, "Okay, I haven't been to Green Bay *(home)* in a long time. How about sending me to Green Bay?" "Well, we're trying. We'll try to get you to Algoma or something." "But I can't get into Algoma." "I know that."

There's only so much cargo on the Great Lakes, and right now there's enough bottoms – or boats – to move it.

Hatch 59

Unloading

Usually when we finish loading and we know we're going to Such-and-Such Dock, we call up the dock boss and say, "Hey, we're going to be there. We're on our way there, and we'll be there in so many hours." That's so everybody can plan ahead. Each dock has a dock boss who comes down and watches the piles so unloading doesn't contaminate the dock's other piles. He keeps an eye on everything as we unload and tells us where he wants the cargo.

Time was, the Pathfinder's cargo holds were built differently than today. The holds had hoppers right in the middle of the barge, and the cargo would feed down to the belt. On the side was a short wall that kept the tunnel separated from the cargo. There were big garage doors that would be rolled up, and side scoops would come in there, unload, one on each side. The vessel hauled more cargo that way, but it was a much slower process. Today, the Pathfinder has slopes all the way to the top. The slopes create big voids on the sides, and probably 2,000 to 3,000 tons of cargo is lost. But the barge is unloaded in half the time.

The Pathfinder has a boom that swings over the side of the vessel. Inside a hold, the cargo falls down onto a belt because of the slopes. The cargo is gravity-fed onto a belt. That belt runs the whole length of the vessel. The cargo then is brought up by way of a conveyor with two belts, dumped on a hopper, dropped onto another belt on the boom, and poured onto a pile on the dock.

Once the cargo is starting to flow out on a dock, the mate is there to take care of ballast because, as the cargo goes out, ballast has to go into tanks to replace the weight.

If you're taking off half your cargo in a hold, you want to put on about half of your ballast. It is measured by heights. Depending on how many feet you have, you can tell exactly how much ballast you have. To the top of the tanks is almost 26 feet from the bottom of the vessel to the top of the ballast tank.

The weight that we're taking out is probably twice as much as the weight we're putting in ballast. We try to coordinate. If we're taking out half of the cargo, we're putting in half of the ballast. If we take out the rest of the cargo, we put in the rest of the ballast. You're doing it simultaneously, that you're taking cargo out and putting ballast in, or vice versa.

Taconite is unloaded from the Pathfinder at Cleveland, Ohio.
Gary Schmidt photo

You don't want to do what's called "blow the ballast tank." There are goose neck vent pipes on deck for the air to release and so water can't go back in easily. If you build up too much pressure in the ballast tanks, you'll blow the tanks. It doesn't take much pressure to blow a tank. Anywhere from three to six pounds of pressure can create a crack or bend a bulkhead and do a lot of damage. There is a goose neck at the forward end of the tank and one at the aft end on each ballast tank. They're about 10 inches in diameter. You have to watch them in the wintertime so that they're not frozen and you're adding water and the air can't escape.

After a trip on Lake Huron, stone is unloaded at Marysville, Michigan.
Jeremy Mock photo

As a hold is unloaded, the deckhands use hoses to wash the cargo down onto the belt and keep the vessel clean for when we get ready to turn around and get our next cargo. We want no contamination.

The old-fashioned way of unloading was by using Huletts *(steam-operated buckets)* that would pull the cargo out of the cargo holds. To unload would take maybe eight or 12 hours. Today, we unload in four hours.

We unload between 4,500 and 5,000 tons an hour. We could unload more. I think the system is built for unloading 5,700 long tons, which is quite a bit of cargo.

Some cargoes like coal will take longer to unload because they're so light that the coal fills the belt up, and you can't unload as many tons per hour. You have more volume than you do tonnage.

For the 2012-2013 season, Dorothy Ann/Pathfinder carried somewhere in the vicinity of 2.8 million short tons. That's mind boggling for one of the smaller ships. I'm one of the smaller ships, not in length but in cargo tonnage.

The tonnage our fleet carries is quite impressive. If you look at the thousand footers, they're doing 60,000 tons in a haul. And there's quite a few of those out there. They run 40 to 50 trips a year, each one. I'm doing shorter hauls. But the thousand footers will run over three million tons a year, every one of them.

***

SIDE TRIP: *While ships run seven days a week, any time of day, their time of arrival at a port in a city can be a problem.*

There are rules and regulations as to bridge hours. Some cities have certain hours during which vessels cannot go through the bridges. But most of the bridges are open for commercial vessels and not so much pleasure vessels.

Stone pours from the end of the Pathfinder's boom at Shiras Dock at Marquette, Michigan. *Gary Schmidt photo*

With a railroad bridge, Amtraks and mail trains have the right of way. If they're within 15 minutes of the bridge when you arrive, you will wait for the mail train/Conrail passenger train. Other than that, if I'm there before the 15 minutes, usually the tenders will open the bridge and let me on through, and they'll hold up the train.

For car bridges, most cities have done away with the bridge hours for the commercial vessels, and the bridges open upon signal.

We give security calls before we come into every port, stating that we are inbound. For instance, Green Bay: "We're at the Green Bay entrance light, and we'll be at Tower Drive Bridge in approximately one hour." That's in case there's another vessel greeting us — coming out of the channel, or coming in. A lot of the times, a lot of the bridges have radios on them, and the tenders will pick up on those call signals. That's especially the case in Cleveland, where all the bridges have radios.

***

Unloading will take up four hours. When we go to the steel mill, unloading takes about three hours. Stone is about 3½ to four hours.

We have to keep ballast water in the barge. If I don't have any ballast in it, my bow will probably go up to around six feet of water. Around six feet of water, my bow thruster tube is out of the water, and I don't have any maneuverability.

***

SIDE TRIP: On the Dorothy Ann, we have two engines strictly for propulsion. We have two generators that are just for electricity, with a third for emergency. The generators on the tug are 200 kilowatt.

The barge has its own electrical system. The barge has a 1,600-kilowatt generator for the unloading system and a 250-kilowatt generator for when we are not unloading, just for lighting.

The barge's propulsion in the bow thruster works off the unloading generator. We usually don't unload and need a bow thruster at the same time. When the big generator is not used for unloading, we transfer the power to the bow thruster, which is a 1,000-horsepower motor that turns the propeller for the bow thruster.

***

I have unloaded three cargoes at three different docks. You have to know the sequence of docks you are traveling to. When you are loading, you have to know what dock you're going to, and which product is coming off first so you don't do harm to the vessel. You figure, "We're going to Toledo, to Ashtabula, to Fairport." I have to know, in order, where I'm starting off with unloading. There are a lot of variations I can do. But you've got to figure it out, and it's a job. That's the first mate's job. He works very hard at it.

And quite often a dock we work with will change orders. We come into a dock prepared, and now the first mate has to get out of bed and get up and change the load plan. But that's his job. He has to consult me. For each plan, he usually consults me. He asks me what our depth should be and talks about the sequence of loading the cargoes and where they're going to.

For unloading at night, we have big floodlights on the boat that light up the area pretty well.

The boom has big floodlights on it, so you light up the pile. We have a camera at the end of the boom, so you can watch the unloading process of the product going into the pile. The guy in the boom shack, from which you control the boom, watches the camera and watches the boom. As the pile is building up, you've got to make sure that it doesn't come up and bury the end of the boom. You have to raise the boom and keep an eye on it.

There are a lot of things to be watching. If you're stable and the boom all of a sudden takes cargo, it tips the boat because you have a lot of weight on the end of that boom. So you make an adjustment with ballast to bring the end of the boom back up.

Now, when we're going from cargo hold to cargo hold to unload, as the product is emptied from one cargo hold, the boom will come up a little bit. As we start to empty the next cargo hold, the boom will go back down again, and it might be heavy. So you've got to be careful that the end of the boom doesn't hit the pile. You've got to have a certain amount of space between the end of the boom and the pile. The mate on watch adjusts the ballast. There's a sequence.

If you're unloading in cargo hold Number 3, cargo hold 3 is over the top of ballast tanks 5 and 6 – so as you're unloading the cargo, you're putting water back in those two tanks. As you're removing cargo, you want to add weight to compensate so not too much stress is put on the vessel.

We have a loading and unloading program on the vessel that tells us how much stress you're putting on the vessel as you're doing this. It's computerized. In the past, they used a formula. I don't know what it is. I just know, if you're taking weight out, you've got to put weight in. A lot of it is just common sense.

We have a ballast schedule. If you're taking product out of cargo hold 4, it's ballast tank 7 and 8. One and 2 are under cargo hold 1. Three and 4 are under 2. Ballast number 9 is the very last, the back rake of the barge where there is no cargo. There is no cargo in the forward peak. We usually leave the forward peak empty at all times, and we put more weight into number 9 to get the stern down.

You can see over the A-frame better when the vessel is in ballast. It puts the barge down farther into the water so you have a better connection system when the pins are extended to connect the tug and barge.

After unloading, there are basic things that are done. They include cleaning the vessel, getting ready for the next product, or, if we've loaded at a port, cleaning the vessel on the outside so you don't contaminate.

***

SIDE TRIP: The guys wear boots, and they wear protective gear all the time. Even in the summertime when it's super hot out, you can't wear shorts. You have to wear long pants or coveralls. You have to wear hard hat gear when you're unloading. We have two great big coolers that we fill with ice water or Gatorade, for electrolytes. A lot of guys like to work without gloves in the summertime, but in the wintertime they all wear gloves.

***

You always have to worry about separation of products. We haul more than one product at one time. When the wind blows, it might blow product over to the next cargo hold where you don't want it. So if you're shoveling product up, you don't want to shovel it into the wrong cargo hold.

Everything has to be cleaned to a degree. When you're unloading, the vessel is completely washed out. The gates that open up underneath the cargo holds and let the cargo onto the belt are washed off. The water comes right from the lake. We open a seacock, which lets the water in. We have a couple of pumps that are equivalent to any fire pump that you see. There's 100 pounds of pressure on them. They're electrically driven.

The cargo that falls off the belt is shoveled back onto the belt, and all that stuff is run off before we unload or load the next product. It's all cleaned totally. That's the main job. Loading and unloading, hosing, and shoveling are constant work. That's known work.

If you're underway, depending on the length of the trip, it depends on what projects you can do if you want to get certain things done. There's a certain amount of painting that has to be done, there's a certain amount of maintenance that has to be done. On the long runs, we get painting done when it's a nice day. There's certain painting on the inside if it's not a nice day. All of our paint is oil based. You try to keep the boat looking decent, and it's got to be fairly clean.

Belts

The Pathfinder is loaded and unloaded using "V"-shaped belts that move product.

When unloading, the cargo is gravity-fed onto a belt. That belt runs the whole length of the vessel. It comes up through an HAC, or High Angle Conveyor, which has two belts. The cargo is slipped in between those two belts, and the conveyor brings the cargo up and around into a hopper. The cargo drops down onto another belt, which is the boom belt. The boom swings out over the side of the barge, and cargo spills off into piles on the dock.

We do wear out belts. We have belt maintenance people come in a couple of times a year. There are a lot of things that can wear out on a belt. The belt is every bit of an inch thick, and in many plies. You just don't replace a belt when gets torn or ripped. Belt maintenance people come in and cut the belt and pull it apart. In different layers, they cut it apart. Then they splice it back together and re-vulcanize it to where you can't even tell that it was torn apart.

The average belt on a self-unloader — the main belt or even a boom belt — lasts approximately 10 years. That's at a cost of maybe half a million dollars to replace on a footer *(1,000-footer)*, and probably a little bit less for me. I'm not sure on the numbers, but I know the belts are expensive. Some are pretty much standardized throughout the fleets, and there is like a fleet insurance policy where there always are a couple of belts on hand that can go to various ships, and of different sizes.

If there are dings and gouges on the outer side, it doesn't really matter. Problems come with contamination. Something may have fallen off a piece of equipment. Steel is our worst fear. If you get a shot of steel and it goes down through the belt and you don't see it, the steel can cut into the belt. As the belt is running, it slices it right down the middle. By the time you stop the belt, you're going to have 200 to 300 feet of a slice, and that's a little tougher repair. It can be repaired, but it's a tougher repair. Once the belt is repaired, it's all

V-shaped belts carry product to a cargo hold of the Pathfinder at Marblehead, Ohio. *Gary Schmidt photo*

pressed and sealed, and the repairmen heat it up. When the repair dries, you can't even tell where that splice is.

Other problems are misalignment and failure of rollers and pulleys.

As the belt travels the length of the ship, it goes up through the loop and comes back down. This is the outer belt. On the inside, there's a shorter belt. As material is dropped onto the belt and cargo comes to a joining point, it gets caught between the two belts and is brought up. It's real tight. There's a hopper that the material drops into. In the hopper are chains. There are wear plates. From that hopper, the cargo drops onto the belt for the boom, which is just a straitlaced boom belt with nothing fancy about it. That boom can turn 90 degrees from its base. The material drops off from the end of the boom.

The A-frame holds all of the mechanism together. The system includes a hydraulic motor, rollers on the belts, a hydraulic device that holds the material tight, a tensioner – all electronics, all on computer, automatically adjusting.

Hatch 61

Dognapping

We were in Ludington, Michigan. We were picking up salt water for a barge. Another captain was on the boat with me. He was my equal. We worked six and six *(six hours on, six hours off)* so he ran his watch, and I ran mine. We went into town in Ludington. On the way back, there were a couple of dogs on the loose, and one of them just kept on following us back toward the boat. So he said, "Well, I could use a dog. Do you think it belongs to somebody?" I said, "I know it belongs to somebody." But he decided he was going to take the dog back anyway. So he took it on the boat with him. And going across Lake Michigan, the dog got seasick. I mean, it threw up all over the room. And we shared a room. So, thanks. As we got to Chicago, he was getting off, and he took the dog home. He thought the dog would be good for his daughter. And it was. The daughter was good with the dog. But his wife was allergic to it. So the son called up the Ludington paper and asked if anybody was missing a Chinese Pug. And somebody said, "Yeah." And so they took the dog to the Badger car ferry *(which runs between Manitowoc and Ludington)*, put it on there, and told the owners that it was coming back over to them.

Weather effects

There are places where you think about weather.

From Whitefish Point to Marquette on Lake Superior in the wintertime can be really unpredictable. Sometimes you might have to run to the north shore and get the right angle on the weather so you can make it. You don't want to get caught in a rolling situation.

And then in the summertime the same place can be flat and calm, and just look like water on a platter. You think back on the same place and remember thinking, "Wow, this is wintertime. This is different."

Great Lakes vessels run in extreme cold and in extreme heat.

There's an interesting thing about the heat and your load when you go through the Welland Canal. *(The canal's maximum permissible draft is 26 feet on average.)* Now, if you're overloaded, you're charged extra. There's a price. You might have loaded at 26 feet, level. As the heat comes on, you'll get a bend in your vessel's steel. Now you might be 26 feet one inch. So you'll see as some boats are going through the Welland Canal that the captains have water run on the deck. The ships have a sprinkler system to keep the steel cooled so the vessel doesn't bend. The bend is on the bottom. What happens is the metal will expand and will bend the ship down *(on the bottom)*. In the wintertime, it can have an opposite effect because the steel is contracting above the water and it's pulling the vessel together.

Wind is a perpetual factor.

Loading at Marblehead can be a mess if it's windy. The wind blows the stone dust into

The Dorothy Ann carves a path through ice.
Gary Schmidt photo

the boat. There's a lot of shoveling the deckhands have to do. It's a tough job. They shovel, and it's still a mess. Marblehead is an open port on Lake Erie. A south wind there is really good because that helps where we're loading. The worst weather we can have is out of the east. If you get anything out of the east, or north and east, with any velocity, it's really hard to load. You stand off and wait for the weather to blow out, or the company sends you to another port to load. If you've started loading, then you're kind of stuck because you've already started a cargo. If you get it loaded far enough, you can kind of hang in there. I'll use engines and bow thrusters and a lot of tricks to help me out. But there are certain points where you can't.

SNAPSHOT: *The Dorothy Ann/Pathfinder is part of the National Weather Service Digital Marine Weather Dissemination System. When possible, weather observation reports are filled out every hour — "and it's got to be sent in six minutes to the hour," Captain Schmidt said.*

The entry form starts with the vessel's radio call sign and password.

The electronic form goes on to blanks to fill in for day of month, time, latitude, longitude, wind speed in knots, direction of wind in degrees of compass, wave height in feet, wave period in seconds, air temperature in Fahrenheit or Celsius (converted automatically in the electronic form), dew point in Fahrenheit or Celsius, barometric pressure in inches or millibars, code for pressure tendency (nine codes), three-hour change in pressure, code for visibility, lake water temperature in Fahrenheit or Celsius, observed present weather, code for past weather (ten codes), total cloud cover in octas (ten possibilities), amount of low and mid clouds present, code for height of lowest cloud base (ten possibilities), and codes of ten possibilities each for low clouds, mid clouds, high clouds, ship's true course, and ship's average speed.

This information is part of a huge electronic network that includes text and graphics for current and forecast conditions.

***

SIDE TRIP: What I usually use is U.S. MAFOR Codes *(see page 317)*. It's a lot easier for me to read a forecast in a five-digit code. That goes a lot faster for me because it's ingrained in my brain what each code number is. You can get the forecasts lake by lake.

***

One of the tools that I use is a Great Lakes forecast map. I use a computer website with NOAA *(National Oceanic and Atmospheric Administration)* weather service maps. The maps give me an idea of what the weather is doing at the present, and then you can advance the maps three hours at a time for the next five days to give you an idea of what's going to be happening. I like that a lot. The website gives me such conditions as sea heights by color code. What I usually use that site for is wind speed and wind direction. The forecast map shows wind speed with flag symbols. Each one of the flags is 10 knots. Half a flag is 5 knots. *(A knot is 1.151 miles an hour.)* The flag shows speed and direction. You can advance the forecast map and see what the weather is going to do in three-hour increments. I use that tool a lot. I can advance it up to five days. For instance, if the weather's going to be strong out of the north coming out of Marquette, I might shoot right straight up to the north shore and work my way back down into the Whitefish Bay. There is no safe harbor between Whitefish Bay Point and Marquette. That's just about all cliffs with no place to go in and hide. That is about 100 miles. You're not going fast. You can't race.

When you're loaded, you have less sail effect on the barge because there's so much

The Dorothy Ann/Pathfinder heads into a patch of ice.
Gary Schmidt photo

Feel forlorn? A lighthouse is cloaked by winter.
Gary Schmidt photo

of the hull that's under the water line that the wind doesn't affect you so much. When you're in ballast and the wind is quite high, there is a sail effect. You may not realize how much it is. I've gone into a port with the wind blowing hard out of the northeast, and I would come in on an angle because the wind is blowing me down. By the time I come in, I'm coming through the gap at a different angle. Ideally, you want to go straight ahead, but you have to take the wind into consideration. You hold the vessel at an angle, and, as the wind blows you down, you keep on bringing it around. You have to play the wind. You have to do that a lot.

The vessel is pretty good into wind on beam up until between 26 and 29 miles an hour. After that, I start to lose it. I can't hold it.

***

SIDE TRIP: ICE BASHING: Many times when I was captain of the Donald C. Hannah, I would take an oil barge from Chicago to St. Joseph/Benton Harbor, Michigan. Once I got

There is a vessel underneath all the white. Thick layers of ice coat the tug Donald C. Hannah during particularly wicked winters in the early 1970s.
Gary Schmidt photo

into St. Joe, I'd unload the barge and then my cargo would be mixed with some other oil, and I'd reload and then head back to Chicago and deliver that oil to somebody else. From the time I left the Chicago locks until I got to St. Joe *(in the southeast corner of Michigan)*, it normally would be four or five hours

One winter when I went over there, the wind had been blowing out of the northwest for a long time, and all the ice was built up down in that part of Lake Michigan. St. Joe had two miles of really heavy duty ice. This ice was as high as the bow of the tug, which was about 14 feet out of the water. I disconnected from my barge and shoved the barge into the ice as best I could. When I'd ram into that ice at pretty good speed and back out, I could see my whole bow print in the ice. It was kind of slushy ice. It was build up. It wasn't packed. It wasn't hard hard, but it was packed because of a big, three-day storm before that. I'd back out and run up a little way and I'd go in as fast as I could and in as far as I could and at the last moment when I wasn't moving ahead anymore, I'd give a twist and break out a great big chunk of ice. It would roll like a growler, like a small iceberg.

It took me 50 hours to do a four-hour run, just to get into St. Joe breaking ice. Four hours over there and the rest of it was breaking to get into the port. It was tiring, let me tell you. You're up in the pilothouse working for six hours, and the next guy would come up and work for six hours. You try to sleep with all that ice breaking, you can't do it. Your room's right there where the tug is breaking ice, and you were just doing the best you could to get a little nap here and there.

*** ***

SIDE TRIP: GEYSERS: While on the Donald C. Hannah, I'd also go to Ludington, Michigan, in winter. We'd come in through the breakwall and into Pere Marquette Lake. We'd go to Dow Chemical, which was far into the lake. Beyond that, there was still more lake, and there would be fish shanties.

When the lake froze, I'd have to break ice. I'd just drop the barge off in the ice, and I'd break a path to the dock. Then I'd make a couple of speed runs.

Well, the Donald Hannah used to throw a big wake – four to five feet, maybe six feet and sometimes more depending on space we were in. When I'd make a speed run, the tug would break the ice for 100 feet on both sides. The ice would just crack it up. If you were lucky and the wind was blowing out of the east, the ice would clear out and flow out into Lake

Captain Schmidt is at the helm of the tug Donald C. Hannah around the time of adventures in ice at Ludington, Michigan.
Photo courtesy Gary Schmidt

Michigan. If you weren't lucky, the ice would re-freeze. Sometimes you'd make two speed runs.

Every time I'd make a speed run toward the dock, I'd see guys from the ice shacks come out and shake their fist at me. I didn't realize that the water was going underneath and then shooting up through their ice holes. One time I ran into a guy who said, "You soaked me so many times." It wasn't intentional. I didn't know that I was doing that. After that, the radio station put out a report when tugs were coming in.

*** *** ***

SIDE TRIP: HUGE WAVE: In the spring of 1973, I was towing the Sea Castle with the Lauren Castle. We were in ballast and headed for Petoskey, Michigan, to pick up a load of cement. There were gale warnings up. I thought I could make it across Lake Michigan and get to protection and get into Little Traverse Bay and go to anchor until the weather subsided. Because you kind of wallow in big waves, the cable on the stern kept rubbing on the stern, and the tow line broke. The barge went aground.

We looked to get to safe haven with the tug. It was a Force 7 gale. We had winds that were 70 and 80 miles an hour. I was trying to ease into the waves. If you go full force into them, you just bury the tug. As I would get into a wave that's starting to crest, I would pull back the engine power and get a little bit better ride and get up to the top and then I'd give the engine a little bit more power, and we'd ride down to the bottom.

Then I looked at this one wave. In the Lauren Castle, the eye level was 18 feet. It wasn't very high off the water, but it was high enough. I was looking under the pilothouse visor to be able to see the top of the wave, and I went to pull back my throttle for more power, and it was already back. We rode it out. This was a huge wave. It was more than 25 feet high.

That is the biggest single wave that I can remember going through. There were several that were big behind it. Most were over 20.

When you get waves that size, and they're running from a long range across a lake, you try to head into them and not take the rest of the ride, the rolling. You ride the wave up until you get the right angle, and then you can take a turn on a wave and then you can head the other way and put the wave on your stern for a while and ride a little bit better.

*** *** ****

It's nice to get off the lake in heavy seas and get into safe haven, especially when you're coming off Lake Superior. If you can round that corner up at Whitefish Point and get into the Whitefish Bay, it's a big relief sometimes, knowing you have to make that turn coming into Whitefish Bay. I've had stern seas that were twentysome feet. Knowing that you have to take seas a little bit on the beam, which you don't want to do, as you're coming around that corner, I've had waves wash across the deck. I've had blue water coming across the deck, and that's kind of scary. You get all that extra weight when the waves are washing over. Things can happen. But you plan on it, and you try to be able to hold your course as long as you can before you make that turn, and you try to keep the rough sea to a minimum of one to two miles until you're back into safe haven again. You really don't want to be in that kind of a sea on a beam sea. But I have done it. It's REALLY nice to get into safe haven when you're in weather like that.

There are times when you just don't go into weather. You don't jump out into 20-foot seas. You just don't do it, not unless you know the wind forecast is on its way down, and it's going to be going down. But if it's still building, you just wait to fight another day.

Most of the time you can sail. There are very few times that you have to go to anchor for the weather, unless it's heading up Lake Huron or down Lake Michigan or up Lake Michigan. Unless it's a true north and south wind, and you're into it, and you're in Chicago and it's due north and you're going to be bucking it for 300 miles, you just don't do stuff like that. Then you take a break. But if you know that it's 20 feet now and in a few hours it's going to be down to 16 and a few more hours it's going to be down to 10 and diminishing, then, yeah, you can take off and take a beating for a little while, and it will come down. The farther north you go the less it will be.

There are circumstances where you just play the weather. You have to do. What you try to do is use the weather to your advantage.

You're always improvising. It doesn't seem like anything's ever the same.

To do what you're doing and playing the weather is a little bit like gambling because you're playing the odds. You play what you think you can get by with, and sometimes it's a little bit of a gamble.

Your job is to keep that ship moving the best you can. You don't want to be lying at anchor. You're not making money when you're lying at anchor. You want to keep it moving, and at all times if you can.

But if you're going to be fighting a sea for 300 miles and it's going to be slowing you down and you're going to be checked back and you're going to be burning fuel and you're not going to be making any more time than if you would've sat at anchor with the engine shut down and you're only going to make four or five more hours, it doesn't make sense to burn up the fuel. There are times when it doesn't make sense to run. But most of the time you do.

Hatch 63

Anchors

We have two anchors on the barge and one on the tug.

I'll anchor for a weather condition.

I'll anchor when a dock is not available. There might be another vessel in the dock, or there may be a problem with the dock, and the dock boss will say he doesn't want us at the dock yet.

I'll anchor for a machinery problem. If there's something not functioning right and you want to get it fixed before you enter a river or a dock – or something's not quite right – you go to anchor and repair a problem.

If terrorists would attack, Homeland Security will order you away from the dock and put you to anchor.

***

SNAPSHOT: On the main deck, we have a big floodlight that we turn on for nighttime. Homeland Security requires that we have something to shine on the anchor so people can't climb aboard at night. That's another thing that was put in since 9/11.

***

What we call a shot for an anchor is 90 feet. I have six shots on one side, which is 540 feet. I have four, maybe five, shots on the other side where the anchor chain is bolted to the bulkhead.

The anchors are two hooks sticking up with a shaft up the middle. Those two hooks will pivot either way. When the anchor is down, the two prongs will hook nicely if you're in sand or a muddy bottom. If you're on rocks, the prongs might skip across the rocks until they find a toehold.

I wouldn't anchor in the middle of the lake. We would drift or float. Many times, we're in over that 540 feet.

On an anchor, you want a scope of about 3 to 1 to your depth. They recommend 5 to 1, but the length depends on how strong the wind is blowing.

If we're in 40 feet of water, I'll put out 120 feet of chain. I'll say, "Give me a shot and a half." Or two shots, depending on how deep the water is.

An anchor fits snugly into the body of the Pathfinder. *Gary Schmidt photo*

If the wind is blowing stronger, I'll add three shots or 3½ shots. That's on Lake Erie.

If we're anchoring off of Stoneport, Michigan, you're anchoring in somewhere between 70 to 100 feet of water. So there you're going to be three and maybe four shots in the water.

If you go to anchor in the St. Marys River, you're going to put out one shot. It's sheltered water.

***

SIDE TRIP: PIECE OF HISTORY: On our way the Dow Chemical Dock at Ludington, Michigan, in the early '80s, I was towing a barge with the tug Donald C. Hannah. We had 1,200 to 1,500 feet of towing cable out. As we got near the dock, I slowed the tug. When you start slowing down with the tug, the barge keeps on traveling from momentum and the cantenary *(curve from hanging)* in the cable drops down lower. You try to pull it up so it doesn't drag. If you slow down too fast, the barge will catch up to you a little bit, and the cable will drag low in the water. As we were going along, we picked up something in the water. As we reached the break wall, we brought the tow line up by winch, and here's another anchor on our line. As we brought the line in, the anchor slid down the cable onto the stern of the tug.

Now we have this big anchor on the tug. It was about seven feet high with flukes about five feet across. It was one with wood on it at the top. The anchor was more than likely from a large, wooden schooner. It was under water for at least 100 years because most of the schooners were off the lakes by the turn of the last century.

As we got into the Dow Chemical Dock *(today owned by OxyChem)*, we told the dock guys that we had an anchor and we needed to get it off. A small crane was brought down to take it off. I was asked, "What do you want to do with it?" I said, "We don't really want it." Dow took it and had some experts down to look at it. We didn't take it off the bottom on purpose, and we don't know where we hooked up with it. We could have dragged it from Chicago all the way up. Who knows? My guess is we probably picked it up in Michigan waters. There are laws about preserving relics on the bottom. You cannot take them or move them. But this thing fell in our lap – literally fell on the tug.

From stories I read, the old schooners had what's called a slip anchor. If they sailed into a port and the conditions weren't favorable at the time, they would drop the anchor with a buoy. If weather came up that was going to push the vessel on shore, they would put up their sails, slip their anchor, and take off and come back and retrieve their anchor later. Or the anchor chain could have broken. When they tried to put the anchor down, they might not have been quite slow enough and as the chain fetched up, it might have snapped.

We don't know what vessel it came off of. There were no markings to indicate what vessel it came from.

Dow got some experts, who preserved the wood. The anchor was put on a base in front of the Dow office in Ludington. *(Today, the anchor is in storage at Historic White Pine Village in Ludington. The museum's description of "70962 anchor" is "84-inch long steel and wood anchor. wood cross bar 111 inches across. large steel ring in center of wood beam, tip to tip of steel anchor hooks is 60 inches. wood greatly deteriorated." A major project is under way at the former Coast Guard station at Ludington. Operating from White Pine Village until scheduled completion in 2014 is the Port of Ludington Maritime Museum. Information as of this writing is at www.historicwhitepinevillage.org).*

*** ***

SIDE TRIP: HOT WIRE: Curly Selvick was captain in 1973 when we were hauling cement at Milwaukee. The weather was rough, and we went to anchor on the north side of the inner harbor. There's a cable the runs from Milwaukee inner harbor out to the lighthouse. It's what powers the lighthouse. As we were picking up the anchor, we must have been moving a little bit, and there was a strain in the chain. I said, "Curly, we've got something hooked on the anchor." He said, "Well, when you get it up in sight, if it's any good, we'll keep it." I said, "Oh, I think it's a power cable." He said, "Drop the hook! Drop the hook!" So we dropped it back down, and the cable released itself, and we did not break or damage the cable.

*** *** ***

SIDE TRIP: IN THE DRINK: Also, with Selvick there was the time I fell in the water. It was 1969, my first year sailing on the tug. Cable was fouled on the anchor, all wound up. We were trying to cut it out with a torch. I couldn't quite reach where the cable was. There's a big shackle that runs through the stem of the barge that a tow line hooks up to in case you have to tow the barge. I had one foot on the tug and one foot on the cable area. I was cutting with the torch, and all of a sudden the shackle fell down the other way, and I went into the water. I fell about 15 feet, feet first. I swam to shore and almost got myself out, but somebody came and helped. We had a rule back then. If you went into the water and guys pulled you out, you owed them a case a beer. So I bought a case of beer for the crew.

*** *** ***

We don't drop anchor at a dock. We're moored there.

We always do what we call clear anchor coming into a dock. You have all the anchors cleared and set to go down. If you have a mechanical failure, or if something weird happens that could disrupt you, you have an emergency plan to drop the anchor and slow the vessel down before you smash into something. For example, a boat might get in your way, and you can't slow the vessel to avoid it.

That's for every port that we go into. Every river we go into, we always clear the anchors. As we approach the confined spaces of the Detroit River or the Cuyahoga River, the anchors are cleared 15 minutes before.

When the anchors are up in their pockets, we have keepers on them so in case something fails, the anchors can't fall when you're under way or the anchors get rattled around by heavy seas.

There are two brake releases. If the bow watch person who is giving distances sees something happen or I can see I'm not going to make a turn in the river, we can drop that anchor. That's standard procedure every time.

The anchor machinery is up forward on the boat in what's called the windlass room, for the anchor windlass that picks up the anchor and puts it back down. There are two chain hawse pipes that the anchor rests in. Through the hull, right directly under the chain, is what we call a pocket. When the anchor comes up, the flukes fit into the pocket that kind of fits flat on the hull of the boat. One link is crosswise from the other link. The chain shoots straight down another pipe that goes down through a couple of decks into what we call the chain locker. It kind of stacks the chain up back and forth. As the chain comes up, there's water that squirts down and cleans off the anchor chain and the anchor as they are coming up through the hull of the ship.

To put the anchor down, you can free wheel it – once you release the brake, it will free wheel to drop the anchor – or we can engage the anchor and we can set it down slowly, the same way we pick it up. Most of the time, we do what we call walking it out of the box. That way, the anchor is free of the anchor box, and it's in a hanging position ready to let go. When we get ready to anchor – while I'm maneuvering and getting the vessel stopped and getting to the position where I want to anchor – two guys are getting the anchor ready to drop free wheel. I'm doing this by verbal command by walkie-talkie. We also have a backup system, the loud hailer. It is very noisy in that anchor windlass room when things are happening. The guys wear head phones, and we have walkie-talkies with head gear so we can communicate.

Once I determine where I want the anchor dropped, I verbally command them to drop the anchor, and they let the anchor free wheel out until it hits the bottom. Then they tell me how much chain there is. For each 90-foot shot, we have a painted area. The first shot has a link painted red, a white link, and a red link. That's 90 feet of chain. The second shot has a link painted red on both ends, and it has two white links in the middle. That's two shots. That's 180 feet. That helps us know about where we're at. The guys will watch the lines as they go out. They'll say, "One shot, two shots," or one shot will go out and it will hit the bottom and stop. They'll report to me, "Okay, we have one shot out of the hawse pipe, the second one is down underneath it in the chain locker yet." I'll make a determination how much I want out depending upon the depth of the water, how hard the wind is blowing, if the vessel is loaded or not loaded, what kind of bottom we have, and the stability of the hooks sticking into the bottom to hold us.

Hatch 64

Growing tomatoes

I'm a nut for fresh tomatoes. I love fresh tomatoes with a salt shaker. The ones you get from the store are green and artificially ripened, and they taste terrible. So I had the guys build a box, and we filled it with dirt. The planter was made from leftover parts boxes for engine parts. We just made the boxes a little bit tighter and drilled holes in the bottom, put a little bit of stone in the bottom, and then I put dirt over the top of the stone. At one of the docks, we had one of the dock guys with a front end loader come down and scoop up a little dirt and just dump it over the side of the barge, and that was good enough. I bought tomato plants and planted them. Because it was a shallow box and, as much water as we have all around us, the wind that goes past dries the dirt out incredibly fast. So every day, the planter had to be watered. Because of the evaporation, I eventually went out and got some mulch. As the plants grew, the buds came out. Because of the lack of bees out on the Great Lakes, I had to take my Q-tip up to the box and artificially pollinate each bud. I took a Q-tip and went across to the next plant. I used the same Q-tip day after day. When new buds came out, I pollinated them as they came along.

I just planted six plants. The tomatoes were plum-size. Out of my six plants, I ended up with 219 tomatoes. And, boy, was I in tomato heaven.

This was on the Dorothy Ann/Pathfinder. I had the planter up on the bow of the Pathfinder so the bow would shield the plants from the wind as we were going forward. The planter was up under the gunnel. I had the guys set up a watering station so I could just take lake water and go up there with two watering cans and water the plants every day.

You bet the tomatoes were off limits. They were Gary's. They were mine. They were off limits. But I let everybody taste them.

At the end of the season, I picked the green ones, about 30 or 40 of them, and I put them in a cardboard box in my window. I just let them ripen on their own, and they did. I had tomatoes up into October.

Captain Schmidt is proud of the tomatoes grown aboard the Pathfinder.
Gary Schmidt photo

Hatch 65

Maintenance and requirements

Painting and maintenance are a constant, ongoing battle. Major maintenance is done during winter, but we have a lot of maintenance to do during the season.

As much as we're moving and as much as we're doing, we don't have a lot of time. All the ships used to, when the crews fit out, get everybody out there to paint the vessel on both sides. They would get it all done at the layup dock. Years ago, crews wouldn't come out to the layup dock as early as they come out now, and the vessels would lay up a lot earlier than what they do now. So a lot of that maintenance could be done at the dock. They had bigger crews, and they would just get the painting done.

Today, when the vessel goes to dry dock every five years, it gets put up, and it gets a re-paint on the outer hull.

The rest of the painting – like the decks and the cowlings *(metal coverings)*, the hatch covers, and then the houses – we can do ourselves. But we do it when we have time to do it. And it's an ongoing, every year, thing. If we don't get it all done this year, we'll work on it next year.

Usually, important areas are painted on a yearly basis, like the decks and hatch covers. The crew is constantly cleaning the vessel, getting ready for the next product. When we're unloading, the vessel is completely washed out. The gates that open up underneath the cargo holds are washed off. Hosing and shoveling are constant work. Because of all the washing down and hosing the decks, material that's on the decks wears the paint off, and the deck gets very slippery. We have to maintain that by cleaning it off, painting it, and putting a non-skid surface on it so you don't slip, fall, and get hurt.

As far as the houses go, we don't have to re-paint every year. We try to get to that when the house starts to look on the dingy side. Then we start renewing the paint. Over time, the paint is put on layer after layer in some places, but on the decks the surfaces get pretty well worn down every year. We try to scrape and brush down to where the bare metal is showing so we can primer that. But if the paint has adhered very well, we'll feather that in and paint up to that area and over it.

Overall, there's a lot of equipment to be maintained. We're self-sustained. Everything is there aboard the vessel. You load yourself, you unload yourself.

Maintenance includes rewinding winches and making sure that the wires are straight on winches, greasing the windlass, greasing all the winches and making sure that everything on them is working properly, setting the clamps on the hatch covers so you clamp them down and they fit properly and maintain a seal.

Rollers on the unloading system wear out and have to be changed. Hydraulics have to be checked because there are parts that are always moving – the gates opening and the gates closing. The lips on gates get damaged when a stone becomes wedged. That might move the seal a little bit so you have product running off onto the belt. That seal might have to be cut off to put a new piece of steel on it. Or sometimes you can bend the seal back into place with a hydraulic ram to make a nice seal again.

The pins that go into the side of the barge and hold us in place have to be greased inside and out. There are grease ports.

Our jockey winches have to be maintained. Any winch has to be maintained.

The motors and the uniflows for the unloading system have to be maintained.

Our pumps – scavenger pumps that pump water out as the guys are hosing down – have to be maintained.

There's belt maintenance, inspections for maintenance.

The boom maintenance includes hosing that off for cleaning for changing products. Inside the hoppers where the loop belt comes up and drops product down into the hopper before it goes on the unloading belt, or the boom belt, are chains that hang down. They're so rocks hit them and not the hard steel on the other side. The chains wear out. Going down past the hardened steel plates you have grating. The material wears the grating out before it gets to the outer plate. As all of this wears down, we have to go in there and hang new chain or cut out those grating plates and put replacements in there. Even the heavy duty hardened steel wear plates wear out. We try to have that done in wintertime, but if we're doing a lot of stone and a lot of bigger stone, those things wear out and chains wear thin and all this stuff finally just gives out and has to be replaced. We do that during the season.

There's rubber skirting so when the stone hits the belt it can't fly off onto the deck. If you start to wear the skirting out and there's a hole, material flows out, and you get a big pile. Several tons of stone will fall out. If it happens while we're unloading, we'll shut down for a half an hour, and we'll replace the skirting. We have certain pieces made up, and we can just unbolt the worn part, set in a new piece, and bolt the replacement section down.

The stone is like a grinder. It just grinds away steel, grinds away everything that's in its way when it's moving with such force – all the time. When you're moving 2.8 million tons through that system, it does a lot of wear and tear. And so there's major maintenance that we do on the run.

In the tunnel, there's wear from water and stone, and little cracks or holes develop. All that gets cropped out and re-done, and we try to do that under way. We'll have the Coast Guard come down and look at the area, and then we'll hire an outside firm to

A crewman heads up a ladder to paint the Pathfinder's pilothouse tower.
Gary Schmidt photo

Washing hatches is a never-ending job aboard the Pathfinder.
Gary Schmidt photo

ride the boat and do the cropping so we don't have any down time.

Steel in separation bulkheads can wear thin. We mark the wear spots and have the panels cropped out and replaced.

We have what we call scavenger pumps down in the tunnel. Eventually, they wear out from material and sands. Sometimes a piece of stone might get in the wrong way and break an impeller *(rotating device that directs liquid)*, and you might have to pull the pump apart for that kind of maintenance.

Sometimes you lose a bearing on a hatch crane. Then the engineers go out to jack it up, pull the wheel off, change the bearing, and put the wheel back on.

There are all kinds of mechanical gear. As the year goes on, things break.

The mechanical maintenance that the engineers do is tremendous throughout the years. They change oils in all the units, all the generators, and the main engines. They change filters. You have two engines on the barge, you have two main engines and three generators on the tug, and the engineers have to maintain that for so many hours.

Things go wrong all the time, little mechanical things, electrical things.

When you're loading, you get a lot of dirt in the winches sometimes. Then the winches get fouled, and they have to be totally cleaned. Even though they're waterproof, some dust gets inside certain areas and you have to change the oils. You have coolers on some of the hydraulic winches and on the hatch crane, too, and the dust fills up into those radiators. The cleaning of that is constant.

We maintain safety equipment, like for the docking chairs and booms that go over the side for sending people over to the dock. The ropes have to be changed every three months whether there's wear or not. It's time-schedule maintenance. We change the ropes well before a wear factor comes in, as a safety measure.

On the jibs, the bearings go out. We're always replacing pulleys. It's a constant battle with maintenance.

We splice cables. Cables wear, especially the midship winch because we have the tracks for our hatch crane and we have rollers that have to go under and then back up and out through a chock. When they go through that, there's a double stress on the cable, and it breaks a little bit easier. Just working. They wear. When they get flat, they might not even be broken yet. But when they get flat, you can see the wear on them. Then sometimes we'll just chop them before they break and put in a new splice. We cut off the extra strands with a torch.

The only access between the Dorothy Ann and Pathfinder is from the exterior. You have to walk over a ladder. In winter, we keep it cleaned off. We have salt and sand. We salt, sand, shovel, break ice. Sometimes we use hot water to melt the ice. We have what we call a donkey boiler on there. It burns a lot of fuel, but we heat the water. And we have to do that sometimes when we're cleaning out the cargo holds in wintertime. We have to heat the water so it doesn't freeze when hitting the already frozen steel.

We have meetings about maintenance. We discuss things that were kind of hazardous to us or that we should look into as being hazardous. We talk about safe or unsafe or practices that we think could be changed to make things safer. It's a meeting of the whole crew.

The company puts out a bulletin on safety issues, and we read it, go through it, and discuss it. And then we discuss what has happened on the vessel during the last month or what things need to be looked at or be included as a safety concern issue.

We have a self-inspection program in hand with the Coast Guard or the American Bureau of Shipping, ABS. That means you go through the vessel and you inspect all your electrical outlets, your lights, and any type of equipment. You make out a report on it, that it's been inspected. If there is something wrong with apparatus, you have to fill in a corrective action report. The next step would be to fix the problem and then report it as fixed. It all goes into a program, and then the Coast Guard and ABS come down and check that program at any time and go through it and then check behind you to see if you actually did all this checking.

And there are audits that go on. For Homeland Security, you have to do a complete inspection at the beginning of the year. We go through the whole boat. We inspect it – everything – for suspicious people being around at fit out, stowaways, suspicious packages. We have to do a complete boat inspection, make sure there's nobody or nothing funky going on. This takes a couple of hours. And then at the end of the year, we do the same thing. We go through another audit and check everything out again and make sure that we're vigilant, and we have enough lights out there covering access to the boat. There are different security levels. There's one, two, and three, three being the highest security. We're at Level 1 most of the time. Sometimes when we go through a drill, we'll simulate MARSEC *(MARitime SECurity)* Level 2. For MARSEC Level 3, operations might be suspended, and the Coast Guard orders you away from the dock. There's so much paperwork, and it's constant.

Hatch 66

Layup and fit out

Maintenance is done every winter.

Layup starts after the closing of the Soo Locks, which is usually around January 15. We have laid up in Sturgeon Bay, Wisconsin; Detroit, Michigan; and Cleveland, Ohio. The company flies you to and from the vessel for layup and fit out.

The vessel goes to a berth in the shipyard. There are a lot of repairs to be done. A lot of equipment has to be gone through. That includes the server for all the computers, which is in the pilothouse. Programs are upgraded. For instance, during the 2013 layup, a new and more powerful computer for the ECPINS was put on board. Crews check the radios, the GPS, the AIS, the gyro and gyro repeater. They go through any discrepancies that I give them. If there's something that's a known problem, they'll check it out. The shipyard tries to get everything done before we have our first cargo, which is between March 1 and March 15.

Starting in September and October leading into the layup season, we meet with the engineers. We go through a check list of things that need to be done, things that have to be done, things that the engineers want to replace or repair. We go through a list, even down to small stuff, of anything that can be done in the off season. We prioritize the list. We get it all set to go so when we do get to the layup dock, the shipyard facility, or ship-side facility that does our repairs, that there is a list. As soon as the vessel is laid up, work can start immediately.

The shipyard gets a crew down there, and guys start doing things that need to be done and get everything prepared for the next season. That includes ordering our supplies for the next year – replacement mooring wires, batteries that have to go into the life rings, batteries that have to go into the survival suits.

Any supplies that we may need for the coming year or things that need to be replaced and fixed are all done. The setup is all prepared before we ever get to that layup dock. Over the winter, that's all repaired, fixed at the shipyard.

Stuff that we just would like to have done – a wish list – doesn't always get done, but the major stuff does get done.

When we lay up, an engineering staff stays aboard. The shipyard has a watchman, and it has an engineer. That engineer might take care of not just the Dorothy Ann. He might take care of other company fleet vessels, too, that are at the shipyard.

To start another season, the vessel goes through an elaborate fit out process.

Coming back to make the ship active, we go through a Coast Guard inspection, which consists of all safety equipment. We go through an ABS inspection. ABS guys examine all repairs that were done during the layoff season. We have to run a boat and fire drill. We have to have a safety meeting and a security meeting at fit out. All of that is before we leave the dock.

The engineer is already there, and engineers have been there all winter. The cook comes in to order supplies and make sure all the food is aboard for when the crew arrives. The crew arrives usually a day before we leave the layup dock. The first mate may come in a couple days early to run the Coast Guard inspection and ABS inspection.

During those inspections, we have to drop the anchor, pick the anchor up, and have all of our safety equipment out and operating. We have to show that

The engines of the Dorothy Ann are started at this control board, which has coverings so buttons aren't accidently pushed when the engines are running.
Gary Schmidt photo

the lights on the life rings and other safety gear all light up with new batteries, that all the equipment is in top shape. Some of the reflectors on life rings may have come off. They have to be rewound. Some of the lines might be rotted. We might put new heaving lines on the vessel. We do what we can to spruce up and paint up the vessel to make it look good again.

As part of the Coast Guard procedure, we have to start the engines and stop the engines. We have emergency shutdowns. We have to demonstrate the fire pumps and shoot water over the side. We have a telegraph system in case communications go out or steering goes out and the engineers have to steer from the engine room. I have a half ahead, full ahead, quarter ahead, half astern, full astern, quarter astern, stop telegraph that I just hit a button. The engineer has to answer in response in the engine room. I can start and stop the engine from the pilothouse, which I have to do. Generators – we switch generators. The generators are set up in emergency sequence. If one fails, the other one automatically starts up, and you lose nothing. If the second one fails, we have an emergency generator that starts up automatically and runs just enough to keep steerage, emergency equipment running, the gyro, emergency lighting, a radar, and a GPS – just bare minimum.

Also during the offseason, we have a captains and chief engineers meeting every year. It's mandatory. There's a certain amount of training that has to do with drug training. Some training is personal training – how to relax yourself, how to get along with people better. People training.

Hatch 67

Dry dock

You have to take the vessel in for a dry docking every five years. You can get a one-year exemption if you have a scuba diver dive under the hull of the tug or barge and check for defects and get an okay. But normally it's five years.

I do not drive the Dorothy Ann or Pathfinder into the dry dock. The shipyards don't want big vessels with their big propellers disturbing the blocks on the bottom. They have tugs maneuver you into place, and you put lines out on both sides, and the shipyard guys position you right over the blocks in a proper spot.

Each vessel on the Great Lakes has its own docking plan of blocks. The blocks are adjustable. The shipyard guys can control the blocks. They can move the blocks in and out. What the shipyards usually do is pump out the dry dock, place the blocks the way they're supposed to be according to the vessel's dry docking plan, center the vessel, mark where the bow is supposed to be and where the stern is supposed to be, and then the shipyard guys settle the vessel in the dry dock – like resting it in a cradle.

The centering is done by wires. After the tugs get you in the dry dock and get you close to your dry docking position, you put lines out on both sides, with winches, and the shipyard guys winch you around and get you into place. They use walkie-talkies. I'm usually on the vessel in the dry dock until it's settled. I'm there to help navigate the vessel in. I might use my wheels *(propellers)* up to the point of where we start to get into the dry dock. Then the shipyard guys put up gangways, and I can get off.

If we're in Sturgeon Bay, usually a couple of Selvick Marine Towing tugs maneuver us in. And Bay Shipbuilding has its own boat that's called the Bay Ship that helps out.

The Dorothy Ann and the Pathfinder could both be put in dry dock at the same time, but they're separated.

When all the water is drained in the dry dock, I always go underneath and look all around. I'm curious. I want to see if I've scraped the bottom and put in little dings. I want to see if there's maybe an oil leak coming off of

The Dorothy Ann stands high and dry in a dry dock at Bay Shipbuilding in Sturgeon Bay, Wisconsin. *Gary Schmidt photo*

something, or see if maybe there are zebra mussels in the sea cocks. I just want to see how much wear and tear there is on the bottom.

Usually when we're in dry dock, my crew is sent home except for the engineers. Engineering stays because anything that's done mechanical or welding wise, that's the engineering part of it. You don't need the deckhands because the painting is done by the shipyard. The shipyard will paint the bottom side. The captain and the mates are not needed. They might be

The Dorothy Ann is braced in dry dock. *Gary Schmidt photo*

needed the day before we leave dry dock or the day we leave. They come back to the boat and get it ready to sail again, clean up and get it shipshape so you're ready to get underway.

Normal dry docking is done for the Coast Guard to inspect the sea cocks, to check on any water transfer from outside to inside, to make sure the gate valves are all in good shape, to make sure that your sea cocks are free of zebra mussels, and to gauge the steel.

The engines are gauged every winter when we're done for the season. Or sometimes if we're having problems, they may be gauged during the season. The engineers look at hours of running time, and then they do a ring gauging that measures how much wear there is on the rings. Throughout the year, they analyze the oil, and they can tell how much steel or copper or whatever metal is in the oil. They can tell what is wearing and where there might be a problem. That's done during the year and at the end of the season. If there are any questions, they mark the pistons or liners or bearings that need to be replaced, and then they'll take care of that in the offseason.

During dry docking, the engineers will just do what the Coast Guard recommends or ABS recommends. They check the hull to make sure that there's no damage, that there are no cracks. They check shell plating for thickness. They check the pressure tanks to make sure the safeties pop off when they're supposed to pop off. They check vents. They check each of the rods that open valves and close valves. They check fuel shutoffs. They go through emergency equipment like the fire pumps to make sure that there's enough pressure going to the farthest place away. The engineers do that every year at fit out also.

Fit out is done after the layoff after everybody has come aboard. We re-fit for the next season. You do that after a dry docking. You re-fit the boat. That means getting supplies, getting everything shipshape, ready to sail again.

There's fit out and lay up. For lay up, you would de-ballast the vessel so, if the vessel goes into a winter layup, the water won't freeze. You make sure that the sea cocks are cleared or have heat on them so valves and pipes don't freeze. All the lines are drained so you don't have burst water lines. We have little drain cocks that we open up and make sure everything is drained. Usually, we pump the sea cocks full of a filler that is a type of biodegradable waxy

Workmen are dwarfed by one of the Dorothy Ann's two propeller pods.
Gary Schmidt photo

grease so they can't freeze and crack and break. We make sure that things are cleaned up, stowed away, and carried off the deck so the sun doesn't rot whatever you have out there. You put away all the safety equipment.

Because the dry docking is usually done in Sturgeon Bay and I live a short run away in Green Bay, I visit the vessel to see how the progress is going. The first day we're in dry dock, I look the vessel over to see if we touched bottom and see what needs to be done on the bottom. But other than that, I'm away from the vessel. Years ago, I sometimes came up there just to show people around, when we could do that. Sometimes I'll come up to visit one of the engineers on the boat and maybe take him out to dinner.

The day before we sail, I come back and sign everybody aboard and make sure that all the supplies that we need are aboard the vessel before we assign work details. We clean up this, clean up that, get the vessel ready for underway.

Any time we are in dry dock or in layup, we have a wish list. For dry docking, it's stuff like making sure the underwater depth sounder is in working order or if a transducer has to be replaced. Unless there's underwater work that has to be done, there's not a big wish list for dry dock unless the dry dock is done during the winter layup period. Then the wish list comes into effect.

The time in dry dock depends on the amount of work that has to be done. Let's say some plate steel may have to be replaced on the barge. With the vessel being more than 60 years old, some parts of steel might wear thin. That kind of steel will be replaced. That's something you may not know until you get into dry dock. You plan for things that you do know, and sometimes the stay may be extended a day or two or maybe even longer. I've seen on other vessels where something major has gone, like a shaft bearing or something is wrong with the shaft itself where it might have to be pulled out. I've seen where a shipyard has taken a boat out of dry dock because a part had to be ordered and wasn't going to be in for a while and put another boat in dry dock. And then when that one's done the first boat goes back in and gets repaired when the parts come.

The company determines the shipyard where the vessel will dry dock. It could be a bid thing, or it might be a position thing, where the company wants you.

The Dorothy Ann has only been dry docked at Bay Shipbuilding. Since I've been on it, the Pathfinder has only been dry docked at Bay Ship also. But we could dry dock at Fraser *(Shipyards, Inc.)* in Duluth, Minnesota, and we can dry dock at Erie, Pennsylvania *(Donjon Shipbuilding and Repair, Inc.)*, and then Toledo *(Ironhead Marine)*, Ohio.

Bay Shipbuilding owns the big graving dock where the ships are built. Bay Shipbuilding tries to build the new ships in the off-winter season. When the shipyard builds, it usually builds modular. It builds super sections inside of a building, and the sections are assembled in the dry dock. The shipyard can put a vessel together pretty fast that way and then clear up the dry dock for dry docking.

The ideal time to dry dock is in the wintertime when you are in layup, but sometimes it's not economical to go into dry dock at that time. It may be economical to go into dry dock when there are no other vessels in line for the dry dock. The company might take you out of service for one or two days in the summertime to do a quick dry docking, or it might end up being six days if there are bottom repairs to do. So the shipyard gets you in and out as fast as it can.

Captain Schmidt stands next to a Dorothy Ann propeller.
Warren Gerds photo

Hatch 68

Mussels

Zebra mussels are kind of a problem.

Sometimes our strainers will fill up with zebra mussels. A generator may overheat on the barge.

***

SNAPSHOT: *Named for the striped pattern on their shells, zebra mussels are an invasive species that arrived in Lake St. Clair in 1988. They upset ecosystems, including on inland lakes.*

***

You have to switch the strainers out. Strainers are put on intake water lines to prevent foreign objects from getting into the main engine or the generators' heat exchangers. You take out the screens that screen the water that's coming in and clean out the zebra mussels. The zebra mussels will fill up a strainer that's at least a foot in diameter, and there are two strainers per side.

If the strainers fill up and start to plug up a system, you can switch a valve to the other side that's empty, and then you can open up the filled side and clean it out. You can shut the water off and clean those zebra mussels out. It's called a dual strainer system.

I think the zebra mussels are being supplanted by some other kind of foreign mussel right now, and they're a little bit bigger mussel than the zebra mussel.

***

SNAPSHOT: *The quagga mussel is another hitchhiker that is invading the Great Lakes. It is about the size of an adult's thumbnail.*

***

The bottoms of the Great Lakes are pretty much covered with mussels now. When you get into shallower water, you suck them up. In the deep water, it doesn't matter.

We have to clean the strainers quite often on Lake Erie. We check the strainers several times a week because of the shallow water, and we're stirring up the bottom. Many days, I'm in two ports on Lake Erie because of short runs. I'll load at Marblehead, and I'll run to Erie and back to Marblehead, and I'll do that in about a 28 to 30-hour period for a round trip. If I run to Cleveland, it's a 20-hour round trip and maybe 24 to Ashtabula.

Dry docking is a good time to make sure that the grids over the sea chests are not filled up with zebra mussels.

The zebra mussels were established when I started on the Dorothy Ann.

Hatch 69

Interlake

I came to Interlake Steamship Company through the AMO *(American Marine Officers)* union.

I was working for another transportation company, and it went out of business. I had just gotten home for the winter. The season was done. The union called me and said that Interlake would like to talk to me, and would it be all right if they gave my phone number to Interlake? And I said, "Yes." I interviewed for the job in February 2000, and I ended up with the job in March 2000.

That particular year it was kind of nice because I got calls from five companies. I didn't have to go out and look. That was a feel-good year for me.

I chose Interlake because it presented a new challenge. I'd worked the smaller tugs and smaller barges, and this was huge. When I walked aboard, I thought maybe I overstepped my bounds a little bit at first. But I adapted to it, and it was nice because I went from something that hauled about 10,000 tons to something that would haul about 23,000 tons. And that's more than doubling the capacity. The tug was much bigger. The company was very nice. It's an aggressive, forward-looking company, and I thought that it was headed in a good direction.

Interlake is privately owned and is dedicated to being here, where some of the other companies are stockholder driven and driven by the stock market and dividends.

This company's sole purpose is to keep its boats sailing and keep this company running. Interlake was started in 1913.

***

SIDE TRIP: *Interlake Steamship Company held its 100th anniversary celebration on Marco Island, Florida, in March 2013.*

We have an annual meeting of masters and chiefs. The celebration was part of the meeting. This year's meeting was huge. It included more people from the office and their families, secretaries, and the whole works. There was a skeleton crew at the office. The shipping season had just started. While we were down there, the Dorothy Ann/Pathfinder put in its first trip.

To last 100 years is a feat. What Interlake does is beyond the grasp of many people. While it is a business, No. 1, it deals with

Captain Schmidt enjoys a laugh during Interlake Steamship Company's 100th anniversary celebration. *Photo courtesy The Interlake Steamship Company*

James R. Barker, Interlake Steamship Company chief executive officer, cuts a cake bearing the image of the ship named for him during the company's 100th anniversary celebration. *Photo courtesy The Interlake Steamship Company*

huge volumes and moves those brutishly huge volumes by a method of transportation that goes back forever in humankind. The system is classic and high tech at the same time.

It is by vessel, and it's cheaper because you can move such a great volume versus a smaller volume in a train or truck.

Interlake started in an extremely bad year for the industry. The Great Lakes Storm of November 1913 cost 12 ships (five of which have never been found) and more than 250 lives. The company weathered storms on water and the economy and accomplished many milestones, including the decision to build the Dorothy Ann/Pathfinder. It was the company's first articulated tug and barge.

All in all, it's been a very satisfactory decision. There has been a learning process with the vessel because there were certain things that weren't correct when it was built, and the company has improved on a lot of necessities – putting on the CP *(controlled-pitch)* wheels *(propellers)* and putting less stress on the gears. At first, the barge didn't have slopes. The vessel could hold more cargo, but it wasn't efficient enough to run that way. Putting in slopes made a big improvement. With that setup, we lost a little cargo room, but we gained a lot of time unloading and loading, plus that was easier. Improvements were made in the tunnel. There was a lot of spillage at first because product would come off the belt too easily. That was all manual labor – to shovel it back onto the belt. But once we got the bugs out of it, it's been very, very successful.

The 2013 annual meeting was different because of scale, number of people, programming, and other activities. There still was normal stuff that we do – the training that has to be done, the meetings throughout the day. But there was some time for fun – sport fishing, golfing, a day at the beach and cookout, every night a dinner. The celebration was more spectacular than other years.

***

Interlake is dedicated to keeping its vessels in tiptop shape. It is dedicated to making the job as easy for the captains and engineers as possible. It's one of the better companies I ever worked for.

Interlake treats its employees extremely well. Everybody has a second chance or a third chance if something doesn't go exactly right, and the company is very loyal to its people, as most of the people are loyal to the company, I think. There are a few people who are not happy. There are always people who aren't happy. But overall it's an extremely good company to work for. I'm very happy with it.

I very seldom go in to the office or headquarters. I have been there a couple of times if I happened to be in the area.

This company is unique in that you don't go to the office much, but the office comes to you. We have ship visits twice a year. We usually go to a spot in the St. Marys River near De Tour, Michigan, off of Drummond Island that's called Black Rock Point. We anchor there, and the CEO of the company, the president of the company, the senior vice president of the company, the vice president of personnel, engineering — everybody — come down to the boat and give us a state of the company, how things are running. It's very, very nice to have people come down like that. They give you what the state of the shipping industry is doing as a whole, give you an idea of what the country's doing as a whole financially, how the company itself is doing as a whole. It's very good. They address the officers in one meeting and the non-officers in another meeting.

Mark Barker, Interlake Steamship Company president, raises a glass for a toast during the company's 100th anniversary celebration. *Photo courtesy The Interlake Steamship Company*

***

SIDE NOTE: To some degree, as the country's economy goes, so does the shipping industry. We feel a lot of the stuff before anybody else does. If you're bringing in raw material to produce steel, if you see that the steel plants are not needing raw materials, that means that they're cutting back, which means that other things are cutting back. That means that manufacturing is not doing as much. The same with construction. If you're not moving construction stone, that means that not much construction is going on. That's another indication that the economy is not doing as well. We kind of see this first hand.

***

Interlake expects me to run its ship, to do it in an efficient manner, to get as much cargo to the customer as possible on each load, to deliver the material on time, and to communicate with our customers and keep them satisfied. Make a profit for the company. Not to waste. To control labor costs. To conserve on fuel when possible. To do a lot of wise business things. Also manage. So, to manage people, to put people at their best position to succeed, which I like to do. I like to dole out responsibility. It makes some people feel more important and do a better job.

I have to use my men efficiently because of the amount of work that they have to do and the amount of time that they can fit that work in a day. And that's managing people. You have to be able to do that in this particular job. We've had some experiments that didn't work so well, but over the years we figured out a pretty good plan by which we keep people kind of fresh — as fresh as you can get working these kind of hours — and still give them a little bit of personal time that they can do things to relax.

Step back a bit. *Captain Schmidt works for a company. He is a manager, and he has to meet expectations. However, he is not a tradition manager in an office building. He's autonomous. A lot of people in a traditional office are managers but not autonomous. Captain Schmidt is in a position where what he says is done.*

There are rules, but they're bendable rules. *(But crew must follow his instructions.)* My expectations of Interlake are that I'm there to perform a job, so I expect a paycheck, the insurance, and job security to a certain point. I don't think I really had a lot of expectations, but as the years went on with this company, it has backed me to the hilt. It has gone way beyond my expectations. Support, communications, pay, everything.

Interlake Steamship Company executives include, from left, Robert Dorn, senior vice president; John Hopkins, vice president; and Brendan O'Connor, director of industrial relations. *Photos courtesy The Interlake Steamship Company*

Training

I don't think my being in the Navy had much to do with sailing on the Great Lakes at all. I was a cook in the Navy. That had no bearing whatsoever with what I do now, except that I like to cook.

My training was by doing. I learned on the job, just like many of the guys on Great Lakes vessels.

I would say there are probably more people coming out of the academies now for officers, but at one time there were more people who worked their way up as a deckhand, to a mate, and so on. And they did it on their own. They studied at home to learn rules of the road, to learn how to load a vessel, how to unload a vessel. All that kind of stuff came from on-the-job training. And you're on the job all the time, for months at a time. It's something learnable.

The hard part is sitting there reading the books when you're trying to do a job. Reading the books and then having to go take a Coast Guard test – that's not easy. Whereas the cadets are in classroom all the time, and they are learning through the books, and they don't have as much practical experience. They get an AB's *(Able Bodied Seaman)* ticket, but to be an AB, you've got to chip a lot of paint and learn how to paint before you can be an Able Bodied Seaman. These guys don't even have to chip paint or do anything like that. There are some advantages to being a mustanger.

The maritime academies are mainly for officer training. Some of them are three years, but most of them are four years. You get a bachelor's degree, besides getting a license. Every summer, you go out on a ship's cruise. It might be for just a month. Sometimes it's longer. But you have to put in so many cruises over that period of time. And through that, the academies teach you navigation, teach you seamanship and, besides readin', writin', and arithmetic, teach you a lot about the marine industry – how to load cargoes to stabilization.

Many people still work their way up, starting as a deckhand. To become a deckhand, all you need to do is get a Coast Guard merchant marine credential. In the process, you need to first get a TWIC card – Transportation

Crewmen gather at the stern of the Dorothy Ann for fire safety training.
Gary Schmidt photo

221

A Dorothy Ann/Pathfinder crewman is lifted in a harness as traveling instructor teaches how to hoist an injured person to safety.
Gary Schmidt photo

Worker Identification Credential. You have to have a physical. You get an FBI background check, a driving record check. They ask you specific questions – "Have you ever been in trouble?" You've got to answer it, and it's all checked. There are passport photos. You have to pay for everything. The process probably takes a couple of months to get all your credentials.

Then you have to go around to the unions or to different companies and apply. When they're shorthanded, that's when they'll give you a call.

And then we'll take new deckhands, and we will train them the way we want to train them. We'll try to see if they fit or don't fit.

You can be a deckhand without any specific training. When you first get on board a ship, you're learning all the time. But it's mostly physical work when you get on board. You're going to be hosing, shoveling, hosing, shoveling, painting, scrubbing. As you get more experience, you're going to be the next guy along. You're going to learn how to run the winches and so on. It's cross training. Everybody learns how to do everything on that vessel.

With Interlake, instead of being called a deckhand, you're called General Purpose Maintenance. That's our classification, even though the Coast Guard has the designations Ordinary Seaman or Able Bodied Seaman or QMED, which is a Qualified Man in the Engine Department. We classify deckhands as General Purpose Maintenance because they can do a little bit of everything. Eventually, you'll learn how to splice cable, you'll splice line. Sometimes the vessel is not moored up against the docks, and you'll run the small boat when we need to ferry the heaving lines to the dock to be able to pull the wires across to moor.

Experienced crewmen are teachers in a sense. They help one another. Everybody wants to make his job easier, so the faster you train somebody behind you, it makes your job easier. You're not pulling all the weight. It's just common sense to help somebody else out. Or at least that's the way I see it.

You become a jack of many trades. It's like cross-training in sports. Everybody does a lot of everything. The reason that you do it that is because if somebody is missing, somebody else can step into a spot.

That's the same with our firefighting teams. We have two firefighting teams. We rotate the people on the teams so they know the next guy's job. If somebody gets injured or if somebody goes down on a fire team, the next person steps up and moves on up.

Sometimes an instructor from American Marine Training Center rides the boat. He'll get on in Marquette and ride all the way to Detroit and maybe Marblehead. He instructs the crew and goes through training drills. We do a lot of training this way. There will be demonstrations of a typical firefight with guys spraying one another to show you how waterproof the gear is. There are demonstrations for evacuating people from the cargo hold if somebody got hurt. We have machines to pick people up and set them down that anybody can use – real easy hand crank winches.

We do a lot of cross training with the deckhands. As they come on board, and, as they've been there a relatively short time – two to three months – then we start moving them on from just hosing and shoveling to maybe running the work boat, maybe starting to learn how to use the winches, how to get on to the hatch crane and be able to work it up and down the deck, and to take the hatches off and put them on. All of the training is in little steps, but you try to train everybody to do everything. That's also, when we unload, learning how to be a gateman.

We are constantly training people to do the next job up. That's so you can step backwards or you can step forward, either way, wherever you are needed, that you can do it, even though you have become an Able-Bodied Seaman. We encourage everybody to be Able-Bodied Seamen. Even though there are only so many Watchman spots or Able-Bodied spots, this company is willing to pay crew members, the minute they get their Able-Bodied Seaman's ticket, pay them right away, even if they are working in an OS or Ordinary Seaman's position. The company pays them AB's wages whether they are working the position or not. That way, we can move people up and down, and we have qualified people at all times. And most of the time, as soon as somebody's able to get an AB ticket on my vessel, he will, and I'm usually carrying more than enough ABs.

To get an Able-Bodied Seaman ticket, a guy has to put in so much time, and then he has to take a Coast Guard exam, which is given at various schools. You can go to school for it, and they prepare you for it, and then they give you the exam. The academy in Traverse City is one of them. In the wintertime, it offers courses. At the end of a course, you'll take the Coast Guard exam for Able Bodied Seaman or Qualified Man in the Engine Department or Tankerman Person in Charge. All of those upgrades have schools for them. You have to go to school for a lot of the positions before the Coast Guard will even let you take an exam.

In the middle of the lake, a vessel doesn't phone a repairman to fix a problem. It has its own repairmen.

The engineers are trained in HVAC, heating and air conditioning. They are trained in diesel mechanics. A lot of them are trained in steam boilers. They are jacks of all trades. They are electricians, they are plumbers, they're the whole works.

There are fabrications all the time. Anything that can help us – even if it's just a piece of steel on a gate that keeps the rocks from flying onto the deck, keeps the rocks on the belt. Whatever we can do to fabricate something to help something along is done. A lot of times, we'll tell engineering what the problem is, and engineering will come up with some kind of a fix for it. We're constantly trying to improve things.

Hatch 71

Rescues

We have rescued people out on the water.

The first time was when I was a mate with Selvick on the Lauren Castle. We were coming down Lake Michigan headed for Chicago. We were out in a gale. It was pretty nasty weather. We were towing the barge Sea Castle with the Lauren Castle. We spotted a red light where there shouldn't be a light. The captain, Orrin Royce, said, "Let's go over and investigate it."

We made a big circle, came back around, and here are two people in a 16-foot runabout.

We had heard reports on them, that they were missing on a trip from Waukegan, Illinois, to Benton Harbor, Michigan. They made it there and were headed back. On the way back, they encountered the weather. They knew they were going to run out of gas. They saw a fish buoy, and they tied up to it. The wind had blown them so far off course that when the Coast Guard was out searching for these people, they were outside the search pattern. Their boat was around Grosse Point down toward Chicago, which is south of Waukegan quite a bit. They were probably 15 to 20 miles off shore. They had been missing for 30 hours. We got them aboard. We took their boat in tow. We called the Coast Guard and said we had the guys in hand and that we were bringing them into Chicago because the weather was too bad to take them anywhere else at that time.

Oh, God, these guys were happy to see us. They told us, "You can keep the boat. We'll just tell insurance that it was lost." "No, no, no, you can have your boat." They were just happy to be on the tug. They could drink the water, but they hadn't had anything to eat. We fed them and got them a hot shower to warm them up. It wasn't bitter cold where they were going to be lost to exposure. They were fine. They were okay.

Here's another thing: They had five flares. Four other vessels that passed when they shot their flares up never saw them. With our tug and barge, we were closer to where they were. We got them into South Chicago, and reporters were down there, and they were interviewing these two guys who were in the boat, but they didn't even mention who rescued them. It was just another nuisance.

The two guys got in their runabout, went to Chicago, filled her up with gas, went back out on the lake, and went up to Waukegan with it, about 30 miles north. But the weather had settled down.

They didn't bring enough gas with them. There are all kinds of problems you can run into, and those storms come up on the Great Lakes. Predicting back in the '70s wasn't all that great. Forecasts weren't very accurate. You were better off watching the barometer.

Another time, when I was on the Triton, we were coming out of Waukegan headed up to Milwaukee, I saw a boat drifting. Its top was up, pointed like a sail instead of a shield. I saw somebody waving, so I went over there and I asked, "Are you in trouble?" A guy said, "Yeah, we're out of gas." As I was talking to him, he wanted gas from us. I said, "I don't have any gas. I'll call the Coast Guard, and I'll stand by for you right here." I called the Coast Guard and told them there were people out there and my position. As I was doing this, people kept coming out of the cabin. Now there were two people on deck. A little while later, there was a third person on deck. And then a woman came out with a child. They didn't have any milk on the boat, and she was wondering if we had any milk. And it kept going on.

There were six people on that boat. They had been out there since the night before. They were out of gas, and they didn't have any supplies with them and not enough diapers and milk for all night. So we gave them what we could, food and water. I stayed until the Coast Guard got there.

Hatch 72

The three-hour tour

Remember the TV show "Gilligan's Island"? Seven people go off on an excursion aboard a small boat and end up as castaways on a deserted island. As the theme song goes, they set sail that day for a three-hour tour. Captain Schmidt was early in his career with the Dorothy Ann/ Pathfinder when one day in July 2001…

I received a call from Captain Mitch Hallin on the Paul R. Tregurtha. He called me up when I was busy handling and left a message saying, "Your brother-in-law is okay." As soon as I could answer the message, I called him back. He said, "Listen, I'm landing at a dock. I can't talk to you right now, but he's okay. I'll talk to you when I get tied up." So he called me back when he was free, and then he told me the story of rescuing my brother-in-law, Pete Cichowski, out in the middle of Lake Superior. Mitch said he had picked up Pete, his son, Petey, and brother, Tony, and everybody was fine, that they were given a ride to Eagle Harbor and the Coast Guard came out and picked them up. That's what I knew at the time. I talked to Pete after that to get the rest of the story. I telephoned him the next day. Then we talked about it once I got home, and I convinced him that he should never go out on Lake Superior again without a GPS.

We now shift gears for the rest of this segment as Pete and Captain Schmidt recount the saga. They are at the kitchen table in Captain Schmidt's house. Pete is a tile installation expert by trade, along with being a do-it-yourselfer supreme. Listen in as the conversation progresses.

Pete: I bought a GPS right after that.

Gary: *(Speaking to you)*: He bought one for himself and one for Tony. *(To Pete)*: Does Tony ever use it?

Pete: I use it. I don't Tony think uses it. I don't think he's been back out, though, either.

Captain Schmidt and his brother-in-law, Pete Cichowski, talk about a grand misadventure on Lake Superior. *Warren Gerds photo*

Gary: It was the very first year I worked for Interlake, and I was so surprised. And then when I told *(executive vice president)* Bob Dorn that it was my brother-in-law, he said, "Well, at least I know where I can send the bill for this."

Pete: There was never a bill. There was an estimate of what it would have been — $40,000-$45,000 for the excursion. I had gone on vacation to Upper Michigan for two weeks. I thought the three of us should go to Isle Royale *(60 miles one way)*, so I worked on Tony's boat. I worked on the motor a bunch. It worked fine. So we kind of planned it. We trailered it all the way to Eagle Harbor *(on the Keweenaw Peninsula)* and fished there for a while. While we were there, the Coast Guard came up to us as we were at the dock. They checked out the boat. We had everything we needed. They checked our compass, our compass worked great.

Gary: The Coast Guard goes through a checklist. You've got to have a fire extinguisher, you've got to have life preservers of a certain type for each person. You have to have an anchor, flairs.

Pete: I think they should make everybody have radar.

Gary: Or GPS.

Pete: When we decided to go that morning, it was really foggy. The whole trip was really foggy. We stayed on Isle Royale for two days.

Gary: An uneventful trip going across?

Pete: No, that was kind of hairy, too. Going there, in the fog, you can't see 100 feet. You can't see the wash behind the boat 100 feet. Like you told us later, we must have put something electrical, like the flashlight, next the compass because the needle went around in circles. Round and round. That's all. We decided to stop. We stopped right in the middle of a shipping lane. Two of us would sleep, and one of us would watch so we didn't get run over. We knew we were in a shipping lane because we could hear the horns when the motor wasn't running. We couldn't hear them when the motor was running unless they were right on top of us. But once we shut off the motor, we'd hear the horns all the time. Four or five vessels passed, at least. We were just stopped. We were not in distress. We could have kept going, we just didn't know which way was where. So we waited until the morning and the sun came up, and we took a bearing off the sun and got right to where we wanted to go. And it was still just as foggy. You couldn't see anything.

So we went northwest from where we were.

Gary: In a general direction?

Pete: In a general direction.

Gary: You know how far that you would be off on a 60-mile run? One degree is one mile.

Pete: Oh yeah?

Gary: Yeah.

Pete: Where we stopped, I figured we were somewhere around 10 miles off shore. We knew we were in a shipping lane because we had seen one boat, and we had heard many boats.

Gary: So it cleared up a little bit and then went foggy again that you could see that one boat?

Pete: It was that close. Way that close.

Gary: So then you finally made it over to Isle Royale.

Pete: We checked out different mines *(ancient copper mines)* and hiked all around. Camped on the shore.

Gary: Where you were, was there a park or a town?

The Paul R. Tregurtha, the longest vessel on the Great Lakes at 1,013.5 feet, came to the rescue of three stranded fishermen, including Captain Schmidt's brother-in-law and nephew. *Photo courtesy The Interlake Steamship Company*

Pete: Rock Harbor, up on the north end.

Gary: So you were able to gas up there before you went back?

Pete: Yeah. Very expensive. Three-something. Back then. It was $3.50 or something a gallon. It was a lot of money to fill that tank up to get back.

Gary: And then on the way back?

Pete: On the way back, there were too many different pilots. Everybody took a different thought of how he was going to get back. We thought if we went a little too much to the left – which is what we did – we would miss the point *(of Keweenaw Peninsula)*. If we went a little bit too much to the right, we would be in Houghton instead of, well… We left Isle Royale at daybreak, and this was about noon when we figured we weren't going anywhere, we were screwed.

Gary: Did you have any extra tanks with you?

Pete:: Nope. We didn't think we needed one.

Gary: How big was your tank that you filled up, 20 gallons, 30 gallons?

Pete: I think it was 30 gallons. That should have been enough if we wouldn't have…

Gary: Yeah. But you did miss the point.

Pete: Yeah, we missed the point.

Gary: And the island's way bigger than the point. The peninsula is big, but if you're coming back and aiming at a point, it's easy to miss the point.

Pete: It's real easy to miss the point.

Gary: And you're figuring gas for the point. If you miss the point, you're going all the way down to Baraga or somewhere around the Huron Mountains on the one side or, the other way, the Apostle Islands or Bayfield or Ashland.

Pete: When we figured out we didn't have enough gas, we shut it down and tried to figure our way.

Gary: Then, once you decided you ran out of gas?

Pete: Then I hailed the Coast Guard, and it wasn't too long that they got back to us. That's when we had problems with the radio where we couldn't hear each other. The speaker on the radio worked. The mike didn't work on the radio when we were trying to call for help. We could hear who we were calling. They couldn't hear us most of the time. So they would try and try. We figured out that they must have heard us once or twice and couldn't hear us anymore. Then we went to the hand-held radios. After talking back and forth a while, our batteries in our two hand-held radios went dead. We could hear them on the boat radio, but they couldn't hear us. I bought Tony a Makita cordless drill battery before we went on the cruise. We had that with us, and we adapted that with wires to one of the handhelds, and that's what finally got us our final talk to the Tregurtha – that hand-held and that Makita battery. We were holding the wires. We didn't know if it would work, but it worked. When we finally got in touch with the Tregurtha by doing that, they were coming out of the Soo, and I was thinking they were only 20 miles out of the Soo, which would put us another 60 or 70 miles away. They said they were going to be a while before they got to us, so we played cribbage until they got there. My brother was so upset that his stomach couldn't take it, and he puked over side the boat just from anxiety. My son, Petey, was all right. He just seemed to go with the flow. It was probably three hours from the time we started getting hold of the Coast Guard until the Tregurtha got to us. We had no idea there was a storm coming up. It was a squall. Before the Tregurtha made it to us, Mitch called us and said, "I've got two blips on the radar. Which one do you think you are?" I said, "Well, where is the other one?" He said it was south of the point from him, so I said, "Nope, we're the other one that's out in the middle, I would say. We're not toward land." We were right. We were out in the middle. We had about 750 feet of anchor line down, and we couldn't touch anything. We were drifting. Mitch told us we were in 1,100 feet of water. So I'm thinking we're close to the middle. When he did come up, he came up out of the fog just like a giant wall, 100 feet high. I don't know how high that is and how loaded he was.

Gary: He was empty. He was in ballast. He was going up to Duluth in ballast.

Pete: He was huge. Just like a wall came out of the fog. You could start to see his lights a little bit, but, you could see the whole thing come. And he came up to us sideways, not bow first. He met us on his starboard side. Put down a gangplank, put down a rope to the eye on the front of the boat. We first went into the galley. They fed us, and we watched TV. We ran out of cigarettes out there, which is really bad. They gave us some cigarettes. We had lots of beer, but we didn't have any cigarettes. We didn't want to drink any beer. The boat was a 26-footer, a Sunray. It hugged right to the side of the Tregurtha. It was amazing. But we didn't make it inside, and it was pouring, and the wind was blowing. We had no idea anything was coming. It was still just as foggy as ever. But the wind came up, and we would have been drenched out there. I don't know how the wind would have taken us with our anchor line down.

Gary: That wouldn't slow you down much at all.

Pete: When we got on board, we were met by two or three guys. They must have been watchmen. They took us to the stern, where everything is. I had no idea that I was even on an Interlake. I didn't know the signature colors of the fleet. After we ate, Mitch took us up to the pilothouse and showed us around. I finally realized, "Oh, this is Interlake." I asked Mitch if he knew Gary. "Yeah, I know Gary." And that's when he must have called you.

Gary: Yeah, he called me up and said, "We've got your brother-in-law. He's okay." And that was the message. I didn't know what the hell was going on.

Pete: Before they got to us – when he saw the two blips on the radar and he asked us where we thought we were – he said, "Listen for the signal." So he blasted three blasts of his horn, about three to five seconds apart. The first time, I thought somebody was messing with us. I was listening – the Coast Guard was in the conversation, too – and it took I'm guessing 45 seconds before we could hear the blasts from when he said he did it. That's an eternity to wait,

Paul R. Tregurtha, vice chairman of Interlake Steamship Company and namesake of the longest vessel on the Great Lakes, jokes during the company's 100th anniversary celebration. *Photo courtesy The Interlake Steamship Company*

because you're listening for a signal. And I thought somebody was screwing with us, maybe that other boat *(blip)* that they saw was blowing their horn – because it was so long between him doing the signal and us hearing it. I was amazed. I had no idea. So he did it again. And then we were convinced that's who we were hearing. We could hear the drone of those diesel motors all the way. I mean, for 40 miles I could hear him coming.

Gary: Yes. The Tregurtha is the largest vessel on the Great Lakes. It's 1,013 feet. It's the largest by seven or eight feet. Those are big, Pielstick engines, big horsepower engines.

Pete: You could hear them a long ways away, for a long time when we were playing cards. On our way to Isle Royale – when we stopped in the shipping lanes and had our motor off – we could hear ship engines, too.

Gary: They have different sounds. All of them are a little bit different.

Pete: And they carry.

Gary: And I think the sound carries better in fog. You can hear it for a long ways.

Pete: It took a couple more hours before the Tregurtha got us about five miles out of Eagle Harbor, and the Coast Guard arrived at the Tregurtha. The Coast Guard gave us gas, gave us one of their walkie-talkies, and escorted us all the way back into the harbor to the boat launch. Then they boarded us, and they wanted to inspect us. We figured we were getting tickets, there was something going to come out of it. And we showed them the piece of paper we had from just three days before, and they just let us go. Got their walkie-talkie back from us. Yes, they said stuff.

Gary: "What were you thinking?"

Pete: Yeah. They had no idea we went to Isle Royale and went through the channel and stopped in the middle of the channel. They read us the riot act, yeah. There was a lot of conversation with them. I was on their boat for quite a while. Tony was driving our boat back, and they were asking a lot of questions on their boat. Then they put me back on our boat and escorted us in. It was quite late, night, by the time we got back into Eagle Harbor. The Tregurtha picked us up at 3 or 4.

Gary: The Tregurtha went on to Duluth. The Tregurtha had radar that could possibly see their boat, pick it up. The Coast Guard, with their small boats, are close to the water. They wouldn't pick up something with the range of the Tregurtha radar.

Pete: When we were stranded, I was extremely nervous, too. I was the one who made the call. I knew that was the only way we were going to get out of there, and it was all because of Gary and knowing the stuff to do when you're out on a lake. Having a marine radio.

Gary: I preached to them about having a radio.
Pete: Many people don't.
Pete: We didn't even name our boat. No name. Yet.
Gary: "This is called Incredible Stupid 1."
Pete: We always kidded about it being the three-hour tour.

***

EPILOGUE: *Captain Mitch Hallin received a Coast Guard commendation for the rescue of the three men. Captain Hallin died of a heart attack May 3, 2002, aboard the Tregurtha.*

Great Lakes Fleet

Vessels on the Great Lakes last longer by far than most planes, trains, and automobiles – and they keep working day in and day out. Old is relative with them.

Being on fresh water lakes, the longevity of the ships on the Great Lakes is great. If a salt water vessel makes it 30 years, she's doing great. It's not unheard of for a vessel on the Great Lakes to be 100 years old, and there is one running out there right now that's over 100 years old. The Medusa Challenger *(also known as St. Marys Challenger, a 551-foot freighter built in 1906)* I believe is the oldest vessel on the Great Lakes now.

The E.M. Ford was cut up three years ago, and she was built in 1898. I worked on a vessel that was built in 1889, the Samuel Mitchell, which became Mel William Selvick as a barge. I worked on it as a barge. The steel was brittle. One time, we came up against the break wall, and it put a little dent in the side of the hull, but it didn't just dent it, it kind of cracked it like a piece of glass. It fractured. Some of the steel they were using back then had too high of a carbon content. It made the steel extremely brittle. That's why some of those boats sank back then in some of those storms. But the new steel is really flexible steel. It's called high-tensile strength steel, and it has a lot of flexibility. They get by with less thickness and more flexibility with it. It just works better.

The vessels have personalities of a kind – a look, shape, and sound.

You get to know a lot of them by sight. There are certain vessels' shapes that you know what they are. If you see a U.S. Steel boat that has a forward end boom, there's only one, John G. Munson. If there's a Bay class thousand footer that has a certain shape to it, you know it's Indiana Harbor, Burns Harbor, American Century, or one of several boats that were built at Bay Shipbuilding – the Walter J. McCarthy Jr. or something like that. You can tell what they are. And if it's one that was built at Lorain, that's our *(Interlake's)* class of vessels, our class of thousand footer. You can tell if it's going to be the James R. Barker or the Mesabi Miner or the Paul R. Tregurtha or maybe the American Spirit. Those type vessels you can tell just by looking at shapes. You know that it's one of those four. After a while, you get to know your different boats. There are a lot of Bay class boats in the Sam Laud, Buffalo, Joe Block *(Joseph L. Block)* that kind of look the same, and you can tell.

An honor roll
(Not all-inclusive)

Vessel	Length	Tonnage
Adam E. Cornelius	680	30,621
Algowood	740	31,750

Vessel	Length	Tonnage
Alpena	520	17,097
American Century	1,000	68,880
American Courage	635	26,992
American Fortitude	690	25,116
American Integrity	1,000	68,320
American Mariner	730	35,583
American Spirit	1,000	66,080
American Valor	767	28,560
American Victory	730	27,552
Arthur M. Anderson	767	28,336
Badger	410	N/A
Buffalo	635	26,216
Burns Harbor	1,000	71,120
Calcite II	605	12,650
Calumet	630	22,064
Cason J. Callaway	767	28,336
Dorothy Ann/Pathfinder	711	23,800
Defiance/Ashtabula	702	30,700
Edgar B. Speer	1,004	69,552
Edward L. Ryerson	730	30,800
Edwin H. Gott	1,004	69,664
Gary L. Ostrander/Integrity	530	17,600
Great Republic	635	27,183
H. Lee White	704	34,247
Herbert C. Jackson	690	27,776
Hon. James L. Oberstar	806	35,280
Indiana Harbor	1,000	68,757
Invincible/Mckee Sons	615	22,288
James R. Barker	1,000	67,475
John B. Aird	730	31,000
John G. Munson	768	28,616
John J. Boland	680	32,772
Joseph L. Block	728	41,664
Joseph Thompson, Jr./Joseph Thompson	707	23,774
Joyce L. Van Enkevort/Great Lakes Trader	845	39,766
Kaye E. Barker	767	29,008
Ken Boothe Sr./Lakes Contender	845	39,766
Lee A. Tregurtha	826	32,884
Manistee*	620	14,900
Manitoba	609	19,093

Vessel	Length	Tonnage
Manitowoc	630	22,064
Mesabi Miner	1,000	67,475
Mississippi	620	15,800
Myron C. Taylor	604	12,450
Ojibway	60	N/A
Olive L. Moore/Lewis J. Kuber	728	21,765
Paul R. Tregurtha	1,013	69,580
Philip R. Clarke	767	28,336
Prentiss Brown/St. Marys Conquest	487	9,520
Presque Isle	1,000	58,240
Roger Blough	858	50,305
St. Clair	770	44,380
St. Mary Challenger	552	12,656
Sam Laud	635	26,216
Samuel De Chaplain/Innovation	536	17,600
Stewart J. Cort	1,000	64,690
Undaunted/Pere Marquette	494	5,750
Victory/James L. Kuber	807	28,560
Walter J. McCarthy	1,000	68,757
Wilfred Sykes	678	24,080

*- The Manistee was the Richard J. Reiss. It was the Richard Reiss for a time. The Richard Reiss was the boat my dad sailed on, and he was on that boat for 38 years. Same thing I haul.

The Philip R. Clarke and Dorothy Ann/Pathfinder share space at the Port of Calcite slip in Rogers City, Michigan. *Gary Schmidt photo*

The Stewart J. Cort passes near De Tour, Michigan. *Gary Schmidt photo*

The Mesabi Miner passes in the St. Clair River near Detroit, Michigan. *Gary Schmidt photo*

The Lee A. Tregurtha heads in the opposite direction at the Soo Locks. *Gary Schmidt photo*

The Canadian vessel Robert S. Pierson meets the Dorothy Ann/Pathfinder at the Soo Locks. *Gary Schmidt photo*

The Herbert C. Jackson approaches on Lake St. Clair. *Gary Schmidt photo*

The Hon. James L. Oberstar passes at Sault Ste. Marie, Ontario, Canada. *Gary Schmidt photo*

The Kaye E. Barker is framed by a Dorothy Ann pilothouse window as the Barker passes on Lake St. Clair. *Gary Schmidt photo*

The tug/barge combination Undaunted/Pere Marquette 41 pass. *Gary Schmidt photo*

The Paul R. Tregurtha, the longest Great Lakes vessel, passes at a distance. *Gary Schmidt photo*

The Canadian tug/barge combination Everlast/Norman McLeod is about to pass in ice. Gary Schmidt photo. *Gary Schmidt photo*

The Charles M. Beeghly, right, passes within feet of the Dorothy Ann/Pathfinder near the Conrail Bridge adjacent to the Levy Dock on the Rouge River near Detroit, Michigan. The Beeghly today is the Hon. James L. Oberstar, which acquired the nickname of performer Jennifer Lopez – JLo. . *Gary Schmidt photo*

The James R. Barker passes. *Gary Schmidt photo*

At the Soo Locks, the 730-foot Canadian vessel Kaminstiqua passes two waiting ships, the Dorothy Ann/Pathfinder, left, and the Paul R. Tregurtha. *Gary Schmidt photo*

Cargo Hold 4 – Maneuvering

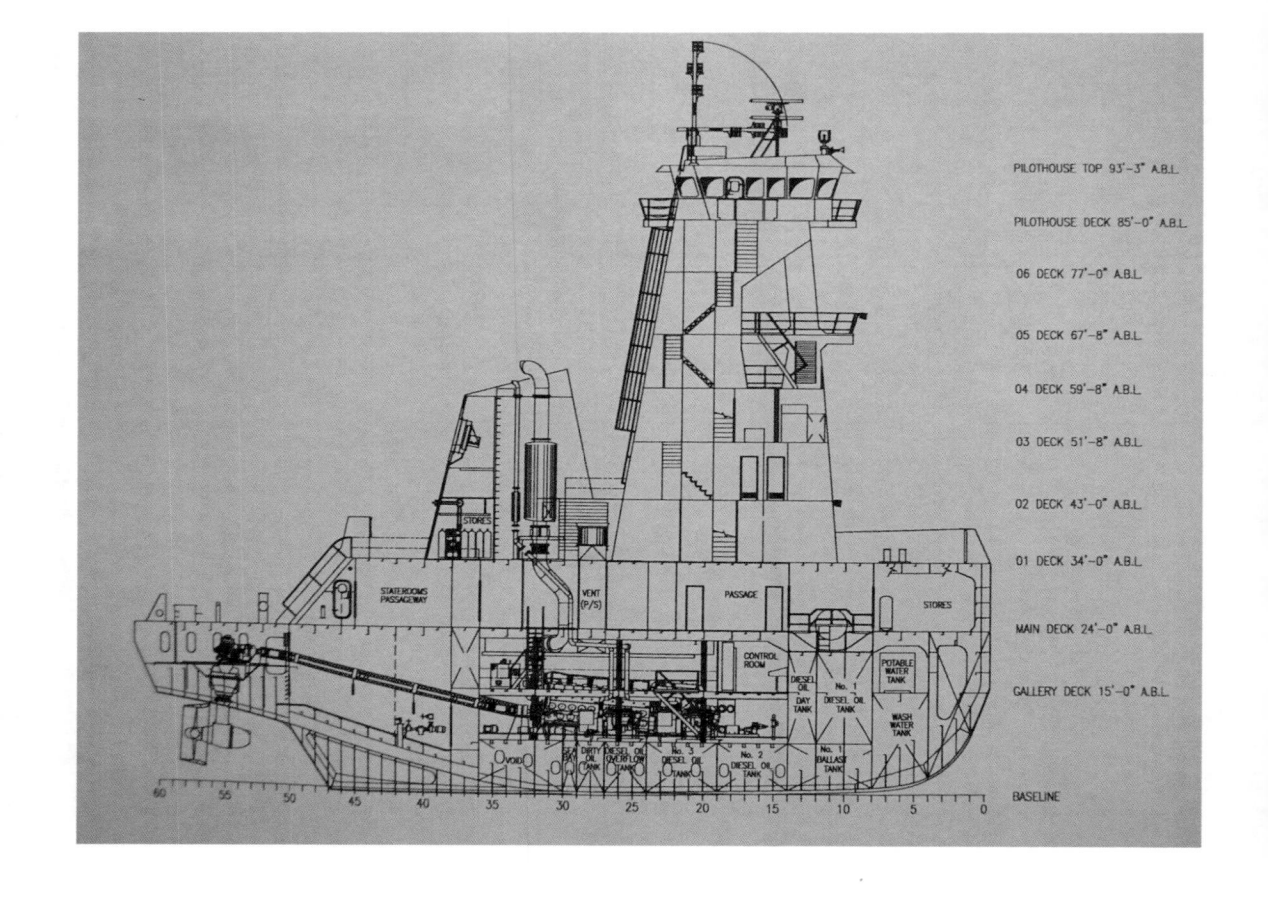

Hatch 73

Cover photo

Captain Schmidt was verbally walking me around the deck of the Pathfinder during one of our interviews. We were well into another of our many sessions at his kitchen table at home. As a prompt for Captain Schmidt, we were using the photograph of the Dorothy Ann and Pathfinder that I chose for the cover of "Real, Honest Sailing." The photo was selected for three key reasons: It shows the full vessel, has work taking place in the scene, and qualifies for a tenet used when printing images in newspapers, magazines, and books — the vessel is pointing toward the side of the page that opens. The direction is a hint to go inside. As Captain Schmidt continued leading me around the deck, step by step, something occurred to me. Now, the photograph had been in the field of play for months, through assorted versions of the cover, always with that photo being crucial. Finally, I noticed that the vessel is not moored next to the dock. The distance is substantial. Suddenly, being a captain on the Great Lakes took a new turn. What follows is a distillation of the questions to Captain Schmidt.

We're at the Levy Dock in Detroit. It's between the Jefferson Street Bridge and the Conrail Bridge, which is right behind me *(out of the picture)*. This is the Rouge River. I've backed in from the Detroit River.

The Dorothy Ann and the Pathfinder are not connected by the pins at this point. We are unloading. We would not be connected when we are loading or when we are unloading. The Dorothy Ann and the Pathfinder

The Dorothy Ann/Pathfinder unloads at the Levy Dock in the Rouge River at Detroit. *Photo courtesy The Interlake Steamship Company*

are connected by the jockey lines. That's all that's holding us. Plus, we have safety lines between us, safety nylons.

We're not up against the dock wall because we're up against a mud bank. There's mud built up on the edge of the river, and we can't get any closer to the work dock. That's the way it is at most docks. Certain docks we can get up alongside, and other docks we are out in the channel just a little bit. We pull up as close as we can get. The channel is so many feet off of each side that is maintained to a certain depth. And if they want this cleaned out up top *(bosses)*, that's up to the docks to clean so many feet out, and most of the docks don't

To get to the optimum spot for unloading at the Levy Dock in the Rouge River at Detroit, the Dorothy Ann must be backed in as far as possible. Captain Schmidt says, "Behind me is the Conrail Bridge. I'm somewhere between 25 and 50 feet from it. If I have to go back to the beginning of the pile (right), I'm real close to it." Note the ladder at the left extending from the Pathfinder for the work boat, seen in the center of the photo with a crewman in it. *Gary Schmidt photo*

want to pay the fees or cannot get permits to do it.

I'm pretty secure to the dock. This area is kind of sheltered. This wouldn't be a problem with wind.

The mud is a factor with putting men on shore.

We have a little work boat that sits in a cradle on the stern of the barge. It's not on the deck right now in the picture. We use a hoist to drop the work boat down to the water with a guy in it. He gets the boat running, and he'll come back to the stern of the tug and pick up another guy. Then we bring the boat to the dock, and a guy gets up on the shore. Now, there will be a dock boss there who has a truck. The guy with the boat will come up toward the shore, and I'll say, "All right, send out wire Number 1," and a heaving line will be dropped down to him. He'll ferry it over to the dock, throw the line up on the shore, and that guy will grab it. The line will be hooked to a truck, and the wire will be pulled up onto the shoreline and hooked to a bollard.

The boat is a 16-foot runabout with a six-horsepower outboard motor. It's a pull crank. We have a little station on the stern of the barge with a 55-gallon drum that is cut in half. The motor is hooked up to the drum and sits in water. We start the motor on the barge. We warm the motor up before we set it up on the work boat and drop the boat in the water. So it's pre-started to where it's easy to start, warmed up, and when we send it down. It's an easy pull.

This is in all conditions, even below zero.

Oh, yeah, it's brutal, there's no doubt. There are some days where it is absolutely brutal. And it's hard on guys. And we have to take breaks and get them warm. There are days that we have gone out in that little boat and had to move ice chunks out of the way to be able to get mooring lines across.

There's another way to get lines across. If we can't use a boat, I can hold the vessel in position, and we'll swing the *(unloading)* boom out. A guy will walk out to the end of the boom over the water, drop the heaving line down to the person there, and then walk the line back and walk it up the deck. On each end, they'll walk the line and tie so we can hook the wire on the bollard.

Docks where we are away from the shoreline we call work boat docks. That's where we put the work boat in. We go to a lot of docks that are work boat docks. Any time we go to Fairport, Lorain, Marine City, this dock and others in Detroit, and some docks along the Cuyahoga River, I have to launch the boat.

There are two deckhands for the work boat. If we have an inexperienced deckhand, he'll be the one who goes on shore and pulls the ropes and ties the vessel up. The more experienced guy will run the boat. But as time goes on, I have all the deckhands on the work boat so they all know how to do it. They all take turns at it. As their duties go, there two things that the deckhands do – take turns at work boat docks, with the boat, and take turns unloading the vessel.

There are three guys on a watch, and they all kind of rotate and take turns with duties at work boat docks. You need one on the boat, one on the dock, the other one who runs a winch while we're running the work boat, and the mate runs the winch on the back until we're tied up.

When you're maneuvering the vessel toward the dock, you're coming up the middle, and you swing the bow over slowly until it can't go anymore. You do the same with the stern. It just comes up against the mud.

As the crew is moving things out, I'm moving the vessel, swinging it in, and swinging the boom out at the same time. Our boom is 260 feet long, and it's off a center post, so you're looking at minus 35. So straight out, at a 90-degree angle to the boat, it's going out there 225 feet.

The docks want you to unload into a specific area. We shift the boat up and down the dock. Sometimes we move the vessel out farther in water. The boom swings to different angles. A lot is dependent on the water levels and how close we can get to the dock. It's not the same every time.

Your pile is only going to be built up to a certain height. You don't want to cave the docks in. There's a weight limitation. The docks are on solid ground, but they are weighted for so much tonnage. It's like with road construction. A road may be made a foot thick, but there's a limitation on truck weights because the cement can break. The same thing can happen with the weight on a dock. The dock boss estimates what your peak is going to be, about 35 feet tall. Some docks are 40 feet tall, and some docks are less than that. The docks know where they want their peaks at. That's something we don't have to figure out. We communicate with the dock boss by walkie-talkie.

As we're making the approach and we get close to where I think the pile is, I estimate where the boom has got to be. As we're making the dock, the boom is going out and water is being put in to stabilize the vessel. It takes us about half an hour or 45 minutes on a work boat dock to tie up.

In the picture, we're unloading a stone that's a clean stone that's been washed. It's called Michigan 6AAs – about a ¾ by ½ inch stone that is used in making concrete. As you see the stone coming off in the picture, there are people up on the barge with the hatches off. They are washing out. As we empty a cargo hold, crewmen wash it so we're ready for the next cargo.

Crewmen who have climbed down a ladder from the Pathfinder prepare to move the work boat as part of the process of tying up at some docks. *Gary Schmidt photo*

That cargo falls onto a belt that goes from forward to aft on the barge. The cargo gets to the A frame, which is called a HAC, a high-angle conveyor, which brings the cargo up through a hatch, drops it into a hopper, which drops the cargo down onto the boom belt, which brings it over the side and feeds the pile on the dock. Everything is gravity feed except for the HAC that brings the cargo up.

This stone came from Stoneport, Michigan. From the time we leave Stoneport until we're tied up and ready to unload at this dock it takes us about 23 to 24 hours one way.

Mississppi River

When I was targeting Hannah Marine as a job that I wanted because I was interested in moving up a little bit from what I was doing with Selvick Towing, I needed my Western Rivers License. I need that with Hannah because of where the company operated. Once you get below Ashland Avenue in the Chicago River, it becomes the Chicago Sanitary Canal, and that becomes the Western Rivers. There's another point between the Great Lakes and the Western Rivers. The Thomas J. O'Brien Lock coming in through South Chicago takes you down the Cal-Sag Channel *(short for Calumet-Saganashkee Channel)*. Hannah's office and shipyard were at the junction between the Cal-Sag Channel and the Chicago Sanitary Canal. So if I wanted to work for this company, I needed to get a Western Rivers License.

The process took Captain Schmidt to Twin City Barge and Towing and a year of work on towboats on the Mississippi River, starting as a deckhand.

Coming off the Great Lakes already running as a captain and going to a deckhand was a real learning experience.

With Selvick, I was just handling one barge or two barges and towing all the time. With the Mississippi River system, you put the barges out in front of you, and you were pushing them all the time, and you were pushing anywhere from one barge on up to 15 barges. One time, we had 17 barges.

The way the Mississippi works, the lock chambers are 600 feet long by 105 feet wide. A typical Mississippi barge is 35 feet wide by 195 feet or 200 feet long. The barges are put together in packs of twos and threes side by side. Then you'll have three rows of these, and that's nine barges. That's what will fit in a lock chamber. From there, you can add another row with what you call a break coupling. You add two more rows of three that will go in the lock with the towboat in the middle of the last six barges.

When you get to a lock that's 600 feet long, you push the first nine barges in, and you have a break coupling where you're able to break the first nine off from the last six. After the nine are dropped down in the chamber as you're going down river, winches on the outside are used to pull the nine barges out and tie them off on the lock wall. The

The Dorothy Ann/Pathfinder is maneuvered through one of five bridges in south Chicago in the Calumet River. *Photo courtesy The Interlake Steamship Company*

deckhand rides down and walks back up a ladder and gets back on the towboat again. The next six are pushed in with the towboat. After they go through the lock, they're reconnected with the nine. They all have 35-foot wires with steamboat ratchets that connect to them and chain links. It takes 125 sets of rigging to connect all of the barges together.

I thought I was pretty good until I started doing this. This is labor intensive. I was able to do the work, but for the first two weeks, we were working six on and six off. That wasn't new to me, but it was full labor on this. I was too tired to even take a shower. I'd fall on my bunk, and I'd go right to sleep. And five hours later, someone is knocking on your door to get up to eat your breakfast and go out and do it again.

We carried different kinds of grains, coal, salt, coke, molasses, sugar, machinery parts. One time, we had a boatload of boats. You never knew what was going to be shipped in these things. It could be general cargo, or it could be stone or gravel. Most of our cargo was coal and salt and gasoline and diesel.

We picked up loads along the way. Assist boats come out, and you just maneuver in the middle of the river, and they come out and say, "We're going to peel off these three loads," and we'd shift barges and rearrange barges. This was night or day.

When we'd get to major ports, assist boats would come alongside the towboat. They refuel you under way, you exchange your groceries under way, you get your fresh water under way from an assist boat. They would come out and tie up. You do all your connecting, get your oils and everything, as you go on down the river. You never really pull into a port. They all come out to you.

Captain Schmidt had to accumulate 90 days of work before he could write for the Coast Guard license. It was six months before he got into the pilothouse. His travels included up the Illinois River into the Chicago water systems. He didn't work long in the pilothouse before he got a call to work for Hannah. While having the license was important to work for Hannah, the Mississippi River experience rippled on for its value with handling – to shift barges, drop off, untie, release, move, and slide into position.

The maneuvering on those towboats *(10 or 12)* was entirely different than what I have on the Dorothy Ann. A nine-foot draft is maintained on the Mississippi River. It's usually at 12 feet or more of water. As the water fluctuates, it does make a difference.

When I was there in 1975, the water was extremely high. Parts of the river were shut down. There was flooding. During high water, you could see the water mark on the houses – a couple of feet from roofs.

You want to be moving faster than the current so you have control. If the current is too much, then you want to be able stop and head into it. You can brake. You have flanking rudders, so you can maneuver yourself against the current a little bit. But when you get down to the locks and you have to stop, you've got to start stopping a long time before you get there.

There are long approach walls because you have vessels going both ways. You might have one locking up while you're waiting to lock down. And you have to wait your turn, and it's a long turn. Every time you get there, it's very long because of all the break couplings and double lockings.

***

SIDE TRIP: A lot of times when it gets foggy in the Mississippi River, you can't go. You just can't maneuver upbound or downbound. What you do is find a place where you can pull over to the bank where you're close enough to tie off to a tree. "Can you see anything yet?" "Yeah, I see a tree coming up. You're two feet from it. Inch forward. All right, you're up against it. All right, we'll try to get a line around this one now."

***

It was maneuvering in current upbound or downbound. It was a whole new learning experience on how to handle multiple tasking barges at one time. The close-quarter maneuvering and handling would give me an edge up on a lot of people, and it's what I like to do. I really like the handling part. I like to maneuver into docks, going up corners and tight corners. It's difficult sometimes, but that's where I get my pleasure, knowing that I can do this stuff and a lot of people can't do this stuff. It's just something I acquired a like for. I became very good down there. I enjoyed it – the ice breaking and year-around navigation. And those were hard winters.

---

57 bridges

With the Western Rivers license, I was able to work for Hannah in the Chicago area out of Lemont, Illinois. You didn't have to open every bridge, and all the bridges in the Chicago system didn't work that well, but you had to know where you were.

The Donald C. Hannah had the hydraulic pilothouse on it that could duck under the bridges. Once you cleared the bridge, hydraulics would lift the house, and you could see where you're at again. You'd drop it down for the next bridge, and then you'd come back up again and see where you're at.

Going down the Chicago Sanitary Canal coming through the Loop, there are 57 bridges. You'd have to duck a lot, but some you didn't have to duck because they were higher bridges. But 57 bridges.

I wrote down all the bridges by name in order. Back in those days, I smoked. As I cleared a bridge, I'd move my cigarette pack down one bridge so I knew where I was. If somebody called me, I could answer. Security calls are very important. You let somebody know you're coming because there are so many spots where you can't pass one another. You have to make arrangements to pass. Two boats won't go into the same bridge at one time. Out of 57 bridges, you wanted to know where you were all the time. I got to know all those 57 bridges by heart in order.

Hatch 75

At the docks

Docking and leaving a dock are never automatic. They're dictated by weather.

The standard operating procedure to leave a dock is one hour before we're finished loading or unloading, the engineers are given a notice so they have time to warm the engines up and get everything ready to leave the dock when the time is there.

I'm given a half-an-hour call before we leave the dock so I can get to the pilothouse, do the necessary tests, and take care of some of my paperwork. My paperwork consists of a ballast report and an arrival or departure report. The arrival or departure report includes tonnages that we've offloaded or loaded, our estimated time of departure, and our estimated time of arrival at the dock. It may include any personnel changes. It may include fuel used during this operation. It also may include drafts. Then there are tests. We have tests to make sure that the radars are working, that the steering is functioning, that the whistle – I usually don't blow the whistle until it's time to depart the dock, but that's part of my thing. Sometimes it's a radio test. I check the navigating lights and make sure all my navigation equipment is operating.

And then I just sit there and wait until I'm told me that we're unloaded and ready to roll. Ready to roll means that crewmen have the boom into place and in the saddle, the hatches are secure, the men are on the dock where they let the lines go, and the paperwork has been gotten from the dock, whether we're loading or unloading. When that happens, I give the guys permission to throw the lines off and then get aboard.

The men get aboard via ladder or, if the boarding ladder doesn't reach a particular part of the dock, we have a long ladder that will go over the side, and the men can climb aboard. The mate moves the boom and puts it in the saddle. At that point, we check to make sure that, once the boom is in the saddle, our vessel is even keeled. If it's not, we may add water to one side or the other to level it out and get what we call a white light.

I give a long blast of the whistle, and we'll back away from the dock or, if we're headed out *(to a distant place)*, we'll just head out.

***

SIDE TRIP: On the ships, you're working Eastern Time Zone all the time. The companies are usually in Eastern Time Zone. When we go to the Central Time Zone, we have to make sure we have that straight. We have to make our ETAs *(estimated time of arrivals)*, and when we talk to dock bosses, we have to make that conversion.

***

Coming to the dock, the standard procedure is engineers are given notice. They go out and start up the loading or unloading generator. That is also connected to the bow thruster and runs the bow thruster, so I have use of the bow thruster.

You communicate with the dock personnel. The dock boss determines exactly where you go. You set up your wires in case you have to shift a little bit or move a little bit. You put the unloading boom over the dock right about where the dock boss wants it, and then you make an adjustment from there. He usually tells you. When we send people ashore to tie up the vessel, we give one of our walkie-talkies to the dock boss, and we have constant communication with the dock.

A crewman is swung toward the dock at Rogers City, Michigan, with a landing boom. *Jeremy Mock photo*

The deckhands are notified to get the deck ready one hour before we will be docking. That means getting the lines or cables ready on the side that we are going to land on. They get the landing boom ready. That's a boom that has a chair on it and a line connected to it that swings over the side. So as I'm making the dock, the guys can swing it out and drop guys down on the dock. That boom can reach out about 20 to 25 feet. I usually wait until I'm within four feet of reaching the dock, then I'll say go ahead and send them over. There are two people involved in it. One has a line figure-eighted on a cleat that he can just let out easily, and one guy that takes him and swings him over the side. So they jump onto this thing from the Number 1 hatch cover, they get on the boom. It extends over the top of the rails and swings a guy over and right out over the side, and he is lower. You can get guys on the dock easily that way before you make the dock and have to try to put a ladder down and hold them.

Some docks don't have enough lighting, so we supply a lot of it. We have floodlights and other lights all over the vessel. Some searchlights when shined down on an angle don't reach corners. We have manual lights that illuminate some areas for the safety of the dockworkers, like where they have to put a cable or line on.

As we're getting into the dock, after the lines and hooks are prepared, and the hooks are prepared, the hatch covers may be removed, depending upon the weather. If it's calm enough, not blowing so hard, we'll take off the hatch covers well before we reach the dock so we're ready to load or unload.

***

SIDE TRIP: For the guys, this is a physical job. Tying the vessel up – mooring the vessel – you're using cables. The cables are one inch in diameter. This is steel cable. It's quite heavy, close to two pounds a foot. They might have to drag that cable on the dock 200 feet. That's a lot of weight. Sometimes if it's longer, we put two people on a cable. For a short distance, one person will handle it.

They're continually shifting wires for moving the vessel. We shift those wires quite often sometimes, moving up and down a dock.

Besides that, when we're loading, there's spillage on deck, all of that spillage is shoveled up. It's shoveled back into the cargo hold. Sometimes it's steel pellets, sometimes it's stone and dust and dirt. Whatever the product is, it needs to be cleaned up and shoveled up and put back into the cargo holds.

The other thing is that, as we are cleaning out, we use inch-and-a-half fire hoses, and they're full of water. They're 150 feet long. You're dragging that with all that water in it to the next cargo hold as you're washing it out. And then you have to pull it again.

It's all manual labor. It's a lot of work.

Some of the guys don't come aboard being physical, but they leave that way. Yes, the work is very physical, and the guys build muscle. It's quite amazing to see some of these kids who come out who are just out of high school or are in college and aboard for a summer job. It's amazing how much muscle they'll put on in two to three months.

On top of it, we have a really nice gym area, workout area, and the younger kids keep up with their workouts. They go to the area in the barge and use the weights or the elliptical or the treadmill or whatever – rowing machines, bicycles, we've got it all. They stay in fairly decent shape.

There are no elevators on the vessel. It's 70 feet up to get to the pilothouse. That's my exercise. I do that maybe five or six times a day. Although it doesn't put a lot of muscle on you, it's good for your cardio vascular system. My legs are pretty good.

There are a lot of steps on the Pathfinder, too. From the tunnel area to the main deck I would estimate is 26 feet, and the pump room is another floor below that. From the main deck to the keel I would estimate it at 35 or 36 feet.

***

I'm called a half an hour before. I get up to the pilothouse. I make sure that the bow thruster is on, things are operating. Once I'm up there and know where we're at and I figure out what I want to do, I send the mate down to the deck so he can get ready to get the guys over the side when we get up alongside.

The mate and the watchman will call distances as I come in and maneuver until I get up alongside. Then we'll send the guys over and tie the boat up.

Once the boat is secure, I call the engineer and let him know that he can shut down the engines. Sometimes, he'll disengage the pins or sometimes I let him say we'll keep it pinned in until we're getting ready to load. It depends upon the weather and where we're at. But most of the time, if it's a load, I have him disengage because we're already inside safe harbor. If we're loading, sometimes we don't disengage the pins – we stay pinned in – until we get to a certain point. And then we disengage, drop the barge down and load it to a certain depth on the stern, re-engage the pin so we don't have to be bouncing around and rocking around in weather.

Once we're secure alongside the dock, the mate, if we're loading, will raise the boom and swing it out of the way so the loaders can load. Or if we are unloading, he will swing the boom over into position where it's supposed to be for unloading.

And, again, I will do my paperwork, which means I'll do an arrival report and, again, that will be tonnages that we have loaded or unloaded and estimated time of departure.

Some docks I back into, some docks I just go head-in.

Some docks I have to turn around and back in because the tug will be in a safe harbor where, if it's turned around the other way, it may not be in a safe harbor. It might be affected by weather. That would be Stoneport, Michigan.

At Port Inland, Michigan, you don't have to back in – you can go in either way – but it's easier to back in when you're light if the weather's not bad. That way, when you're coming out, if the weather's bad, you can head out into the weather and not take too bad of a beating.

Some docks are longer than others. At some docks, the loaders move up and down the docks. At other docks, the

Some docks are scenic, as this one at Fairport Harbor, Ohio. Crewmen are taking a break from washing down a cargo hold through an open hatch. *Gary Schmidt photo*

loaders are stationary, and you have to move the vessel up and down the dock.

The Shiras Dock in Marquette, Michigan, is short, and you have to back into it. A thousand footer would not go into that dock. But other big vessels – 800 feet long – have to back in also.

For some docks where our company does business, which vessel goes there depends upon the size of the vessel. It's a matter of who can do it. I'll definitely take all the Cuyahoga loads. There's only one other vessel in our fleet that can do Cuyahoga, and that would be the Herbert C. Jackson. It's a single screw with a stern thruster and a bow thruster, and the Jackson can do it, but it would be much harder for him to do it than for me.

I have an advantage of having a midship winch. I can pull my vessel in on a short dock because my bow is sticking way out. It would be really hard to run a cable that far to hold your bow around. But that's what some boats have to do. I'm fortunate where I can just tie up with two stern cables and a midship cable, and it works out just right for me and holds me in the spot where I need to be for that Shiras Dock. Some docks I back into, some docks I just go head-in.

There are a lot of different ways to make a dock. Weather dictates it. On a nice day, it's kind of automatic. When I go into Marblehead, which is an open dock to Lake Erie – and weather from all directions – I must have 30 different ways to make that dock.

When I'm docking, sometimes I use my Z-drive and my bow thruster at the same time.

And I use them for effect. Say I'm making a left-hand turn. If I start shoving my stern so it goes to the right, that means my bow is going to go to the left. If I'm in the turn and I'm already tight to the bank with the bow and I don't want it to go anymore left, I'll use that bow thruster, and I'll shoot my bow to the right. I'm shooting my stern to the right so my bow doesn't go to the left very fast. I want to maneuver for effect as I'm going around the corner.

It's the same way with making a dock. I'll use the bow thruster to push the barge toward the dock as I'm trying to push the stern of my tug into the dock at the same time. Because if I'm pushing my stern into the dock, that means that my bow is going to the right, and I want it to go to the left. So I'm pushing both over to the left at the same time as I make a dock. As you get in, it's a feel – you let the bow thruster off, you let the bow fall out a little bit, you stop your stern, and everything kind of coasts in – and then you give it a little shot just to stop it so it doesn't fall in hard.

I have to keep in mind which side of the vessel we should dock on. The boom swings out either way 90 degrees, port or starboard. There's no difference except that the ballast control panel we use most is on the port side. It's a lot easier to run ballast and be able to watch your boom and watch what's going on from what we call the boom shack, where the controls are for the boom. We have controls for the boom on both sides of the barge. A computer on both sides tells you how the cargo is running. But the ballast is all on the port side. And you have to load ballast as you're unloading. You have to unload ballast as you're loading. If you go to your starboard side to watch your boom as you're unloading, you're not seeing your ballast. It is a visual thing. So starboard side docking is a little bit harder than a port side docking.

With a vessel the size of the Dorothy Ann/Pathfinder, there are places around the outside of the vessel that you can't see.

If you're looking forward, there are some blind spots. But we have a bow camera that takes care of blind spots. It can look down to the water, and you can see any vessel in front of you at any time. It's adjustable. I can turn it completely around, 360 degrees.

Ice is an obstacle. It depends on if you're loading or unloading. If you're unloading, you're swinging a boom over a certain area, and it doesn't matter if there's ice in between you and the dock. But if you're loading and you have a short boom and it can only go so far, then you've got to get the ice out of the way, and you have to be up against the dock and be able to shift back and forth so the vessel can stay there. So you've got to do a lot of work cleaning the ice out of your way so that you can move along the dock to load.

With my Z-drives, I work it, clean it out, use one Z-drive to wash the ice away and one to pull myself backward. With the wheel wash on the one Z-drive, I'll wash the ice and water back and forth and not have as much power on the Z-drive. I'll use a little more power on the other Z-drive to pull me back against the dock, and, as I'm going back, I'll wash that ice out of my way.

A lot of times if there's a tug at the dock or in the port that we're going to, we'll order a tug out to break the ice up and help clean it out. But at some places, there are no tugs, so you have to do it yourself. You do the best you can. It's not always perfect.

There are tugs in many major ports. There are tugs in Chicago and Cleveland. Cleveland will send tugs as far as the next ports on Lake Erie. They'll go to Ashtabula or maybe have one tug sitting over in Ashtabula because a lot of boats go in and out of there and need ice assistance. A tug out of Cleveland might be put there for the end of the sailing season. Toledo has its fair share of tugs. There are a couple in Green Bay. Ports that need tugs have tugs – where you might need that assistance.

Everything is slower when it's snowy or there's ice. It takes more people. It takes longer to do the job. Everything is slower. It's twofold to do almost anything.

If it's so difficult, why doesn't everybody just go home?

Because the companies have customers they want to satisfy. Tugboats traditionally can do a lot of icebreaking. In the past, there was little pipeline oil delivery, so a lot of the fuel oil, heating oil, and gasoline was shipped by barge. This was back in the '70s. These were essentials. If a place like Mackinac City, Michigan, was running low on gas, we would try to accommodate our customers. They paid a premium for it. Sometimes working winters was a break-even situation, but it kept the customer base.

Commotion

You do have noises when docking. A massive vessel is coming up against the dock. It's steel against wood in most cases. Sometimes it's steel against rubber. And we have powerful engines. And there's a lot of weight in the vessel. There's a lot of creaking. If you're going up against wood and you're hard on that wood, it'll smoke. Rubber on the dock will make noises and creak. A lot of times, the rubber that's attached to the dock is attached with cable, so you'll hear the scraping of the cable against the side of the hull. There's the revving of the engines when you have to give the vessel a shot of power. The running winches make a lot of noise.

But all this depends on the conditions. If the weather is decent, there's a lot less scrambling. But when the weather is bad, you might need to get a wire out, and you need to get it now.

I try to stay away from yelling. There a lot of people who are hollerers and screamers. I'm not one of them. I take a different approach because the more desperate the situation, if you sound anxious and desperate to the guys, it makes them more anxious and desperate. You try to keep it as calm as possible. If things aren't going right, just tell them, "Well, let's start it over. Let's start from scratch, and do it by doing this first." Or, "Let's not do it exactly like that. Let's try a different approach." Does it happen all the time? No. You can't stay calm all the time.

I'm fortunate. We don't have to holler. I have a walkie-talkie for everybody on the vessel, so everybody carries one. We make sure that communication is essential. On some larger vessels, watchmen and mates will have walkie-talkies and not deckhands, and they have to shout to deckhands what do to.

Hatch 76

Driving

Driving a car is one thing. Driving a tractor is another. Driving a bus is another. Driving an 18-wheeler is another. Driving a train is another. Driving a boat is another. Driving a ship like the Dorothy Ann/Pathfinder includes 7,200 horsepower, a front end more than 600 feet ahead of you, the "road" more than 70 feet below you, crewmen giving you information on walkie-talkies, gauges and screens around you, and controls in hand to operate a bow thruster and two propellers, independently, in 360-degree arcs as you guide 13 other people and 50 million pounds safely in all weather, night and day.

I have my hands on both controls when I'm maneuvering. Those compass drives go 360 degrees either way. On top of those controls are the throttles that change the speed up and down. They're like little balls.

I have a screen that tells me my rpm's *(engine revolutions per minute)* and the percentage of power I'm using. The screen also tells me what degrees that my pods are at one way or the other. Also, at eye level as I'm looking out the window, I have that same information on either side of the window that I can glance at – one for the port and one for the starboard drive. I don't have to be looking down to see what my hands are doing. I can be looking out the window and just glance at either side and see what my pods are doing and make sure they're in the right configuration.

As I'm maneuvering and looking out, I'm seeing whether my bow is turning fast enough. If it's not, I'll put more angle on my thruster and bring my stern over, which will bring my bow over, or I'll give it some bow thruster movement. To engage the bow thruster, I use a lever that is right next to the two throttle levers.

With control systems like these, the Dorothy Ann/Pathfinder commands full attention to drive. *Gary Schmidt photo*

Nothing is done really fast, but it seems like it's fast sometimes. It might be turtle slow, but it sure looks like it's going faster than what you want it to sometimes. And when you're trying to stop what you're doing or reverse the action, it seems awfully fast.

***

SIDE TRIP: *While the Dorothy Ann is a priority, the Pathfinder is not out of mind.* We have somebody aboard the barge just about all the time. The watchman makes rounds up there. During the daytime, there's always somebody out there working. At night, they're making rounds about every hour, a general walk-through looking for anything that's not right – no water leaking, that somebody didn't leave a valve open that might be flooding the bottom. There's a certain way they make rounds. They check all the voids that way. Any communication is by walkie-talkie. They call up and say, "Everything is good on the barge."

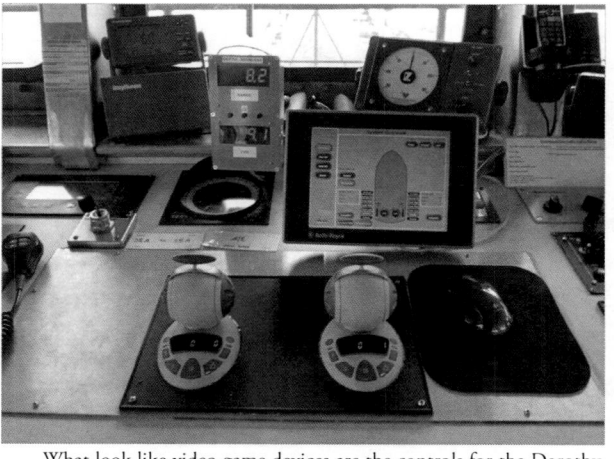

What look like video game devices are the controls for the Dorothy Ann's twin 3,600-horsepower engines. *Gary Schmidt photo*

***

Maneuvering so much so often, I do most of my stuff by feel. There are some times when I do certain things by points, like when I'm getting ready to back into the Rouge River. There is a certain landmark that I have where I start my maneuver. I know I'm going to be about 400 to 500 feet off the bank of the river, and there is a conveyor belt that I'm looking at. When I'm looking at it straight out the starboard window, I start my maneuver, and I start it to a certain point, giving the engine so many rpms because I've done the maneuver enough that I know, "This is what I need to do to do this maneuver," and come out just about perfect every time. And there are variables. The wind will play a factor, and sometimes current will play a factor. But the maneuver comes out pretty close most of the time. Other times in other places, everything is by feel.

When I'm going upbound in a river, I'm looking out the window and can just tell if the vessel is not moving fast enough, my hand automatically turns. It doesn't seem like I have to think about it too much. It's just doing it. You're just concentrating on what's happening out there, and you respond accordingly.

When I make an adjustment with my hands, I watch to see that the vessel is doing what I want it to do. If it's starting to go too fast, I might respond a little bit by counteracting what it's doing. It's all feel.

There are no foot pedals. I'm doing more listening than speaking. I have guys on the vessel, and they are telling me what's going on, and I'm processing what I'm seeing with what they're telling me and responding to that with my hands. Sometimes I'll acknowledge them. Most of the time, I just say, "Keep talking. I'm listening to you. I hear you. Just keep talking." A lot of times I don't say, "OK, OK." Or if they're not responding fast enough sometimes I'll ask, "What do you have now?" But most of the time, it's just them speaking.

This takes place day or night. Visibility is a big thing. I have search lights and other lights that help me see the bank. But maneuvering during the day is so much easier than doing it at night, just because of being able to see what you're doing. It seems to take a little longer at night. You don't do things quite as fast. When you see what you're doing, you probably do it a little bit quicker – not quite as cautious because you can see what's going on.

A monitor tells the captain details of the pitch, direction, and power of one of the Dorothy Ann's propellers. *Gary Schmidt photo*

Currents are a factor. Currents change because of rain, because of no rain. Sometimes you have a wind that's blowing off the lake that might be pushing the water up the river instead of the current coming out of the river. That changes things a little bit. And when you have a rain storm, you're aware of the rivers that flood or have a swifter current than would be normal. Some rivers aren't affected much by rain storms, like the St. Clair/Detroit River and St. Marys River. The Cuyahoga River is affected. It's a really narrow river, and with the Cuyahoga Valley being cemented in and all the water going to the river, that thing can swell up in a hurry, and you can get currents up to four miles an hour. In a small river, that's running quite hard.

Current in the Cuyahoga River can run either way. If you have a good rain, everything will run out. If you have a good wind, it can be blowing it all in. Both situations make you drive the boat differently, steer it differently.

What really gets me is that as you're making a turn in the Cuyahoga River on a bend, when you have the current running inbound, it sets you down on the inside corner. When you have a stronger current coming out, it has a tendency to come off the side and want to blow you to the outside. An outbound current is a lot easier to run because you can use more power against it. You're not picking up a lot of speed, but you use more power against it and you can maneuver better. A current coming with you wants to throw your stern all over the place, and it's very, very hard to steer.

Also, the current does not run down the middle. If you have a curvy river and you have a straight stretch, that river is running and hits a bank and the current wants to shoot you across to the opposite bank, and it's faster and stronger. You want to read the currents. You want to stay in the center if you can. But if you can make more speed, you'll read the river and take the slacker water.

In another area, when you come under the Blue Water Bridge in Port Huron, the current is at its strongest point in the whole Detroit River system. It runs right about three to four miles an hour. When you're doing 10.5 miles an hour with a loaded barge, and all of a sudden you're doing 14.5 miles an hour and you have to maneuver that, that is a lot. That's overtaking you, and you have to be aware of what's happening at all times when you're picking up speed like that. If the current gets a hold of you, if you're downbound coming around that corner, if you get over too far, it'll push your stern over and want to push you right into the bank.

With the Z-drives, the vessel is extremely maneuverable. I can turn it around 180 degrees within its length within a very short period of time, less than a minute. To stop it, you don't reverse the engines but turn the pods the other way and just pull it backwards.

To back out of or back into places, my Z-drives are turned around so they're facing in the opposite direction, and they're pulling me. Because of the uniqueness of them pulling me, I can pull my stern one way, I can pull my stern the other way, and the vessel maneuvers very well. The bow kind of follows around. I am controlling the bow thruster as well. I might have to give the throttle a little extra with the

Buttons on a panel will light to alert the captain to a possible malfunction. *Gary Schmidt photo*

bow thruster once in a while to get it moving a little faster or to slow it down so it doesn't move quite as fast, but it follows the tug pretty well.

With Z-drives, the force is not pulling you straight. I can pull myself to the port or to the starboard real easy, forcing the vessel over one way or the other. It maneuvers very nicely in tight quarters that way.

I have my controls for the throttle and the direction all in one ball for the starboard and all in one ball for the port, and which ever way I point the ball, that pod is going to take me that way.

The bow thruster control is a separate lever that gives me a right or a left. I can push it to the right, and it will push me to the right. If I push it to the left, it will push me to the left.

The propulsion system was recently upgraded. It went from a fixed wheel – meaning that the propeller blades were at a certain angle – to a variable pitch. The pitch can be changed, which is a more efficient system. It's easier on gears, it's quieter. You change the pitch to change your speed. You change the pitch so you have no pitch whatsoever, so you're just kind of hovering. You can reverse the pitch so you're pulled backwards. It's another variable.

We used to have trouble with the gears in our Z-drives on the propulsion side from engaging the clutch and disengaging the clutch, and that's kind of hard on it. A variable pitch counteracts that. The wheel is engaged all the time. What you're doing is changing the pitch – zero pitch, meaning that you're not going anywhere, up to 90 or 100 percent pitch, which gives you full power, full propulsion. That way you're not engaging or disengaging the clutch, which puts a lot of strain on the clutch. It's just engaged all the time, which is easy on the gears. That was something like a $2½ million upgrade. It's a nice system. I like it very much.

***

SIDE TRIP: *As with any type of boat, lights are important. Captain Schmidt discussed some.* If something happens – you lost propulsion or steering – there are two red lights you turn on. They mean "not under command." There are different phases of towing lights. If you're towing ahead with a vessel behind more than 200 meters, you have three white

A waterlogged piece of wood more than three feet long once jammed in the Dorothy Ann's propeller pod. *Gary Schmidt photo*

towing lights on the mast. If you're towing less than 200 meters astern, that's two white lights on the mast. On some vessels that are connected like I am, we display regular steam vessel or motor vessel lights.

***

Sometimes there is communication with the engine room. If something is not working properly or something is not happening the way it's supposed to happen, I'll call the engine room to report it, and the engineers will look into it or fix it or explain what's happening and tell me not to worry about it. A lot of little things can happen. A lot of times, it's just indicators or a false alarm somewhere or some kind of alarm going off and you just want to know what's going on.

(The engine is in the lower part of the Dorothy Ann and is under his control in the pilothouse.) It's controlled by electronics, by wire.

Under way, there's always a mate in the pilothouse. I'm up there, as the captain, in all confined spaces – rivers. Making a dock or leaving a dock, the captain will be up there also. Or I may be up there at any time I think I need to do something like making a new route or charting the waypoints.

Stuck

We were in Cleveland, Ohio, and a waterlogged piece of wood was kicked up off the bottom and got stuck in the wheel. The barge is loaded deeper than the tug. Whatever comes off the bottom of the river flows up, and you pull it in through the wheel. Most of the time when something goes through the wheel, you can hear it. You hear a little rumble. Most of the time, it doesn't get stuck. This time it got stuck. I might have been shifting the engine out of gear as the wood came in there and jammed. I couldn't shake it out, so I had to have a scuba diver down. He got it out, just worked it out.

One time we picked up a tire off the bottom. It got around one of the hubs *(blades)* of the wheel *(propeller)*. How it got underneath there I don't know. It wrapped itself around, so there was a real wobble. It was out of balance. We had to get a diver, and he pulled the tire off. As it came up, we saw it was a Pathfinder tire *(a heavy-duty kind, as for an SUV)*.

Hatch 77

Speed

I have a speedometer. It's called GPS. It's very accurate. It gives me my speed all the time.

With the old way, you used a stopwatch on a given known mile. For instance, there was a mile measure in the St. Clair River if you were downbound past Stag Island. There were two posts a mile apart. You'd take a stopwatch out. You knew approximately how fast you were going, but the current might change that a little bit. You would do your test and figure out how fast you were going. If you were doing close to 12 miles an hour, that's what you wanted. The Coast Guard

The 7,200-horsepower Dorothy Ann churns water while maneuvering near the Shooters restaurant dock in the Cuyahoga River in Cleveland, Ohio. *Gary Schmidt photo*

used to check your speed all the time. It would set up radar spots and make sure that you were doing the speed limit. If you were speeding excessively, you would be fined.

Nowadays with GPS, you get a constant reading. If you get into a narrow spot in a river, you pick up speed because the water is rushing through there a little bit faster. When the river widens out, you have less current. As you get to a narrow spot, like near Courtright Light from Port Lambton, Ontario, to St. Clair, the speed can pick up as much as a mile an hour. It's usually about eight to nine tenths faster. Now, with GPS, you can see that.

The speed on the GPS goes up by tenths. I can read the speed in miles per hour or in knots. If it's miles per hour, it's 12 miles per hour. If it's knots, it's 10.4 knots. You watch that. I don't worry about a tenth or two tenths of a mile an hour. But if it gets close to four tenths of a mile an hour, then you pull the throttles back a little bit. You try to keep the speed as close to 12 miles per hour as you can. If you are excessively speeding, the Coast Guard will call you and tell you.

***

SIDE TRIP: I use miles per hour for the office, mainly. It just makes it easier for the paperwork that we have to pass on. Aboard ship, it's a lot easier to use nautical speed because your charts, your radars, radar plotting, and anemometer are in nautical miles. But the office wants miles per hour because this is the way it was done for 100 years. And just with a push of a button, I can change readings from knots to miles per hour. We have to use the knots for our weather observations that we send in to NOAA Weather.

***

There are speed limits because big vessels throw big wakes. You can do wake damage. As you are going into a narrow area, and if somebody has a little slip with a parked boat, you suck the water out from underneath the boat and pull it out. As you go by, water floods back in. You can move large vessels back and forth. If you go too fast, you can break vessels loose from their moorings.

A lot of vessels will request a checkdown as you're passing, especially ones in a fuel dock. You don't want to pull anything away from a fuel dock. That's really bad.

At certain docks, especially one at Marine City St. Clair Aggregates Levy Dock, I'm 30 feet off the dock with my wires there. If somebody goes by really fast, you've got to tend the winches because the wake will pull you and suck you around in surges, and your cargo pile won't be the same. You might have to shut down operations so you don't contaminate other piles with your stone because the piles are close together. I request a checkdown there, and I request a checkdown at fuel docks and Blue Water Aggregate. Also, when a ship goes by, it pulls you and you move up and down the dock a little bit. That's when breakages happen with winches, when there is some odd movement. Even in locks. You have the winches set, and you can get a surge if the lock gates open too fast. Most of the time at locks, I'm sitting up in the pilothouse and running the engines and helping stop because you don't have much play room in the locks.

My top speed in the Cuyahoga River is right around three miles an hour. I look at the GPS and watch the speed. If I'm coming into a turn, speed is misleading when you're looking out and you're going slowly. And I have certain speeds that I want to make certain bends at. I'm watching the speed as part of doing everything else.

In the Cuyahoga, we put the engines on a fixed 600 rpms. Another reason I'm looking at the GPS and looking at speed is because that sound is constant, and it is a little bit different factor than I was used to without fixed rpms. By sound, I used to know the engine speed and the rpms as they went up and down.

You're looking at the response, too. Is the bow coming around fast enough? Is the stern swinging over where it should be, or is it swinging over too fast where you might clip something back there? That's where your speed comes in.

On the open water, we set the rpms at our maximum, 850. Your miles per hour changes according to if you're heading into the wind, if you have a following wind, the depth of your barge, and current. All of those are factors in your speed. I can have a load coming out of Marquette and have an average speed of 10.7 miles an hour, but I can go over 11.5 miles an hour and I can go down to nine point something miles an hour if I'm heading into a sea with high winds.

I seem to make better speed in cold water. I think some of it has to do with the algae that grows on the ship's side. It looks like grass and gets to be six to eight inches long. That furry stuff slows you down. More resistance. At the end of summer, our speed is less. Once you've been through ice in Fall, that scrapes it all off, and you increase your speed.

Pins

As you leave the galley and go forward on the Dorothy Ann, you come into the pin room. A pin that we connect the tug and barge with is a massive piece of steel that's connected to a big hydraulic cylinder.

Each pin weighs about 14 tons. That's how much steel is in it. It's a massive piece of steel that keeps us connected to the barge when we're pushing.

On the Triton, the connection was with lines and cables. I had Kevlar lines, which are stronger than steel and lighter than cable. The 1½-inch cable that we were using was so heavy that it was hard for the small crew that I had to pull those lines. We replaced most of the cable with the Kevlar lines, and one guy could lift that. It's that light. It would take two to three guys to lift off the other cable.

A pin on the Dorothy Ann/Pathfinder sounds very much different from what it is. Don't think pin, as in an everyday safety pin, think PIN, as in something extremely large.

The pin is a connection system. The system is built from within. It starts with heavy steel in the center of the tug. I'm talking a mass of steel maybe a foot thick with four-inch steel gussets on it. This steel is connected to a hydraulic ram. The hydraulic ram is connected to what we call a pin.

The inner core of the pin is a 24-inch diameter stock steel, which is solid steel. Built off of this is a round cylinder that is connected in many points welded together in gussets to a five-foot cylinder, which is probably inch-thick round steel, which slides in and out of a corresponding five-foot diameter tube by way of a hydraulic system.

On the outer side of the tug is two feet of steel that has bushings on the end, and then there's a head on it which is bolted together. These heads have fingers that, as they are pushed out, match fingers on the barge. Both sides become connected so solidly that if the barge and the tug were to roll, they would roll as one.

The Dorothy Ann and Pathfinder are called an articulating tug and barge for the simple reason that, as the tug moves up and down to weather, the connection system can move. The system has bearings in it to help it move up and down and slide around.

What Captain Schmidt calls a pin is massive mechanism that weighs 14 tons and is five feet in diameter. *Gary Schmidt photo*

Shown detached, the connection system is visible between the Dorothy Ann and Pathfinder. *Gary Schmidt photo*

A crewman climbs the ladder between the bow of the Dorothy Ann and the stern of Pathfinder, an extension of which can be seen wrapping around the Dorothy Ann in the background. *Gary Schmidt photo*

The pins are on the forward end of the Dorothy Ann. They connect at the aft of the Pathfinder. In weather, the tug will be in the notch and its stern will go up and down. The barge might move, but the barge doesn't move much. It's mostly the tug. But if the connected vessels roll side to side, we'll roll as one. But if we're heading into seass, the tug will go up and down, but the bow will stay steady with the barge. You get some weird motions sometimes.

For a long time, I always was a little leery because the setup didn't look like much. Then I saw the pins out and on the ground. The two 14-ton steel connection assemblies couldn't be fit on a semi truck when they were taken out to be re-turned and have new bearings put on. Only one pin could fit on a semi trailer at a time.

The pins are maybe 16 feet long. They are five feet in diameter, and they have a core piece of steel that runs down the center that's two feet solid steel core. Really heavy, heavy steel is built out around it to make another cylinder. This thing is just massive. Close to 16 feet of a pin is within the vessel.

There's a button that engages the hydraulics. When you push the button, the pins start to extend. They have to fit into a corresponding notch and be even on both sides. You can't have a list in the barge when trying to engage. The fit will be off by what they call a tooth, and then put a six-inch list into the tug or into the barge. You wouldn't want that to happen. You have to visibly see the attachment. Usually when we are getting close to finishing unloading or finishing loading, the mate on watch will pin in the tug. When that is happening, I am getting things prepared to leave the dock, doing the reports. There are ballast reports that have to be sent in every time we ballast or de-ballast. I get the log book ready. I check out the equipment in the pilothouse, the whistles, the navigation lights, and steering system – making sure everything's a go before we turn the wires loose and leave the dock. That's when crewmen pin in or un-pin.

When we extend the pins, it's done very slowly. But there is a fast retract. There's an emergency button if you ever have to disconnect in a hurry. Let's say the barge broke in half, and you wanted to get out of that barge notch – you didn't want to go down with the barge – you just hit a red button, and it retracts instantly. That's done with nitrogen gas accumulators. The system retracts in a matter of a second or two. All that weight, in seconds. Sometimes you feel a jolt. The fast retract makes a lot of noise, too. It scares a lot of crewmen when they are fresh aboard. They're not used to that noise. I'm usually awake when the pins are extended or retracted. I'm getting ready to leave the dock or getting to the dock. Other people are sleeping, and they say it is quite startling sometimes.

I developed a comfort level in learning how to trust the pins. At first, I didn't know if they could break or what kind of seas they could take. I was told the pins could handle up to somewhere around 20-foot waves. We've had the vessel out in seas that were over 20 feet, and the system performs well.

Z-drives

Distinguishing the Dorothy Ann from many vessels is its propulsion system. Captain Schmidt usually uses the nickname Z-drive.

It is actually what is called a compass drive, which means it can turn 360 degrees. I think people just shortened it up with a catchy name, Z-drive. But it is a compass propulsion system. It can turn 360 degrees, with the propeller on the inside of a cowling, which gives it thrust. The water comes in around it.

The system has no stops. I can keep on going in a circle, turn it one way or turn it the other way.

A "Z" is formed in its design. Off the engine is a shaft. There's a clutch and a Cardan knuckle. It looks exactly like the knuckle on your car drive shaft, you're universal. But this is a huge universal. From the engine, that shaft goes up a shaft alley with a lot of bearings supporting it along the way. The top gear box of the Z-drive has another Cardan knuckle system. Off the gear box is a shaft that goes down and hooks into the propellers in the cowling.

The engines are in the lower part of the Dorothy Ann. They are under the captain's control in the pilothouse by way of an electrical system.

I have two Z-drives. They operate independently, or I can operate them in tandem.

Driving on the lake, the Z-drives are used in tandem – 90 percent of my engine rpms, about 850 rpm, with the variable pitch propellers at 100 percent pitch. But when I'm maneuvering, I'm never in tandem.

I have the capability to set the speed and just be able to use the variable-pitch propellers, and the engines will stay at the same speed. I have three speeds. One is set for 600 rpms, one's set for 800, and one's set for maximum rpms. There is another setting where it just goes by what I do off the controls. I can set my controls from 0 to 100 percent pitch. Gauges on my Z-drive will tell me what percentage – what I call for. I might call for 50, and it'll tell me I'm using 50 or 51 or 52 or 60 percent. On the other hand, there's another gauge that tells me how much engine rpms I'm using, if I'm using 80 or 90 percent. In the middle, it will show me the direction that my thruster is thrusting. If it's straight ahead, it'll be 360 or 0. If I turn it around, it's going to be 90 degrees. When I'm

One pod of the Dorothy Ann's propulsion system dwarfs workmen at Bay Shipbuilding in Sturgeon Bay, Wisconsin. *Gary Schmidt photo*

maneuvering, I've gotten into the habit of using the Z-drives at 45-degree angles.

At that angle, the thrust is outward. That slows me down. But if you want the power again instantly as you're maneuvering to a dock, you can just straighten the Z-drives out, and that will bring you ahead again.

I can slow down even faster if I turn by turning my drives transverse, which is 90 degrees, with both pods shooting water out to the side of the vessel. That

The captain can see exactly where the Z-drive pods are directed when he operates the Dorothy Ann's propulsion system. *Gary Schmidt photo*

will give me almost zero propulsion ahead, even though I'm still turning the engines at 600 rpms with 50 percent on the variable pitch propellers. It saves the steps of trying to adjust the throttles and the pitch all the time as you're maneuvering to a dock.

Maximum pitch on the propellers may be 20 degrees. There are a couple of modes. There's fixed mode where I control the pitch all the time, like if I'm running a straight 850 rpms. But if I am using the variable pitch where the engine is controlling the pitch by computer, as I bring the rpms up, the pitch automatically is advanced so it can't overwork the engine.

In other words, Captain Schmidt has multiple motions going on his head for the variables available in the starboard and port propellers – speeds, propeller angles, and pod angles. This does not compare with anything in everyday normal life.

It's very hard. The only thing you can compare a Z-drive with is the old outboard motors that were able to swing in a circle. If you really wanted to, you could put two outboards on a small boat and turn them around, and you could do the same kind of maneuver. If you want your bow to go to the right, you steer your stern to the left. And vice versa.

To back out of places, the Z-drives are turned around so they're facing in the opposite direction, and they're pulling me out. Which ever way I pull the tug's stern, the vessel maneuvers very well. The bow of the barge kind of follows around. You might have to give the barge a little extra with the bow thruster once in a while to get the bow moving a little faster or to slow it down so it doesn't move quite as fast, but the barge follows out pretty well. With Z-drives, the vessel maneuvers very nicely in tight quarters. I am controlling the bow thruster as well.

I have my controls for the throttle and the direction all in one ball for the starboard and all in one ball for the port. Which ever way I point the lever is the direction the vessel will go. The bow thruster is a separate lever right next to the others that gives me a right or a left. I can push it to the right, and it will push me to the right. If I push it to the left, it will push me to the left.

Sometimes there is communication with the engine room. If something is not working properly or something is not happening the way it's supposed to happen, I'll call to report it to the engineers. They'll look into it or fix it or say this is what's happening and not to worry about it. A lot of little things can happen with indicators or alarms, and you just want to know what's going on.

(Prior to the Dorothy Ann): The Triton had straight shafts with rudders behind them. Walking aboard the Dorothy Ann, the Z-drive system was new. This was a new situation I had to learn. But I've learned a lot.

Bow thruster

There's one bow thruster on my vessel. It's on the Pathfinder. A 1,000-horsepower motor that operates the bow thruster runs off the barge's 1,600-kilowatt generator. A 16-cylinder CAT *(Caterpillar engine)* drives the generator, which is a lot of power. That's satisfactory power, but captains always want more juice. More is better. But it is very sufficient. It does the job.

The bow thruster is on the part of the hull that's just forward of where cheeks start to bend in to the bow. It's

Many vessels navigate with the aid of a propeller at front called a bow thruster.

forward of the collision bulkhead, which is a separation from the bow to the cargo areas with watertight integrity so in case of an accident you don't flood the whole system. A watertight hatch takes you right from the cargo area into the bow thruster area. Below the water level is a tube that's 3½ feet in diameter that runs all the way across the ship. In the middle of the space is a variable-pitch propeller. You can go forward or reverse with it.

The propeller is driven by the electric motor. A shaft on the motor leads right straight down to the bow thruster and watertight gearing. The variable pitch is hydraulic in nature. The pitch one way pulls the bow to the right. Pitch the propeller the other way, and it will throw the bow to the left. The motor is driven by our unloading generator. We usually don't unload and need the bow thruster at the same time.

The bow thruster is controlled several different ways. I can control it from the pilothouse. Up there, I have a forward station and an after station for the bow thruster. When I'm backing up, I can still have the use of the bow thruster in the stern station. You can also control the bow thruster from the barge. There's a little house up forward on the focsle just above the windlass room that has a lever if somebody needs to run the bow thruster from up forward. When we go into Charlevoix, we take the tug out of the notch and one guy operates the bow thruster from the barge as other guys pull it back into position on the dock with cables.

There's heavy duty grating on both sides of the bow thruster – steel bars in three by six-inch grating. I have gotten stuff caught up in it. A line has gone through the grating and wound up in the thruster. We have to go down in there. We can tip the vessel so the bow thruster is out of the water. There's an inspection hatch that you can go down inside and into the tube from inside the vessel. We've also lost that grating one time, probably from ice, probably from not being welded on well.

In the Interlake fleet, most of the vessels have bow and stern thrusters. They're single screwed, which means that they don't have the maneuverability of a Z-drive. They use the stern thruster to throw their stern one way or another as they're going through a bridge to keep the vessel centered.

My first time using a bow thruster was on the St. Marys Cement, but it was a lot smaller. It was diesel operated, and it only ran about 250 horsepower. The thousand footers in the Interlake fleet have a 1,500-horsepower bow thruster – big horsepower.

Bow thrusters make maneuvering easier. When steering with a straight shaft and rudders, you use your engine a lot, and your stern doesn't swing over as fast, and your bow doesn't come back over the other way as fast.

At the controls

Imagine you are Captain Schmidt, and you are headed to Marquette, Michigan, to pick up a load of taconite. Imagine it's a calm and sunny summer day on Lake Superior as you guide the Dorothy Ann and Pathfinder. This is how you handle the vessel as you come off the lake at your usual 12 miles an hour to ease down to zero to tie up at a dock on your starboard (right) side. You're handling a vessel more than two football fields long.

Once you come around the break wall, you're lined up on the ore dock so when you're approaching and coming past the end of the dock that you're no more than 20 feet off the dock. As you're coming in there, you want to be slowing down. You pull your throttles back to about 50 percent. At 50 percent, you're doing about 600 engine rpms. When you pull your throttles back, the variable-pitch propellers are in the non-fixed mode. As you're pulling the rpms back on the engines, the pitch of the propellers is coming back automatically. You bring the throttles back to 50 percent, the rpms are right at 600. At that point, at 600 rpms, I might go into a fixed mode where the rpms are going to stay the same at 600 rpms, but now I can adjust my pitch to 100 percent or I can adjust my pitch down to zero percent, and the engine will still run at 600 rpms. With the engine running steady, I'll take my 100 percent pitch and bring it back to 50 percent or even lower. This slows me down a bit more. Now, as I'm slowing down, I take the Z-drives out of tandem so they aren't working together and are working individually. I will start angling the drives at about 40 degrees. As I turn the drives so they are facing outboard from their sides, that will slow me down more. An angle of 45 degrees will be the same as working one engine straight ahead instead of two engines straight ahead. Then if I need to slow the vessel down, I might go transverse. That means that the Z-drives are shooting 90 degrees out on either side of the vessel. That will be almost like stopping. It's like zero pitch. But if I need to jockey the vessel just a little bit one way or the other, I can change one drive. If I change one drive to ahead, I can push my stern over with the other drive. That will bring my bow in a little bit closer. Then if I want it to stop the motion, I'll just bring the Z-drives back to transverse, or to 45s. That will bring me straight ahead as I'm starting to slant the vessel in a little bit. Then I use my bow thruster as I'm

The Dorothy Ann/Pathfinder eases into the historic dock at Marquette, Michigan. *Rod Burdick photo*

Captain Schmidt stands as he maneuvers the Dorothy Ann/Pathfinder.
Jeremy Mock photo

coming in. Maybe now I want my bow to stay in place. I use my bow thruster against the dock, and I'll take my port drive and put the angle out at 90 degrees and the other drive at maybe a 45, so I'm still coming ahead a little bit. As I'm doing that, the thrust is pushing my stern over a little bit more, and the bow thruster is pushing my bow over a little bit more, and I'm coming in on the dock. I'm crabbing in toward the dock a little bit more. If it's happening too fast, I'll take the bow thruster off and just let the bow coast a little bit. I'll take the stern drives and put them both at 45 so I'm just coming ahead. Or maybe at transverse, so it's really slow ahead. Now I'm getting close to where I want to start landing. I'm two or three feet off. I might bring the bow thruster over just so the bow comes up against the dock real easy. I'll swing the guys over onto the dock. My stern still might be four or five feet off, and the bow will be riding along the dock. As I'm doing that, I'll take my starboard engine, and I'll turn it back to 180 degrees. It'll start slowing me down. I'll put my port drive on about a 45 ahead so the thrust is still driving my stern over just a slight bit and bringing the stern up against the dock. Once it starts coming up against, I'll bring the port engine to a 45 in reverse, which would be 135. As I'm doing that, the action is dragging me backward but holding my stern in a little bit. The other drive will still be backing me up. We'll just coast ahead to where we want to be, and I'll say, "Throw out a cable." We get close, and we'll work ahead on that cable just a little bit. Then we'll get out the other cables as we're doing that and then make the final adjustment with the cables. I'll just stop the engines, here we are, we're parked. We're where we want to be. That's Z-drive maneuvering.

The process of making a dock at Marquette – from the time I check down the engines about one mile off the dock until I reach the dock, putting the men on the dock, getting the cables out, and being all secure in position for loading – is half an hour.

I'm in total concentration. It's like tunnel vision. I'm listening to my guys giving me distances on the walkie-talkie, and I'm looking out windows and doing what I'm doing. There are blind spots. When we get up close to the dock, within 20 feet, I can't see how many feet are down there off the dock. I estimate. I can tell pretty close where we are. But at 20 feet, I can no longer see anything between the barge and the dock. Then we get in closer – three feet to two to one foot and then up against. Once you're up against, you hold the bow in with the bow thruster, and once your stern is up against, you hold it in with the port stern drive. Then you maneuver with the starboard drive. If you want to go ahead a little bit or go back a little bit, you maneuver ahead and back with the starboard drive and hold yourself up against the dock. That's where the noises come in from sliding along the dock and creaking up against wood, or rubber, or steel.

You can't make a dock fast. If you make a mistake, there's going to be damage – a lot of damage because of the weight of everything, the mass. So everything is slow.

The Marquette dock is protected from weather. The dock is high up off the water, close to 100 feet. Up on top of the dock is where the railroad workers are. We're way down on the lower part of the dock, tying up and where we shift the vessel. Then the chutes swing down and start filling you up.

Ports and docks

To communicate as we're coming into a port, we give security calls on channel 16 VHF, our radio, to let other vessels know that we're coming in.

When we are talking to the facilities that we are approaching, our company has already been in contact about our arrival. Then I give them a final, sometimes 12-hour ETA *(estimated time of arrival)*, sometimes a four-hour ETA. Sometimes they just want an hour call. I try to give them as much heads up notice as possible. Some docks, like in Cleveland when I'm picking up iron ore pellets and taking them up the Cuyahoga River to the steel mill, want a 3½-hour call. The heads-up time is different at various unloading facilities. It depends upon how far the dock boss lives away from the facility. Some want 2½ hours, some want two, some want one hour. Most of them want one hour.

The contact is by telephone. I have a lot of telephone numbers. I have a phone book with just companies and people who we work with and contact people. It's put out by Interlake, and I update it. As people come and go everywhere, you scratch out "John" and put in "Chris." And you usually write in there that Chris, instead of a one-hour notice, wants an hour-and-a-half notice. We build a little database on that kind of stuff and keep it fluid. I have it in the computer and on paper. As the company gives me a new contact number, I put into my phone contacts and an email as it came in from the office. And then I take that email and add it to my phone book under that company's name and write in that person's name and number. I keep that in two places – in my office and in the pilothouse.

***

SIDE TRIP: For communicating with the office, if it's immediate, we use wireless telephone, Verizon, for instance. If we're out in cellular wasteland where there is no Verizon, we have satellite telephone, and we can always get through. If the message is not urgent, it goes through our email system, which is wireless Verizon again. There is ship's mail also. It's mail that I send out on the mail boat or at some port that we're at. With a hard copy of payroll to be sent to the office, I might go to a post office and send it off. That's usually express mail or priority mail in a hard envelope, flat rate. I also send the same payroll off via our email system so the office has an early copy so it can get some of the work done. But a lot of the ship's mail has to go by snail mail.

***

My main job is the stone job. The stone docks are mainly in Michigan and Ohio, Marblehead being the most frequented by my vessel. *(Marblehead, Ohio, is in the southwest corner of Lake Erie.)* I probably do at least 80 trips a year out of Marblehead, Stoneport *(Michigan, northwest corner of Lake Huron)*, Calcite *(Michigan, northwest corner of Lake Huron)*, Drummond Island *(southeast of Sault Ste. Marie, Michigan, at the mouth of the St.*

Marys River), Cedarville *(northern Michigan in the tip of Lake Huron)* and Port Inland *(northern Michigan)*. Sometimes we go to a Canadian port to load stones, Meldrum Bay *(at top of Lake Huron)*. About 80 percent of my cargoes are stone. Most of the stone loading docks are single facilities, like Marblehead, Stoneport, and Cedarville.

Scores of ports have many docks, with some docks being privately owned and some being part of operations of a port authority.

There are a lot of docks in the Cuyahoga River that I go to. At the lakefront is a loading facility for taconite that we take up the river. Others are Mid-Continent Coal and Coke, the River Dock *(stone)*, West Third Street *(stone)*, and, across from that, Cuyahoga Road Products *(stone)*. Osborne Dock has a couple of docks I go to, Upper Osborne and Lower Osborne. Mittal Steel Dock has three different docks that I go to. Chicago is the same way – many, many docks that I go to. I go to couple of docks in Milwaukee. At Toledo, there are at least four docks that I've been to. I've been to at least three docks at Ashtabula.

Going into a dock to unload, you may be carrying more than one cargo. You talk to the facility person as to how he wants the product, where he wants the product. Even at a single dock, there usually are several different products. Like Osborne, I could bring in as many as eight different products there. Not at one time, but it has eight different spots to dock there, and you have to know where they are.

At ports, it's first come, first served. If you are in the port, and you're on your way out, there are certain places you can pass and certain places you can't. Sometimes you just have to wait until another vessel clears the river. Or we decide on a place where we can pass and say the first one to this spot pulls over and the other guy will go on by. But you do make passing arrangements. There are certain places where you just can't get two vessels in there.

Large cities have a port authority with docks that it operates, but those docks aren't necessarily the ones the Dorothy Ann/Pathfinder goes to.

For instance, the Port of Cleveland owns a lot of dockage in the outer harbor. It owns almost 2,000 feet of dock that salt water vessels can come in and load and unload. There are a couple of slips that they can come into, and each one is numbered. Then you go into the river, and many of those docks are privately owned.

The company deals with the port authorities. At Cleveland, we go into the port for special things, like putting on supplies. One time, we went in there for minor repairs. Another time, we went in for potable water. We were out of water, we were in the river, and we couldn't use river water.

The Pathfinder unloads at Severstal Steel on the Rouge River in Detroit, Michigan. Note the Christmas tree at the end of the Pathfinder's boom where the taconite is pouring off. *Gary Schmidt photo*

Hatch 83

Cuyahoga Old River Bed

Taking a load of stone from Marblehead, Ohio, east to Ontario 4 Dock in the Cuyahoga River Old River Bed in Cleveland takes me about 5½ to six hours from dock to dock. When I get one mile from the entrance, I check down – check my engines – and slow down as I come to the river. At the break wall at the river mouth, I want to be down to about five miles an hour and still going down.

As I get in past the break wall and through the basin, I enter the entrance, which used to be the canal and is the mouth of the Cuyahoga River now. The old river bed entrance was blocked off years ago.

As I come in, I'm getting down to three miles an hour as I'm passing the old Coast Guard station. As I get up to the first railroad bridge – the Norfolk Southern number 1, a lift bridge – I'm down to a mile an hour. On a right-hand turn into the old river bed, there's Shooters Restaurant right on the upstream corner. As we come around the corner, the next dock is Christie's Cabaret. At the end of Christie's Cabaret is a slip at Lafarge Cement Dock. This corner is very, very difficult. First of all, I'm usually loaded to about 23 feet 6 inches to come into this dock, and that's my maximum depth. I may be touching mud and structure underneath on the bottom. I'm just sliding along and may be pushing mud to some degree.

The east side of the Cuyahoga River was called The Flats. There used to be taverns and restaurants, and they are being torn down. Across on the other side is where Shooters is. As I'm coming around on the eastern bank, my stern is 10 to 15 feet off. My bow is off of Shooters about 20 feet. As my center comes around at Ontario 2 Dock on the turn, I'm usually four to five feet off – maybe eight feet if I'm lucky. On top of that, there might be a boat at the Lafarge dock there. His stern sticks out quite a ways, and passing is really difficult. As I continue, maneuvers are really, really tight. I'm doing less than a half a mile an hour. Once I make that, I start making stern room.

There's a little tree on the next bank straight ahead of me. I try to line up on it to straighten myself up. I'm pretty much in the middle of the river by the time I'm coming up straight.

The next turn, where all the railroad tracks are near the Cargill Salt Dock, has big, heavy tires all the way around the corner. This is

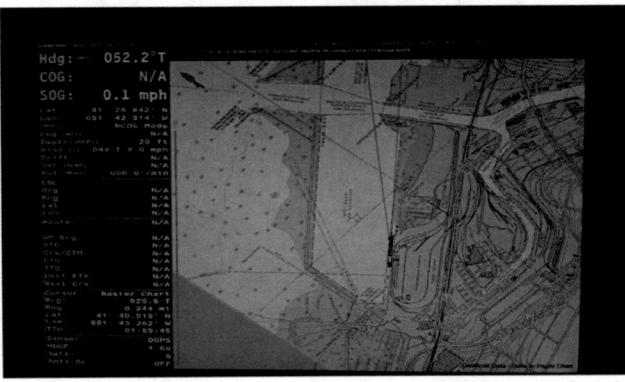

An ECPINS image shows the layout of the Cuyahoga Old River Bed on the right. *Jeremy Mock photo*

Ontario 4's Dock. As I'm making the turn off the tree, my bow is within 40 feet of the dock in front of me, and now I've got to start swinging my stern to clear the Willow Street Bridge as I'm making this turn. I end up staying about eight feet off a knuckle on the Ontario 4 Dock. My bow, on the Cargill Salt Dock, is about 20 feet off, and my stern is about 10 feet off as I come around the corner. I have to make it a very sharp turn to dock on the port side along the Ontario Stone Dock.

If I'm coming in real deep because of my load, I have to lighter *(lighten the load)* at the first part of the dock before I can go up into the next part of the dock.

Once I'm on a little straight stretch at Ontario 4, I swing my bow in and swing the guys over to catch lines. There are several trees I have to watch out for along this bank, so I can't swing my cargo boom too early. Once I get the people on the dock, I come in and swing my stern in, and we get a couple of lines out. I start working ahead. As we clear the trees, we start swinging the cargo boom out.

We unload maybe two cargo holds. Sometimes we put a whole load there. For example, let's say we're going to dump half the load there. That lighters it up. We'll unload cargo holds one and three, get our bow wires back in, and then I'll shift up along the dock. We'll throw our wires off and leave the guys on the dock. Next, we shift up around the corner to unload a different kind of stone or sand – a heavier stone, a drain stone, or a sandy type of stone.

We've laid up over winter at the shipyard there. The Great Lakes Shipyard is at the end of the navigation on the south side of the old river bed. We back in. We tie up the barge on one side. Then the tug is taken out of the notch and tied at the dock right alongside.

There is a slip where the shipyard has a floating dry dock. They built Z-drive tugs here at that dock also. They do topside repair and small dry dockings. I think they re-planked the Nina there – *(a replica of the Christopher Columbus ship of the Nina, the Pinta and the Santa Maria fame)*.

The Cuyahoga

The South Chicago is a challenging river, going in and out, especially with a 700-foot vessel. I'm not unique to that. There are a lot of 730-foot vessels that go in there and load coal and drop off products, and it's challenging to all of them. There's a lot of barge traffic, the river is narrow, and bridges don't always open on time. But Cleveland probably is the most challenging of the ports that I go to a lot. The Cuyahoga River has a lot of docks where we unload, and the river is the most challenging of my maneuvering.

I'm basically driving two football fields. A football field is 300 feet long, not counting the end zones, and the Dorothy Ann and Pathfinder together are more than 700 feet. Our thousand footers on the Great Lakes are three football fields long.

The Dorothy Ann/Pathfinder is the longest vessel to go up and down the Cuyahoga River. It's more maneuverable than other vessels because of the compass drives.

We normally make 120 to 130 trips in a season from mid-March through mid-January. Just for the Cuyahoga River, we did about 70 trips one recent year.

The Cuyahoga is a narrow river, and we snake along it for about four miles. Current is a big factor. It can run either way.

I come in at the break wall on Lake Erie at Cleveland. While I have gone into the old riverbed and unloaded there, we take most of the products along the busy part of the Cuyahoga.

In spring, we do a shuttle from Whiskey Island on the Cleveland outer harbor to the Areclor Mittal Steel mill. We do about 20 trips in spring alone.

At Whiskey Island, we'll load ore to go up all the way the whole navigation channel. It takes about four hours to load us.

The Cuyahoga River winds through Cleveland, Ohio.

We'll be hauling a little over 15,000 short tons, or about 13,000 long tons. Our load on any day depends on the water level and if the river has been dredged recently up at Mittal. Our stern will be about 21 feet deep, and our bow can be anywhere from 16½ to 19 feet deep – a variance of almost 1,100 tons that we may take up that river – according to current, rain status, water levels, and silting at the dock.

The first trip is always an experiment. We always go up there light, paying attention to what the depth sounders say, and how far we can push up at this depth, and what we think we can carry on our next trip. Then we increase the load by six-inch increments until we're comfortable getting a full load up there. Then we mark down what our maximum is for that season. The situation is always brand new because, with the melt and run off in the springtime, you get some pretty good rushes of water carrying a lot of silt. The navigational, controlled

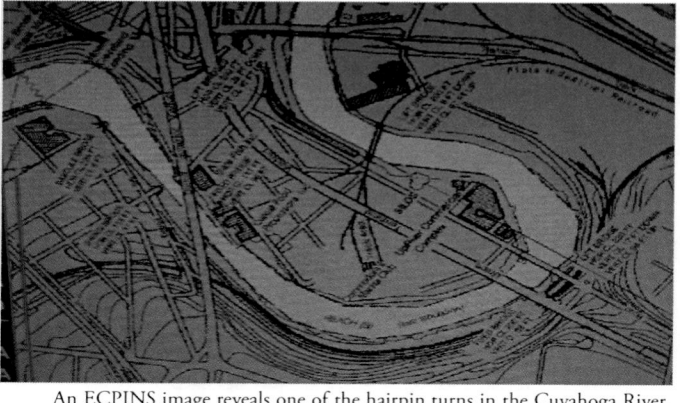

An ECPINS image reveals one of the hairpin turns in the Cuyahoga River.
Jeremy Mock photo

depth of the navigational channel ends right at Arcelor Mittal. The rest of the river is not dredged. It's more of a canoe area going up farther. The runoff carries a lot of silt down, and as soon as it hits that drop off where it's been dredged, the sediment drops right there and fills that in. That's what we have to watch for.

We make a trip a day. If we can make a trip up and back fast, we get a little bit of down time at night to do some cleaning, sanitary work, sweeping the tunnels up, and keeping the boat as clean as you can. It's a little lighter pace. And you get the vessel prepared for morning to reload at the dock.

We're going back and forth. Once we unload at Arcelor Mittal, I'll back out the river. It takes me about three hours to back out. The maneuvering all the way up to the top of the river is about 3 hours and 15 minutes. Going back out to Whiskey Island is around three hours.

The river has hairpin turns. When I make the first 90-degee turn, I have 20 feet of room off my stern, about 30 feet off my side, and anywhere from 45 to 60 feet over my bow. When you make that turn, you've got to stay kind of in the middle of the river.

Up the river a bit is another turn. If there's any current, it's really hard to push the vessel through there. Sometimes I have to go full speed just to get through the nearby bridge. In places, the river is deep at the bank, but it has mud flats.

On another curve, I'll have 12 feet off my stern as I'm coming off, less than 20 feet off my side and about 45 to 50 feet for my bow.

I have guys spotting for me the entire time. There'll be a person in the pilothouse with me for distances off my stern. Usually the first mate will take all the corners on the inside, meaning the corners that are closest to the vessel on whichever way I'm turning it. That could be port side, could be the starboard side, whatever the turn is. I'll have a guy on the bow. He moves to where the bow is going to be closest to the bank. Let's say I'm making a left hand turn, the mate would be on the port side, and the guy on the bow would be up on the starboard side. There also are guys out there getting the deck ready. If I need a guy for another position report – on the starboard side midship – I'll put him across from the mate. I have four people for position reports. They are out there no matter what the weather is. We communicate with walkie-talkies. They talk in order. The guy in the bow might say, "Cap, you have 200 feet over your bow." The guy on the port side might say, "You're about 25 feet off the next knuckle." The guy on the starboard side says, "You've got a lot of room on the starboard side" because I'm making a left-hand turn. The guy watching my stern will say, "You've got eight feet, 12 feet, 16 feet." You've got to come in to those kinds of distances where you're really close.

The walkie-talkies have re-chargeable batteries. Everybody has a charger in his room. When the guys go off watch, they plug their battery in right away. The walkie-talkies are good. They have a microphone that comes off. When it's raining, the microphone could short out, but we have learned how to protect it with a plastic bag that we put over the top of the microphone, and you can hear through it just fine. But wind will rattle it a little bit. You have to protect the microphone from the wind to some degree to talk, but it works well. The positioning of the people is very important to me because they are communicating by walkie-talkie the whole time. I don't talk to them a lot unless I need a repeat on something. I'm constantly listening. They're trained to tell me if they think we're going too fast, and, even though I know I'm going too fast for a reason, they may not, but they still tell me that. And I want them to tell me that. I don't ever tell them, "don't tell me that."

Captain Schmidt knows he may seem to be going too fast but he's really not because he's ready to make a maneuver in a split second. The maneuver just has to be made.

Right. And they're giving me that information, which is good because it might be a reminder that I might be going too fast. So I never tell them not to tell me something. The more the better. I can sort through what I don't need.

Physically, I am maneuvering the pods. I'm steering the vessel as it's going up the river – and moving the throttles and adjusting speeds and changing directions and using bow thrusters and putting all the information together to maneuver through the corners. This could be at night, or during the day. In some places, the river runs east and west. The sun can bother me. Sometimes it's early morning and the sun is coming up, and it's blinding me as it's coming right down over the water and into my eyes. Or the sun can be setting. It can get to you at some of these curves. I can hardly see a thing. The other people are my eyes, especially when I'm backing out of the river. I don't ever turn around in a river. You go up forward, and you come out backwards. When I'm coming out backwards, I hardly look at the bow. I'm just listening to the people tell me how much room I have and adjusting the bow and the bow thruster and adjusting my stern. I can see my stern usually by adjusting as we go along and listening to what they're telling me. I depend totally on those distances, and I get upset when they don't do it right. I have them pretty well trained. I don't want to know that I've got eight feet on one side, I want to know that I'm eight feet and opening or eight feet and holding. I want some kind of dynamic of what it's doing. So that's what we do. I've had them trained a long time to do that kind of stuff.

Sometimes I have an audience. Seagulls follow us. There are many seagulls in this river. They're after the fish we churn up. People like to watch. There's a little restaurant/tavern called Wipple's, and customers all watch as I'm coming around. I have my big Packers player up on the Dorothy Ann. I get a lot of reaction, especially when I come through The Flats, where all the bars are. Cleveland Browns Stadium is near. I get a lot of reaction. I like to give it to them, too. The last two times I put my Packers player up, the Packers got beat by the Browns. I get boos every time I go through there. "BOOOOO!"

***

SIDE TRIP: SHOOTERS CORNER: Shooters on the Water restaurant has a dock for small craft to come in and tie off. When we're coming into the harbor, we have to give our security calls. Shooters is one of the places we call because it is near a red zone, and boats can't tie up in a red zone. Any place they call a red zone, small craft cannot tie up, legally. But they do. There's a little bit of a red zone near Shooters where boaters tie up at, that they shouldn't. Shooters is not a red zone, because it is a restaurant. We just have to call in advance and let Shooters know that we're coming in, and hopefully they can get the boats out of the way. And they tell people to get

A crowd gathers at the popular Shooters restaurant on the Cuyahoga River.
Shooters on the Water photo

their boats out the way, but people don't want to set down their drinks sometimes and go move their boats right away. We've had troubles getting past Shooters. They are part of the nuisances in this part of Cuyahoga River. There are a lot of nuisances in the Cuyahoga River. One time, a guy was working on his boat tied up at Shooters. He was not really having lunch, but he was working on his boat. He could move his boat, but he needed help doing it. And I'm coming in there. And I'm thinking. "He's got to move his boat," because we had given advance notice. I see him in there, and he's got his engine compartment opened up and doing nothing. Finally, I just had to have my guys tell him, "You *have* to move the boat, or you're going to get crushed." I didn't go in right away. Then I started going, and I thought, "Well, maybe I can get around him, maybe I can't." I couldn't get around him. I had to stop. People at Shooters helped him out, towing the boat back, but it was really a show. You can call it a shit show if you want. That's what it was. Finally, they got the boat tied.

As I come up around the corner by Shooters, my stern is five feet off of Shooters' dock. The dock is built out over the water, so there's room underneath. It's built out of pine. Timbers run vertically up and down along the dock so the small craft don't get hung up underneath the dock. The boats can slide up, because the river does go up and down quite a bit. I've had my stern just touch these things. They're not screwed or bolted in. There's nothing supporting the bottom part. And I come up. If you touch it at all, you just crack it loose. That's a little damage report. But it's not much of damage. The company has a good rapport with the owners at Shooters. Usually, nothing much is said about it. But it does happen because it is very tight.

***

When we're ready to leave Whiskey Island, we call the Norfolk Southern bridge and say we'll be needing an opening. We have Amtrak and mail trains that we have to contend with. If the trains are within 15 minutes of the bridge and are going to be at the bridge before me, the bridge tender cannot open the bridge. I've waited there half an hour to 45 minutes sometimes for one train after another. This is a main railroad line. It follows the Lake Erie coast all the way. If the bridge is open before I get there, I can make the turn coming in at right about 2½ miles an hour.

Ahead, I go underneath the Cleveland Memorial Shoreway Bridge, I'm still going pretty good and making about two miles an hour. When we clear that bridge, on the east side is the Samsel Supply warehouse where we get our supplies.

*** *** ***

Highlights

Here are glimpses of what Captain Schmidt encounters as he progresses along the Cuyahoga River.

Concerts take place in the Jacobs Pavilion at Nautica on the west bank of the Cuyahoga River. *Nautica Entertainment Complex photo*

➪ I come upon the Nautica Pavilion. They have a tent there, and they have concerts right on the riverfront. This is another nuisance. It has a dock. Sometimes as I'm coming around the bend in the river there, a concert will be going on. There will be all kinds of little boats tied up with folks listening to the concert, and I have to get them out of the way. A band was playing there one time that I think was The Spinners – I'm not real sure about remembering the name of the band, but they were doing songs that we knew; you could hear them – and all these boats were around in the river there. The singer was singing away, and I had to give a whistle *(blow the ship's horn, which is LOUD)*. I'm 20 feet off the pavilion as I come around. I didn't mean to scare the guy, but I guess I did. He was singing, and he about jumped out of his pants. He mentioned something about, "Whoa, what was that?"

➪ I also have to blow the whistle for the Center Street Bridge. It's a swing bridge that swings both ways. You can't advance too far because the bridge always swings toward you so, as you're clearing it, they can clear up street traffic faster. This is a slow bridge; it doesn't move real fast.

➪ If I look up through the Center Street Bridge and get up onto the next bank, there's a telephone pole. If I'm dead on that telephone pole, I'm usually right in the middle of the river as I come through the bridge.

➪ The old Commodore's Club is now called Rivergate Park. Here are all the crew boats that run the river. It's another nuisance. You've got to be careful because their dock sticks to them.

➛ My stern is going to be about 30 feet off the bank as I make my approach to Columbus Road. There is a lift bridge that I have to call in for it to lift. My stern would just be clearing the Columbus Road Bridge, and I can start picking up speed a little bit again and I can get it up to almost two miles an hour. We go past the Medusa Dock. This is another place where if you're meeting somebody, if it's not a large vessel, he can tie off and you can get around. But it's very right and very slow.

➛ At the end of the Medusa Dock is a railroad bridge. It's open 99 per cent of the time, but every once in a while they'll drop it down and run a couple trains across. A tender will be there to open the bridge on demand.

The Dorothy Ann/Pathfinder is about to make a turn in the Cuyahoga Old River Bed. A bridge that is no longer in use is up. Cleveland Browns Stadium is at the left, Christies Cabaret is center right off the bow of the Pathfinder, and downtown Cleveland and the 57-story Key Tower is at the right.
Jeremy Mock photo

➛ The bridges in Cleveland are tended well. *(In 2011, Cleveland employed 21 bridge tenders, according to WEWS-TV.)* Some of the tenders roam. They'll take care of two bridges. And they have time to drive. Once they clear one, they might drive down to the next one to take care of it. And they'll let you know if that's happening.

➛ Coming into Collision Bend, on the left side is the Sherwin-Williams research and corporate headquarters. It's a very nice place – tennis courts, basketball courts, walking trails. They have it set up nice for their employees. You notice stuff like that as you go up the river.

➛ As you're making the turn, there are some small craft that are tied up right on the turn, and they're there year 'round. People live on the boats, so you don't want to get too close to the boats. I try to keep my starboard side 30 to 35 feet off of the small craft that are permanently docked there.

➛ At the top of the hill is where the rock and roll restaurant is. Hard Rock Café has a great big guitar sticking up in the air, so you can't miss it.

➛ Next is a 125 to 135-degree turn in a very short way. I do a power turn. That means I can flip my Z-drives over and really push my stern over. As I'm doing this, I'm turning my bow to the port so I'm trying to hold it up over to this side, because I'm turning and wanting to push my bow down onto it.

➛ We have unloaded coke at the Mid Continent Coal and Coke Dock. If I'm coming up with stone, we usually drop stone off at the River Dock just past Mid Continent. River Dock is a work boat dock for us. I can't get the guys off. I can't get up against the dock. So

The 700-plus foot Dorothy Ann/Pathfinder would reach to about the height of the notch on Cleveland's 947-foot Key Tower in the left background. Imagine the vessel in the tight quarters and turns of the river in the foreground. *Jeremy Mockj photo*

I drop the work boat off right across from the Mid Continent Dock. The work boat guys tie off right in between two bridges, walk to the dock, and get ready to catch lines for me. I have a little delay. The guys have to walk a quarter of a mile or more.

⇨ There are several spots on the River Dock that we would be tying up. It has a ground hopper. There's a tunnel underneath, just with holes in the ground. You unload right over the top of the holes, and the product goes onto the belt at a slow speed. It's a very long unload. It's about a nine-hour unload that way.

⇨ The Norfolk Southern number 2 bridge is a lift bridge that I have to call in for. We'll lift the bridge up, the folks in my forward bow mast will clear the bridge, and then will tie off. The tug will be on the other side of the bridge after it is lowered. The Dorothy Ann and the Pathfinder are straddling that bridge. When I'm done unloading, I have to pull my cables back, swing my bow in, and then call the bridge and tell the tender to lift it up so we can head out.

⇨ As soon as we clear the Norfolk Southern number 2 bridge, you have the high overhead bridge of the I-90 Vanderbilt Freeway Bridge. Sometimes we're parked underneath the I-90 Bridge to unload stone at Cuyahoga Road Products. Sometimes we unload heavy drain stone, which is big, two by four-inch stone. Most of the time, we drop off a pea-sized crushed stone. We have to shift ahead and unload, and shift ahead and unload, until we get all the product off.

⇨ As we get into the Marathon Dock, I have to slow it down pretty good – about a mile an hour. A lot of times, there'll be a barge tied up at the Marathon Dock. And this makes passing extremely tight. Then it's about a half a mile an hour.

⇨ Once I clear the Marathon Dock, it becomes the Osborne Dock for quite a ways. And they're in the turns. There are probably eight or ten different piles that I can go to, and I haul to all of them.

⇨ The old Jefferson Street Bridge is a real slow turn. The bridge is no longer there, but the old abutments are. On the right hand side is a marine construction company. Vessels tie up there. Across from it is the Upper Osborne Dock, where the ore is unloaded on the way up. Some of the vessels going to the Arcelor Mittal Upper Dock will unload lighter there a little bit so they can get all the way up the river and unload the rest of the product. Two railroad bridges are right next to each other. It's really tight. I'm seven feet on one side and maybe 12 feet on the other and eight feet on the stern until I get through. We call the bridges the Twin Bridges. They're railroad bridges. One is abandoned and torn out. The other one is a jackknife bridge. It just lifts up on one side as a single-span bridge. But it never opens all the way. It's always on an angle like a partially opened jackknife. When I'm going through it, my pilothouse misses it by about 25 feet. I'm real close to it – closer than what I want to see because of my height.

The Dorothy Ann/Pathfinder is about to pass under another set of bridges – Norfolk Southern number 2 and I-90 – while making a turn in the Cuyahoga River. *Jeremy Mock photo*

➪ There's a lot of traffic. Cleveland has a lot of traffic. You can meet somebody in Marathon Bend. I've had boats tied up there, waiting. We've shifted. The other boat will back out alongside of me. I'll be backed up where my stern is almost touching the side. Once the other vessel gets alongside of me, I'll shift all the way up, and the captain can make it around me.

➪ At West Third Street is a real good meeting place. You can tie up, and, as another vessel is coming around, you can miss everything. You can meet somebody in Collision Bend. You can tie up, and the vessel can make it around the corner. It gets alongside of you, you shift up, and it makes it on through. There are only a few places you can meet.

➪ There's a turning basin. Across from the turning basin is the Mittal Lower Dock on the starboard upstream side. There's barely enough room to turn around, and that takes me more time than it does to back the vessel out. There is plenty of room in turning basin, but you're still making a turn with a heavy boat. You can't put your stern too far into the turning basin because it's on the shallow side. It's probably 17 feet or less draft in there. That is OK when you're empty. I can get the barge in there to turn it around, but I can't get the tug in there.

➪ Near the turning basin are cooling towers. It's where they cool the steam that comes off the steel plants. Water is constantly running out and cooling. That becomes a nuisance in cold because it produces steam, and you can't see through it sometimes. Depending on which way the wind is blowing, it'll block your vision quite a bit.

➪ At the end of the navigation channel is a red light for a water discharge or intake. I don't remember what it is, but we can't block the spot. Our bow reaches to 10 feet of the red light only if we can make it. When the river is silted in, we don't make it within 150 feet of that light.

➪ From the red light back, we're probably 550 feet to where the loading boom is. The dock crew has a spot. We'll unload the ore into that spot just about all the time. The facility has a couple of gantry cranes – bridge cranes – that shift up and down. They'll take the ore from that area so when we come back with the next load they'll have a clear spot for us. Then we can dump our new load in the same spot.

➪ It takes us about three hours to unload at Mittal. And then we head out. Heading out is easier than going up because we're in ballast *(carrying water in ballast tanks for*

After a delivery at Arcelor Mittal Steel, the captain uses controls in the rear of the Dorothy Ann pilothouse to back the vessel 3½ miles out of the Cuyahoga River. *Gary Schmidt photo*

balance). I can make better speed. I can see where my stern is, and I listen to my guys a lot. I have a camera up forward that I can see in a monitor in the pilothouse. I can see how much I'm swinging and how I'm making bridges in the pilothouse. It's a little bit easier to maneuver when the vessel is light, versus a heavy vessel.

*** *** ***

As I am maneuvering the vessel, I am standing. If I'm making the full trip from the break wall to the upper dock at Mittal Steel, it's three to 3½ hours one way, and that's about a four-mile trip. You're just on the whole time. When I leave, it's usually, again, three to 3½ hours to back out of there from the same spot.

It can be nerve wracking. It does weigh on you, and you feel the tension from some of that stuff. Sometimes if you haven't had enough sleep, it can be very irritating, too. But it's something that I do, and it's something that I really do enjoy most of the time. It's like any job, the job gets to you every once in a while, but overall I really like what I do a lot.

I have "up" days pretty often. The trip is quite difficult. When you get a lot of trips in a row, it's quite hard. I don't mind it. I kind of like it. I like being busy. I don't like the long runs where I'm trying to invent stuff to do that I don't need to do.

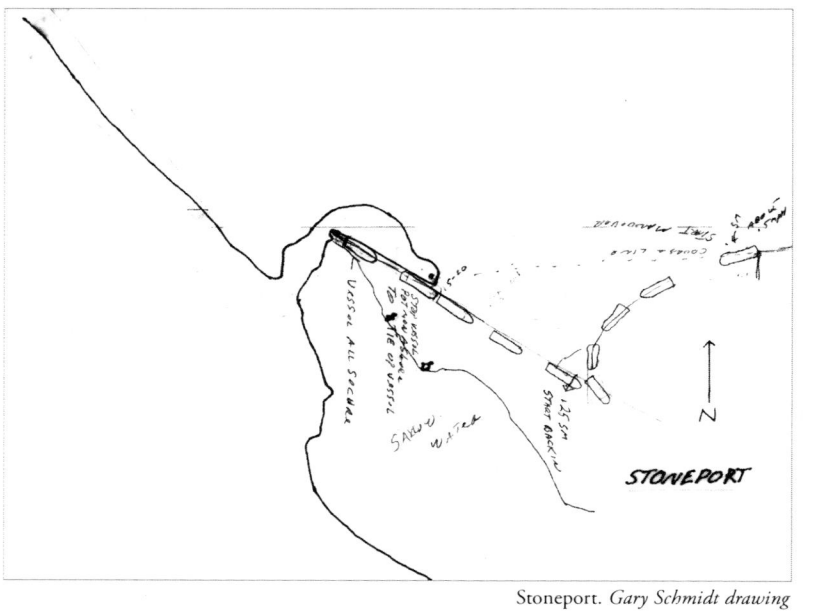

Hatch 85

Tricky docks

Any Great Lakes dock that you would try to maneuver the Dorothy Ann/Pathfinder into could lead to disaster. Captain Schmidt masters them all with a certain amount of ease that comes with experience. He blends smarts, power, and finesse to move inordinate tons of floating weight to the correct spot. But some places get his attention more than others. These are three.

Wind-blown headaches: Stoneport, Michigan

As I approach Stoneport, I check my engines when I am 1.5 miles from the loading dock. At .4 of a mile, I start my turn. When I have turned and am 180 degrees from the dock, I start backing. At that point, I am .25 miles from the dock, which is fringed by shallow water. As I back alongside of the dock, I stop and put a deckhand ashore to catch the cables as we near the end of the dock. This maneuver is fairly easy most of the time. It can get very hard when the wind is out of the north or northeast when it is blowing more than 25 miles an hour.

Stoneport. *Gary Schmidt drawing*

Out of the notch: Saginaw River, Michigan: Bay City Aggregate Dock

About one mile from the Saginaw River Front Range Light, I check my engines to slow down to about five to six miles an hour by the time I reach Front Range Light. I proceed at that speed until I reach the Coast Guard station. Then I check to dead slow so I'm almost stopped by the time my bow reaches the Essrock Cement Dock. Then I start to back into the Bay Aggregate Dock. As I'm turning and backing, my stern is about five feet off the corner of the Bay Aggregate Dock. My bow is 15 to 30 feet off the Essrock Cement Dock. My starboard quarter is about four to six feet off the upstream side of the Bay Aggregate Dock. Once inside of the slip, I stop about half way down the dock and take the tug off the notch and tie off on the upstream side of the slip. Then my deckhands move the barge with the mooring cables to the very end of the slip. When we are finished unloading, we move

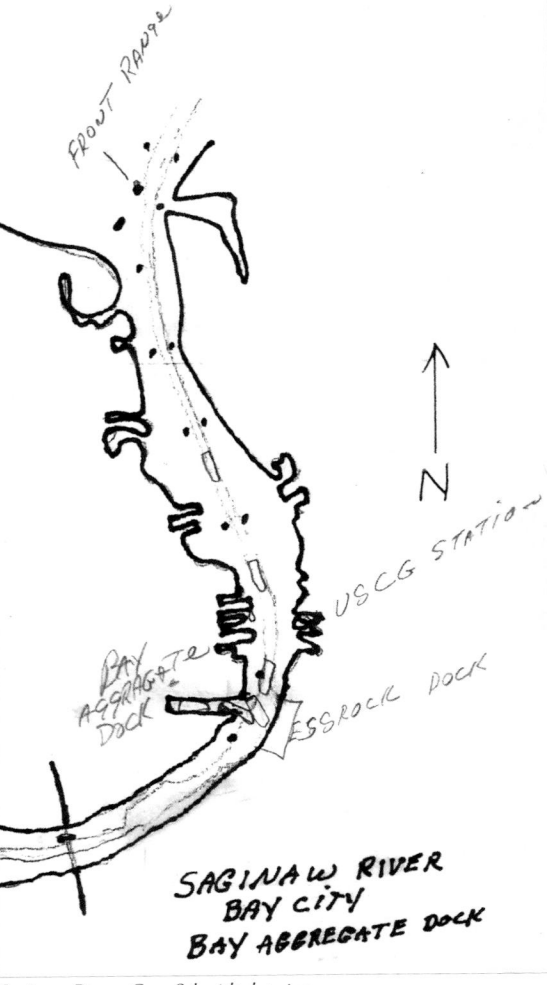

Saginaw River. *Gary Schmidt drawing*

The Dorothy Ann docks next to the Pathfinder at Bay City Aggregate, where space is limited. *Gary Schmidt photo*

the barge back out to the middle of the slip and put the tug back into the notch of the barge and re-connect.

A "Gary maneuver": Rouge River, Detroit, Michigan: Levy Dock

I have to back the vessel into the Rouge River. That is probably close to three-quarters of a mile to the Levy Dock. I back the vessel in because there's a bridge at the stern of the Dorothy Ann. The spot is next to the place where the dock boss wants me to unload. If I were to drive forward to this dock, I couldn't get into that spot. I have to back up to be able to reach that area of the dock. A thousand footer could do this, but he would need tug assistance. Any other steamboat that doesn't have a Z-drive could not do this.

The Rouge River is off the Detroit River, which has a fairly good current running south. The river is more than half a mile across. As I am coming down the Detroit River, about 500 feet off the bank, I have spots on the dock at Zug Island where I make my turn to back in. When my pilothouse is even with a conveyor belt on Zug Island, I give my Z-drive a hard over and I use my bow thruster to throw my bow one way and my stern thrusters to throw my stern the other way toward Zug Island. I maneuver the vessel around until I'm in position where I'm just missing a buoy at a slight upward angle. Across the way is a slip on the Canadian side, the Morton Terminal. When I'm backing in, I want to be looking right down that slip.

All the time, I'm back in I'm pushing my bow around. I'm backing slowly. When I get to a bridge, there's a slight turn. It's a very tricky maneuver. I'm the one who invented it. It is a Gary maneuver. I taught it to several people. I had another experienced captain I was working with, and he was just learning my boat, and he said, "You will never do this with any other boat on the Great Lakes."

The maneuver was created out of necessity. To unload here, I knew I had to back in. The first time I did it, it wasn't exactly what I wanted, but I got by with it. And then I refined the maneuver. I found points that worked and the amount of power that could be put on the engine, 600 rpms, and just maneuvered around. You pick spots. You have spots to do a certain maneuver. It's by memory. And I teach it by memory. If somebody else wants to write it in their maneuvering books, that's fine. But I'm a visual guy when it comes to handling. It's all visual. A lot of captains have a lot of marks that they use for every maneuver. I'm more of a how-is-it-shaping-up, how-is-it-looking person.

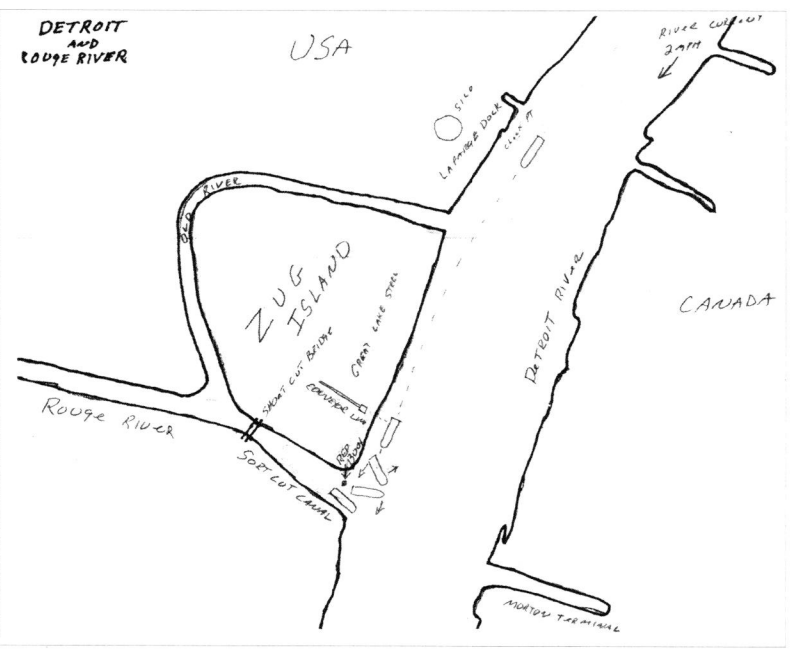

Rouge River. *Gary Schmidt drawing*

Seen from the passing Lee A. Tregurtha, Captain Schmidt maneuvers the Dorothy Ann and Pathfinder in the Detroit River as he prepares to back the vessel into the Rouge River at the left. *Captain Brad Newland photo*

Because of the nature of the Dorothy Ann, I am doing a lot of maneuvering. I do a lot of maneuvering that these other boats couldn't possibly do.

Hatch 86

Advice

One day when Captain Schmidt and I were toward the end of our interviews for this book, his cell phone sang out, "I'm your captain, I'm your captain." It was Jeremy Mock calling from aboard the Dorothy Ann/Pathfinder in Lake Erie. He was seeking advice.

He was going into Fairport Harbor. He's going up into the basin. He was concerned about wind.

It's one of the docks where we take the tug out of the notch so we can get the barge in position to get the stone where the dock boss wants it. Jeremy had a south wind of more than 20 miles an hour. He wanted to know how that would affect the light tug. And the wind does affect the tug to some degree. But a south wind is not too bad there because you get protection inside the harbor. Once you get inside, you lose a lot of that wind. The direction is great. As long as the direction is out of the south, you don't have much problem. What we do is we get into the basin, and we put the bow of the barge up into the corner of the basin. We just ease it in there. You're only doing one or two tenths of a mile an hour until the bow comes up against the bank. Then we push into the bank, and we hold the barge into a certain area. We get out two cables to kind of hold us into place there, and we back the tug out of the notch and get on the side of the barge, and we tie off on the side of the barge. We push the stern of the barge in with the Z-drives and push it up against the bank. Once we get close to the bank, we get out the other two cables, and then we pull ourselves back into position and push it in all the way and hold the barge with cables and swing our boom out.

We use fendering when we have adverse winds, when you can't control the vessel the way you want to control it. There is a sail effect of the wind blowing you down onto the barge. You have a big sail effect with that big, tall tug pilothouse. The wind will blow the tug faster than it's blowing the barge. We have car tires and rope finders aboard the vessel. You try to put fendering in between the vessel and the dock. It cushions the blow of the steel against steel, and you don't do any damage.

That dock wants the load as far out onto the dock as possible. We unload into the area where it wants the pile.

When we're unloaded, you do the same thing. You shift yourself all the way up to the front with the wires. You throw off your three and four wire and your two wire, and you're just being held by pulling your bow up against the bank up front. You take your other Z-drive and slowly just pull yourself out until your stern is clear of all of where you wouldn't be able to stay in the notch, the obstruction, until you get out toward the end of the river, and then you untie the tug. You back up, and you get the tug back into the notch, and you put on your jockey wires.

As you're doing that, if you have an adverse wind, like an east wind, it will blow you back into the dock quite hard. You might get the stern of your tug into a bad area. So, once you get the barge out there far enough, you've got to get back and get in the notch, and get pinned in. Once you're pinned in, you can work yourself back out into the middle of the river.

Jeremy has done that maneuver many times, but he hasn't faced that kind of wind.

Hatch 87

Nuisances

A husband and wife from De Pere, Wisconsin, were talking about their love of sailing on Green Bay and Lake Michigan in their pleasure boat. Upon hearing about the Dorothy Ann and Pathfinder, they spoke in admiration of the aura and scale of large Great Lakes working vessels. The husband said, sheepishly, "We're probably nuisances to them."

There are a lot of nuisances out there.

You get boats that don't want to move out of your way in confined space.

In the Detroit River, there will be a ton of vessels that'll be fishing, and they're right in the middle of the river. When you're in motion, you don't have a choice one way or the other. You've got to go. What I try to do is aim for their stern and figure they eventually will move forward. But you just don't know what they're going to do. You blow them a proper saluting signal or passing signal. I very seldom blow a danger whistle, and it has to be dangerous before I'll blow that. You try to give them the proper whistle signal. Sometimes they move, sometimes they don't. You just don't know. There's no communication. Most of them don't have radio. Some of them do. And if they do, they don't even listen to you, or they don't respond. They're fishing. A lot of times, the people have their back to you. They don't care. And you've got to watch out for them because you just don't know what they're going to do.

Sailing vessels out on the Great Lakes think they have the right of way all the time, and most of the time they do have a right of way. But at the same time, they want to challenge you. It seems like when they see a big vessel, they want to come over to look at it. They want to see what's going on with it. And so they come at you. And you don't know what their intentions are. You don't even know if they see you. I've had vessels, especially sailing vessels, at night that must tie down their wheel and just go. You blow your whistles, and you shine it with lights, and you just have no idea what they're going to do.

***

SIDE TRIP: The Army Corps of Engineers runs the locks. It's in charge of dredging, basically getting rid of silt that builds up. The corps is in charge of a lot of things. I use its website a lot. You can see the last time that the Corps did soundings for a port and get all the soundings at low water datum. That determines how to load your vessel. That's pretty important to have that information.

While the Corps is in charge of dredging, that's usually contracted out. You have to work around the dredging. Some dredges require that you slow down because their barges are tied off alongside of them. If they're just tied off on lines, and if you go by too fast, you'll break their lines loose. Others are spudded down *(tied to a piling)*. They're pretty safe, and they don't move too much. They're just an inconvenience. They aren't a real nuisance. You know they're there, and you know what you've got to do to get around them.

The dredging is no more of a nuisance than a small craft that can be in your way, or they're no more of a nuisance than a bridge that doesn't open for you. It's something that's got to be done, and it's something that you work around.

***

I've had close encounters with a lot of sailing vessels over the years. I remember one time early in my career, coming down Lake Michigan, one of the mates was on watch. He said he saw something out of the corner of his eye go across the bow. He got on the radio and said, "Anybody out there better turn on your lights." All of a sudden, the whole area lit up with lights, and here we were in the middle of the Chicago-Mackinac sailboat race *(Chicago Yacht Club's Race to Mackinac, about 325 miles)*. They were all trying to get an advantage. That was back in the days before the Coast Guard escorted the sailboats. Today, the situations are not as bad as they were because communication is much better and radars are much better and all the equipment is much better. You can keep an eye on the boats a lot better.

There are risks in coming too close. I suppose I might swamp a small boat. I doubt it. If you're going in the same direction, you might pull a small boat with you from suction. It might suck it over to you. But most of the time, a small boat can maneuver away from you easily enough. A lot of times, the bow wash will push a small boat away.

That happened with one of those personal watercraft. Three guys were jumping my wakes in the St. Clair River and having fun. Then they'd gather in a huddle and talk about it for a minute, and then they'd come back around and start jumping my wakes again and go back in front of me. And they'd go right in front of me. One time, they go out in front of me, and I keep on coming, and they're not moving, and they're not moving. All of a sudden, I saw one guy throw a rope to the other guy. He had a breakdown and couldn't get his machine running. He put the rope onto the handle bar, and the other guy took off real quick and pulled the guy right over on his side and put him right in the water. So now I know I've got a problem. This guy was in the way. I really turned sharp. This was right up by a dangerous corner, the southeast bend in the St. Clair River. I was lucky enough that my wake pushed him away, or I could have gotten him bad. Everybody was good, everybody was safe, but it sure did scare the living dickens out of me.

Some people are curiosity seekers. At the dock, with Homeland Security, boats aren't supposed to come close. We're supposed to keep a vigilant eye out for anything like that, for terrorists, which is a bunch of hooey. At the dock, there really isn't too much of a nuisance.

Hatch 88

The radar story

Back when I was on the Donald C. Hannah, we were given the opportunity to test prototype radar for Sperry Rand. It was river radar. This was the early '80s. The concept was that it didn't have a strong magnetron that sends out a really strong signal, but it would pick up a weaker signal and had a better receiver and could really give you clarity and definition on a radar screen. We had been using it for quite a while, and it was fantastic. It was one of the best radars that you could tune in and pick up details on buoys and boats. I could even distinguish as little as four feet between the walls in the Chicago Sanitary Canal and the side of the barge at the head of it. When you can see that clear of a definition, that's great.

We had been using the radar for quite a while, and one particular time it was foggy in the Chicago River. It was about 5 in the morning. I was headed down toward the Chicago Sanitary Canal.

***

SNAPSHOT: *The Chicago Sanitary and Ship Canal is a shipping link between the Great Lakes, by way of Lake Michigan, and the Mississippi River. The canal is 28 miles long and includes locks, dams, control stations, and spillways. It is on the National Register of Historic Places. Built in the early 1900s, the canal combines ship access and sanitation as part of the Chicago Wastewater System.*

***

I was light tug. I didn't have a barge in front of me, so I was just moving right along. All of a sudden, I picked up a target. It looked to me like it was a small runabout or small boat, maybe a 16 to 20-foot runabout, and maybe going fishing. As approached it, I slowed down. My fog whistle was on and blowing every two minutes. As I'd get down close to him, he'd take off. He'd pick up and speed on, and he'd run real fast for a mile, maybe two miles. And then, as I was going down the river, I'd catch up to him again. I'd blow my whistle, and, sure enough, he'd start up again and he'd take off again. And, man, this kept on going on and on every mile or two miles. And I'd be blowing my whistle at him to let him know I'm coming, and he'd take off. Finally, after four or five times like that, we got to a spot where all of a sudden the fog cleared. And when it cleared, I could see I was blowing my whistle at a Canada goose. That's how good the radar was. I had no idea it could pick up a Canada goose and make it look like a small boat.

***

ETC: Usually with a radar, you get one or two years out of a magnetron. With that Sperry Rand, we got 11 years before it was changed out. Sperry Rand people did check back on it. They wanted to know how the reception was, did I have any problems with it, what I liked about it, what I didn't like about it. To get the prototype, we just happened to be in the right spot at the right time. One of the guys from Sperry Rand was on hand when we needed radar. At the same time, we were a good test vessel because of our activity on the Chicago Sanitary Canal, and then running over to South Chicago Indiana Harbor. Going into Indiana Harbor, we had barges that were 60 feet wide and bridges that were 60 feet wide. We had very little room for error. As the bridges were older, you had a little more room because boats came up against the pilings on the bridge. The boats kind of pushed the pilings out a little bit, so you might have had 61 feet or 62 feet.

Accident

We went to the Shiras Dock in Marquette Harbor, Michigan, about 1 or 2 o'clock in the morning. It was my first time in there. We backed into the dock, which is the power plant. It's a very narrow channel, and you have to be pretty precise. You have to stay within the channel. It's shallow on both sides. We backed in all right and unloaded stone.

We left at 6 o'clock in the morning. It was just light. I was maneuvering my stern to clear the buoys, and we hit something. I didn't know what it was at the time. I felt the boat lift a bit. As I went out of the pilothouse, I looked behind the vessel, and I could see, "Wow, that's oil." Something happened, so we went to anchor. We put out oil booms around the boat.

We had to put our work boat in the water. We have oil absorbing booms. They're about 40 feet long, they float, and they can be clipped together. They have great big magnets that you put onto the hull. You put the booms around the boat and make sure no oil escapes and that oil is absorbed into an absorbent pad that floats on the water. It ran from the stern of the barge all the way around the Dorothy Ann to the other side stern to enclose the whole vessel. Any oil that comes up around the hull would be caught inside the boom. We captured residue. We had stopped all oil coming out of the vessel.

The third mate was up there just watching what was going on, which was very, very nice. When something goes wrong, it's nice to have the extra hands readily available. I got out the checklist. In that process, you have to call the Coast Guard and the national response center, if there's oil in the water, which we did. We notified the company. We did the best we could to stop any further leaks on the vessel.

The chief was involved, and my first mate. Everybody responded on board as well as could be expected. We did everything by the book. The company ordered divers to come out to look at the bottom and see what happened. It called in somebody to do the cleanup. The Coast Guard was involved and had a helicopter fly over and look things over. It had various boats.

When the diver went down and came back up and said, "The Z-drive is missing," I was just ashen, to know that I knocked off the Z-drive. I didn't know what I had hit.

In the process, the executive vice president and our company lawyer came up as support, to investigate and assist with everything. They were great support. They were really nice.

Within two hours, anybody who is involved in an accident or oil pollution spill or anything on that order – anybody who was involved or on watch at the time – has to take an alcohol test. And within 24 hours, you have to take drug test, a pee test. You go to a hospital, and they have professionals do a test on you. All passed, and everybody was cleared of any alcohol or drugs.

Divers went down again in the channel to find the Z-drive, to make sure no more oil would leak out of it. They found that there was no more oil. The oil that came out was the reserve oil in the tank to the Z-drive. As soon as this happened, I notified the engineer, and he saw that the supply was going down and shut the supply tank off. So no more oil came out of the boat.

We had just overhauled those Z-drives the winter before, so they were just like brand new. The seals were all tight. So when the Z-drive fell off and went onto the bottom, no oil leaked out, no water got into it. It was quite amazing the way it broke off the way it did.

With the Dorothy Ann in the background, its torn-off Z-drive rests near the rudder it struck. *Gary Schmidt photo*

We lost approximately 80 gallons of oil. The oil was a pretty close to hydraulic oil. It spread fairly thin on top of the water, so 80 gallons of oil looked like a square mile of rainbow-colored water.

The pollution control people came up.

***

SNAPSHOT: *The National Response System is the government mechanism for emergency response to discharges of oil and release of chemicals into navigable waters and the environment.*

***

Divers went down and found the Z-drive. When they found the Z-drive, they found a rudder right next to it. I have no rudders. The rudder fell off another vessel.

The rudder fell off at a 90-degree angle with the blade sticking up in the mud. When I maneuvered and I turned, I came right into the back of that rudder that was stationary in the mud, and it was just enough to tear the Z-drive right off.

So the Coast Guard got involved in the accident, and ABS, and the Environmental Protection Agency. The company sent the Crisis Response Team, and it really helps. It's a great support. More companies ought to do it. I've been with companies that you're sort of on your own. You have an accident, you fill out all reports, you get some support verbally, but that's about it. They don't send anybody. The Interlake team deals with the Coast Guard. It will deal with getting the divers and whoever they need there to take care of the situation. I filled out the form 2692, which is the Coast Guard accident report.

You have to report weather conditions and site visibility and give an accounting of what happened and how it happened. Each person who saw or was involved in the accident has to make a statement in writing. I've got a whole file and sub-files of this accident.

What happened after that is we went back to the ore dock where we were supposed to load, but now I'm down to only one Z-drive. We got permission from ABS to run with one Z-drive, which we had done in the past when one had failed on us. The Coast Guard came down to see what I could do with it. So I had to go out and do sea trials with the boat empty. After we loaded, they wanted more sea trials, and the Coast Guard was satisfied. We were able run with one Z-drive until the other Z-drive was overhauled. I've handled the vessel with one Z-drive in the past. The boat still responds better than any rudder boat. Z-drives are tremendously maneuverable.

We went into dry dock, the Z-drive was repaired, and we were on our way.

The entire oil cleanup had to be paid for, the loss of time with the boat, cargoes lost. Eventually, the company came to an agreement with another company.

This was a major accident, and the repair was substantial. It was a very expensive thing. I'm glad to find that I didn't do anything wrong.

Hatch 90

Best teacher

The person who was Captain Schmidt's best teacher probably didn't know it.

Curly Selvick. Curly Selvick not so much taught me, I learned from watching a lot.

Every time that he would handle – if I didn't have to be out on the barge or I was off for lunch – I was in the pilothouse watching his every move because that's what I wanted to do.

I also learned a little bit from Orrin Royce. He was a captain for a while for Selvick.

A lot of my learning how to operate a vessel was by trial and error. If this didn't work, let's try something else. And when you do it from an early age, you seem to learn faster.

When you're operating hands-on – when you're doing the operating yourself – you learn the characteristics of the boats and how they handle in general. Some of the guys who came up through the ranks on steamboats might have been a wheelsman at one time and then a watchman and then a mate as he worked his way up. It might be years and years and years before he got to handle a boat. I had a guy who came off of the Niagara, which was a suction dredge in Saginaw Bay. His job was eliminated. They got rid of the boat, so he came over and he was going to operate a tugboat. Well, he came from telling the wheelsman how to steer. He'd say, "Ten degrees left rudder," or "Half ahead," or "Quarter ahead," or "Give 'er a shot," but he never had his hands on the wheel itself. He knew how to handle a boat, but when he came to a tugboat, and he had to push the throttles himself and steer the boat himself, he was always late or early. He couldn't get it from the brain to his hands. Eventually, I gave up trying to teach him. I was teaching how to handle a tugboat. I finally said, "Start giving yourself commands. Instead of just trying to steer the boat and react to what the situation is, look out there and say, 'OK, 10 degrees left rudder. Give my starboard engine half ahead.'" And once he started to give himself commands and his hands were working to his commands, well, then he started to be able to handle a little bit. But in a situation like that, teaching somebody like that is very hard. Everybody learns at a different rate and a different style.

Going back to Curly Selvick, I'd been running first mate for a while, and he didn't think I was quite ready to handle the boat yet. I was still pretty young. I was 25 or 26 years old. Curly would handle the boat in the rivers. When we would run in the open water, he would get somebody to run in the open water.

We were on the Lauren Castle. It was 1,200 horsepower, single screw with rudder and propeller, and pilothouse control.

Curly was an exceptionally good boat handler, so he would handle the barges. When we'd bring a job in, we'd anchor the barge, get the tow line taken in, and then we'd go in and pick up Curly. We'd come back, and we'd make up *(connect)* to the barge, and then he'd push it up in really tricky places.

The Milwaukee River is very, very tight where we had to go up, into the Menominee part of the Milwaukee River: The Milwaukee River and the Menominee River fork at Plankinton Avenue. If you go up the Menominee River, you go straight ahead, but then it goes off to the Menominee Canal and off the Menominee Canal it branches off. You go to the Burnham Canal. There are three waterways coming off the Menominee. Where it takes a sharp left and goes up the Menominee Canal is right at the Post Office in Milwaukee. You've got a 90-degree turn there. Then when you go up the canal, you go maybe about two or three city blocks, and you take a right, and you're going up the Menominee Canal. That's where all the grain silos are. In the Burnham Canal, you take another left, and it would be another 90-degree turn, and then another right, turn, and it would be another 90-degree turn, and up there were cement plants. The first one was Lafarge now but at the time was Huron Cement. You have to go through a tiny swing bridge, and only have about 46 feet. It was very narrow, and we had a very narrow barge that would go up through it. Once you got through that, it was Miller Compressing on the right-hand side and on the left-hand side was the Penn-Dixie Cement plant, our customer at the time. Being in those tight corners with all the turns and bends is where I learned from Curly. Eventually we were in a corner where you couldn't make the turn with the length that we were with the tug and the barge together. You'd run out of room. Your stern would be up against one side, and your bow would be up against the other side. You have facing wires off the stern, one off of each side, that connect you to the barge. We used to take the port wire off, and we'd push the stern around as we were advancing. Once we got around – with a bridge in the mix – we'd have a channel on both sides, and, we'd connect that wire again. You'd be up far enough, and then you'd have to make it down through a little passage. It was 46 feet. It was real tight stuff, and Curly was exceptionally good at it. I learned a lot from just watching him do that.

Hatch 91

Relief

Jeremy is known by everybody as Monk. His real name is Mock. Jeremy came aboard the vessel I think in November of 2000. He was just out of the Marine Corps. He was in pretty good shape and gung-ho. You knew he was a Marine. Tough. He was fearless, absolutely.

As he got about four years under his belt on the boat, he decided that this is what he wanted to do, and this was his job. He has accomplished a lot, once he went and got a license. He studied on his own, with Paul

In recent years, Jeremy Mock, whose nickname is "Monk," was relief captain aboard the Dorothy Ann/Pathfinder. *Gary Schmidt photo*

Berger, who was first mate on the vessel at the time. They were kind of friends. They lived in the same area, and Jeremy would go over to Paul's house and study. Paul would teach him what he could teach him. Jeremy took the license test on his own and passed it, did everything he needed to do.

At one time, I had two guys on the vessel who had a mates license but neither one of them had a masters license. I told them it was a competition between the two of them. I said, "Whoever gets their license first, I'll start breaking him in, start teaching him how to handle." As time went on, Jeremy is the one who got his masters license first. Then I started to proceed to teach him how to handle a vessel – driving. And it takes patience because you see all the mistakes that someone is making and sometimes you can't explain exactly how it is that he should do this. I've done it for so long that it's automatic. I don't even think about how I'm doing something. I just know that I'm doing it. To express that and try to teach him how to do it was something. I would correct him and tell him, "No, this is wrong," and he accepted the criticism really well and he learned a lot.

As time went along, finally the position opened up where he could start relieving. After so much time and him coming around so well, I couldn't be more proud of a person for what he has accomplished – starting out as a deckhand and working his way up to mate and to second mate and to first mate and on up into the relief captain's job. And now he'll be the master of that vessel.

He's very well liked. He's accomplished the handling part of it very well. Very knowledgeable. Somebody who comes up that way does well, I think – a mustanger versus somebody who comes the academy. Somebody coming out of the academy, not being a deckhand, has kind of a drawback to start with. It's a little different attitude. Whereas somebody who has actually gone out and hosed down, shoveled, has scraped paint, painted, and knows the ins and outs of the system before he ever becomes a mate – some of those deckhands are teaching mates how to pump ballast off or helping them out with this and that until they learn their job. Jeremy came up knowing his job.

It took Jeremy about 10 years to work up to being relief captain. When I'd leave the vessel for vacations, I'd tell Jeremy, "If you have any problems whatever, don't hesitate to call me at home and I'll give you a hand." And that's the first thing he did. Any problems he had, he'd give me a call. Once you have that trust, knowing that he's going to ask you questions if something tough comes up, or a weather problem, or anything else that he's not really sure of, I didn't worry about him at all. The fact is, after the first two times that he handled the boat without me, I didn't give it a thought. "You've got a problem, give me a call. I'd do what I can to help you out." And he did.

Now he doesn't call so often. He doesn't need to. But he still calls me. We just talk to talk. And I like that. I appreciate that. And we've become friends instead of master/mate. It's deeper than that.

Appendix

Dorothy Ann/Pathfinder Glossary

AB: Able-Bodied Seaman, a U.S. Coast Guard designation. On the Dorothy Ann, the position is General Purpose Maintenance Rated, GPMR, for company payroll purposes.

ABS: American Bureau of Shipping: A service for marine safety.

Aft (versus stern): A direction, as "to the rear." The stern is the place, the rear end. Example: When the crewman went aft, he eventually wound up at the stern.

AIS: Automatic Identification System. An electronic tracking system used on ships and by vessel tracking services for identifying and locating vessels.

AMO: American Marine Officers: Union of merchant marine officers in the United States.

Articulated: A mechanical connection between two units (the Dorothy Ann and Pathfinder) that allows for movement.

Ballast: Water that is used to balance the vessel.

Ballasted conditions: A vessel is carrying no cargo and is balanced with water in tanks.

Barge: A vessel used for carrying freight, as the Pathfinder.

Beam: The greatest width of a vessel.

Boat versus ship: While used interchangeably by Captain Schmidt, he makes a distinction: "You can put a boat on a ship, but you can't put a ship on a boat." The Dorothy Ann/Pathfinder is a ship.

Bollard: A short, thick post on a wharf or ship used for stabilizing with ropes.

Boom: An apparatus to move something. The Pathfinder has a 260-foot off-loading boom for product. The Pathfinder has two personnel-landing booms, one on each side near the bow. There are five stiff-leg cargo booms, two on the Dorothy Ann and three on the Pathfinder, that stick out over the water and swing back over the ship and have chain hoists connected to them.

Boom: A temporary floating barrier used to contain an oil spill.

Bow: Front of a vessel.

Bow thruster: Propulsion system on the front of a vessel.

Bulker: Ship that carries bulk product.

Bulkhead: An upright partition that divides a vessel into compartments and adds structural rigidity.

Buoy: An anchored float in water that marks a location, indicates a navigational channel, and warns of danger or a hazard.

Cable, wire, line: A line can be made of manila or nylon. Wire is considered wire, wire rope or cable. Cable is heavy woven wire for mooring a vessel.

Capstan: An apparatus used for hoisting weights with heavy line by winding a spool-shaped cylinder manually or by motor.

Chandlers: Ship provisioners – with food, maintenance supplies, cleaning compounds, rope, and so on.

Chart datum: A measure of water depth. It's the level from which defined depths on nautical charts are measured.

Chock: A heavy fitting through which anchor or mooring lines are guided.

Deckhand: Beginning level sailor who does a lot of labor and works his or her way up; career details: www.iseek.com.

Dock: A protected area in which vessels moor. The term often denotes a pier or wharf.

Downbound/upbound: The directions for movement of vessels in the Great Lakes area as designated by the St. Lawrence Seaway Development Corporation. Downbound is eastward, and upbound is westward.

Draft: The depth of water a vessel draws.

Dry dock: A place in a shipyard in which a vessel is secured and water around it drained so exterior maintenance can be done.

Dunnage hatch: A place for storage.

EMD: Electro Magnetic Diesel, the type that drives the Dorothy Ann.

Fiddley: The iron framework around a hatchway opening.

Fit out: The time of preparing a vessel for sailing, with everything in place and in prime running order.

Galley: Kitchen area.

GPS: Global Positioning System. An electronic, satellite-based navigation system that provides location and other information.

Great Lakes: The massive body of fresh-water lakes that include Lake Erie, Lake Huron, Lake Michigan, Lake Ontario and Lake Superior. The lakes are in the domain of Canada and the United States.

Great Lakes Maritime Academy: At Traverse City, Mich. www.nmc.edu/maritime/.

HAC: A high-angle conveyor system used for moving product on a belt.

Hatch: An opening in a deck fitted with a watertight cover.

Hold: A compartment below deck in a large vessel for carrying cargo.

Hull: The main body of a vessel.

Knots versus miles an hour: One knot equals 1.151 miles an hour. Knot is generally used in nautical situations.

Laker: A bulk freight-carrying vessel on the Great Lakes.

Lat long: Latitude and longitude readings.

Latitude: The distance north or south of the Equator measured and noted in degrees.

Layup: The period when a vessel is not in operation, preferably in winter so annual maintenance can be done.

Light tug: Running a tug by itself, not towing or pushing a barge.

Lighter: Lighten the load.

Line: A rope or cordage used aboard a vessel.

List: The angle a vessel leans to a side.

Log: A record of courses and operation of a vessel.

Longitude: The distance in degrees east or west of the meridian at Greenwich, England.

Loud hailer: A powered speaker. Aboard the Dorothy Ann, it has more than one function. It is the speaker system within the vessel that is used for emergency alarm. Aside from speaking into it, it simulates a ship's whistle, a gong or bell, a fog horn that could be put on an automatic cycle. The vessel also has loud hailer separate from the emergency system used for speaking to personnel on deck.

Make a dock or making a dock: Captain Schmidt's expression for maneuvering to a dock.

Miles an hour versus knots: One mile an hour equals .869 knot.

Mackinac Bridge: The 26,372-foot span between lower Michigan and Upper Michigan. Also, the dividing line between Lake Michigan (to the west) and Lake Huron (to the east).

MAFOR Code: The MArine FORecast five-digit system simplifies weather forecasts.

MARSEC: Abbreviation for MARitime SECurity, designated by levels of importance.

Mill scale: A substance formed on the outer surfaces of plates, sheets or profiles when they are being produced by rolling red hot iron or steel billets in rolling mills.

Modoc whistle: A steam whistle, now out of use, made from a longer piece of steel pipe. It had a flutter reed in it to create a sound like the war whoop sound of the Modoc Indian. Its purpose was to warn other tugs and vessels that a raft of logs was in the area; the unique sound was useful because it could not be misunderstood as to its meaning.

Notch: The area where the Dorothy Ann and Pathfinder are connected.

Octas: A cloud cover over one-eighth of the sky.

Pins: In the case of the Dorothy Ann/Pathfinder, large-scale interlocking equipment.

Pitch: Angle on propellers.

Plimsoll marks: A set of load-line markings on a cargo vessel.

Port (direction): Left side of vessel facing forward. Starboard is right side.

Port (place): A harbor, a haven. Where ships dock. A port may have one dock or many docks.

Purple K: Fire retardant.

Rudder: A vertical plate or board for steering a boat.

Running lights: Lights required to be shown on boats under way between sundown and sunup.

Sail effect: The change of direction caused by wind blowing against the side surface of a vessel.

Sault Ste. Marie, Michigan, United States of America/Sault Ste. Marie, Ontario, Canada: Twin cities that are adjacent to the Soo Locks. The name is pronounced Sue Saint Marie.

Screw: A vessel's propeller.

Sea cock: A through-hull valve, a shutoff on a plumbing or a drain pipe between the vessel's interior and water outside the hull.

Secure: To make fast.

Self-unloader: A vessel that needs no shore-side equipment to empty.

Soo Locks: MacArthur Lock: southern most; handles vessels up to 800 feet long. Poe Lock: handles the Great Lakes' thousand-foot freighters. These are the active locks.

Starboard (direction): The right side of vessel facing forward. Port is left side.

Stern: The rear of a vessel.

Strapping table: A chart used to convert readings of liquid levels in the tanks of a barge to volume measurements of that liquid.

Taconite pellets: Processed (enriched) iron ore.

Trim: The fore and aft balance of a boat.

Ton: One of three weights used on the Great Lakes: A short ton is 2,000 pounds, a long ton is 2,240 pounds, and a metric ton is 2,204.6 pounds.

Towing: Captain Schmidt says, "When I'm pushing with the Dorothy Ann, it's considered towing. Whether pushing ahead, towing astern, or pushing alongside is all considered towing."

Tug: A boat (that comes in many sizes) that moves vessels by pushing or towing.

Turnout gear: Also called bunker gear. Outer protective clothing for firefighters.

TWIC Card: Transportation Workers Identification Credential. It's a necessity for access to secure areas.

Wake: The moving waves in the track or path of a vessel.

Walkie-talkie: A two-way device for communicating over short distances.

Waypoint: A reference point used for navigation. Latitude and longitude coordinates specify the point.

Welland Canal: The 26-mile ship canal in Canada that allows vessels to bypass Niagara Falls. The canal connects Lake Ontario and Lake Erie.

Wheel: The propeller of a vessel.

Whistle: Ship's horn. Captain Schmidt often refers to the horn as a whistle.

Windrows: Where the wind has blown the ice up in piles, or rows of piles.

Z-drives: The twin power linkage for propelling the Dorothy Ann is in the shape of a "Z." It's also called a compass drive because the propelling pod can turn 360 degrees.

Standing Orders

- Each watch on the lake will have a line of position on the chart with 2-hour position using GPS and radar
- In meeting or passing situations, if possible without danger to ship, maintain a Closest Point of Approach of 1 mile or more
- Blow passing or meeting signals or communicate signals over VHF at all times
- Call Captain 30 minutes prior to entering port
- Before entering rivers or port check steering and throttles
- In fog, use whistle signals and notify Captain of present position, visibility, and traffic present
- If ship starts to work in a sea, notify Captain
- If any major change in weather reports or if weather increases to strong or if gale or storm warning are issued, notify Captain
- When running boom off, notify Captain. Give wind and sea conditions
- If at any time you are not sure of orders or if situations, call Captain

CHECK LIST FOR DECK CREW
ENTERING PORT
- Before entering break wall or rivers
- Clear anchors
- Make ready landing chair or work boat (check gas, put in plug)
- Rig ladder
- Turn on and check winches
- Rig winch wires to proper side
- Ready heaving line
- Pop hatch clamps
- Remove hatch covers (weather permitting)
- Get work vests ready
- Put on hard hats

CHECK LIST FOR DECK CREW
LEAVING PORT
- Upon departure, secure the deck
- Stow all gear (life vests, heaving lines, etc.)
- Secure hatch crane
- Secure work boat
- Secure boarding ladders
- Clamp all hatches
- Secure work lights
- Secure MG sets
- When clear of break wall
- Secure anchors
- Make rounds (check for water leaks, and anything unusual)

- Secure all port lights
- Secure all water tight doors and hatches

FIRE
- Call Master
- Sound General Alarm   time: _____
- Make announcement of location of fire
- Shut fire dampers
- Fix ship's position   lat: _____ long: _____
- Maneuver to reduce wind age including slowing, running with wind, or putting the wind on the beam
- Contact nearest Coast Guard and any other ships in the area

NOTES
- Type and location of fire: _____
- Time team on scene: ┐┐┐┐┐┐┐┐┐┐┐┐┐┐┐┐┐┐┐┐┐┐_____
- Time fire is out: _____
- Is a re-flash watch set: ____ if not, why: _____
- Other notes:

MAN OVERBOARD
- Throw life ring over side
- Sound General Alarm   time: _____ Make announcement on PA
- Push and hold for 3 seconds MOB button on Northstar GPS
- Switch to hand steering, slow to half speed, and put drives 40 degrees

TOWARDS the side man went over
- Post lookouts to help keep man in sight
- Update Master with actions taken
- Initiate emergency VHF broadcast to vessels in area
- Prepare work boat for launching as rescue boat

NOTES
- Position of man overboard   lat: _____   long: _____
- Time back at position of man over: _____
- Time search pattern initiated: _____
- Time rescue boat launched: _____
- Time person recovered: _____
- Time and name of other vessels on scene: _____
- Time released from search by Coast Guard: _____

CHECKLIST FOR ENTERING DOCKS OR RIVERS
- Check notice to mariners
- Have local chart out and ready
- At 1 hour out
- Notify duty engineer
- Security call (note all traffic)
- Get water gauge (log it in ship's log)

- Check times for deck call out
- Call dock for 1 hour notice
- At 30 minutes out
- Call Captain
- Call Engineer for big generator on barge
- Security call
- Clear anchors
- Prepare decks (including chair, work boat, heaving lines, cables, boarding ladder, hatch   clamps, etc.)
- At 15 minutes out
- Check steering, bow thruster, search lights
- Just before entering port, go bay to bay

CHECK LIST FOR LEAVING DOCKS OR RIVERS
- 1 hour prior to departure
- Call Engineer
- 30 minutes prior to departure
- Call Captain
- Before departure
- Get water gauge (log it in ship's log)
- Get weather report
- Get all charts out and ready for next voyage
- Check all navigation and safety equipment
- Test steering gear and lights
- Give security call (note all traffic)
- Upon departure
- Have deck crew secure tug and barge for sea
- Leaving break wall or river
- Secure anchors
- Call Engineer, go sea to sea

Websites

http://www.weather.gov/dmawds/
Digital Marine Weather Dissemination System of National Weather Service/National Oceanic and Atmospheric Administration
Includes 18 text sites for conditions and forecasts and 25 graphics-driven sites that include the five individual Great Lakes

http://www.ecfr.gov/cgi-bin/text-idx?c=ecfr&tpl=%2Findex.tpl
Federal regulations, current and updated

http://coastwatch.glerl.noaa.gov/modis/region_map.html
Satellite images, over time, of the Great Lakes as a whole and individually

http://glakesonline.nos.noaa.gov/glcurrents/Composite_gl0101.html
Currents of Cuyahoga River (Cleveland, Ohio) at Center Street Swing Bridge
This site is specific to the needs of the Dorothy Ann/Pathfinder

http://www.lre.usace.army.mil/
U.S. Army Corps of Engineers Detroit District
News and topics of interest in the region

http://www.lrb.usace.army.mil/
U.S. Army Corps of Engineers Buffalo District
News and topics of interest in the region

http://boatnerd.com/
BoatNerd, a highly organized collection of knowledgeable Great Lakes and St. Lawrence Seaway enthusiasts
Detailed sites about vessel passage, news and information, with photo galleries, shopping, and much more.

http://ais.boatnerd.com/
Specific site of BoatNerd
Interactive vessel passage maps by which movements and locations of individual ships may be found.
Also,
Marinetraffic.com/ais/
For ship movements globally

www.lcaships.com
Lakes Carriers' Association
Information and news of 17 members and more

www.maritimehistoryofthegreatlakes.ca

Site of Maritime History of the Great Lakes, with numerous links

www.duluthshippingnews.com

Site of Duluth Shipping News, with current news and videos on the industry and vessels

www.eagle.org

Site of American Bureau of Shipping, which sets standards for vessels

www.americansteamship.com

Business site for 18 American Steamship Company vessels

www.keyship.com

Business site for nine-vessel Great Lakes Fleet/Key Lakes, Inc.

www.interlake.com

Business site for 10 vessels of Interlake Steamship Company/Lakes Shipping Company, Inc.

Museums/Attractions
(Among others)

Door County Maritime Museum
120 North Madison Avenue, Sturgeon Bay, Wisconsin
(920) 743-5958 • www.dcmm.org
Plus: Tours of tug John Purves

Dossin Great Lakes Museum
100 The Strand Drive on Belle Isle, Detroit, Michigan
(313) 833-5538 • www.glmi.org
Plus: Pilothouse of freighter William Clay Ford

Great Lakes Lore Maritime Museum
367 N. 3rd Street, Rogers, Michigan
(989) 734-0706 • www.gllmm.com
Plus: Honors those who served the shipping industry

Great Lakes Shipwreck Museum
18335 North Whitefish Point Road, Paradise, Michigan (Whitefish Point Light Station)
(906) 635-1742 • (888) 492-3747 • www.shipwreckmuseum.com
Pluses: Objects of fateful vessels, including Edmund Fitzgerald

Lake Superior Maritime Visitor Center
600 South Lake Avenue, Duluth, Minnesota
(218) 720-5260 • www.lsmma.com
Pluses: Pier History tour, historicf Fresnel Lens

Marine Museum of the Great Lakes
55 Ontario Street, Kingston, Ontario, Canada
(613) 542-2261 • www.marmuseum.ca
Plus: Tours of Alexander Henry, former Canadian Coast Guard icebreaker; located in former Kingston Dry Dock

Marquette Maritime Museum and Lighthouse
300 North Lakeshore Boulevard, Marquette, Michigan
(906) 226-2006 • www.mqtmaritimemuseum.com
Plus: Collection of lighthouse lenses

William G. Mather Museum

601 Erieside Avenue, Cleveland, Ohio
(216) 694-2000 • www.glsc.org/mather_museum.php
Plus: Tours of restored 618-foot freighter

SS Meteor Maritime Museum

300 Marina Drive, Superior, Wisconsin
(715) 394-5712
www.superiorpublicmuseums.org/ssmeteor/NewMETEORMAIN.htm
Plus: Tours of last whaleback ship in the world

SS Col. James M. Schoonmaker/Willis B. Boyer Museum Ship

International Park, 26 Main Street, Toledo, Ohio
(419) 936-3068 • www.willisboyer.org
Plus: Tours of 617-foot freighter

Soo Locks

312 W. Portage Avenue, Sault Ste. Marie, Michigan
(906) 632-7020 • www.saultstemarie.com/soo-locks-46/
Pluses: View large vessels traversing the locks between Lake Superior and Lake Huron; visitor center movie and other attractions; boat tours of locks

Museum Ship Valley Camp

501 E. Water Street, Sault Ste. Marie, Michigan
(888) 744-7867 • 906) 632-3658
www.saulthistoricsites.com/museum-ship-valley-camp-3/
Plus: Tours of freighter with 100 exhibits in cargo holds

Welland Canal

Welland Canals Centre, 1932 Welland Canal Parkway, St. Catherines, Ontario, Canada
(905) 984-8880 • www.stcatharines.ca; also, www.wellandcanal.com
Pluses: Watch ships work their way through Lock 3 (of eight); extensive collection; scenic H20 Highway

Wisconsin Maritime Museum

75 Maritime Drive, Manitowoc, Wisconsin
(920) 684-0218 • www.wisconsinmaritime.org
Plus: Tours of World War II submarine Cobia

Ship Signals

Entering a channel or a blind comer: One prolonged blast

Turning to starboard: One short blast

Turning to port: Two short blasts

Reverse propulsion: Three short blasts

Danger: Five short and rapid blasts

Open the draw bridge: One prolonged then one short blast

Sailing in fog: One prolonged followed by two short blasts

Greeting: One long, two short

Master's salute: Two long, three short. "A master might be saluting the shipyard when he departs with a new vessel. It might be a master to master salute."

Departing dock slip: One prolonged blast

Emergency general alarm: Prolonged, of 10 seconds or more

Abandon ship: Six short blasts

MAFOR Codes

An abbreviation of MArine FORecast, this is a North American code used in the transmission marine weather forecasts.

Time period
- 0 - Existing weather conditions at the beginning of the forecast period
- 1 - Forecast valid for 3 hours
- 2 - For 6 hours
- 3 - For 9 hours
- 4 - For 12 hours
- 5 - For 18 hours
- 6 - For 24 hours
- 7 - For 48 hours
- 8 - For 72 hours
- 9 - Occasionally

D: Code figure for forecast direction of the wind.

Wind direction
- 0 - Calm
- 1 - Northeast
- 2 - East
- 3 - Southeast
- 4 - South
- 5 - Southwest
- 6 - West
- 7 - Northwest
- 8 - North
- 9 - Variable

Fm: Code figure for forecast speed of the wind

Wind speed
- 0 - Beaufort Number 0-3 (0 - 10 knots)
- 1 - Beaufort Number 4 (11 - 16 knots)
- 2 - Beaufort Number 5 (17 - 21 knots)
- 3 - Beaufort Number 6 (22 - 27 knots)
- 4 - Beaufort Number 7 (28 - 33 knots)
- 5 - Beaufort Number 8 (34 - 40 knots)
- 6 - Beaufort Number 9 (41 - 47 knots)
- 7 - Beaufort Number 10 (48 - 55 knots)
- 8 - Beaufort Number 11 (56 - 63 knots)
- 9 - Beaufort Number 12 (64 - 71 knots)

W1: Code figure for forecast weather.

Weather
- 0 - Moderate or good visibility (greater than 3 nautical miles)
- 1 - Risk of ice accumulation on superstructure (air temperature between 0 and -5 degrees Celsius
- 2 - Strong risk of accumulation of ice on superstructure (air temperature below -5 degrees Celsius
- 3 - Mist (visibility 1/2 to 3 nautical miles)
- 4 - Fog (visibility less than 1/2 nautical mile)
- 5 - Drizzle
- 6 - Rain
- 7 - Snow or rain and snow
- 8 - Squally weather with or without showers
- 9 - Thunder storms

2: Identifies the group as a supplementary group. The 2 group is valid for the same period as the group that immediately precedes it. V: is the code figure for the forecast visibility.

Visibility
- 0 - Less than 50 meters
- 1 - 50 - 200 meters
- 2 - 200 - 500 meters
- 3 - 500 meters to 1/2 nautical mile
- 4 - 1/2 to 1 nautical mile
- 5 - 1 to 2 nautical miles
- 6 - 2 to 5 nautical miles
- 7 - 5 to 12 nautical miles

S: Code figure for forecast sea state.

State of sea
Height in Meters
- 0 - Calm (glassy)
- 1 - Calm (rippled) - 0.0 - 0.1
- 2 - Smooth (wavelets) - 0.1 - 0.5
- 3 - Slight - 0.5 - 1.25
- 4 - Moderate - 1.25 - 2.5
- 5 - Rough - 2.5 - 4
- 6 - Very rough - 4.0 - 6
- 7 - High - 6.0 - 9
- 8 - Very High - 9.0 - 14
- 9 - Phenomenal – more than 14

Sample codes

Lake Erie 11670: The numbers, in order, stand for Great Lakes, three-hour time period, wind from the west, 48 to 55 knots, forecast of moderate or good viability more then three nautical miles.

Lake Michigan 12156: The numbers stand for Great lakes, six-hour time period, wind from the northeast, 34 to 40 knots, forecast for rain.

Lake Superior South Central* 13877: The numbers stand for Great Lakes, nine-hour period, wind from the north, 48 to 55 knots, forecast for snow.

*-Codes for the individual lakes may be broken down into sections as conditions apply.

Security Levels

MARSEC
MARitime SECurity system of United States Coast Guard for terrorist threats to nautical facilities and vessels.

Levels
1 (Yellow): Minimum appropriate security measures.

2 (Orange): Additional protective security measures due to heightened risk of an incident.

3 (Red): Specific security measures when an incident is probable, imminent, or has occurred.

To Cap

For those who've spent a life at seas, they've come to understand that there is no death – only life. There is no loss – only difficult gifts.

–Unknown

Captain –

It will be three years on January 15th since I stepped an unknown foot aboard this tug. A fill-in hitch of less than a week to pad the account after an abysmal sailing year. An opportunity to possibly solidify a humbled sailor's chance at resurrecting a once-promising career was, at best, a fleeting thought. I said yes to that lay-up gig to maybe, hopefully, have my name thrown in the relief hat that's passed around the fleet every other month. If I let myself believe in just that much, then maybe I'd have another paycheck around June. Besides, the crew on the Lee A. didn't hesitate to inform me of the "trashfinders" perils.

It only took one day to realize that this was a real boat. That you can work on the Dorothy Ann and let your effort speak for itself. No games, just real, honest sailing. And for the first time in a great while, my confidence re-surfaced. I knew that all I needed was to perform my job to the best of my ability. Because the architect who shaped this method of simplicity from tasks that others made so difficult, was a captain of true integrity. And I knew you would notice that all I wanted was to learn.

And you did notice. Along with the chance you took on me came a level of faith that I never expected. Knowing that you trust me is one of the greatest compliments I have ever received. Working for you as a deckhand, a mate, and a student has been an honor and a privilege, and I could never thank you enough for giving me the push I needed to find myself again.

I have carried the quote I opened with since fishing in Alaska. It has always puzzled me, trying to hash out its meaning. But as the last few days have become increasingly harder to say goodbye and more difficult to choke back my emotions, just to express my gratitude to you, I've begun to understand its simplicity. You will always be here. I just wish we had more time.

– Sincerely,
Kevin J. Bower

Warren Gerds and Captain Schmidt work on details of this book at the kitchen table of Captain Schmidt's home in Allouez, Wisconsin. *Warren Gerds photo*

Gary Schmidt photo